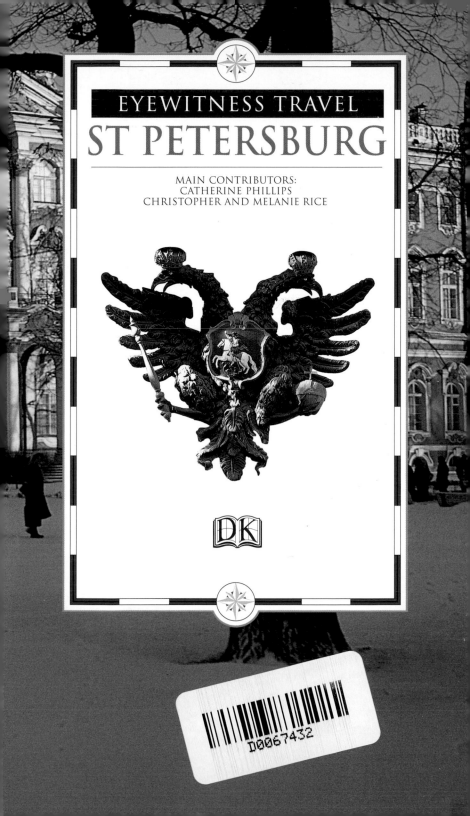

EYEWITNESS TRAVEL
ST PETERSBURG

MAIN CONTRIBUTORS:
CATHERINE PHILLIPS
CHRISTOPHER AND MELANIE RICE

DK

LONDON, NEW YORK,
MELBOURNE, MUNICH AND DELHI
www.dk.com

PROJECT EDITOR Anna Streiffert
ART EDITOR Marisa Renzullo

EDITOR Ella Milroy
US EDITORS Mary Sutherland, Michael T. Wise
DESIGNERS Gillian Andrews, Carolyn Hewitson,
Paul Jackson, Elly King, Nicola Rodway
VISUALIZER Joy Fitzsimmons
MAP CO-ORDINATORS Emily Green, David Pugh
PICTURE RESEARCH Brigitte Arora
DTP DESIGNERS Samantha Borland, Sarah Martin, Pamela Shiels

MAIN CONTRIBUTORS
Catherine Phillips, Christopher and Melanie Rice

PHOTOGRAPHERS
Demetrio Carrasco, John Heseltine

ILLUSTRATORS
Stephen Conlin, Maltings Partnership, Chris Orr & Associates,
Paul Weston

Reproduced by Colourscan, Singapore
Printed and bound by South China Printing Co. Ltd., China

First American Edition, 1998
13 14 15 16 10 9 8 7 6 5 4 3 2 1

Published in the United States by
DK Publishing, Inc., 375 Hudson Street,
New York, New York 10014
Reprinted with revisions 2000, 2001, 2004, 2007, 2010, 2013

Copyright 1998, 2013 © Dorling Kindersley Limited, London

PUBLISHED IN GREAT BRITAIN BY DORLING KINDERSLEY LTD.
A CATALOG RECORD FOR THIS BOOK IS AVAILABLE FROM THE LIBRARY OF CONGRESS.
ISSN 1542-1554
ISBN 978-0-7566-9500-2
THROUGHOUT THIS BOOK, FLOORS ARE REFERRED TO IN ACCORDANCE
WITH EUROPEAN USAGE, I.E. THE "FIRST FLOOR" IS ONE FLOOR UP.

*Front cover main image: Golden dome of St Issac's Cathedral
with statue of St Nicholas*

MIX
Paper from
responsible sources
FSC
www.fsc.org   FSC™ C018179

**The information in this
DK Eyewitness Travel Guide is checked regularly.**
Every effort has been made to ensure that this book is as up-to-date as
possible at the time of going to press. Some details, however, such
as telephone numbers, opening hours, prices, gallery hanging
arrangements and travel information are liable to change. The
publishers cannot accept responsibility for any consequences arising
from the use of this book, nor for any material on third party
websites, and cannot guarantee that any website address in this
book will be a suitable source of travel information. We value the
views and suggestions of our readers very highly. Please write to:
Publisher, DK Eyewitness Travel Guides, Dorling Kindersley,
80 Strand, London WC2R 0RL, UK, or email: travelguides@dk.com.

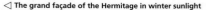
◁ **The grand façade of the Hermitage in winter sunlight**

CONTENTS

**Bronze model of ship, a symbol
of St Petersburg**

INTRODUCING
ST PETERSBURG

**Petersburgers enjoying the snow
outside the Admiralty**

ST PETERSBURG
AREA BY AREA

Little Stable Bridge crossing the Moyka river

Golden statues of the Grand
Cascade at Peterhof

TRAVELLERS' NEEDS

SURVIVAL GUIDE

15th-century icon of St George and
the Dragon, Russian Museum

St Isaac's Cathedral, lavishly decorated inside with more than
40 different stones and minerals

HOW TO USE THIS GUIDE

This guide will help you to get the most from your visit to St Petersburg, providing expert recommendations as well as detailed practical information. *Introducing St Petersburg* maps the city and sets it in its geographical, historical and cultural context, with a quick-reference timeline on the history pages giving the dates of Russia's rulers and significant events. *St Petersburg at a Glance* is an overview of the city's main attractions. *St Petersburg Area by Area* starts on page 54 and describes all the important sights, using maps, photographs and illustrations. The sights are arranged in two groups: those in the central districts and those a little further afield. The guided walks reveal three characteristics of the city – the canals, the Neva and the islands. *Beyond St Petersburg* describes sights requiring one- or two-day excursions. Hotel, restaurant, shopping and entertainment recommendations can be found in *Travellers' Needs*, while the *Survival Guide* includes tips on everything from transport and telephones to personal safety.

FINDING YOUR WAY AROUND THE SIGHTSEEING SECTION

Each of the seven sightseeing areas is colour-coded for easy reference. Every chapter opens with an introduction to the area it covers, describing its history and character. For central districts, this is followed by a Street-by-Street map illustrating a particularly interesting part of the area; for sights beyond the city limits, by a regional map. A simple numbering system relates sights to the maps. Important sights are covered by several pages.

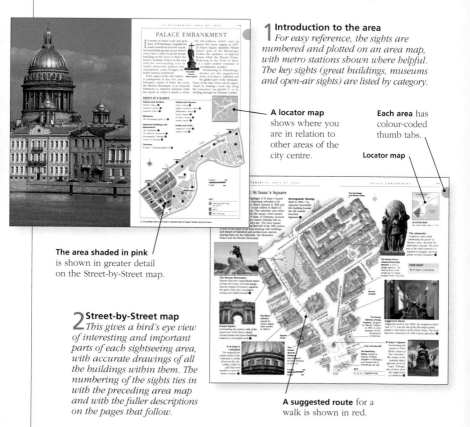

1 Introduction to the area
For easy reference, the sights are numbered and plotted on an area map, with metro stations shown where helpful. The key sights (great buildings, museums and open-air sights) are listed by category.

A locator map shows where you are in relation to other areas of the city centre.

Each area has colour-coded thumb tabs.

Locator map

The area shaded in pink is shown in greater detail on the Street-by-Street map.

2 Street-by-Street map
This gives a bird's eye view of interesting and important parts of each sightseeing area, with accurate drawings of all the buildings within them. The numbering of the sights ties in with the preceding area map and with the fuller descriptions on the pages that follow.

A suggested route for a walk is shown in red.

ST PETERSBURG AREA MAP

The coloured areas shown on this map *(see pp14–15)* are the five main sightseeing areas into which central St Petersburg has been divided for this guide. Each is covered in a full chapter in the St Petersburg Area by Area section *(pp54–131)*. They are also shown on other maps throughout the book. In St Petersburg *at a Glance (pp32–49)*, for example, they help you locate the most interesting museums and palaces or where to see the city's many delightfully designed bridges. The maps' coloured borders match the coloured thumb tabs on each page of the section.

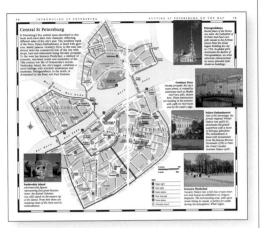

Numbers refer to each sight's position on the area map and its place in the chapter.

Practical information lists all the information you need to visit every sight, including a map reference to the Street Finder maps *(pp238–45)*.

3 Detailed information on each sight
All the important sights are described individually. They are listed to follow the numbering on the area map at the start of the section. The key to the symbols summarizing practical information is on the back flap.

A Visitors' Checklist provides the practical information you will need to plan your visit.

Story boxes highlight unique aspects or historical connections of a particular sight.

4 St Petersburg's major sights
These are given two or more full pages in the sightseeing area in which they are found. Buildings of interesting architecture are dissected to reveal their interiors; museums and galleries have colour-coded floorplans to help you find important exhibits.

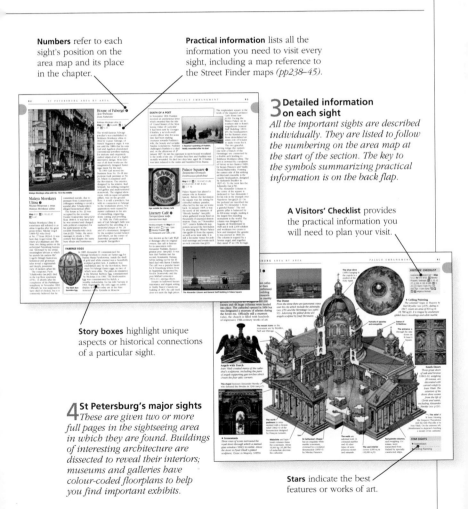

Stars indicate the best features or works of art.

INTRODUCING
ST PETERSBURG

FOUR GREAT DAYS IN ST PETERSBURG

In just over 300 years St Petersburg has had many faces. Peter the Great's folly, built on a swamp and intended to turn Russia's face towards the West, soon became a magnificent city reflecting the majesty of the Russian Empire. Then it was the "cradle of the Revolution", where Lenin came to power. During the Second World War it was a symbol of

The Victory Monument

national pride. Today it is Russia's cultural capital, with a wonderfully preserved heritage and an international arts programme. Taken together, these four itineraries encompass the city's sight-seeing highlights. Individually, they show the influences that shaped the city: imperial, Russian and Soviet. The price guides include the cost of travel, food and admission.

Rastrelli's masterly main staircase at the Winter Palace

IMPERIAL CITY

- Art and opulence
- Grand squares and views
- Remembering Rasputin

TWO ADULTS allow at least 6,000 roubles

Morning
The day starts at the centre of the city with the Baroque **Winter Palace** (see pp92–3), once the official residence of the imperial family and now the heart of the **Hermitage** museum (see pp84–93). Concentrate on the magnificent state rooms, where the Tsars received important guests. Do not miss the view over vast **Palace Square** (see p83), which incorporates the glorious sweep of the General Staff Building, formerly home to the state ministries and now part of the museum. Walk along the embankment to **Krokodil** (see p186) for lunch.

Afternoon
Head back along Galernaya ulitsa to **Senate Square** (see p78) – the **Bronze Horseman**, a statue of Peter the Great, rears up at its centre. There are fine views across the river to Vasilevskiy Island, lined with rich mansions and handsome institutions.

Turn round, and take in **St Isaac's Cathedral** (see pp80–81), topped by a gilded dome. It took from 1818 to 1858 to construct this colossal structure, which, since the Soviet era, has been designated a museum.

Under 1 km (half a mile) west, the **Yusupov Palace** (see p120) has an exhibition on Grigoriy Rasputin, the "holy man" murdered here by Prince Felix Yusupov. Dine at nearby **Bella Vista** (see p188) with views across River Neva or, for a more modest outlay, at **1913** (see p185) – the year the Romanovs celebrated 300 years on the throne.

RUSSIAN CITY

- Icons and incense
- A traditional lunch
- Shopping for souvenirs

TWO ADULTS allow at least 4,800 roubles

Morning
This itinerary takes in the best traditional Russian sights of a city where European influences can be more evident than Russian. Start at the **Russian Museum** (see pp104–7), the world's finest collection of Russian art. Marvel at the **Church on Spilled Blood**'s (see p100) interior, then enjoy a traditional Russian lunch at **Kalinka-Malinka** (see p187).

The Russian Revival-style Church on Spilled Blood

Afternoon

Inspired by the morning's sights, nip across to the **Souvenir Market** *(see p199)*, which sells everything from icons to fur hats.

Then take the green metro line from Gostinyy Dvor to Ploshchad Aleksandra Nevskovo to **Alexander Nevsky Monastery** *(see pp130–31)*. Many notable Russians, including Tchaikovsky and Dostoevsky, are buried here. As the afternoon fades, you may like to attend a magical candlelit choral service at the Church of the Annunciation. Round off the day with a visit to nearby **Slavyanskiy stil** *(see p199)*, a shop selling wonderful Russian linen.

In the evening, visit the ballet *(see pp202–3)* or dine among folk dancers at **St Petersburg** *(see p188)*. For both, book ahead.

A FAMILY DAY OUT

- **Awesome views**
- **Gruesome specimens**
- **Food in a forest**
- **Skating or the circus**

FAMILY OF 4 allow at least 4,500 roubles

Morning

The day starts with a stiff climb up to the colonnade of **St Isaac's Cathedral** *(see pp80–81)* for panoramic city views. Then cross the Neva to the **Strelka** *(see pp58–9)* of Vasilevskiy Island to take in one of the museums there *(see p60)*: the **Zoological**, the **Institute of Russian Literature** or the **Kunstkammer**.

A pleasant walk across the river takes you to Petrogradskaya *(see pp64–73)*. Head to the inexpensive **Pelmeni Bar** for a filling lunch or, for something lighter, try vegetarian **Troitskiy Most** *(see p193)*.

Afternoon

The focus of Petrogradskaya is the **Peter and Paul Fortress** *(see pp66–7)*, with its opulent cathedral and grim history. Attractions include the tombs of the Romanovs, prison

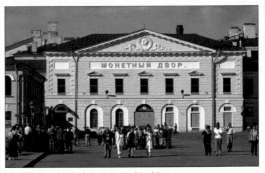

The still-operational mint at Peter and Paul Fortress

cells, displays on the history of the city, Peter the Great's rowing boat, and a rampart climb. In summer, the park surrounding the fortress has all kinds of family attractions. Also in the park is **Zver** *(see p185)*, a restaurant surrounded by trees where adults can relax while their children run around.

After supper, take the metro to Krestovskiy Ostrov, then a short walk to the western spit of **Yelagin Island** *(see pp136–7)*, where there are fine sunsets and an ice rink in winter. Or, if it is too cold, make a visit to the **Circus** *(see p201)*.

SOVIET CITY

- **Revolutionary heritage sites**
- **Monuments to the People**
- **Soviet-themed dining**

TWO ADULTS allow at least 2,700 roubles

Morning

To indulge a fascination for Leningrad, "Cradle of the Revolution", start at the city centre's edge at the **Smolnyy Institute** *(see p128)*, home of the Revolution and later of the Communist Party. Opposite, catch bus No. 46 and ride past the monument to Dzerzhinsky, father of the Soviet secret police, past the **Field of Mars** *(see p94)* where the dead of the Revolution are buried, and across the river to the **Museum of Russian Political History** *(see p72)*. The **Cruiser Aurora** *(see p73)*,

whose guns sounded the 1917 Revolution, is moored a short distance away. For lunch, try Georgian **Salkhino** *(see p185)*.

Afternoon

A little further north, the small **Kirov Museum** *(see p72)* is devoted to the head of the city's Communist Party, Sergey Kirov, whose assassination in 1934 prompted a wave of executions.

To appreciate the Soviet glorification of the People's achievements, take the metro to Moskovskaya and the **Victory Monument** *(see p131)*, whose awesome underground Memorial Hall shows life during the Siege of Leningrad. Then take the metro back to Tekhnologicheskiy Institute and ride the red line between Avtovo and Ploshchad Vosstaniya, where each station tells a part of the history of the city *(see p224)*. Finally, dine at **Kvartirka** *(see p187)* or **Russian Kitsch** *(see p184)*.

The Avtovo metro station celebrates post-war car production

Putting St Petersburg on the Map

The Russian Federation, or Russia as it is usually known, is the world's largest country, covering an area of 17.4 million sq km (6.7 million sq miles). Situated in its north-west corner, St Petersburg is Russia's second city, with a population of just under five million. Once Russia's capital and known as its "Window on the West" *(see pp20–21)*, the city was built on the marshy lands where the Neva joins the Gulf of Finland. Of the 12 countries bordering Russia, Estonia and Finland are St Petersburg's closest neighbours.

Murmansk

Ponoy

WHITE SEA

Arkhangelsk

Sev. Dvina

FINLAND

Ljusnan

NORWAY

Ladoga

M18

OSLO

Dalälven

HELSINKI

M10

Vologda

ST PETERSBURG

SWEDEN

TALLINN

M11

Novgorod

Yaroslavl

STOCKHOLM

ESTONIA

M10

M8

Pskov

Lovat

Volga

M9

RIGA

LATVIA

MOSCOW

DENMARK

BALTIC SEA

A12

M1

COPENHAGEN

LITHUANIA

Tula

KALININGRAD

VILNIUS

Orsha

M20

Hamburg

MINSK

POLAND

BELARUS

Gomel

BERLIN

E77

WARSAW

M13

GERMANY

Odra

Pripyat

M3

Kharkov

PRAGUE

M17

KIEV

Dnepr

CZECH REPUBLIC

UKRAINE

Munich

VIENNA

SLOVAKIA

Dnestr

M20

M23

BRATISLAVA

AUSTRIA

MOLDOVA

BUDAPEST

E60

CHISINAU

Odessa

Drava

SLOVENIA

HUNGARY

ROMANIA

ITALY

CROATIA

BLACK SEA

BOSNIA-HERZEGOVINA

BELGRADE

BUCHAREST

SARAJEVO

SERBIA

MONTENEGRO

KOSOVO

ADRIATIC SEA

SKOPJE

ROME

TIRANA

MACEDONIA

ALBANIA

TURKEY

GREECE

KEY

▬▬	Motorway
▬▬	Major road
═══	Minor road
────	Railway
▪─▪─	Country boundary

0 kilometres　180

0 miles　　　180

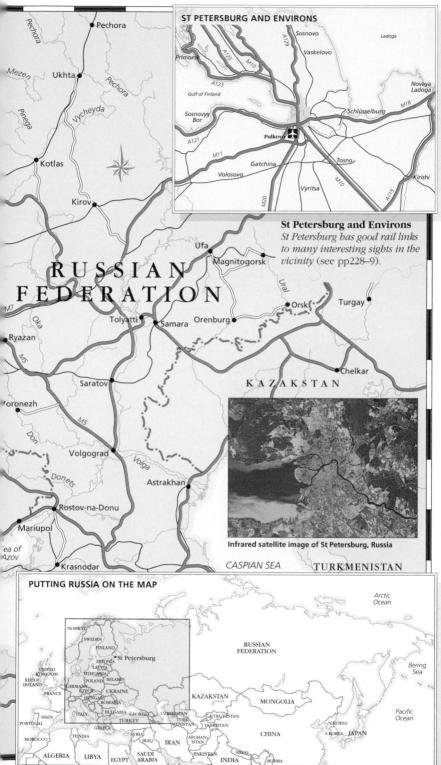

ST PETERSBURG AND ENVIRONS

Pechora

Pechora

Mezen

Ukhta

Pechora

Vycheyda

Pinega

Kotlas

Kirov

RUSSIAN
FEDERATION

M7

Oka

Ryazan

M5

Voronezh

Don

Donets

Mariupol

Sea of
Azov

Krasnodar

Ufa

Magnitogorsk

Tolyatti   Samara   Orenburg   Orsk   Turgay

Ural

KAZAKSTAN

Saratov

Volgograd   Volga

Astrakhan

Rostov-na-Donu

Chelkar

CASPIAN SEA   TURKMENISTAN

St Petersburg and Environs
*St Petersburg has good rail links
to many interesting sights in the
vicinity (see pp228–9).*

Sosnovo   Ladoga

Primorse   Vaskelevo

A125   M10

A129

Gulf of Finland   A123

Novaya
Ladoga

Sosnovyy
Bor   Schlüsselburg   M18

A121   Pulkovo

M11   Gatchina   Tosno   Kirishi

Volosovo   M10

M20   Vyritsa   A115

Infrared satellite image of St Petersburg, Russia

PUTTING RUSSIA ON THE MAP

Arctic
Ocean

NORWAY
SWEDEN
FINLAND
ESTONIA   St Petersburg
LATVIA
LITHUANIA
UNITED   POLAND   BELARUS
KINGDOM
REP OF   GERMANY
IRELAND   CZECH   UKRAINE
FRANCE   HUNGARY
ROMANIA

RUSSIAN
FEDERATION

Bering
Sea

SPAIN   ITALY   BULGARIA   GEORGIA   UZBEKISTAN
PORTUGAL   GREECE   TURKEY   TURK   KYRGYZSTAN
MENISTAN   TAJIKISTAN   N KOREA   JAPAN
MOROCCO   TUNISIA   SYRIA   IRAQ   AFGHAN   S KOREA
ISTAN
ALGERIA   LIBYA   EGYPT   SAUDI   IRAN   PAKISTAN   NEPAL   BURMA
ARABIA   INDIA

KAZAKSTAN   MONGOLIA

CHINA

Pacific
Ocean

Central St Petersburg

St Petersburg's five central areas described in this book each have their own character, reflecting different sides of the city's past. The southern bank of the Neva, Palace Embankment, is lined with glorious, stately palaces. Gostinyy Dvor, to the east, has always been the commercial hub of the city with shops, bars and restaurants lining Nevskiy prospekt. To the west lies Sennaya Ploshchad, a mixture of romantic, tree-lined canals and reminders of the 19th-century low life of Dostoevsky's novels. Vasilevskiy Island, the city's largest, combines a naval heritage with scholarly institutions and museums. Petrogradskaya, to the north, is dominated by the Peter and Paul Fortress.

KAMENNOOSTROVSKIY

UL LENINA
PUSHKARSKIY PER
UL MIRA
ULITSA KROPOTKINA
UL VOSKOVA Uл ВОСКОВА   SYTNINSKAYA UL
BOLSHAYA PUSHKARSKAYA
UL MARKINA   КРОНВЕРКСКИЙ ПРОСПЕКТ
КРОNVERKSKIY PROSPEKT

PETROGRADSKAYA STORONA

Gorkovskaya Ⓜ

UL LIZY
CHAYKINOY PER
TATARSKIY PER
MYTNINSKAYA

ALEKSANDROVSKIY PARK

ZOO SAD

KRONVERKSKAYA NAB КРОНВЕРКСКАЯ НАБ

PR

PROSPEKT DOBROLYUBOVA

✝
SS Peter and Paul Fortress

Neva

Mal Neva Мал Нева

TUCHKOV MOST

NABEREZHNAYA MAKAROVA НАБЕРЕЖНАЯ МАКАРОВА

SREDNIY PROSPEKT СРЕДНИЙ ПРОСПЕКТ

TUCHKOV
PEREULOK
BUGSKAYA
TIFLISSKAYA UL

The Institute of Russian Literature

Rostral Columns

BIRZHEVAYA PLOSHCHAD

BIRZHEVOY MOST

VASILEVSKIY OSTROV

Ⓜ
Vasileostrovskaya

KADETSKAYA LINIYA
6-YA LINIYA 6-Я ЛИНИЯ
7-YA LINIYA
UL REPINA
BOLSHOY PROSPEKT UL REPINA

Menshikov Palace

BIRZHEVOY PROEZD

DVORTSOVYY MOST

DVORTSOVAYA NAB

NAB РЕКИ MOYKI НАБЕРЕЖНАЯ РЕКИ МОЙКИ

MILLIONNAYA

The Hermitage & Winter Palace

PLOSHCHAD SHEVCHENKO

UNIVERSITETSKAYA NAB УНИВЕРСИТЕТСКАЯ НАБ

Бол Нева

BLAGOVESHCHENSKIY

ADMIRALTEYSKAYA NAB

The Admiralty

ADMIRALTEYSKIY PR

NEVSKIY PR

Admiralteyskaya Ⓜ

The Bronze Horseman

MALAYA MORSKAYA ULITSA

NAB   NABEREZHNAYA РЕКИ MOYKI НАБЕРЕЖНАЯ РЕКИ МОЙКИ

Kazan Cathedral

St Isaac's Cathedral

ISAAKIEV-SKAYA PL

Bol Neva

ANGLIYSKAYA

NABEREZHNAYA

GALERNAYA ULITSA
KONNOGVARDEYSKIY BULVAR
KONNOGVARDEYSKIY BULVAR
UL YAKUBOVICHA

PLOSHCHAD TRUDA
UL TRUDA
POCHTAMTSKAYA UL

BOLSHAYA MORSKAYA ULITSA
UL KRYUKOVA KANALA
NABEREZHNAYA REKI MOYKI

PEREULOK PIROGOVA
PRACHECHNIY PEREULOK
UL DEKABRISTOV

GRAZHDANSKAYA ULITSA

KAZANSKAYA ULITSA

NAB РЕКИ MOYKI НАБЕРЕЖНАЯ РЕКИ МОЙКИ

PEREULOK ANTONENKO

GRIVTSOVA

Sadovaya Ⓜ

SENNAYA PLOSHCHAD

Sennaya Ploshchad Ⓜ

Spasskaya Ⓜ

VOZNESENSKIY PR ВОЗНЕСЕНСКИЙ ПР

ULITSA

NABEREZHNAYA KANALA GRIBOEDOVA

SADOVAYA ULITSA
GLINKI

KORSAKOVA UL

GRIBOEDOVA

САДОВАЯ УЛ

MOSKOVSKIY PR

ULITSA EFIMOVA

Mariinskiy Theatre

PR RIMSKOVO

St Nicholas' Cathedral

SHCHEPYANOY PEREULOK

YUSUPOVSKIY SAD

PER BOYTSOVA

NABEREZHNAYA REKI FONTANKI НАБЕРЕЖНАЯ РЕКИ ФОНТАНКИ

Fontanka Фонтанка

Vasilevskiy Island
Adorned with figures representing four great Russian rivers, the Rostral Columns (see p60) stand on the eastern tip of the island. From here there are sweeping views of the Neva and its embankments.

Petrogradskaya

Burial place of the Romanov tsars, the Cathedral of SS Peter and Paul (see p68) stands in the fortress where Peter the Great began building the city in 1703. Its gilded spire dominates the skyline of Petrogradskaya, an area otherwise characterized by many splendid Style-Moderne buildings.

Gostinyy Dvor

Nevskiy prospekt, the city's main artery, is crossed by waterways such as Moyka river (see p36), shown here. These intersections are bustling in the summer, with cafés on river boats and by the water's edge.

Palace Embankment

Part of the Hermitage, the former imperial Winter Palace (see pp92–3), dominates this grand waterfront with a burst of Baroque splendour. The embankment is lined with monuments from the famous Bronze Horseman (p78) to Peter the Great's modest Summer Palace (p95).

Sennaya Ploshchad

Yusopov Palace (see p120) has ornate interiors and houses an exhibition on Gregory Rasputin. The surrounding area, with quiet streets lining its canals, is perfect for walks during the atmospheric White Nights.

KEY

■	Major sight
■	Main sight
M	Metro station
🚢	River boat pier
🚓	Police station
✚	Orthodox church

0 metres 600
0 yards 600

Map labels: SAMPSONIEVSKIY MOST · PETROGRADSKAYA NAB · PETROGRADSKAYA ULITSA · POSADSKAYA ULITSA · UL KUYBYSHEVA · UL KUYBYSHEVA · PESOCHNAYA UL · Cruiser Aurora · Kshesinskaya Mansion · PETROVSKAYA NAB · TROITSKIY MOST · Trinity Bridge · Нева · NAB KUTUZOVA · Summer Palace · SUVOROVSKAYA PLOSHCHAD · NAB LEBYAZHYEVO KANALA · Field of Mars · FONTANKA · Church on Spilled Blood · Engineers' Castle · Russian Museum · GRIBOEDOVA · INZHENERNAYA ULITSA · ITALYANSKAYA ULITSA · SADOVAYA ULITSA · KLENOVAYA ULITSA · NABEREZHNAYA REKI FONTANKI · Nevskiy Prospekt 2 · Nevskiy Prospekt 1 · НЕВСКИЙ ПРОСПЕКТ · Gostinyy Dvor · PER KRYLOVA · ITALYANSKAYA UL · KARAVANNAYA UL · SADOVAYA ULITSA · LOMONOSOVA · UL ZODCHEVO ROSSI · APRAKSIN PEREULOK · TORGOVYY PER · NABEREZHNAYA REKI FONTANKI

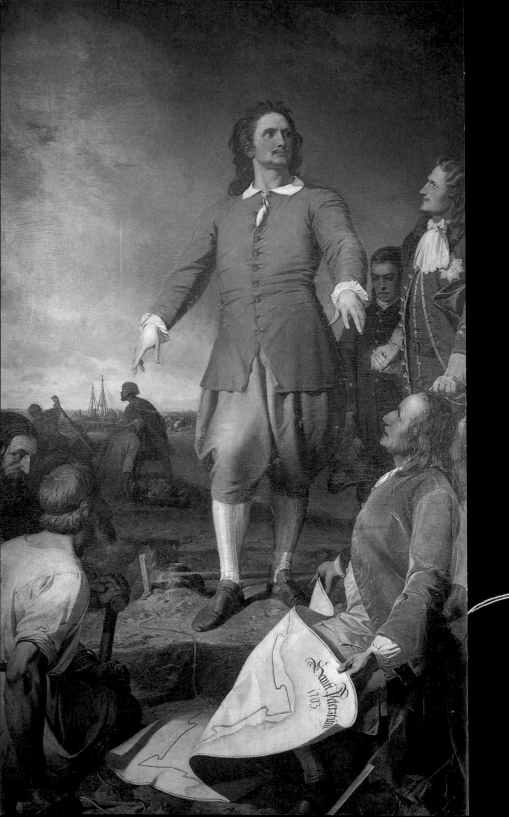

Saukt Petersburg
1703

THE HISTORY OF ST PETERSBURG

*F*ounded in 1703, within ten years St Petersburg had become capital of the vast Russian empire and quickly gained a reputation as one of Europe's most beautiful cities. In the 20th century it underwent three name changes, three revolutions and a 900-day siege. For a city less than 300 years old, it has an amazing history.

Some 850 years before St Petersburg became capital of Russia, local Slavic tribes invited the Viking chieftain Rurik to rule them. His successor founded Kiev, which grew into a great princedom. In 988 Grand Prince Vladimir adopted Orthodox Christianity with profound consequences; Orthodoxy was to become a cornerstone of Russian identity. Paradoxically, Russia only emerged as a united entity during the 250-year domination of the Muslim Mongols. In 1237 these fierce tribes conquered all the principalities except Novgorod. In the 14th century the Mongols chose Moscow's power-hungry grand prince, Ivan I (1325–40), to collect tribute from other subjugated principalities. This sealed the fate of the Mongols for, as Moscow thrived under their benevolence, she also became a real threat.

Ivan IV "the Terrible"

Within 50 years, an army led by Moscow's Grand Prince Dmitriy Donskoy won a first victory over the Mongols, and the idea of a Russian nation was born.

During the long reign of Ivan III (1462–1505) the Mongols were finally vanquished and Moscow's prestige increased. Ivan the Terrible (1533–84) was the first to be called "Tsar of All the Russias". Yet his reign, which began in glory, ended in disaster. Ivan killed his only heir, and the so-called Time of Troubles followed as Russia came under a succession of weak rulers and Polish usurpers invaded Moscow.

THE FIRST ROMANOVS

To end this strife, in 1613 the leading citizens chose Mikhail Romanov to be tsar, thus initiating the 300-year Romanov rule. Under Mikhail, Russia recovered from her upheavals, but his greatest legacy was his son Aleksey. Intelligent and pious, Aleksey modernized the state, encouraging an influx of foreign architects, codifying laws and asserting the power of the state over the church.

Mongol warriors in a 14th-century manuscript illustration

TIMELINE

800	1000	1200	1400	1600
862 Rurik establishes Viking stronghold at Novgorod	**1147** Moscow is founded		**1480** Ivan III stops paying tribute to Mongols	**1605–13** Time of Troubles
863 Cyril and Methodius create early version of Cyrillic		**1462–1505** Reign of Ivan III		
	1108 Town of Vladimir is founded	**1223** First Mongol raid	**1242** Alexander Nevsky defeats the Teutonic Knights	**1613** Mikhail Romanov becomes first tsar of the Romanov dynasty
988 Prince Vladimir converts to Orthodox Christianity			**1533–84** Reign of Ivan IV the Terrible	
		1240 Mongol rule established in Rus	**1598** Boris Godunov claims title of tsar after 12 years as regent	

Boris Godunov

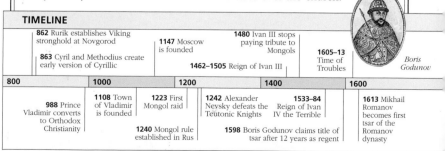

◁ **Peter the Great instructing his workers during the building of St Petersburg (Alexander von Kotzebue, 1862)**

PETER THE GREAT

In the transition from a medieval to a more modern state, the future Peter the Great, founder of St Petersburg, was born. After his father Aleksey's death, Peter's childhood was overshadowed by severe rivalry between his mother's family, the Naryshkins, and that of his father's first wife, the Miloslavskiys. At the age of ten Peter ascended the throne, but the Streltsy Guards, influenced by the Miloslavskiys, started a bloody revolt. As a result his sickly half-brother Ivan became his co-tsar, and Ivan's sister Sophia their regent. The memory of seeing his family brutally killed caused his hatred of Moscow and distrust of its conservative, scheming society.

When Ivan died in 1696, the 24-year-old Peter had grown to a giant of a man with a tempestuous combination of willpower and energy. Long hours

Peter the Great (1682–1725)

spent drilling toy soldiers as a child developed into a full-scale reform of the Russian army. But Peter's dream was of a Russian navy. In 1697, he went on a European tour to study shipbuilding and other wondrous achievements. To everyone's dismay the young tsar spent more hours working at the docks than socializing at court. On his return to Russia he lost no time in bringing in westernizing reforms.

A NEW CAPITAL

It was Peter's determination to found a northern port with an unrestricted passage to the Baltic that led to war with Sweden, at the time one of the strongest countries in Europe. By May 1703 Peter had secured the Neva river and began to build the Peter and Paul Fortress and a shipyard opposite *(see pp20–21)*. Only an autocrat with Peter's drive could have succeeded in building a

View of St Petersburg in the early 17th century, with the Admiralty shipyard to the left

TIMELINE

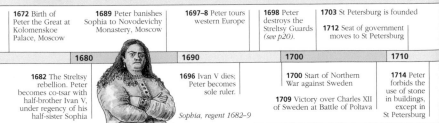

1672 Birth of Peter the Great at Kolomenskoe Palace, Moscow

1689 Peter banishes Sophia to Novodevichy Monastery, Moscow

1697–8 Peter tours western Europe

1698 Peter destroys the Streltsy Guards *(see p20)*.

1703 St Petersburg is founded

1712 Seat of government moves to St Petersburg

1680

1690

1700

1710

1682 The Streltsy rebellion. Peter becomes co-tsar with half-brother Ivan V, under regency of his half-sister Sophia

1696 Ivan V dies; Peter becomes sole ruler.

1700 Start of Northern War against Sweden

1709 Victory over Charles XII of Sweden at Battle of Poltava

1714 Peter forbids the use of stone in buildings, except in St Petersburg

Sophia, regent 1682–9

LIFE AT ELIZABETH'S COURT

When Elizabeth was not busy looking over architectural plans, she would lie around on her bed, gossiping with a group of ladies whose chief task it was to tickle her feet. Her restless nature meant that her courtiers had to endure endless hunts and skating parties, and were required to keep her company at all hours. Her riotous cross-dressing masquerades were notorious, as was her vast wardrobe, allegedly containing over 15,000 dresses.

Tsarina Elizabeth going for a stroll at Tsarskoe Selo, surrounded by eager courtiers

THE PETTICOAT PERIOD

For most of the rest of the 18th century Russia was ruled by women, whose taste did much to set the celebrated architectural tone of St Petersburg.

During the brief reigns of Peter's wife Catherine I (1725–27) and his grandson Peter II (1727–30), the court abandoned this frontier city for the more comfortable life in Moscow. But when the throne passed to Anna, daughter of Peter's co-tsar Ivan, she decided to create a recognizably European court in St Petersburg. Anna was 37 at the time, and had spent most of her life in Germany. This was obvious in her choice of ministers and favourites, of whom many were German. Fashion and style, however, were imported from France and opera from Italy. Though she herself was serious, plain and somewhat cruel, Anna did much to put the court on a footing with the most frivolous in Europe, as well as encouraging a flowering of culture.

Tsarina Elizabeth, daughter of Peter the Great, was the ideal successor to this twittering court. Elizabeth was

city on this fetid bogland, where building materials were in short supply and disastrous floodings regular. More than 40,000 Swedish prisoners-of-war and peasants laboured and perished here, their bones contributing to the city's foundations.

Whether or not it was always Peter's intention to make this his new capital, it only became possible after his decisive victory at Poltava in 1709 put an end to the Swedish threat. St Petersburg was named capital of Russia in 1712 and, by Peter's death in 1725, there were 40,000 inhabitants in the city and many more in the surrounding labour encampments.

Elizabeth (1741–61)

attractive, energetic and cheerful, a combination that endeared her to almost everyone, especially the Guards who helped secure her place on the throne. She left the affairs of state to a series of well chosen advisors. The only element of seriousness lay in Elizabeth's perhaps surprising piety, which at times led her to retire temporarily into a convent. Her chief legacy is the splendid Baroque architecture she commissioned, mainly designed by her favourite architect Rastrelli *(see p93).*

1721 Peace of Nystad ends war with Sweden		**1738** Russia's first ballet school is founded in St Petersburg	**1745** Tsarevich Peter marries the future Catherine the Great	**1757** St Petersburg Academy of Arts is founded
1733 Cathedral of SS Peter and Paul is finished after 12 years' work				
1720	**1730**	**1740**	**1750**	
1717 Peter travels to Holland and France	**1730–40** Reign of Anna	**1741** Anna's successor Ivan VI is deposed; Elizabeth takes power, supported by Guards' officers		**1754** Rastrelli's Winter Palace is begun
1725 Catherine I is empress after death of Peter the Great	**1727–30** Reign of Peter II	*Anna Ivanovna, daughter of Ivan V*		

A Window on the West

Determined to drag his country out of the medieval period, and inspired by the few Westerners he met in Moscow, Peter the Great was the first tsar to travel to Europe. He returned with many ideas for reforms and architectural novelties which he put into practice in his new city. In 1710, when the Swedish threat was over, the reluctant imperial family and government were moved to this chilly, damp outland. But Peter was adamant and soon a rational street plan, stone buildings and academies made St Petersburg a thriving capital in which fashions and discoveries from Europe were tried out before filtering through to the rest of Russia.

EXTENT OF THE CITY

■ 1712   □ Today

PLAN OF THE NEW CITY

This map of 1712 shows Peter's original plan for his capital, with Vasilevskiy Island as centre. This was abandoned due to the hazards of crossing the Neva, and the city spread out around the Admiralty instead.

The Carpenter Tsar
During his 1697–8 tour of Europe, Peter (to the left in this picture) spent months at the Deptford Docks, labouring with his men to learn the basics of ship building.

Based on Amsterdam, the original city grid was meant to follow a strict network of canals but this had to change *(see p57)*.

Menshikov palace

New Fashions
Peter's desire to Westernize Russia led to a rule forcing his courtiers to have their bushy beards shaved off.

THE STRELTSY REBELLION

As a result of a malicious rumour that Peter's relatives planned the murder of his half-brother Ivan, in 1682 the Streltsy Guard regiments invaded the Kremlin. A horrifying massacre took place in front of the 10-year old Peter who saw his adviser and members of his family murdered. This traumatic event is probably what caused Peter's facial tic and certainly his wish to build another capital city. In 1698 he took a terrible revenge by torturing over a thousand Streltsy Guards to death.

Brutal murders in the Kremlin, 1682

The Battle of Poltava
The struggle with Sweden for control over the Baltic led to the Great Northern War. Nine years after the embarrassing defeat at Narva, Peter the Great's army reforms bore fruit. In 1709 he won a decisive battle over Charles XII at Poltava, and thereby Russia's first victory over a major European power.

WHERE TO SEE PETER THE GREAT'S CITY
Some of the buildings from the earliest days of St Petersburg still exist in the city centre, including the rustic Peter the Great's Cabin *(p73)*, the Summer Palace *(p95)* and the Baroque Menshikov Palace *(p62)*. Much of Peter and Paul Fortress *(pp66–7)* also dates from this time. It is also well worth visiting Monplaisir, Peter's first home at Peterhof *(p150)*.

Peter the Great's workshop, the Summer Palace

Kronwerk (outer defence walls)

Peter and Paul Fortress

The port was here until the 1880s.

Admiralty

Summer Palace

Wine Goblet
The tsar, who could hold his drink, enjoyed pressing alcohol on his guests until they passed out. This elegant crystal goblet belonged to his close friend Alexander Menshikov and is engraved with his coat of arms.

Marshy soil and a lack of local stone made construction difficult. Thousands of labourers died during the first stages.

Catherine I
After an unsuccessful first marriage, Peter was drawn to a Lithuanian girl who had followed the army back from the wars in 1704. Her healthy good looks were brought to the tsar's attention by Alexander Menshikov (see p62). Although only two daughters survived, their marriage was happy and Catherine succeeded Peter as the first woman on Russia's throne.

Mice Bury the Cat
Coloured woodcuts, lubki, *served as political cartoons in Peter's day. The tsar was always portrayed as a cat on account of his moustache.*

CATHERINE THE GREAT

Catherine, a German princess, was chosen by Elizabeth as wife for her successor, the petty-minded Peter III. When Peter ascended the throne in

1761 Catherine had resided in Russia for 18 years and was fully fluent in Russian. She had made it her duty to steep herself in the Russian culture which she later came to adore. Six months into Peter's reign, Catherine and her allies in the Imperial Guard deposed the tsar. He was assassinated within days and she was crowned Catherine II.

Catherine the Great in 1762

By Catherine's death at the age of 67, her reputation as an enlightened leader *(see p24)* had been overshadowed by her illiberal reaction to the news of the French Revolution in 1789 and by scandalous rumours concerning her later love-affairs. However, she left a country vastly enlarged after successful campaigns against Turkey and Poland.

WAR AND PEACE

During the Napoleonic Wars, under Catherine's grandson Alexander I, Russia finally took her place alongside the other great European powers.

Despite his part in the murder of his father Paul, much was expected of the new tsar who was in thrall to the ideals of enlightened government. Russia was by now desperately in need of reform. Of particular concern was the plight of the peasantry, who were tied to the land in serfdom.

However, the necessities of war subsumed everything, and no inroads were made against the Russian autocracy during Alexander I's reign.

Determined to harness the wave of Russian patriotism, Alexander joined Britain and marched against Napoleon in Austria in 1805. After the crushing defeat at the battle of Austerlitz, however, the inexperienced tsar retreated, his army having lost 11,000 men.

At the Peace of Tilsit, signed in 1807, Napoleon divided Europe into French and Russian spheres, lulling Alexander into a false sense of security. In 1812 the French emperor invaded Russia, but was defeated by its size and climate. The Russian army followed his forces to Paris, taking part in the allied campaign which led Napoleon to abdicate in 1814. In celebration, Alexander commissioned a series of imposing public edifices in a fitting Empire style.

Murder of Paul I, 1801. Despite all his precautions, Catherine's unstable, paranoid son was murdered in a coup in his own fortified palace *(see p101)*

TIMELINE

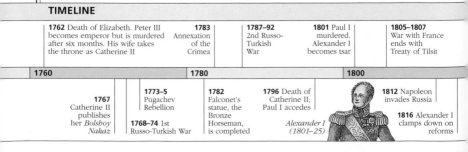

1762 Death of Elizabeth. Peter III becomes emperor but is murdered after six months. His wife takes the throne as Catherine II	1783 Annexation of the Crimea	1787–92 2nd Russo-Turkish War	1801 Paul I murdered. Alexander I becomes tsar	1805–1807 War with France ends with Treaty of Tilsit

1760   **1780**   **1800**

1767 Catherine II publishes her *Bolshoy Nakaz*	1773–5 Pugachev Rebellion / 1768–74 1st Russo-Turkish War	1782 Falconet's statue, the Bronze Horseman, is completed	1796 Death of Catherine II; Paul I accedes / *Alexander I (1801–25)*	1812 Napoleon invades Russia / 1816 Alexander I clamps down on reforms

Decembrist rebels defeated by tsarist troops, 1825

THE DECEMBRIST REBELLION

Officers of the Russian army who had witnessed the freedoms of democratic Europe were frustrated by Alexander's failure to consider constitutional reform. When his stern brother Nicholas was declared tsar in 1825, these liberals rallied their soldiers to support the older brother Constantine, who had given up his rights to the throne, in the hope that he would be more open-minded. They made a stand on 14th December on what is now Senate Square *(see p78)*. Troops loyal to the tsar were instructed to fire on the rebels, killing hundreds before the leaders surrendered. The new tsar, Nicholas I, treated them with the severity which was to become the hallmark of his reign. Five leading figures were hanged, and over a hundred exiled to Siberia.

A CITY OF RICH AND POOR

For much of the 19th century, a walk along Nevskiy prospekt offered a microcosm of an increasingly divided society. Striding past drunks, beggars and prostitutes, the city's courtiers, cocky young officers and leading citizens headed for shops selling imported fashionable accessories, or to the distinguished delicatessen Yeliseev's to buy caviar and champagne. They often lived above their means, mortgaging their serfs and lands to keep up with the astronomical costs of their luxurious lives. This was also a city in which the salary of a low ranking government clerk was never sufficient to feed a family. In the countryside, tension was growing among the serfs tied to the large estates of the aristocracy. With such blatant inequality, growing pressure for political reform was inevitable.

After the unrelenting autocracy of Nicholas I, the "Iron Tsar", liberals welcomed the reign of his fair-minded son Alexander II. In 1861, the tsar passed the Edict of Emancipation, abolishing serfdom, but requiring peasants to buy their land at far from advantageous terms. Thus industrialization finally took off as peasants flocked to the big cities to work in factories, only to be met by even worse living conditions.

THE NAPOLEONIC INVASION

Napoleon's Grand Army of 600,000 men reached Moscow in September 1812, after the victory at Borodino, but was defeated by the tactics of non-engagement devised by the great Russian hero General Kutuzov. Finding himself in a city abandoned by its rulers and set on fire by its people, and with the Russian winter ahead, Napoleon was forced into a retreat over the frozen countryside. He eventually reached the border, with only 30,000 men left alive.

French army retreating from Moscow 1812

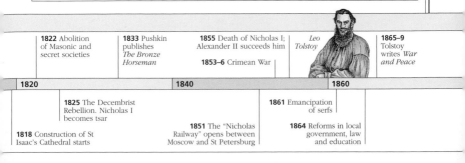

			Leo Tolstoy	
1822 Abolition of Masonic and secret societies	**1833** Pushkin publishes *The Bronze Horseman*	**1855** Death of Nicholas I; Alexander II succeeds him **1853–6** Crimean War		**1865–9** Tolstoy writes *War and Peace*

1820		1840		1860	
	1825 The Decembrist Rebellion. Nicholas I becomes tsar			**1861** Emancipation of serfs	
			1851 The "Nicholas Railway" opens between Moscow and St Petersburg	**1864** Reforms in local government, law and education	
1818 Construction of St Isaac's Cathedral starts					

The Enlightened Empress

Born a minor German princess, Catherine II was a learned and energetic woman. She recognized the importance of the great Enlightenment philosophers Voltaire and Diderot, with whom she corresponded. She bought impressive collections of European art for the Hermitage *(see pp84–93)*, libraries for Russia's scholars and talked much about reducing the burden on Russia's serfs. However, a peasant uprising in the 1770s and news of the French Revolution in 1789 put paid to her liberal notions and, when she died, the majority of Russians were just as badly off as before.

EXTENT OF THE CITY

▨ 1790   ☐ Today

Royal Guards Swear Allegiance
On 28 June 1762, Catherine usurped the throne of her unpopular husband Peter III in a palace coup. The guards regiments flocked to support her and the tsar was assassinated on 6 July.

The Temple alludes to Catherine's passion for Neo-Classical architecture.

A medal is presented to Count Orlov for his victory over the Turks at Chesma in 1770.

CATHERINE THE GREAT

Catherine II "the Great" (1762–96) pursued an expansionist foreign policy. Russia's first naval victory, leading to the annexation of the Crimea, is commemorated allegorically on this fabric.

Count Alexey Orlov, brother of Catherine's one-time lover Grigoriy, played an important role in her takeover of the throne.

Catherine's Instructions
In 1767 the 36-year-old Catherine published her 22-chapter Great Instruction (Bolshoy Nakaz). *The book is a collection of ideas on which a reform of Russia's legal system was to be based.*

Pretender Pugachev
The greatest threat to Catherine's reign was caused by the Cossack Pugachev who claimed to be Peter III. He was arrested, but escaped to lead a widespread peasant uprising which broke out in 1773 and only ended with his execution in 1775.

The New Academy of Sciences

Catherine, who founded over 25 major academic institutions in Russia, also commissioned new buildings for those already existing. Quarenghi built the Neo-Classical Academy of Sciences in 1783–5.

WHERE TO SEE THE NEO-CLASSICAL CITY

Catherine had the Marble Palace *(see p94)* and the Tauride Palace *(p128)* erected for two of her lovers, and added the Small and Large Hermitage and the theatre *(p84)* to the Winter Palace. Her architect Cameron designed the Cameron Gallery and the Agate Pavilion at Tsarskoe Selo *(p150)* and Pavlovsk Palace *(pp158–61)*.

Grecian Hall at Pavlovsk, created by Charles Cameron in 1782–6

Catherine is portrayed as Pallas Athena, goddess of wisdom and warfare, with her attributes of a shield and helmet.

Empire-Style Vase (1790)

Porcelain was much prized at court. In 1744 the first Russian producer, the Imperial Porcelain Factory, opened in St Petersburg.

The fabric, used for a screen, was made by the Pernons factory, Lyons, in 1770.

Mikhail Lomonosov

A philosopher, historian, linguist and scientist, Lomonosov (1711–65) personified the intellectual enlightenment of 18th-century Russia (see p61). This sculpture of him as a boy by the seashore refers to his fisherman origins.

Grigoriy Potemkin (1739–91)

Of all her lovers, Catherine respected and admired Prince Potemkin the most. He was a successful general and an influential counsellor. They remained friends until his death.

Alexander II was murdered by a revolutionary group in 1881. Tragically, he is said to have had the plans for a Russian parliament in his pocket

THE DEATH OF TSARIST RUSSIA

Pressure for reform had built up such a head of steam that in 1881, when still no radical changes had taken place, a revolutionary group murdered Alexander II. The reign of Alexander III was one of rabid reaction. The press was under strict censorship and the secret police more active than ever. But workers began to get organized and opposition was growing. Nicholas II took over a country on the verge of breakdown, in spite of the rapid industrialization of the 1890s. The unsuccessful war with Japan (1904–5) was followed by "Bloody Sunday". On 9th January 1905 a peaceful demonstration carried a petition to the tsar only to be met by bullets. News of the massacre spread like wildfire and the 1905 Revolution broke out with strikes all over Russia. To avert further disaster, Nicholas II promised basic civil rights and an elected Duma (parliament) with the right to veto legislation. However, the tsar simply dissolved the parliament whenever it displeased him. This high-handed behaviour, along with the royal family's unpopular intimate friendship with Rasputin *(see p121)*, further damaged the Romanovs' reputation.

The outbreak of World War I brought a surge of patriotism which the tsar sought to ride. But, by late 1916, Russia had lost three and a half million men, morale at the front was low and food supplies at home scarce.

Red Army badge

WORLD OF ART MOVEMENT

The oppressive political climate at the turn of the century did not prevent art from flourishing. A small group of St Petersburg artists, including Bakst and Benois, grew into an influential creative movement under the inspired leadership of Sergey Diaghilev. Western art was introduced in their stylish *World of Art* magazine, while their stage designs and costumes for the Ballets Russes *(see p118)* brought Russian culture to the west.

Costume design by Leon Bakst, 1911

REVOLUTION AND CIVIL WAR

In February 1917 strikes broke out in the capital, now renamed Petrograd. The tsar was forced to abdicate, his family put under arrest and a Provisional Government set up. But revolutionaries returning from exile organized themselves and, in October, an armed revolution overthrew the government *(see pp28–9)*.

TIMELINE

1881 Alexander II is assassinated by the "People's Will" group. Alexander III becomes tsar.

1902 Lenin publishes *What is to be Done?*

1898 Social-Democratic Workers' party is founded. Russian museum opens

The Romanov family in 1913

1913 300th anniversary of Romanov rule

1880

1900

1881–2 Anti-semitic pogroms

1887 Lenin's brother is hanged for attempt on the tsar's life

1894 Alexander III dies, Nicholas II accedes

1903 Pro-violence Bolsheviks (under Lenin) secede from Social-Democratic Workers' party

1904–5 Russo-Japanese War

1905 The 1905 Revolution is followed by the inauguration of the first Duma in 1906

1914 Outbreak of WWI; St Petersburg changes name to Petrograd

The leading Bolshevik party proved to be as careless of democracy as the tsar but, in March 1918, they kept their promise to take Russia out of the war. The army was desperately needed at home to fight the developing civil war. The Bolsheviks (Reds) found themselves threatened by a diverse coalition of anti-revolutionary groups which came to be known as the "Whites", initially supported by foreign intervention. It was the threat of the Whites rallying opposition around the royal family that led to their execution in July 1918. But the Whites were a disparate force and, by November 1920, the last troops had abandoned the struggle, leaving a devastated Soviet Russia to face two years of appalling famine. To manage, Lenin had to revise his aggressive "War Communism" nationalization project. His slightly milder New Economic Policy allowed for private enterprise.

The imperial palaces around St Petersburg were totally destroyed by the Germans in World War II. This photo shows Pavlovsk (see pp156–9) in 1944

THE STALIN YEARS

In the five years after Lenin's death in 1924, Joseph Stalin used his position as General Secretary of the Communist Party to eliminate all rivals. He then established his long dictatorship.

The terror began in earnest with the collectivization of agriculture which forced the peasants to give up all livestock, machinery and land to collective farms. During this time, and in the ensuing famine of 1931–2, up to 10 million people are thought to have died.

A first major purge of intellectuals took place in urban areas in 1928–9. Then, in December 1934, Sergey Kirov, the party leader in Leningrad, was assassin-

Joseph Stalin on a propaganda poster from 1933

ated on the secret orders of Stalin (see p72). Blamed on an anti-Stalinist cell, the assasination was used as the catalyst for five years of purges throughout the country. By the time they were over, some 15 million people had been arrested, many sent to the Gulag (labour camps) and over a million executed.

Stalin's purge of the Red Army boded badly for World War II, for he had got rid of three quarters of his officers. When the Germans invaded Russia in 1941 they cut off Leningrad in less than three months, subjecting the city to a 900-day siege (see p131) which left more than two million people dead, half of them civilians. Leningrad came to be known as a "Hero City".

The Germans were eventually defeated, but the Russian people, who lost 20 million souls to the war, were subjected to a renewed terror by Stalin, which lasted until his death in March 1953.

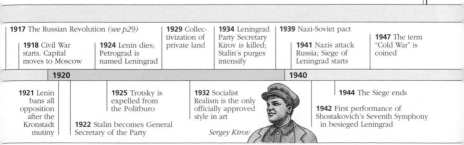

1917 The Russian Revolution *(see p29)*		**1929** Collectivization of private land	**1934** Leningrad Party Secretary Kirov is killed; Stalin's purges intensify	**1939** Nazi-Soviet pact	**1947** The term "Cold War" is coined
1918 Civil War starts. Capital moves to Moscow	**1924** Lenin dies; Petrograd is named Leningrad			**1941** Nazis attack Russia; Siege of Leningrad starts	

1920				**1940**	
1921 Lenin bans all opposition after the Kronstadt mutiny	**1925** Trotsky is expelled from the Politburo	**1932** Socialist Realism is the only officially approved style in art		**1944** The Siege ends	
	1922 Stalin becomes General Secretary of the Party	*Sergey Kirov*		**1942** First performance of Shostakovich's Seventh Symphony in besieged Leningrad	

The Russian Revolution

St Petersburg is known as the cradle of the Russian Revolution, a central event in the history of the 20th century. After the 1917 February Revolution which led to the abdication of Tsar Nicholas II, the Provisional Government declared a political amnesty. Exiled revolutionaries such as Lenin and Trotsky flooded into the city. By setting up a network of Workers' and Soldiers' Soviets, representative councils elected by the people, they established an alternative government. In October, when soldiers had deserted from the front in droves, the revolutionary leaders decided on an armed uprising which brought the Communists to power.

EXTENT OF THE CITY

■ *1917*   □ *Today*

The Ex-Tsar

Nicholas II, seen here clearing snow at Tsarskoe Selo during his house arrest in March 1917, was later taken with his family to Yekaterinburg where they were murdered.

Looting was tempting for the mob of sailors and soldiers, especially in the palace's well-stocked wine cellars.

Soldier of the Red Guard

STORMING THE WINTER PALACE

Late on the evening of 25 October 1917 the battleship *Aurora (see p73)* fired some blank shots at the Winter Palace. The Red Guard, trained by Trotsky at the Smolnyy Institute, stormed the palace. Their aim was the arrest of the Provisional Government, unsuccessfully defended by 300 Cossacks.

The Cossacks, who defended the palace with some cadets and members of the Women's Battalion, were too few to offer any serious resistance.

Lenin, Leader of the People

A charismatic speaker, as shown in this painting by Victor Ivanov, Lenin returned from exile in April to lead the Revolution. By 1918, his Bolshevik faction had shown their determination to rule.

Revolutionary Plate

Various ceramics with revolutionary themes, mixed with touches of Russian folklore, were produced to celebrate every occasion, in this case the Third International.

Leon Trotsky

The intellectual Trotsky played a leading military role in the Revolution. In 1927, during the power struggle after Lenin's death, he was exiled by Stalin. In 1940 he was murdered in Mexico by a Stalinist agent.

Propaganda

One hallmark of the Soviet regime was its propaganda. Artists were employed to design posters spreading its message through striking graphics. War Communism during the Civil War (1918–20) was encouraged by posters such as this one, extolling the "Workers' and Peasants' Defence".

Avant Garde Art

Even before 1917, Russia's artists had been in a state of revolution, producing the world's first truly abstract paintings. A great example of this new movement is Supremus No. 56, painted in 1916 by Kazimir Malevich.

Ministers of the Provisional Government tried to keep order but were arrested.

New Values

Traditions were radically altered by the Revolution; instead of church weddings, couples exchanged vows under the red flag. Loudly trumpeted sexual equality meant that women had to work twice as hard – at home and in the factories.

TIMELINE

1917 The February Revolution	**March** The tsar is persuaded to abdicate. Provisional Government is led by Prince Lvov	**October** Bolsheviks storm Winter Palace after signal from *Aurora* and expel Provisional Government	**March** Bolsheviks sign Brest-Litovsk peace treaty with Germany. Capital is moved to Moscow

1917

1918

July Kerensky becomes Prime Minister of Provisional Government

Cruiser Aurora

1918 January Trotsky becomes Commissar of War

December Lenin forms the CHEKA (secret police)

July Start of Civil War. Tsar and family are murdered in prison at Yekaterinburg

The Washington Dove of Peace, a Russian caricature (1953) from the days of the Cold War

THAW AND STAGNATION

Three years after Stalin's death his successor Nikita Khrushchev denounced Stalin's crimes at the Twentieth Party Congress and the period known as "The Thaw" began. Political prisoners were released, and Solzhenitsyn's *One Day In the Life of Ivan Denisovich,* about life in the Gulag, was published.

In foreign affairs, things were not so liberal. Soviet tanks invaded Hungary in 1956 to prevent the country seceding from the Warsaw Pact and, in 1962,

Khrushchev's decision to put nuclear missiles on Cuba brought the world to the brink of nuclear war.

When Leonid Brezhnev took over in 1964, the intellectual climate froze once more and the persecution of political dissidents was stepped up. The first ten years of his regime were a time of relative plenty. But beneath the surface a vast black market and network of corruption was growing. The party apparatchiks, who benefited most from the corruption, had no interest in rocking the boat. When Brezhnev died in 1982, the politburo was determined to prevent the accession of a younger generation. He was followed by 68-year-old Yuriy Andropov and, when he died, 72-year-old Chernenko.

GLASNOST AND PERESTROIKA

When 53-year-old Mikhail Gorbachev announced his policies of *glasnost* (openness) and *perestroika* (restructuring), when he took over in 1985, he had no idea what would follow and that the end of the Soviet Union was in sight.

For the first time since 1917 the elections to the Congress of People's Deputies in 1989 contained an element of genuine choice, with rebels such as Boris Yeltsin and human rights campaigner Andrey Sakharov winning seats. In 1991, local elections brought nationalist candidates to power in the

Mikhail Gorbachev and George Bush

FIRST IN SPACE

It was under Krushchev that the Soviet Union achieved her greatest coup against the West, launching the first Sputnik into space in 1957. That same year the dog Laika was the first living creature in space, aboard Sputnik II. She never came down again, but four years later Yuriy Gagarin made spectacular history as the first man in space, returning to a hero's welcome. The Soviets lost the race to put a man on the moon, but their space programme worked as powerful propaganda, backing up the claims of politicians that Russia would soon catch up with and overtake the West.

Sputnik II and the space dog Laika, 1957

TIMELINE

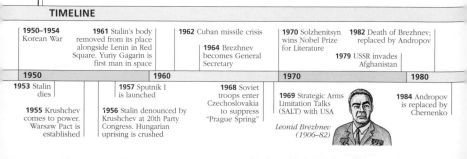

1950	1960	1970	1980
1950–1954 Korean War	**1961** Stalin's body removed from its place alongside Lenin in Red Square. Yuriy Gagarin is first man in space	**1962** Cuban missile crisis **1964** Brezhnev becomes General Secretary	**1970** Solzhenitsyn wins Nobel Prize for Literature	**1982** Death of Brezhnev; replaced by Andropov
			1979 USSR invades Afghanistan	
1953 Stalin dies	**1957** Sputnik I is launched	**1968** Soviet troops enter Czechoslovakia to suppress "Prague Spring"	**1969** Strategic Arms Limitation Talks (SALT) with USA	**1984** Andropov is replaced by Chernenko
1955 Krushchev comes to power. Warsaw Pact is established	**1956** Stalin denounced by Krushchev at 20th Party Congress. Hungarian uprising is crushed		Leonid Brezhnev (1906–82)	

Demonstrations on Palace Square during the 1991 coup

travel, others cry out for a return to Communism and the albeit limited social protection it offered.

The social problems are still being resolved. Major international companies flooded in, and by early 1999 relative stability had been achieved. The elections of December 1999 dramatically reduced the power of the Communists, bringing in young liberal reformers and confirming optimism about Russia's future. The religious revival continues, and churches of all denominations have been restored to their original purpose.

republics, and democrats in the major Russian local councils. Russia and the Baltic Republics seceded from the Soviet Union, while the people of Leningrad, always in the vanguard of progressive movements and led by the reformist lecturer in law, Anatoly Sobchak, voted to restore the city's original name, St Petersburg.

The new Russian State Emblem

With his momentous victory in the election for President of the Russian Republic, Yeltsin was able to deal the death blow to the Soviet Union. It came after the military coup against Gorbachev in August 1991, when Yeltsin's stand against tanks in Moscow made him a hero. In St Petersburg no tanks were on the street, but nonetheless Sobchak rallied supporters of democracy. By the end of the year, the Soviet Union no longer existed.

In March 2000, Vladimir Putin was elected President of the Russian Federation, and re-elected in 2004. Dmitry Medvedev became President in 2008, with Putin as Prime Minister. In 2012, Putin and Medvedev switched roles, much to the dismay of many Russians who took to the streets in protest.

ST PETERSBURG TODAY

The economic reforms which Russia has undergone since 1991 have widened the gap between rich and poor and, while some revel in the new opportunities for work and

A church wedding, popular again since religion has gained new importance among the young

1989 USSR leaves Afganistan	1990 Gorbachev is elected President of the USSR and awarded the Nobel Peace Prize	1998 Nicholas II is reburied with his family in SS Peter and Paul Cathedral on 17 July	2004 Putin is re-elected as President for the second term	2008 Georgian–South Ossetian Conflict; Russia recognises the independence of Abkhazia and South Ossetia	
	1990	**2000**		**2010**	**2020**
	2000 Putin becomes President of Russia			2008 Medvedev becomes President of Russia; Putin becomes Prime Minister	2012 Putin becomes President again and Medvedev, Prime Minister
	1991 Yeltsin becomes President of Russia. Dissolution of the USSR on 25 December		2004 Beslan Siege; 300 people killed in a Beslan school by Chechen rebels		

ST PETERSBURG AT A GLANCE

A city built on water, St Petersburg offers beautiful scenery and a wide range of sights. The Peter and Paul Fortress *(see pp66–7)*, the city's first building, contrasts with Baroque monasteries and Neo-Classical palaces. The city's short but stormy history is reflected in many of its museums, which display everything from Catherine the Great's fine art collection in the Hermitage to memorabilia of the Revolution in the Kshesinskaya Mansion *(see p72)*.

To help you make the most of your stay, the following 12 pages are a time-saving guide to the best museums and palaces and the most interesting of the many bridges and waterways. The cultural figures that made St Petersburg a city of importance are also featured. Below is a selection of sights that should not be missed by any visitor.

ST PETERSBURG'S TOP TEN ATTRACTIONS

Russian Museum
See pp104–7

Mariinskiy Theatre
See p119

Nevskiy Prospekt
See pp46–9

Stieglitz Museum
See p127

Church on Spilled Blood
See p100

The Hermitage
See pp84–93

Cathedral of Our Lady of Kazan
See p111

St Isaac's Cathedral
See pp80–81

Cathedral of SS Peter and Paul
See p68

Alexander Nevsky Monastery
See pp130–31

◁ **The Neo-Classical Kazan Cathedral with its impressive semi-circle of granite columns**

St Petersburg's Best: Bridges and Waterways

Like its waterbound sisters, Amsterdam and Venice, St Petersburg is built around a network of canals and rivers which are still the life-blood of the city. They contribute to its unique atmosphere by creating eerie mists which rise from the ice-laden waters in winter and, in summer, a glittering mirror of façades during the glowing sunsets and bright White Nights.

Bridges, necessary for communication between the islands, were also an excellent means to adorn the city with decorative sculptures, elaborate lampposts and wrought-iron work.

A walk or a boat trip *(see pp134–5, pp226–7)* is the best way to enjoy them.

Winter Canal
Laid out in 1718–20, this narrow canal is crossed by three bridges and Yuriy Velten's Hermitage Theatre foyer (1783–7).

Blagoveshchenskiy Bridge
Rebuilt in 1936–8, this bridge still retains its original cast-iron seahorse railings, designed by Bryullov.

Lion Bridge
One of the earliest of its kind, this pedestrian suspension bridge dates from 1825–6. Its cables are anchored inside four cast-iron lions, by sculptor Pavel Sokolov.

Egyptian Bridge
This bridge spanning the Fontanka was decorated in the Egyptian style fashionable at the time of its construction, in 1826.

Malaya Neva

Vasilevskiy Island

Bolshaya Neva

Palace Embankment

Moyka

Kanal Griboedova

Sennaya Ploshchad

Fontanka

| 0 metres | 500 |
| 0 yards | 500 |

Trinity Bridge

The ten-arched Trinity Bridge (1897–1903) is famous for its Style-Moderne lampposts and railing decorations, the work of the skilful French engineers Vincent Chabrol and René Patouillard.

Swan Canal

This tree-lined canal (1711–19) leading out to the Neva is named after the swans which were once drawn to its peaceful waters.

Bridge Passage

Cleverly designed to span the confluence of the Moyka and the Griboedov, the Theatre and Small Stable bridges were constructed by Traitteur and Adam in 1829–31.

Petrogradskaya

Neva

Gostinyy Dvor

Anichkov Bridge

This three-span bridge, carrying Nevskiy prospekt across the Fontanka, was built in 1839–41. At each corner are Pyotr Klodt's impressive sculptures of men taming wild horses.

Lomonosov Bridge

The distinctive domed granite towers, built in 1785–7, originally contained the bridge's opening mechanism. The bridge was rebuilt in 1912, but the towers were kept.

Bank Bridge

Dating from the same time as the Lion Bridge, and designed by the same team, this bridge is adorned by four magnificent cast-iron griffons. Its name derives from the nearby former Assignment Bank.

Exploring St Petersburg's Bridges and Waterways

A boat trip on St Petersburg's canals and waterways is one of the highlights of any visit to the city. From the Anichkov Bridge the river boats *(see p226)* loop along the Neva, Fontanka and Moyka rivers, taking in many impressive bridges and landmarks. Alternatively, you can choose your route to explore the city's rich architectural heritage by taking a water taxi *(see p227)*. A pleasant wander along the embankments of the Griboedov Canal leads past imposing 19th-century apartment houses and fancifully decorated bridges. In winter it is sometimes possible (but not advisable) to walk on the frozen Neva.

The ice-laden Neva river in front of the Peter and Paul Fortress

THE NEVA AND ITS BRANCHES

Greatest of St Petersburg's numerous waterways, the Neva flows from Lake Ladoga in the east through the city to the Gulf of Finland, a distance of only 74 km (46 miles) in total. Vasilevskiy Island, one of more than 100 islands in the Neva Delta, divides the river into two separate branches, Bolshaya (Great) Neva and Malaya (Small) Neva.

Icebound for at least four months of the year, the Neva usually shows the first signs of cracking in March. The official opening of navigation is announced by the port authority in early spring. Before the Revolution the event was marked with great ceremony. The Commander of the Peter and Paul Fortress *(see pp66–7)*, at the head of a naval flotilla, would scoop some icy water into a silver goblet which he presented to the tsar in the Winter Palace *(see pp92–3)*.

RIVERS AND CANALS

Inspired by Amsterdam, Peter the Great kept the many streams of the delta as canals, which also helped to drain the swampy ground. As the city grew, new ones were dug to improve the canal network.

The **Moyka** originally flowed from a swamp near the Field of Mars *(see p94)*. In the 19th century the aristocracy lined its quays with impressive Neo-Classical mansions which are still their main attraction. Canal boats and barges ply the 7-km (4-mile) long **Fontanka**, widest and busiest of the waterways, which was once the border of the city. These two rivers are linked by the **Kryukov Canal**, dug in the 18th century.

The **Griboedov Canal**, first known as the Catherine Canal in honour of Catherine the Great, was designed to move cargo from Sennaya Ploshchad. Today the atmosphere here is more tranquil. The stretch of water running south from the Lion Bridge is particularly picturesque. The narrowest waterway is the **Winter Canal**, just to the east of the Winter Palace. Nearby is the delightful **Swan Canal** which runs along the Summer Garden *(p95)*.

Steady industrial growth in the 19th century prompted the construction of a new canal, the **Obvodnyy**, in 1834, to take the increasing number of heavy cargo barges and supply water to the city outskirts.

NEVA BRIDGES

The most central of the Neva bridges is the **Palace Bridge** (Dvortsovyy most). The present structure, built early in the 20th century, replaced a seasonal pontoon bridge which linked the mainland to Vasilevskiy Island. The other

View of the Moyka and its south bank with a water taxi in foreground

Peter the Great Bridge, crossing the Neva near Smolnyy Institute

bridge to this island, **Blago-veshchenskiy Bridge** (Blago-veshchenskiy most, see p63) was the first permanent bridge over the Neva. Once known as Lieutenant Schmidt Bridge, it returned to its original name in 2007. The **Trinity Bridge** (Troitskiy most, see p73) was built in 1897–1903 by the French Batignolles company. At 582 m (1,910 ft), the Trinity Bridge was the Neva's longest, until the construction of the **Alexander Nevsky Bridge** (Most Aleksandra Nevskovo) in the 1960s, which is some 900 m (2,950 ft). Between these two is the **Liteynyy Bridge** (Liteynyy most) built in 1874–9. In 1917, the city authorities tried to prevent rebel workers crossing the Neva from the Vyborg Side by raising the central bridge span. The tactic failed since the re-volutionaries decided to cross on foot over the frozen ice.

Near the Smolnyy Institute is the **Peter the Great Bridge** (Most PetraVelikovo), also known by its Soviet name Bolsheokhtinskiy most. It has a central drawbridge and distinctive steel twin arches, erected in 1909–11.

From April to November almost all Neva bridges are raised at night to give ships access to the Volga (see p209).

DECORATIVE BRIDGES

In the beginning, wooden bridges spanned the canals and rivers of St Petersburg. They were usually known by their colour – red, blue, green, and so on. The **Red Bridge** (Krasnyy most) which carries Gorokhovaya ulitsa over the Moyka, has pre-served its original name. Built in 1808–14, this iron bridge is decorated with picturesque lamps on four granite obelisks. Lamps are also a feature of the **Lantern Bridge** (Fonarnyy most) which crosses the Moyka river near to the Yusupov Palace (see p120). Here the gilded lampposts are shaped to look like treble clefs. **Singer's Bridge** (Pevcheskiy most) at the other end of the Moyka takes its name from the choir of the nearby Glinka Capella. Its engineer, Yegor Adam, also designed the lace-like patterning of the railings.

At the junction where the Griboedov meets the Moyka is an interesting ensemble, formed by the wide **Theatre Bridge** (Teatralnyy most) and

Lamppost, St Panteleymon's Bridge

Small Stable Bridge (Malo-Konyushennyy most). The latter is cunningly designed to look like two bridges.

Among the more attractive bridges is Georg von Traitteur's pedestrian **Bank Bridge** (Bankovskiy most), crossing the Griboedov. Its cables are held up by two pairs of gold-winged griffons. The **Lion Bridge** (Lvinyy most), also by Traitteur, uses a similar device; in this case the suspension cables emerge from the open jaws of four proud lions.

St Panteleymon's Bridge (Panteleymonovskiy most, see p99) spans the Fontanka near the Summer Gardens. It was Russia's first chain bridge (1823–4). The Empire-style decoration has survived and includes gilded fasces and double-headed eagles perched on laurel wreaths. Next to the Nevskiy prospekt, the **Anichkov Bridge** (Anich-kov most) is famous for its four vibrant bronze sculptures of wild horses and their powerful tamers, all of them in different poses. Further down the Fontanka, framed by a handsome Neo-Classical square by Carlo Rossi, is the **Lomonosov Bridge** (Most Lomonosova) with its unusual stone turrets.

The **Egyptian Bridge** (Egipetskiy most) spans the Fontanka close to the Kryukov Canal. It is ornamented with bronze sphinxes and bridgeheads resembling the entrance to an Egyptian temple. Originally constructed in 1826, the bridge collapsed under the weight of a passing cavalry squadron in 1905 but was rebuilt in 1955.

A 19th-century illustration of one of the many floods in St Petersburg

A CITY UNDER WATER

Peter the Great should have known it was a bad idea to found a city here. The first flood, just three months after he started the fortress in 1703, swept away his building materi-als. The water rises dangerously high on average once a year, but four floods, in 1777, 1824, 1924 and 1955, wrought massive damage. In 1824 the whole city went under water and 462 buildings were totally destroyed. This inspired Pushkin's poem The Bronze Horseman (see p78). Markers showing record waterheights can be found by the Winter Canal and the Peter and Paul Fortress. In 1989 construction of a dam was begun to prevent future destruction.

St Petersburg's Best: Palaces and Museums

St Petersburg boasts more than 90 museums, many of them housed in palaces or other buildings of historical importance. Some are well known throughout the world, such as the Hermitage which began as Catherine the Great's private collection of European art. Others, including the Russian Museum and the Summer Palace, highlight local art, history and culture. Some of the most evocative museums are those commemorating the lives and work of famous artists, writers and musicians. This selection represents the most interesting in each category.

Petrogradsk

The Hermitage

Incorporating the breathtaking state rooms of the Winter Palace, the world-famous Hermitage holds nearly three million exhibits which range from Fine Arts to archaeological finds.

Malaya Neva

Vasilevskiy Island

Menshikov Palace

This grandiose Baroque palace on Vasilevskiy Island is testimony to the power of Peter the Great's friend and advisor, Prince Menshikov.

Bolshaya Neva

Palace Embankment

Sennaya Ploshchad

IMPERIAL COUNTRY PALACES

To escape the pressures of the capital, successive Russian rulers built sumptuous retreats in the rural hinterland of St Petersburg. These offer a fascinating insight into the lifestyle of the Romanov dynasty.

Tsarskoe Selo's Catherine Palace was built by Rastrelli in a flamboyant Baroque style.

Peterhof's palace and pavilions are enhanced by the splendid cascades and fountains adorning the attractive grounds.

0 km   15

0 miles   15

Pavlovsk's Great Palace is set in an extensive naturalistic landscaped park, embellished with ponds, pavilions and monuments.

Kshesinskaya Mansion
Built for a prima ballerina of the Mariinskiy Theatre, this attractive Style-Moderne mansion now houses the Museum of Russian Political History containing souvenirs from the Revolution.

Summer Palace
Interiors and furniture, such as Peter the Great's original four-poster bed, give an idea of the tsar's relatively modest lifestyle.

Neva

Stieglitz Museum
A rich collection of applied art is displayed in Messmacher's magnificent building, which was inspired by palaces of the Italian Renaissance.

Gostinyy Dvor

Russian Museum
Carlo Rossi's Mikhaylovskiy Palace is the splendid setting for an outstanding collection of Russian art, ranging from medieval icons to contemporary paintings and sculptures. This semi-abstract work Blue Crest *by Vasily Kandinsky dates from 1917.*

Pushkin House-Museum
Period furnishings and personal belongings such as this inkstand recreate the atmosphere of Alexander Pushkin's last home.

0 metres	500
0 yards	500

Exploring St Petersburg's Palaces and Museums

The city's palaces range from imperial excess to the tasteful homes of the nobility, while art museums cover the fine and applied arts and folk crafts. The history of St Petersburg, from its foundation as Peter the Great's "window on the West" to its role as the "cradle of the Revolution", is covered by a variety of museums while its culture is documented in the apartments of writers, composers and artists. More specialist interests, from railway engines and military paraphernalia to insects and whales, also find reflection in the wealth of museums.

**Bedroom in the Chinese Palace
(1760s), Oranienbaum**

**Peter the Great's Summer Palace
overlooking the Fontanka**

PALACES

The fabulous wealth of imperial St Petersburg is reflected in the magnificence of its palaces. No trip to the city is complete without a visit to at least one of the spectacular out-of-town imperial summer residences, **Peterhof** *(see pp148–51)*, **Pavlovsk** *(see pp158–61)* or the Catherine Palace *(see pp152–3)* at **Tsarskoe Selo**. These palaces, built and added to in the last 200 years of Romanov rule, illustrate the extravagance of the imperial court and the wealth of the empire's natural resources. An abundance of gold, lapis lazuli, malachite, marble and other precious minerals decorates many of the rich palace interiors. The palace parks and grounds are landscaped and filled with follies and monuments.

At the centre of the city, the **Winter Palace** *(see pp92–3)* is home to the Hermitage art museum and epitomizes the opulence of the court. Peter the Great's more intimate

Summer Palace is nearby *(see p95)* and makes a pleasing contrast. Peter's friend and counsellor, Prince Alexander Menshikov, also built two sumptuous residences, the **Menshikov Palace** *(see p62)* on Vasilevskiy Island, and his summer palace at **Oranienbaum** *(see p146)*, Lomonosov.

Overlooking the Moyka river is the **Yusupov Palace** *(see p120)* which is famed as the murder scene of Rasputin, the extraordinary peasant who exerted his malign influence over the Russian court.

For those in search of a tranquil setting, a pleasant day can be spent exploring the **Yelagin Palace** *(see p126)* and the island of the same name.

ART MUSEUMS

One of the world's greatest collections of Western art is housed in the **Hermitage** *(see pp84–93)* which is home to some 3 million pieces of art. With collections ranging from Egyptian mummies to Scythian gold, Greek vases,

Colombian emeralds and a vast and dazzling array of Old Master, Impressionist and Post-Impressionist paintings, it is essential to be selective.

The **Russian Museum** *(see pp104–107)* is a showcase for Russian art, including the 20th-century avant-garde and the folk crafts which influenced it. Exhibitions from its holdings are also in the **Mikhaylovskiy Castle** *(see p101)*, **Marble Palace** *(see p94)* and **Stroganov Palace** *(see p112)*.

The **Academy of Arts** *(see p63)* exhibits work by past students as well as models of the city's notable buildings.

There are fascinating displays of applied arts from around the world in the **Stieglitz Museum** *(see p127)* which includes ceramics, wood carving, ironwork and embroidery. Its interiors and the glass-roofed exhibition hall are equally impressive.

***The Cyclist* (1913) by Natalya Goncharova, Russian Museum**

HISTORY MUSEUMS

St Petersburg's dramatic 300-year history is proudly recorded in a number of the city's museums. The **Cabin of Peter the Great** *(see p73)* was the earliest building to be constructed in the city and it offers an intriguing insight into the surprisingly humble lifestyle of this tsar.

A group of historic sights lies within the Peter and Paul Fortress. The **Cathedral of SS Peter and Paul** *(see p68)* houses the tombs of all but two of Russia's tsars since Peter the Great. The preserved cells of the grim **Trubetskoy Bastion** *(see p69)* act as a reminder of the hundreds of political prisoners to be confined within the fortress walls. In the **Commandant's House** *(see p69)*, the courthouse where prisoners were once interrogated, an exhibition looks at medieval settlements in the area, while the **Engineer's House** *(see p68)* focuses on daily life in St Petersburg before the Revolution.

A wealth of revolutionary memorabilia, including Stalin era posters and a huge propaganda stained-glass panel, can be found in the **Museum of Russian Political History**. The museum is located within the Kshesinskaya Mansion *(see p72)* which, in 1917, housed the Bolshevik headquarters. The **Cruiser Aurora** *(see p73)* also played a part in the Revolution, having fired a warning shot before the storming of the Winter Palace in October 1917.

For an impression of the prestigious pre-revolutionary school where poet Alexander Pushkin was a student, some of the class rooms of the **Lycée** at Tsarskoe Selo *(see p155)* have been restored to their 19th-century appearance.

On the southern outskirts of the city, in Victory Square *(see p131)*, the **Monument to the Heroic Defenders of Leningrad** poignantly evokes the Siege of Leningrad (1941–4) and acts as an important reminder of the great hardships endured by St Petersburgers during World War II.

Office of Leningrad party secretary Sergey Kirov, Kirov Museum

SPECIAL INTEREST MUSEUMS

Remnants of Peter the Great's legendary "cabinet of curiosities" can be found in Russia's oldest museum, the **Kunstkammer** *(see p60)*. Housed under the same roof is a **Museum of Anthropology and Ethnography**, displaying a large collection of artifacts from all over the world. For natural history, the **Zoological Museum** *(see p60)* encompasses most known life forms, including a unique collection of molluscs and blue corals.

The **Institute of Russian Literature** *(see p60)* houses manuscripts from Pushkin to Mayakovskiy. The **Artillery Museum** *(see p70)* covers military hardware, from pikes to ballistic missiles. Train enthusiasts will find plenty to enjoy in the **Railway Museum** *(see p123)*, including an 1835 engine built for the Tsarskoe Selo railway.

The **Museum of Musical Life** in the Sheremetev Palace *(see p129)* displays period

18th-century violin and score in Museum of Musical Life, Sheremetev Palace

instruments and explains the role of the Sheremetev family as leading music patrons in 19th-century St Petersburg. A stunning array of beautiful stage costumes are on display alongside photos, set designs and other theatrical ephemera in the **Theatre Museum** which is situated on Ostrovskiy Square *(see p110)*.

HOUSE-MUSEUMS

A handful of evocative museums commemorates some of the city's most famous residents. The **Pushkin House-Museum** *(see p113)*, the **Nabokov Museum** *(see p122)* and the **Dostoevsky House-Museum** *(see p130)* recapture something of the life and character of their former residents.

The **Anna Akhmatova Museum** in the former service quarters of the Sheremetev Palace *(see p129)* traces the dramatic life of the poetess who lived here for many years.

For an insight into the life of a powerful Communist official of the 1930s, visit the **Kirov Museum** *(see p72)*. The museum is devoted to the popular leader whose assassination on Stalin's orders initiated the Great Terror *(see p27)*.

Outside the city in **Repino** *(see p146)*, the house of the painter Ilya Repin is set in beautiful woodland on the Gulf of Finland.

Celebrated St Petersburgers

As the residence of the Russian imperial family and court from the early 18th century, St Petersburg was the focus of patronage and an almost boundless source of wealth. It was the perfect seed bed for creativity and the flowering of ideas. Institutions such as the Academy of Arts, the University, the Kunstkammer and the Imperial School of Ballet trained generations of cultural figures and scientists to the highest standards. So successful were they that, by the dawn of the 20th century, St Petersburg had become one of the most important cultural centres in Europe.

Grigoriy Kozintsev
Director Kozintsev confirmed his reputation in the West with his interpretation of Shakespeare's Hamlet (1964), made at Lenfilm (see p70).

Nikolai Gogol
A merciless satirist of St Petersburg society, Gogol lived on Malaya Morskaya ulitsa (see p82) for three years.

Petrogradskay

Malaya Neva

Vasilevskiy Island

Bolshaya Neva

Ilya Repin
This outstanding realist painter is seen here teaching life drawing at the Academy of Arts (see p63) where he was a professor.

Sennaya Ploshchad

Pyotr Tchaikovsky
Tchaikovsky graduated from the Conservatory (see p120) in 1865 and went on to compose his world-famous operas and ballets.

Anna Pavlova
A prima ballerina at the Mariinskiy Theatre (see p119), Pavlova took Paris by storm in 1909 when she toured in Les Sylphides with the Ballets Russes.

Alexander Pushkin
The great poet, who sketched this self-portrait on a manuscript, died in the flat which is now a house-museum (see p113).

Sergey Diaghilev
Driving force behind the Ballets Russes, Diaghilev also produced the influential World of Art *magazine in his flat on 45 Liteynyy prospekt. He is shown here with* Jean Cocteau (left).

Neva

Palace Embankment

Anna Akhmatova
The poetess' most famous poem, Requiem, *is a powerful and moving indictment of the Stalinist regime. Akhmatova, seen here in a portrait by Nathan Altman, lived in the service quarters of the Sheremetev Palace (see p129).*

Gostinyy Dvor

Dmitriy Shostakovich
Shostakovich's Seventh Symphony *was broadcast live on the radio from the Great Hall of the Philharmonia (see p98) in August 1942, while the city was under siege. Many testified to its role in boosting the morale of the besieged citizens.*

Fyodor Dostoevsky
The novelist Dostoevsky lived for many years among the slums of Sennaya Ploshchad (see p122) which provided the setting for his greatest work, Crime and Punishment.

0 metres	500
0 yards	500

Remarkable St Petersburgers

The streets of St Petersburg are redolent with literary and artistic associations. Fascinating art collections, house-museums, theatres and concert halls evoke the memory of famous St Petersburgers. The world of the 18th-century genius Lomonosov and 19th-century writers Pushkin and Dostoevsky can be imagined. So too, can the spirit of Russian ballet when dancers such as Anna Pavlova and Vaslaw Nijinsky thrilled the Mariinskiy audiences. During these early years of the 20th century, writers, musicians, dancers and painters flocked to St Petersburg, bringing with them a wealth of creativity.

Symbolist "Silver Age" poet, Andrei Bely (1880–1934)

WRITERS

Considered the father of modern Russian literature, **Alexander Pushkin** (1799–1837) was simultaneously intoxicated by St Petersburg's beauty and sensitive to the underlying climate of political suspicion and intolerance which constrained writers in the wake of the Decembrist rebellion of 1825 *(see p23)*. **Nikolai Gogol** (1809–52) responded to these constraints by satirising the status quo. In *The Nose*, he targeted the city's bureaucrats with their inflated sense of self worth and mind-numbing conformity.

Another aspect of the city altogether is revealed by **Fyodor Dostoevsky** (1821–81). His novel *Crime and Punishment*, one of more than 30 works set in the city, takes place against a backdrop of squalor in the notorious slums of Sennaya Ploshchad *(see p122)*. The story of the murder of an old moneylender was based on a real crime and the novel's publication in 1866 was blamed for a series of subsequent copy-cat killings.

Poetry, which flourished in the "Golden Age" of Pushkin, only regained its ascendancy over the novel in the "Silver Age" during the first decade of the 20th century. Some of the most exciting poets of the period, including **Aleksandr Blok** (1880–1921), **Andrei Bely** (1880–1934) and **Anna Akhmatova** (1889–1966), gathered at The Tower, a flat overlooking the Tauride Gardens *(see p128)*. Bely later wrote *Petersburg*, one of the earliest stream-of-consciousness novels. Akhmatova is honoured by a museum in the Sheremetev Palace *(see p129)* while one of her protégés, **Joseph Brodsky** (1940–96) went on to receive the Nobel Prize for literature in 1987. Brodsky became the bête-noire of the Leningrad literary establishment in the 1960s. The refusal of the authorities to publish his poetry, which they condemned as decadent, finally forced him to emigrate in 1972.

MUSICIANS

The first important composer to emerge from the nationalist movement was **Mikhail Glinka** (1804–57), the earliest composer of Russian opera. In 1862, the Conservatory *(see p120)* was founded by **Anton Rubinstein** (1829–94) and this became the focus of musical life in St Petersburg. **Nikolai Rimsky-Korsakov** (1844–1908) taught here for 37 years and together with composers such as **Modest Mussorgsky** (1839–81), and **Aleksandr Borodin** (1834–87), he was part of "the mighty handful". They were a largely self-taught group aiming to develop a musical language based on Russian folk music and Slav traditions. Many of the operas premiered at the Mariinskiy *(see p119)*.

One of the musical geniuses of the 20th century was **Igor Stravinsky** (1882–1971). He spent much time abroad but, as works like *The Rite of Spring* testify, his cultural roots were firmly in his homeland.

The city's most important concert venue is the Great Hall of the Philharmonia *(see p202)* where **Pyotr Tchaikovsky**'s (1840–93) *Sixth Symphony* was premiered in 1893 and **Dmitriy Shostakovich**'s (1906–75) *Seventh Symphony*, his most famous work, was performed in 1942.

Portrait of composer Mikhail Glinka painted by Ilya Repin in 1887

The Circus (1919) by avant-garde artist Marc Chagall

ARTISTS

From the 18th century, the Academy of Arts *(see p63)* was the centre of artistic life in St Petersburg. **Dmitriy Levitskiy** (1735–1822), **Orest Kiprenskiy** (1782–1836), **Silvestr Shchedrin** (1791–1830), and Russia's first internationally recognised artist, **Karl Bryullov** (1799–1852), were all trained here.

In 1863, a group of students rebelled against the Academy and went on to establish the Wanderers movement *(see p106)*. To some extent the Academy and the Wanderers became reconciled when the most versatile of these artists, **Ilya Repin** (1844–1930), was appointed professor of painting at the Academy in 1893.

Five years later **Sergey Diaghilev** (1872–1929) and painter **Alexandre Benois** (1870–1960) launched the *World of Art* magazine *(see p107)*, proclaiming "Art for art's sake". Another collaborator, **Leon Bakst** (1866–1924), designed the most famous of the Ballets Russes costumes. Bakst also taught **Marc Chagall** (1889–1985) who later settled in France and had a profound impact on art in the West as well as in Russia. Other members of the Russian avant-garde include **Kazimir Malevich** (1878–1935) and **Pavel Filonov** (1883–1941).

Works by all of these artists can be seen at the Russian Museum *(see pp104–107)*.

DANCERS AND CHOREOGRAPHERS

The skills of Russian dancers are legendary and the performances of the Mariinskiy (Kirov) Ballet Company continue to enthral audiences all over the world. Since 1836 the dancers have been trained at the former Imperial Ballet School *(see p110)*. In 1869–1903 the outstanding choreographer at the Mariinskiy was **Marius Petipa**. He inspired a generation of dancers including **Matilda Kshesinskaya** *(see p72)*, **Vaslaw Nijinsky** (1890–1950) and the legendary **Anna Pavlova** (1885–1931). Petipa's successor, **Mikhail Fokin** (1880–1942), is famous as the principal choreographer of the Ballets Russes *(see p119)*. The Mariinskiy tradition was revived after the Revolution by another graduate of the Ballet School, **Agrippina Vaganova** (1879–1951). Her groundwork paved the way for a new generation of dancers including **Rudolf Nureyev** (1938–93) and, modern dancers **Galina Mezentseva** and **Emil Faskhoutdinov**.

FILM DIRECTORS

The Lenfilm Studios (see p70) were founded in 1918 on the site where the first Russian cine film had been shown in 1896. In its heyday Lenfilm produced 15 movies a year. Its two most remarkable

Poster for *The Youth of Maxim* (1935) directed by Kozintsev

directors, **Grigoriy Kozintsev** (1905–73) and **Leonid Trauberg** (1902–90), first joined forces in 1922 and began making short experimental films. The pair then went on to direct *The New Babylon* (1929), remarkable for its montage and lighting effects, and *The Maxim Trilogy* (1935–39). Kozintsev's versions of *Hamlet* (1964) and *King Lear* (1970), with music composed by Shostakovich for both films, mark the height of his success in the West.

SCIENTISTS

The great polymath Mikhail Lomonosov

The foundations of modern Russian science were laid in the 18th century by **Mikhail Lomonosov** (1711–65) *(see p61)* who worked for over 20 years in the Kunstkammer *(see p60)*. His treatise, *Elementa Chymiae Mathematica*, published in 1741, anticipates Dalton's theory of the atomic structure of matter.

In 1869, **Dmitriy Mendeleev** (1834–1907), a professor of chemistry, compiled the Periodic Table of Elements. Many people believe that the world's first radio signal was sent by **Aleksandr Popov** (1859–1906) from the laboratories of St Petersburg University on 24 March 1896.

In 1904, the world-famous physiologist **Ivan Pavlov** (1849–1936) won the Nobel Prize for medicine for his theory of conditioned reflexes, which he demonstrated by experimenting on dogs and their hearing responses.

Nevskiy Prospekt
From the Admiralty to the Griboedov Canal

A pleasant stroll along this first stretch of
St Petersburg's main artery reveals a wealth of
attractive buildings. A profusion of architectural
styles ranges from the Baroque Stroganov Palace
to the magnificent Neo-Classical Cathedral of Our
Lady of Kazan and the striking Style-Moderne
Singer House. The stately avenue was once
known as the "Street of Tolerance", referring to
the clutch of churches of different denominations
that were established here in the late 18th and
early 19th centuries. *(See also p108.)*

Literary Café
*Once called the Wolf and Beranger,
this café was known for its fashionable
clientele. Pushkin left from here
for his fatal duel in 1837 (see p83).*

**Admiralty
(p78)**

**Palace Square *(p83)* and the
Hermitage *(pp84–93)***

The 1760s apartment blocks at Nos. 8
and 10 are an example of early
St Petersburg Neo-Classicism.

ADMIRALTEYSKIY PROSPEKT

N E V S K I Y   P R O S P E K T

BOLSHAYA MORSKAYA ULITSA

MALAYA MORSKAYA ULITSA

ZELENYY

Admiralty Garden
*This garden was laid out in
1872–4. Near the fountain
are busts of composer Mikhail
Glinka, writer Nikolai Gogol
and poet Mikhail Lermontov.*

**St Isaac's Cathedral
(pp80–81) and
Astoria Hotel *(p79)***

BOLSHAYA MORSKAYA ULITSA

0 metres	100
0 yards	100

School No. 210
*This school carries a sign,
dating from the Siege,
warning, "Citizens!
This side of the street is
more dangerous during
artillery bombardment".*

Aeroflot Building
*Marian Peretyatkovich's severe granite
building (1912) is uncharacteristic of the
city's architecture. The upper storeys were
inspired by the Palazzo Medici in Florence;
the arcades by the Doge's Palace, Venice.*

STAR SIGHT

★ Cathedral of Our Lady
of Kazan

LOCATOR MAP

NEVSKIY PROSPEKT

НЕВСКИЙ ПРОСПЕКТ

Dutch Church Building
*The Dutch church was housed behind
the central Neo-Classical portico of Paul
Jacot's seemingly secular building
(1831–7). The elongated wings are still
occupied by offices, flats and shops.*

Stroganov Palace
*The façade of this splendid Baroque
palace, one of the oldest buildings
on the street (1753), is embellished
with sculptural ornaments and the
Stroganov coat of arms (see p112).*

The Fashion House
*Marian Lyalevich designed this
building for Mertens Furriers
in 1911–12. The impact of the
Neo-Classical arches is
heightened by
the beautiful
plate glass.*

NAB REKI MOYKI

BOLSHAYA KONYUSHENNAYA UL

MALAYA KONYUSHENNAYA ULITSA

N E V S K I Y   P R O S P E K T

Singer House was built
for the Singer Sewing
Machine Company in
1902–4 by Pavel Syuzor.
The building is distin-
guished by a glass globe
on a conical tower.

KAZANSKAYA ULITSA

KAZANSKIY MOST

→ Continued
(pp48–9)

The Lutheran Church
(1833) was an important
centre for the evangelical
community. Converted into
a swimming pool during the
Soviet era, it is once again
open as a church *(see p112).*

KANAL GRIBOEDOVA

The Griboedov Canal,
originally known as the
Catherine Canal, was renamed
in 1923 after the 19th-century
Russian playwright
Aleksandr Griboedov.

**★ Cathedral of
Our Lady of Kazan**
*Ninety-six Corinthian col-
umns, arranged in four rows,
form an arc facing Nevskiy
prospekt. Andrey Voronikhin's
design was inspired by
Bernini's colonnade for St
Peter's in Rome (see p111).*

Nevskiy Prospekt
From the Griboedov Canal to the Fontanka

Nevskiy Prospekt has been the main focus for St Petersburg's shopping and entertainment since the mid-18th century. As the prospekt continues towards the handsome Anichkov Bridge on the Fontanka river, cafés, bars, restaurants and cinemas sit alongside three historic shopping arcades, the Silver Rows, Gostinyy Dvor and Passazh. Bustling with life, this stretch of the avenue also has many sights of historic and architectural interest, including the Anichkov Palace.

Passazh Arcade
This popular shopping mall is covered by a glass canopy stretching 180 m (590 ft). The arcade opened in 1848 and was reconstructed in 1900.

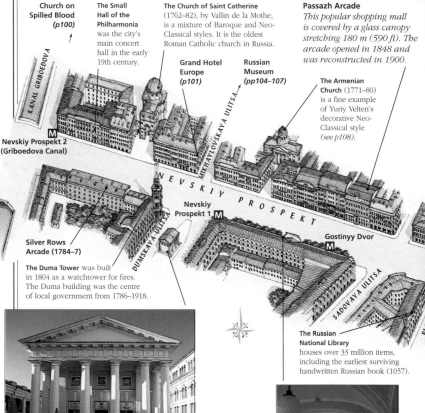

Church on Spilled Blood *(p100)*

The Small Hall of the Philharmonia was the city's main concert hall in the early 19th century.

The Church of Saint Catherine (1762–82), by Vallin de la Mothe, is a mixture of Baroque and Neo-Classical styles. It is the oldest Roman Catholic church in Russia.

Grand Hotel Europe *(p101)*

Russian Museum *(pp104–107)*

The Armenian Church (1771–80) is a fine example of Yuriy Velten's decorative Neo-Classical style *(see p108).*

KANAL GRIBOEDOVA

MIKHAYLOVSKAYA ULITSA

NEVSKIY PROSPEKT

Ⓜ **Nevskiy Prospekt 2** (Griboedova Canal)

Nevskiy Prospekt 1 Ⓜ

DUMSKAYA ULITSA

Silver Rows Arcade (1784–7)

Gostinyy Dvor Ⓜ

SADOVAYA ULITSA

PLOSHCH

The Duma Tower was built in 1804 as a watchtower for fires. The Duma building was the centre of local government from 1786–1918.

The Russian National Library houses over 33 million items, including the earliest surviving handwritten Russian book (1057).

Portik Rusca Perinnyie Ryadi
Now standing alone, the six-columned portico by Luigi Rusca was originally the entrance to a long arcade of shops. The portico was dismantled during the construction of the metro and rebuilt in 1972.

★ **Gostinyy Dvor**
This striking arcade has been St Petersburg's main bazaar since the mid-18th century (see p108). It houses more than 300 outlets which sell everything from clothes and cosmetics to souvenirs and chocolates.

| 0 metres | 100 |
| 0 yards | 100 |

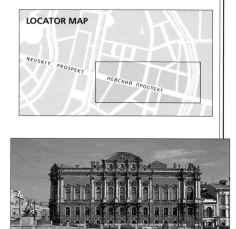

LOCATOR MAP

NEVSKIY PROSPEKT

НЕВСКИЙ ПРОСПЕКТ

★ Yeliseev's
Famous for its beautiful Style-Moderne decor, this building is home to Yeliseev's delicatessen, and also houses the Akimov Comedy Theatre (see p109).

STAR SIGHTS

★ Yeliseev's

★ Gostinyy Dvor

Beloselskiy-Belozerskiy Palace
Now a cultural centre and offices, this sumptuous palace was designed in Neo-Baroque style by Andrey Stakenschneider in 1847–8. The red façade is decorated with Corinthian pilasters and atlantes upholding balconies.

Quarenghi's Stalls were built in 1803–6 as trading rows. They were then handed over to the imperial chancellor and became known as the Cabinet.

Number 66 was occupied by the music publishers Bessel and Co in the 19th century. Tchaikovsky was one of many composers who frequented their offices.

NEVSKIY PROSPEKT

OSTROVSKOVO

FONTANKA

ANICHKOV MOST

FONTANKA

Alexandrinskiy Theatre

A statue of Catherine the Great stands in Ostrovskiy Square *(see p110).*

Moskovskiy railway station

The Anichkov Palace was first built as a present from Tsarina Elizabeth to her lover, Aleksey Razumovskiy. It later became the winter residence of the heir to the throne *(see p109).*

Anichkov Bridge
Four dynamic bronze statues of rearing horses and their tamers adorn this well-known landmark. They were designed in the 1840s by Pyotr Klodt (see p35).

ST PETERSBURG THROUGH THE YEAR

Whatever the weather, Russians are always ready to celebrate and consequently take their public holidays very seriously. Flowers have great symbolic significance, from mimosa for International Women's Day, to lilac to mark the beginning of summer. Every official holiday, as well as some local festivals such as City Day, are celebrated both in the centre of town and in the many

Lilac, a symbol of summer

different districts, with regattas, parades and fireworks at night, when the torches on the Rostral Columns *(see p60)* are lit. Classical music is the central theme of a large number of festivals each year, attracting talented performers from all over the world. But even without an official holiday, Russian people love to get out and about, whether to ski or ice-skate in the winter months or gather mushrooms in late summer and autumn.

SPRING

Spring has set in for good when the first sunbathers gather on the beaches outside the Peter and Paul Fortress *(see pp66–7)* and when, in early April after the waterways have thawed, the city's bridges open to allow ships through.

To warm themselves up after the months of cold, locals celebrate "maslennitsa", the making of pancakes *(blini)* prior to Lent. They then gather bunches of willow as a symbol of the approaching Palm Sunday. On the eve of Lent, "Forgiveness Sunday", it is common practice to ask for-giveness of those you might have offended during the year.

Once the snows have gone, the first trips to the *dacha*, or country house, are made to put the gardens in order.

Candles lighting up Russian Ortho-dox church during Easter service

tradition to say *s prazdnikom* (congratulations on the holi-day) to everyone. There are even special performances and concerts and, however sexist it may seem to non-Russians, it is a very popular day.
From the Avant Garde to the Present *(Ot avangarda do nashih dney)*, mid-Mar. A cele-bration of 20th-century art and music in a city-wide festival.
Easter Sunday *(Paskha)*. The dates on which Lent and Easter fall change every year. On Easter Sunday, St Peters-burg churches are filled with worshippers, the evocative sound of ethereal music and chanting and the smell of incense. Russians tradi-tionally greet each other with *Khristos voskres* (Christ is risen), to which the reply is *Voistine voskres* (He is truly risen).

mid-Apr. As warm clothing and heavy boots are laid aside after the cold winter months, the public flock to concert halls throughout the city.
Cosmonauts' Day *(Den Kosmonavtiki)*, 12 Apr. Space exploration was one of the glories of the Soviet Union and this occasion is celebrated with fireworks at 10pm.

MAY

Labour Day (International Workers' Solidarity Day *(Den Truda)*, 1 May. Public holiday.
Peterhof Fountains *(Fontany v Petergofe)*, first weekend in May. Bands and orchestras accompany the switching on of the famous fountains at Peterhof *(see p151)*. **Victory Day** *(Den Pobedy)*, 9 May. After a sombre ceremony at Piskarevskoe Cemetery *(see p126)*, smartly dressed veterans fill Nevskiy prospekt *(see pp46–9)* and Palace Square *(see p83)* in commemoration of the Nazi surrender in 1945. **City Day** *(Den goroda)*, last week of May. A great variety of events, mainly taking place around the Peter and Paul Fortress *(see pp66–7)*, mark the founding of the city on 27 May 1703.
Musical Olympus International Festival, late May/early Jun. Young musicians from all over the world are accompanied by St Petersburg's most famous orchestras.

Early sunbathers on the banks of the Peter and Paul Fortress

MARCH

International Women's Day *(Mezhdunarodnyy zhenskiy den)*, 8 Mar. Men rush around the city buying flowers for their womenfolk. It is a

APRIL

Musical Spring in St Petersburg *(Muzikalnaya Vesna v Sankt-Peterburge)*,

Proud war veteran on Victory Day

AVERAGE DAILY HOURS OF SUNSHINE

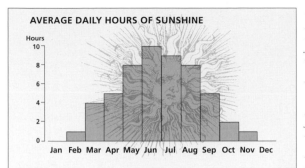

Hours

10
8
6
4
2
0

Jan Feb Mar Apr May Jun Jul Aug Sep Oct Nov Dec

Sunshine Hours
St Petersburg's climate can vary dramatically from hot, sunny days and occasional heavy downpours during the summer months, to winters with sub-zero temperatures and snow. From mid-June to mid-July, it never gets dark. During the winter months the days are extremely short, but there can be days of bright sunshine.

SUMMER

A lilac in flower is the real symbol that warm weather has set in and there is an air of excitement once the Field of Mars *(see p94)* comes into bloom. Throughout the warm months, the city is deserted at weekends when people go off to their *dacha,* which is usually a summer house outside the city.

St Petersburg's main festive season is during the acclaimed White Nights in June, when the sun hardly sets and it never quite gets dark. Concerts, ballets and other performances take place all over the city, which fills with thousands of visitors *(see p201).* The most favoured place to be at nighttime is on the embankments of the Neva, which are crowded with revellers watching the bridges being raised around 2am.

JUNE

International Protection of Children Day *(Den Zatschity detey),* 1 Jun.

Performances and events for children are held throughout the city.
Russia Day *(Den Rossii),* 12 Jun. The day Russia became "independent" of the Soviet Union is marked with fireworks at 10pm.
Trinity Sunday *(Troytsa),* 50 days after Easter. Believers and atheists alike go to tidy the graves of their loved ones and raise a glass of vodka for their souls.
The White Nights Swing, Jazz Festival, mid-June. A large jam session supported by local and visiting musicians for anyone with an interest in jazz.
Stars of the White Nights, Classical Music Festival *(Zvezdy Belykh nochey),* Jun. This is the original White Nights festival, with first-class opera, classical music and ballet concerts performed at all major venues.
White Nights, Rock Music Festival *(Belye nochi),* late Jun. Numerous outdoor rock concerts are held at the Peter and Paul Fortress *(see pp66–7).*

Russian battleships moored on the Neva, Navy Day

Festival of Festivals *(Festival-festivaley),* last week in Jun. This is an international non-competitive film festival showing the best international films released over the past year. The festival attracts film stars from all over the world.
Tsarskoe Selo Carnival *(Tsarskoselskiy karnaval),* last weekend in June. Funny costumes, music and mayhem fill the centre of Tsarskoe Selo *(see pp152–5).*

JULY

Sporting Competitions. St Petersburg is a popular sporting venue for numerous international events, offering everything from tennis to figure skating and yachting.
Navy Day *(Den Voenno-morskovo Flota),* first Sun after 22 July. The Neva resembles a shipyard, with submarines and torpedo boats adorned with flags and bunting.

AUGUST

With schools on holiday and temperatures at their highest, this is a quiet time, with most families escaping to their *dacha* outside the city.

Bridge opening in front of the Peter and Paul Fortress on a White Night

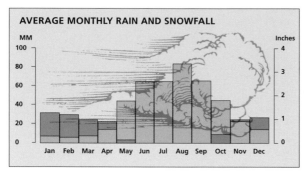

AVERAGE MONTHLY RAIN AND SNOWFALL

MM | Inches

■ Rainfall (from axis)
□ Snowfall (from axis)

Rain and Snow-fall Chart

St Petersburg summers are humid and wet, but the downpours are a welcome relief from the summer heat. In winter frequent snowfalls build up to create metre-high drifts, usually not thawing until late March.

AUTUMN

City life begins to gain pace as people return from their *dacha* and families begin to prepare for the start of school.

In September, when theatres re-open after the summer break, the city's cultural life resumes. The Mariinskiy (Kirov) returns from touring, and new plays and operas are premiered. October marks the start of the festival season, with guest musicians and theatre groups from all over the world taking part.

The crisp autumn weather is ideal for gathering mushrooms.

Chanterelle mushrooms

Popular hunting spots can be found to the northwest of the city around Zelenogorsk and Repino *(see p146)*. Enthusiastic mushroom-gatherers rise early to hunt for chanterelles, oyster mushrooms, *podberyozoviki* (brown mushrooms) and *podosinoviki* (orange-cap bolens). The locals are skilled in identifying edible mushrooms while amateur pickers should be aware of the dangers of poisonous ones. An activity with fewer potential side-effects might be a trip on the hydrofoil to Peterhof *(see pp148–51)* to see the magnificent fountains before they are switched off for the winter.

Children dressed up for the first day of school

SEPTEMBER

Knowledge Day
(Den znaniy), 1 Sep. The city is full of children heading for their first day back at school, laden with flowers.

OCTOBER

International Theatre Festival Baltic House *(Baltiyskiy dom)*, Oct. Actors, clowns and pantomime artists gather from the Baltic countries to perform in theatres and on the streets with two weeks of mayhem.

NOVEMBER

Day of National Unity, 4 Nov. A reminder that the Russian Federation is a multi-national country with various religions and political parties.
Sound Ways, Modern Music Festival *(Zvukovyye puti)*, mid-Nov. A chance to catch up with some of the most avant-garde trends in jazz and contemporary classical music from Russia and the rest of Europe. Musicians invited from abroad abound, and many of Russia's most renowned performers refuse international engagements in order to take part in this exciting home-grown festival.

Autumn colours in the park at Tsarskoe Selo

AVERAGE MONTHLY TEMPERATURE

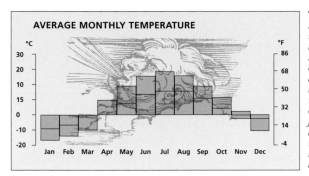

°C / °F

30 / 86
20 / 68
10 / 50
15 / 32
0
-10 / 14
-20 / -4

Jan Feb Mar Apr May Jun Jul Aug Sep Oct Nov Dec

Temperature Chart

St Petersburg's climate is maritime and milder than might be expected. Summers are warm and often punctuated with hot days as early as May, though during the winter months temperatures often fall well below freezing. St Petersburg's average minimum and maximum temperatures throughout the year are shown in this chart.

WINTER

As the ice thickens on the waters and the snow deepens, people head for the outdoors once more. Children's sledges are not expensive to buy, and all other equipment can be hired. Cross-country skiing needs no lessons to make it fun. Tsarskoe Selo *(see pp152–5)* and Pavlovsk *(see pp158–61)* parks provide ski and sledge hire at the ski bases *(lyzhnaya baza)*. Skates can be hired for use in the rink at Moskovskiy Park Pobedy, by Park Pobedy metro station in the south of the city, and also at the Central Park of Culture and Rest (Krestovskiy Ostrov metro station).

The truly hardened members of the local "walruses" swimming club break the ice by the Peter and Paul Fortress *(see pp66–7)* every day to take an early morning dip.

In the midst of winter activities come New Year and Christmas. New Year is the big holiday, while Christmas itself is celebrated according to the Orthodox calendar, on 7 January. Many people also still

Sledging on the frozen Neva outside the Hermitage *(see pp84–93)*

Drilling a hole through the ice for winter-time fishing

celebrate Old New Year, which falls on 14 January. A seasonal delight is the Christmas ballet, *The Nutcracker*, at the Mariinskiy Theatre *(see p119)*.

DECEMBER

Constitution Day *(Den konstitutsii)*, 12 Dec. When Yeltsin's new constitution replaced the Brezhnev version, a new constitution day replaced the old one. Fireworks are set off all over town at 10pm.
Musical Encounters in the Northern Palmyra *(Muzykalnyye vstrechi v Severnoy Palmire)*, Dec–Jan. This classical music festival is the last one of the year and is made even more magical by the backdrop of snowy streets and frozen waterways outside.
New Year's Eve *(Novyy god)*, 31 Dec. Still the biggest holiday of the year, New Year's Eve is best celebrated with the local "champagne", Shampanskoye *(see p183)*. This is considered to be a family celebration, with people dressed as Grandfather Frost (the Russian equivalent of Santa Claus) and the Snow Maiden, the traditional bearers of gifts.

JANUARY

Russian Orthodox Christmas *(Rozhdestvo)*, 7 Jan. Christmas is celebrated in a quieter fashion than Easter, with a traditional visit to an evening service on Christmas Eve (6th), when the church bells ring out all over the city.

FEBRUARY

Defenders of the Motherland Day *(Den zashchitnikov rodiny)*, 23 Feb. The male equivalent of Women's Day. Men are congratulated and given flowers and presents.

PUBLIC HOLIDAYS

New Year's Day (1 Jan)
Russian Orthodox Christmas (7 Jan)
International Women's Day (8 Mar)
Easter Sunday (Mar/Apr)
Labour Day (1 May)
Victory Day (9 May)
Independence Day (12 Jun)
Day of National Unity (4 Nov)
Constitution Day (12 Dec)

ST PETERSBURG
AREA BY AREA

VASILEVSKIY ISLAND

It was Peter the Great's intention that Vasilevskiy Island (*Vasilevskiy ostrov*), the largest island in the Neva delta, was to be the administrative heart of his new capital. However, lack of access (the first permanent bridge was not built until 1842) and the hazards of floods and stormy crossings led to the abandonment of Peter's project, and the centre grew up across the river around the Admiralty (*see p78*) instead. The island's original street plan, based on canals that were never dug (*see p20*), survives in the numbered streets known as lines

Allegorical sculpture of Neptune on the façade of the former Stock Exchange

(*linii*), which run from north to south. The focal point of the island is at the east end with the fine ensemble of public buildings around the Strelka, or "spit". The rest of the island developed with the spread of industrialization in the 19th century and it became a middle-class haven. There was also a thriving German community here which is reflected in the several Lutheran churches. Today much of the island has a sedate air, with tree-lined avenues, museums and some attractive 19th-century architecture.

SIGHTS AT A GLANCE

Museums
The Institute of Russian Literature ❷
Kunstkammer ❹
Menshikov Palace ❻
Zoological Museum ❸

Streets and Bridges
Blagoveshchenskiy Bridge ❿
Bolshoy Prospekt ❼

Historic Buildings and Monuments
Academy of Arts ❾
Rostral Columns ❶
Twelve Colleges ❺

Churches
St Andrew's Cathedral ❽

KEY

| Street-by-Street map See pp58–9 |
| M Metro |
| Tram stop |
| River boat stop |

0 metres 400
0 yards 400

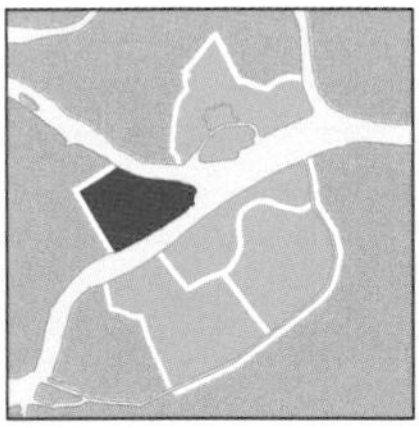

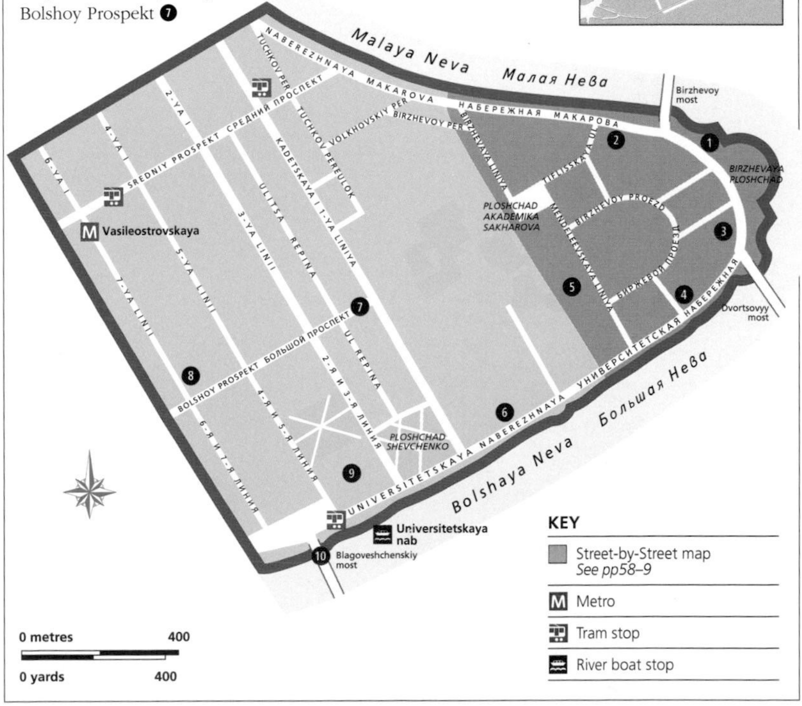

◁ One of the two imposing 14th-century BC sphinxes situated in front of the Academy of Arts

Street-by-Street: the Strelka

The eastern end of Vasilevskiy Island is known as the Strelka, or "spit". Once St Petersburg's main centre of commerce, it has become an area of learning. The Academy of Sciences and St Petersburg University are both situated here, as are various museums, institutes and libraries, housed in the former warehouses and customs buildings. The nautical theme is preserved in the two Rostral Columns. In front of these lighthouses is a lawn, a popular spot for newly married couples to have their picture taken. From here there are views across the Neva towards the Peter and Paul Fortress *(see pp66–7)* and the Hermitage *(see pp84–93)*.

The old Stock Exchange and Rostral Columns from across the Neva

The Lomonosov Monument honours Mikhail Lomonosov (1711–65), who taught at the Academy of Sciences.

Twelve Colleges
Originally erected to house the 12 ministries of Peter the Great's government, they now form the main building of St Petersburg University ❺

The Academy of Sciences was founded in 1724. The present building was constructed by Giacomo Quarenghi in 1783–5.

★ Kunstkammer
The Kunstkammer houses Peter the Great's collection of biological curiosities. Its tower, crowned by a sundial, is a St Petersburg landmark ❹

Zoological Museum
With over 1.5 million specimens the museum is one of the finest of its kind in the world. The exhibits include a set of stuffed animals that belonged to Peter the Great and a world-famous collection of mammoths ❸

Palace Embankment

STAR SIGHTS

★ Kunstkammer

★ Rostral Columns

Academy of Sciences Library was founded in 1714 with Peter the Great's personal book collection. It now has over 17 million volumes.

Sakharov Monument

LOCATOR MAP
See Street Finder, map 1

The New Exchange Bazaar was designed by Quarenghi in the early 19th century. At the time a busy market filled its Neo-Classical loggias. Today students have replaced the shoppers, as the building houses departments of the university.

The former Stock Exchange was built in 1805–10 as the focal point of the Strelka. It was modelled on a Greek temple.

BIRZHEVOY MOST → Peter and Paul Fortress

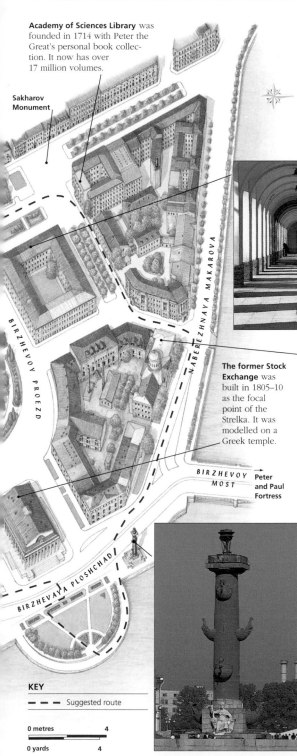

NABEREZHNAYA MAKAROVA

BIRZHEVOY PROEZD

BIRZHEVAYA PLOSHCHAD

KEY

- - - Suggested route

0 metres 4
0 yards 4

The Institute of Russian Literature
Housed in a building built in 1832, this literary museum, also known as Pushkin House, holds more than 70 books, prints and manuscripts ❷

★ **Rostral Columns**
Originally lighthouses guiding ships through the busy port of St Petersburg, these imposing 32-m (105-ft) high columns are a distinctive feature of St Petersburg's skyline. They are still lit for Navy Day (see p51) and other festivals ❶

Rostral Columns ❶

Ростральные колонны
Rostralnye kolonny

Birzhevaya ploshchad. **Map** 1 C5.
🚌 7, 10, 24, 47, 191, K-187,
K-209, K-252. 🚊 1, 7, 10, 11.

Situated on the Strelka
before the former Stock
Exchange, the impres-
sive twin russet-coloured
Rostral Columns were
designed as lighthouses
by Thomas de Thomon in
1810. During the 19th
century the oil lamps were
replaced by gas torches
which are still lit on
ceremonial occa-
sions. The columns
are decorated with
protruding ships'
prows in celebration
of naval victories.
The monumental
figures around the base
represent four of
Russia's rivers, the Neva,
Volga, Dnieper and Volkhov.

**Rostral Column
on the Strelka**

The Institute of Russian Literature (Pushkin House) ❷

Институт русской
литературы (Пушкинский
Дом)
*Institut Russkoy Literatury
(Pushkinskiy Dom)*

Naberezhnaya Makarova 4.
Map 1 C5. **Tel** 328 0502. 🚌 7, 10,
47, 187, K-209, K-252. 🚊 1, 7, 10,
11. ⏰ 11am–4pm Mon–Fri. 📷 ♿
English. **www**.pushkinskijdom.ru

Founded at the beginning
of the 20th century, this
museum houses numerous

manuscripts and exhibits
connected to Russia's
greatest poet, Alexander
Pushkin. Known as
Pushkin House, the
museum focuses on
preserving the legacy
of Russian literary
culture from the distant
past to the present. The
museum has grown
into an unrivalled
repository of rare
and unusual artifacts
connected with some of
Russia's greatest writers,
including Turgenev,
Gogol, Dostoevsky,
Tolstoy and Blok.
A room is
dedicated
to the Silver
Age poets,
displaying
work by Anna
Akhmatova and
Mikhail
Bulgakov.

Today Pushkin House
contains more than 3 million
autographed manuscripts,
including 12,000 pages from
Pushkin alone. In addition to
more than 700,000 books and
print editions reflecting the
history of Russian literature,
the museum also preserves
thousands of images,
paintings, drawings and
objects. Many of these are on
view in the galleries, which
are decorated with period
furniture. In addition to the
archives, the institute also
publishes new scholarly
editions, which are on sale at
the museum.

Visitors who wish to take an
English-language tour of the
museum should be sure to
phone ahead.

Manuscripts on display at the Institute of Russian Literature

Zoological Museum ❸

Зоологический музей
Zoologicheskiy muzey

Universitetskaya naberezhnaya 1/3.
Map 1 C5. **Tel** 328 0112. 🚌 7,
10, 24, 47, 191, K-187, K-209.
K-252. 🚊 1, 7, 10, 11. ⏰
11am–6pm Sat–Thu. 📷 (free Thu).
📷 🎫 ♿ English. **www**.zin.ru

Housed in a former customs
warehouse designed by
Giovanni Lucchini in 1826,
this museum has one of the
world's largest natural history
collections containing more
than 1.5 million specimens.
Some of the stuffed animals
belonged to Peter the Great's
Kunstkammer collection,
including the horse he rode at
the Battle of Poltava *(see p18)*.

Dioramas recreate natural
habitats for giant crabs,
weasels, polar bears and blue
whales. The museum is
renowned for its collection of
mammoths. One prized carcass
was exhumed from the frozen
wastes of Siberia in 1902 and
is almost 44,000 years old.

Weasel in the Zoological Museum

Kunstkammer ❹

Кунсткамера
Kunstkamera

Universitetskaya naberezhnaya 3.
Map 1 C5. **Tel** 328 0812. 🚌 7, 10,
24, 47, 191, K-187, K-191, K-209,
K-252. 🚊 1, 7, 10, 11. ⏰ 11am–
6pm Tue–Sun. 📷 🎫 English.
www.kunstkamera.ru

The delicate, sea green lantern tower of the Baroque
Kunstkammer ("art chamber")
is visible across this part of
Vasilevskiy Island. The building, by Georg Mattarnoviy, was
constructed in 1718–34 to ex-
hibit Peter the Great's infamous
Kunstkammer collection.
While touring Holland in 1697
Peter attended the lectures of

The restrained Baroque façade of the Kunstkammer (1718–34), Russia's first museum

Frederik Ruysch (1638–1731), the most celebrated anatomist of his day. He was so impressed with Ruysch's collection of rarities that on a return visit in 1717, he purchased the entire collection of over 2,000 anatomical preparations. He transported it to St Petersburg and exhibited it to a wide-eyed public, who were enticed by free glasses of vodka. At the time, Peter's collection also included bizarre, live exhibits of deformed or unusual people, including an hermaphrodite. This, Russia's first museum, also included a library, an anatomical theatre and an observatory.

Today the Kunstkammer houses the Museum of Anthropology and Ethnography, with the remnants of Peter's bizarre collection on display in the central rotunda. Included are the heart and skeleton of Peter's personal servant, "Bourgeois", a giant at 2.27 m (7.5 ft), and a cabinet of teeth extracted by the tsar who was an enthusiastic amateur dentist. Most gruesome of all is the collection of pickled oddities which include Siamese twins and a two-headed sheep.

The halls surrounding the *Kunstkammer* collection contain exhibitions on the peoples of the world. Often neglected by visitors, these marvellously old-fashioned displays present an informative range of artifacts, from an Inuit kayak to Javanese shadow puppets.

Twelve Colleges ❺

Двенадцать коллегий
Dvenadtsat kollegiy

Universitetskaya naberezhnaya 7.
Map 1 C5. 🚎 7, 24, 47, 129, K-187, K-209. 🚊 1, 10, 11. ⬤ to public.

This distinguished Baroque building of red-and-white stuccoed brick is almost 400 m (1,300 ft) in length. It was intended for Peter the Great's newly streamlined administration of 12 colleges or ministries. The single, uninterrupted façade was designed to symbolize the government's unity of purpose, while the curious alignment, at right angles to the embankment, is explained by Peter's unrealized plan for a large

Mikhail Lomonosov (1711–65)

square with an unbroken view across the Strelka. Another popular theory is that Prince Menshikov changed the plan in Peter's absence so that the building would not encroach on his grounds. Domenico Trezzini won the competition for the design in 1723, but subsequent bureaucratic wrangling delayed its completion for 20 years. The building's function gradually changed and in 1819 part of it was acquired by St Petersburg University. A string of revolutionaries, including Lenin in 1891, were educated here. Among the famous Russian lecturers to teach here were the chemist Dmitriy Mendeleev (1834–1907) *(see p45)* and the physiologist Ivan Pavlov (1849–1936) *(see p45)*.

Overlooking the Neva, outside the Twelve Colleges, is an engaging bronze statue of the great 18th-century polymath Mikhail Lomonosov (unveiled in 1986). The son of a fisherman, Lomonosov was the first Russian-born member of the nearby Academy of Sciences. A "universal genius", he wrote poetry, systematized Russian grammar and was a pioneer in mathematics and the physical sciences. Thanks to his scientific discoveries, the art of porcelain, glass and mosaic production began in Russia.

A section of the west façade of Trezzini's Twelve Colleges

The southern façade of Prince Menshikov's 18th-century palace

Menshikov Palace ❻
Меншиковский дворец
Menshikovskiy dvorets

Universitetskaya naberezhnaya 15.
Map 5 B1. *Tel* 323 1112. 🚌 7, 24,
47, 191, K-209. 🚎 1, 10, 11. 🚐
1, 10, 11. ⬜ 10:30am–6pm
Tue–Sat; 10:30am–5pm Sun. 🎫 🎦
compulsory (English, French, German
available).

The ochre-painted Baroque
Menshikov Palace, with
its beautifully carved pilasters,
was one of the earliest stone
buildings in St Petersburg.
Designed by Giovanni Fontana
and Gottfried Schädel for the
infamous Prince Menshikov,
the palace was completed in
1720. The palace estate originally extended as far as the
Malaya Neva river to the north.
  Prince Menshikov entertained
here on a lavish scale, often
on behalf of Peter the Great,

PRINCE MENSHIKOV

A leading advisor, com-
rade-in-arms and
friend of Peter the
Great, Aleksandr
Menshikov
(1673–1729)
rose from hum-
ble origins to
his position as
the first governor
of St Petersburg.
After Peter's death
in 1725, Menshikov
engineered the ascension
of Catherine I (Peter's wife,
and Menshikov's former
mistress) to the throne, thus
maintaining his power until
her demise. His notorious
extravagance and venality
eventually caught up with
him. Accused of treason,
he died in exile in 1729.

---

who adopted the palace as a
pied-à-terre. Guests would
cross the Neva by boat and
arrive to the grand welcome
of a liveried orchestra.
  The palace is now a branch
of the Hermitage *(see pp84–
93)* with exhibitions on early
18th-century Russian culture,
revealing the extent to which
Peter the Great's court was
influenced by Western tastes.
  The compulsory tour begins
on the ground floor; besides
the kitchen there are displays
of Peter's cabinet-making
tools, period costumes, sturdy
oak chests and ships' com-
passes. Adorning the beautiful
vaulted hallway are marble
statues imported from Italy
which include a Roman Apollo
dating to the 2nd century AD.
  Upstairs, the secretary's
rooms are decorated with 17th-
century Dutch engravings of
Leyden, Utrecht and Kraków.
A series of breathtaking rooms
are lined with hand-painted
blue and white 18th-century
Dutch tiles. Tiles were
not only fashionable,
but also easy to
keep clean.
  In the tiled bed-
room of Varvara
(Menshikov's
sister-in-law and
confidante) is a
German-made
four-poster bed,
with a Turkish
coverlet woven from
cotton, silk and silver
thread. Hanging behind it is
an exquisite 17th-century
Flemish tapestry.
  Menshikov and Peter often
received guests in the aptly
named Walnut Study which
has Persian walnut panelling
and commanding views of
the Neva. Paintings hang from
coloured ribbons, as was the

fashion, including a late
17th-century portrait of Peter
the Great by the Dutch
painter Jan Weenix. The
mirrors were a novelty at that
time and such displays of
vanity were anathema to the
Orthodox Church.
  The Great Hall, decorated
in gold and stucco, is where
balls and banquets were held.
On one famous occasion, it
was the setting for a "dwarfs'
wedding" which Menshikov
arranged for the amusement
of his royal master.

The fine, Style-Moderne *apteka*,
just off Bolshoy prospekt

Bolshoy Prospekt ❼
Большой проспект
Bolshoy prospekt

Map 1 A5. Ⓜ *Vasileostrovskaya.*
🚌 6, 7, 41, 42, 128, 151, 152,
K-124, K183, K-346, K-350, K-690.
🚐 10, 11.

This imposing avenue was
opened early in the 18th
century to connect Menshikov's
estate to the Gulf of Finland.
  The mix of architectural
styles ranges from the elegant
Neo-Classicism of St Catherine's
Lutheran Church (1768–71) at
No. 1 to the simple Troyekurov
House (No. 13, 6-ya liniya) in
17th-century Petrine Baroque.
  Other buildings of note include St Andrew's food market
(1789–90) and two Style-
Moderne edifices. One is the
former pharmacy, or *apteka*,
(1907–10) around the corner
on 7-ya liniya, and the other
is Adolph Gaveman's Lutheran
orphanage at No. 55 (1908).

The Academy of Arts (1764–88) on the Neva embankment, an example of early Russian Neo-Classicism

St Andrew's Cathedral ❽

Андреевский собор

Andreevskiy sobor

6-ya liniya 11. **Map** 5 B1. *Tel 323 3418.* 7, 24, 42, 100, 128, 151, K-62, K-154, K-183, K-200, K-349, K-690. 10, 11.

First built on the initiative of Peter the Great's second wife, Catherine I *(see p21)*, who donated 3,000 roubles towards its construction, the original church was destroyed by fire.

The present Baroque church with its distinctive bell tower was constructed by Aleksandr Vist in 1764–80. The most stunning feature of the interior is the carved 18th-century iconostasis which incorporates icons from the original church.

The treasure of St Andrew's Cathedral, its beautiful Baroque iconostasis

Next door is Giuseppe Trezzini's small Church of the Three Saints (1740–60) which is dedicated to SS Basil the Great, John Chrysostom and Gregory of Nazianzus.

Academy of Arts ❾

Академия Художеств

Akademiya Khudozhestv

Universitetskaya naberezhnaya 17. **Map** 5 B1. *Tel 323 3578.* 7, 47, K-62, K-124, K-154, K-350. 10, 11. ◯ *11am–6pm Wed–Sun.* www.rah.ru

Founded in 1757 to train home-grown artists in the preferred Western styles and techniques of art, the Academy spawned a galaxy of talent, including the great painter Ilya Repin *(see p42)* and architects Andrey Zakharov (1761–1811) and Andrey Voronikhin (1759–1814).

The innate conservatism of the Academy tended to discourage innovation and experiment and in 1863 a band of 14 students walked out of their graduation exams in protest. They went on to found a realist art movement and became known as the Wanderers or *peredvizhniki (see pp106–7)*.

The imposing Academy, built between 1764–1880 by Aleksandr Kokorinov and Vallin de la Mothe, is an example of the transition from Baroque to Neo-Classicism. Still an art school, it exhibits the work of students past and present, including canvases, architectural drawings and models of many of the city's notable buildings, such as the magnificent Smolnyy Convent *(see p128)*.

The splendid Neo-Classical halls and galleries, though faded, retain something of their original grandeur. Of note are the Conference Hall on the first floor, with its ceiling painting by Vasiliy Shebuev, and the adjoining Raphael and Titian galleries, adorned with copies of Vatican frescoes.

Flanking the river stairs outside the Academy are two sphinxes from the 14th century BC. Discovered among the ruins of Thebes in ancient Egypt, they were installed here in 1832. The faces are thought to bear a likeness of the pharaoh Amenhotep III.

Blagoveshchenskiy Bridge ❿

Благовещенский Мост

Blagoveshchenskiy Most

Map 5 B2. 6, K-154, K-350.

Opened in 1842 with this name, this was the first permanent crossing of the Neva. In 1855 the bridge was renamed Nicholas Bridge but in 1918, after the revolution, it was called Lieutenant Shmidt Bridge to commemorate a sailor who led an uprising of the Black Sea fleet in 1905. Reconstruction carried out in 1936–8 incorporated Aleksandr Bryullov's original railings, adorned with sea horses and tridents. In 2007 the bridge reverted to its original name.

PETROGRADSKAYA

The city was founded on the northern banks of the Neva river in 1703, at the height of the Great Northern War (*see p18*). Building began with the construction of a wooden fortress and Petrogradskaya, or the Petrograd Side, soon became a marshy suburb of wooden cabins occupied by craftsmen working on Peter the Great's new city.

Nearby, the area around Trinity Square was originally a small merchants' quarter centred around a now demolished church and St Petersburg's first stock exchange.

Detail on bridge to Peter and Paul Fortress

Petrogradskaya was sparsely populated until the late 1890s when the construction of the Trinity Bridge (Troitskiy Most) made the area accessible from the city centre. The bridge caused a housing boom at the height of a fashion for Style-Moderne architecture which is still in evidence today. The population quadrupled and the area became very popular with artists and professionals.

The highlight of the area, which is still largely residential, is the Peter and Paul Fortress.

SIGHTS AT A GLANCE

Museums
Artillery Museum **7**
Cabin of Peter the Great **13**
Commandant's House **4**
Cruiser Aurora **12**
Engineer's House **2**
Kirov Museum **10**
Kshesinskaya Mansion **11**
Trubetskoy Bastion **6**

Gates
Neva Gate **5**
St Peter's Gate **1**

Cathedrals
Cathedral of SS Peter and Paul **3**

Streets, Squares and Parks
Aleksandrovskiy Park **8**
Kamennoostrovskiy Prospekt **9**
Trinity Square **14**

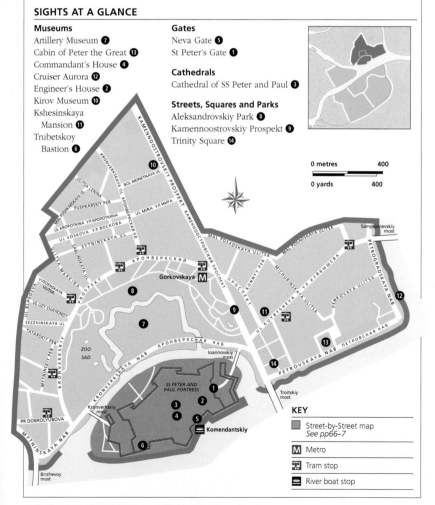

| 0 metres | | 400 |
| 0 yards | | 400 |

KEY

	Street-by-Street map *See pp66–7*
M	Metro
	Tram stop
	River boat stop

◁ The Baroque Cathedral of SS Peter and Paul in the Peter and Paul Fortress

Street-by-Street: Peter and Paul Fortress

The founding of the Peter and Paul Fortress on 27 May 1703, on the orders of Peter the Great, is considered to mark the founding of the city. It was first built in wood and was later replaced, section by section, in stone by Domenico Trezzini. Its history is a gruesome one, since hundreds of forced labourers died while building the fortress and its bastions were later used to guard and torture many political prisoners, including Peter's own son Aleksey.

The cells where prisoners were once kept are open to the public, alongside a couple of museums and the magnificent cathedral which houses the tombs of the Romanovs.

The Archives of the War Ministry occupy the site of the "Secret House", a prison for political criminals in the 18th and 19th centuries.

Artillery Museum *(see p70)*

Kronverkskiy most

Zotov Bastion

Trubetskoy Bastion
From 1872–1921 the dark, damp, solitary-confinement cells in the bastion served as a grim prison for enemies of the state. Today, the bastion is open to visitors ❻

The Mint, founded in 1724, still produces ceremonial coins, medals and badges.

The Naryshkin Bastion (1725) is where the noon cannon is fired. The tradition began in 1873, stopped after the revolution and was resumed in 1957.

The beach is popular in summer and in winter, when members of the "walruses" swimming club break the ice for an invigorating dip.

Commandant's House
For 150 years this attractive Baroque house was the scene of interrogations and trials of political prisoners. It now houses a museum of local history ❹

Neva Gate
This riverside entrance, also known as "Death Gateway", leads to the Commandant's pier from which prisoners embarked on their journey to execution or exile. The Neva river's flood levels (see p37) are recorded under the arch ❿

★ Cathedral of SS Peter and Paul

Marbled columns, glittering chandeliers and painted decor combine with Ivan Zarudnyy's carved and gilded iconostasis to create a magnificent setting for the tombs of the Romanov monarchs ❸

The Boat House is now a ticket office and souvenir shop.

Golovkin Bastion

The Grand Ducal burial vault is the last resting place of several Grand Dukes shot by the Bolsheviks in 1919 and of Grand Duke Vladimir who died in exile in 1992.

LOCATOR MAP
See Street Finder, map 2

St Peter's Gate
The entrance to the fortress, by Domenico Trezzini, completed in 1718, features the Romanov double eagle with an emblem of St George and the dragon ❶

STAR SIGHT

★ SS Peter and Paul Cathedral

| 0 metres | 100 |
| 0 yards | 100 |

Ioannovskiy Ravelin contains a ticket office.

Ivan Gate, in the outer wall, was constructed from 1731–40.

Ioannovskiy most

Kamennoostrovskiy prospekt, Gorkovskaya Metro and Trinity Bridge

Statue of Peter the Great by Mikhail Chemiakin (1991).

Peter I Bastion

KEY

— — — Suggested route

Engineer's House
This building, dating from 1748–9, houses temporary exhibitions of artifacts used in everyday life in St Petersburg before the revolution ❷

St Peter's Gate ❶
Петровские ворота
Petrovskie vorota

Petropavlovskaya krepost. **Map** 2
E3. M *Gorkovskaya.* 🚌 46, 49,
K-46, K-76, K-223.

The main entrance to the
Peter and Paul Fortress is
through two contrasting arches.
The plain Neo-Renaissance
Ivan Gate (1730s) leads to the
more imposing St Peter's Gate
(1708–18), an ornate Baroque
structure with scrolled wings
and a rounded-gable pediment.
Domenico Trezzini redesigned
the Peter Gate, retaining Karl
Osner's expressively carved
bas-relief which allegorizes
Peter the Great's victory over
Charles XII of Sweden *(see
p18)*. It depicts St Peter
casting down the winged
sorcerer Simon Magus.

Peter Gate, entrance to fortress

Engineer's House ❷
Инженерный дом
Inzhenernyy dom

Petropavlovskaya krepost. **Map** 2 D3.
Tel 232 9454, 230 0329.
M *Gorkovskaya.* ⭕ 11am–5pm
Thu–Mon, 11am–4pm Tue. 🎫
🎟 *English.* **www**.spbmuseum.ru

The Engineer's House, built
in 1748–9, has a changing
exhibition which gives a
fascinating glimpse of daily
life in St Petersburg before
the Revolution. Architectural
backdrops and historical paintings give way to an engaging
miscellany of artifacts, ranging
from model boats to duelling
pistols and court costumes.

In 1915 there were more
than 100 outlets selling musical
instruments in the city and the

**An accordion and organ surrounded by Style-
Moderne furniture, Engineer's House**

museum displays an excellent
collection which includes
phonographs, gramophones,
symphoniums and piano
accordions of the period.

A section on vintage tech-
nology features Singer sewing
machines, typewriters, Bakelite
telephones and box cameras.

Cathedral of SS Peter and Paul ❸
Петропавловский собор
Petropavlovskiy sobor

Petropavlovskaya krepost. **Map** 2 D4.
Tel 230 6431. M *Gorkovskaya.*
⭕ 10am–7pm Mon–Fri, 10am–
5:45pm Sat, 11am–7pm Sun. 🎫 🎟
English. **www**.spbmuseum.ru

Domenico Trezzini designed
this magnificent church
within the fortress in 1712.
Employed by Peter the Great,
who wished to turn his back
on traditional Russian church

architecture,
Trezzini produced
a Baroque
masterpiece of
singular elegance.
The bell tower was
completed first to
test the foundations
and this served as
an excellent view-
point from which
Peter could oversee
the construction
work of his new
city. The cathedral
was completed in
1733, but was badly
damaged by fire in 1756
when the soaring 122-m
(400-ft) spire was struck by
lightning. The gilded needle
spire, crowned by a weather-
vane angel, remained the
tallest structure in St Petersburg until the building of a
TV transmitter in the 1960s.

The interior, with its glittering chandeliers, pink and
green Corinthian columns and
overarching vaults, is a far cry
from the traditional Russian
Orthodox church. Even the
iconostasis is a Baroque flight
of fancy. This masterpiece of
gilded woodcarving was
designed by Ivan Zarudnyy
and executed in the 1720s by
craftsmen from Moscow.

After Peter's death in 1725,
the cathedral became the last
resting place of the tsars. The
sarcophagi are all of a uniform
white Carrara marble, except
the tombs of Alexander II and
his wife Maria Alexandrovna,

Cathedral of SS Peter and Paul, with Dvortsovyy most in foreground

which are carved from Altai jasper and Ural rhodonite. Peter the Great's tomb lies to the right of the iconostasis.

The only tsars who are not buried here are Peter II, Ivan VI and Nicholas II. In 1998 a controversial decision was taken to rebury the remains of the last Romanov tsar, his wife and children, and the servants that died together with them, in a chapel by the entrance to the cathedral.

The Grand Ducal Mausoleum, where relatives of the tsars are buried, was added to the northeast of the cathedral at the end of the 19th century.

Commandant's House ❹
Комендантский дом
Komendantskiy dom

Petropavlovskaya krepost. **Map** 2 D4. **Tel** 230 6431. **M** *Gorkovskaya*. 🔲 11am–7pm Thu–Mon, 11am– 6pm Tue. 🌐 📷 *English*.

Dating from the 1740s, the plain brick, two-storey Commandant's House served both as the residence of the fortress commander and as a courthouse. Over the years, political prisoners, including the Decembrist rebels *(see p23)*, were brought here for interrogation and sentencing.

The house is now a museum, with a ground-floor exhibition on medieval settlements in the St Petersburg region, and temporary exhibitions upstairs.

Neva Gate ❺
Невскине ворота
Nevskie vorota

Petropavlovskaya krepost. **Map** 2 E4. **M** *Gorkovskaya*.

This austere river entrance to the fortress was once known as the "Death Gate". Prisoners to be transported to the even more notorious Schlüsselburg Fortress (to the east of St Petersburg) for capital punishment, or to a "living death" in penal servitude, were led down the granite steps and taken away by boat. The appropriately dour, grey gateway dates from

Neva Gate leading from the river into the Peter and Paul Fortress

1730–40 (reconstructed in 1784–7) and is unornamented apart from an anchor in the pediment. In the archway, brass plaques mark record flood levels. The catastrophic inundation of November 1824 is the one commemorated in Pushkin's poem, *The Bronze Horseman (see p78)*.

Trubetskoy Bastion ❻
Трубецкой бастион
Trubetskoy bastion

Petropavlovskaya krepost. **Map** 2 D4. **Tel** 230 6431. **M** *Gorkovskaya*. 🔲 10am–7pm daily. 🌐 📷 *English*.

Peter the Great's son, the Tsarevich Aleksey, was the first political prisoner to be detained in the grim fortress prison. Unjustly accused of treason in 1718 by his overbearing father, Aleksey escaped abroad only to be lured back to Russia with the promise of a pardon.

Instead, he was tortured and beaten to death, almost certainly with Peter's consent and participation.

For the next 100 years prisoners were incarcerated in the much feared Secret House, since demolished. In 1872 a new prison block opened in the Trubetskoy Bastion which has existed as a museum since 1924. On the ground floor there is a small exhibition of period photographs, prison uniforms and a model of the guardroom. Upstairs are 69 isolation cells, restored to their original appearance, while downstairs there are two unheated, unlit punishment cells where the recalcitrant were locked up for 48 hours at a time. Once every two weeks, all detainees were taken to the Bath House in the exercise yard for de-lousing. Here prisoners were also put in irons before being carted off to penal servitude in Siberia.

POLITICAL PRISONERS

The fortress' sinister role as a prison for political activists continued until after the Revolution. Generations of rebels and anarchists were interrogated and imprisoned here,

Leon Trotsky (1879–1940) in the Trubetskoy Bastion

including Leon Trotsky in the wake of the 1905 Revolution. Other prominent detainees were the leading Decembrists in 1825 *(see p23)*, Dostoevsky in 1849 *(see p123)* and, in 1874–6, the anarchist Prince Pyotr Kropotkin. In 1917 it was the turn first of the tsar's ministers, then of members of the Provisional Government. Then, in the Civil War *(see p27)*, the Bolsheviks held hostage four Romanov Grand Dukes who were subsequently executed in 1919.

Rocket launcher in the courtyard of the Artillery Museum

Artillery Museum ❼

Музей Артиллерии

Muzey Artillerii

Alexandrovskiy Park 7, Kronverkskaya Embankment. **Map** 2 D3.
Tel 232 0296. Ⓜ *Gorkovskaya.*
⭘ *11am–5pm Wed–Sun.* ⬤ *last
Thu each month.* 📷

This vast, horseshoe-shaped
building in red brick stands on
the site of the Kronverk, the
outer fortifications of the
Peter and Paul Fortress *(see
pp66–7)*. Designed by Pyotr
Tamanskiy and constructed in
1849–60, the building was
originally used as the arsenal.

More than 600 pieces of artillery and military vehicles
include tanks and the armoured
car in which Lenin rode in
triumph from Finland Station
(see p126) to Kshesinskaya
Mansion *(see p72)* on 3 April
1917. There are uniforms,
regimental flags, muskets and
small arms dating to medieval
times, as well as several rooms
devoted to World War II.

Aleksandrovskiy Park ❽

Александровский парк

Aleksandrovskiy park

Kronverkskiy prospekt. **Map** 2 D3.
Ⓜ *Gorkovskaya.* ♿

The park's unique character
as a centre of popular culture
and entertainment was
established in the year 1900
with the inauguration of the
Nicholas II People's House.
This was where pantomime
artists, wild animal trainers,
magicians and circus acts

entertained the crowds, while
the more serious-minded were
drawn to the lecture halls,
reading galleries and tea
rooms. The *pièce de résistance*
was the magnificent domed
Opera House (1911), where
the legendary bass singer,
Fyodor Chaliapin, sometimes
gave performances.

Today the Opera
House offers less
highbrow entertain-
ment, as its change
of name to Music Hall
suggests. The adjoin-
ing 1930s buildings
include the innovative
Baltic House Theatre,
the Planetarium and a
waxworks museum.

The park still draws crowds
on summer weekends and
public holidays, although some
of the attractions, especially
the zoo, are rather tawdry.

Kamennoostrovskiy Prospekt ❾

Каменноостровский проспект

Kamennoostrovskiy prospekt

Map 2 D2. Ⓜ *Gorkovskaya or Petrogradskaya.* 🚌 *46, K-30, K-76, K-223.*

Developed during the con-
struction boom of the late
1890s, this eye-catching avenue
is noted for its Style-Moderne
architecture. The first house,
at No. 1–3 (1899–1904) was
designed by Fyodor Lidval.
The multi-textured façade,
windows of contrasting shapes
and sizes, ornate iron balconies and fanciful carvings
are the most typical features
of this Russian version of Art
Nouveau. The neighbouring

house (No. 5) was once occupied by Count Sergey Witte,
a leading industrialist who
negotiated the peace treaty
with Japan in 1905 *(see p26)*.

Situated just off the start of
the avenue is the city's only
mosque (1910–14). Designed
by Russian architects, its minarets, majolica tiling and the
rough granite surfaces of the
walls are fully in keeping
with the surrounding
architecture. The mosque
was, in fact, modelled on the
Mausoleum of Tamerlane in
Samarkand and involved
Central Asian craftsmen.

At No. 10 is the tall portico
of the Leningrad Film Studios
(Lenfilm). It was on this site,
in May 1896, that the Lumière
brothers showed the first moving picture in Russia. Since its
founding in 1918, some of the
most innovative Soviet film
directors such as Leonid Trauberg and Grigoriy
Kozintsev *(see p45)*
have worked there.

At the intersection
with ulitsa Mira, each
house has indivi-
dually designed
turrets, spires, reliefs
and iron balconies
forming a handsome
Style-Moderne
ensemble. Other buildings of
interest include No. 24
(1896–1912), with its red
brick majolica and terracotta
façade; No. 26–28 where
Sergey Kirov lived *(see p72)*;
and on the corner of Bolshoy
prospekt, the "Turreted House"
with its Neo-Gothic portal.

**Griffon, No. 1–3
Kamennoostrovskiy**

**Turreted House (1913–15),
Kamennoostrovskiy prospekt**

Style-Moderne in St Petersburg

In vogue throughout Europe from the 1890s to the 1900s, Art Nouveau marked a break with imitation of the past. The movement, known as Style-Moderne in Russia, began in the decorative arts and was then reflected in architecture, where it led to an abundance of ornamental elements. Inspired by new industrial techniques, artists and architects made lavish use of natural stone and brick, wrought iron, stucco, coloured glass and ceramic tiles.

Kshesinskaya Mansion railing detail

Dominated by sinuous and undulating lines, with a predominance of floral- and vegetal-inspired elements, even traditional forms such as doors and windows are distorted or given unexpected curves.

In fin-de-siècle St Petersburg, the Style-Moderne flourished as the city underwent a building boom, particularly on Petrogradskaya. The city became a showcase for the talents of leading architects such as Fyodor Lidval and Aleksandr von Gogen.

Kshesinskaya Mansion *reveals von Gogen's relatively severe version of Style-Moderne. Asymmetrical in composition, it is enlivened with wrought iron and glazed tiles (see p72).*

Yeliseev's *is evidence of the skill of Gavriil Baranovskiy, who made excellent use of industrial techniques in the creation of large window spaces. The rich exterior detailing is matched by elegant shop-fittings and chandeliers inside (see p109).*

28 Bolshaya Zelenina ulitsa *is one of the most outstanding examples of the use of stylized animal and fish motifs and a variety of surface decoration techniques. Fyodor von Postel's 1904–5 apartment block is reminiscent of the work of his contemporary, the Catalan architect Gaudí.*

1–3 Kamennoostrovskiy pr *is the work of St Petersburg's master of Style-Moderne, Fyodor Lidval. Delicate details such as floral and animal reliefs stand out against a background of discreetly elongated proportions and unusual window shapes.*

Singer House *(1910–14) reveals Pavel Syuzor's use of an unusually eclectic mix of architectural styles. Ornate Style-Moderne wrought-iron balconies and decorative wooden window frames combine with elements of Renaissance and Baroque revivals.*

Portrait of Sergey Kirov (1930s), in the Kirov Museum

Kirov Museum ⑩
Музей С. М. Кирова
Muzey S M Kirova

Kamennoostrovskiy prospekt 26–28, 4th floor. **Map** 2 D1. *Tel 346 0217, 346 0289.* **M** *Petrogradskaya.* ☐ *11am–6pm Thu–Mon (5pm Tue).* 🈂 *English.* **www.spbmuseum.ru**

From 1926–36 this flat was home to one of Stalin's closest political associates, Sergey Kirov. As the charis-matic first Secretary of the Leningrad Communist Party, Kirov soon gained national importance. His increasing popularity led Stalin to see in him a potential rival. On 1 December 1934, Kirov was gunned down at his office at the Smolnyy Institute *(see p128)* by Leonid Nikolaev, a party malcontent. Stalin used the assassination as an excuse to launch the Great Purges *(see p27)*, although most histo-rians believe Stalin himself was behind Kirov's murder.

Kirov acquired the status of a martyr after his death, with

countless buildings named in his honour. His apartment, preserved as it was in his life-time, is an example of the near cult status awarded Party leaders, with documents and photographs chronicling his political career, and a touching array of memorabilia including his clothing and favourite books.

Kshesinskaya Mansion ⑪
Особняк М. Кшесинской
Osobnyak M Kshesinskoy

Ulitsa Kuybysheva 4. **Map** 2 E3. *Tel 233 7052.* **M** *Gorkovskaya.* ☐ *10am–6pm daily.* ● *last Mon of month.* 🈂 🈂 *English.* **www.polithistory.ru**

This remarkable example of Style-Moderne architecture was commissioned for prima ballerina Matilda Kshesinskaya. Designed in 1904 by the court architect, A von Gogen, the building is almost playfully asymmetric with a single, octagonal tower. Most eye-catching of all are the many contrasting building materials with bands of pink and grey granite, cream-coloured bricks, delicately ornamented iron railings and majolica tiles.

The most impressive interior is the splendid recital hall with its pillared archway and palms. Nearby, the Kshesinskaya memorial room has some of the dancer's possessions, inclu-ding sketches of Nicholas II.

In March 1917 the mansion was commandeered by the Bolsheviks and became their headquarters and, on Lenin's return to Russia *(see p126)*,

he addressed the crowds from the balcony facing the square. The mansion, previously home to a museum glorifying the October Revolution, now houses the Museum of Russian Political History. On the first floor the Bolshevik Party secretariat and Lenin's office have been faithfully restored. Upstairs is a fascinating collection of memorabilia from the revolutionary era, including Communist posters, Nicholas II coronation mugs and even a police file on Rasputin's murder *(see p121)*.

The museum has temporary exhibitions covering political history, taking in the theory and consequences of perestroika and the policies of contemporary parties.

MATILDA KSHESINSKAYA

One of the finest prima ballerinas ever to grace the stage of the Mariinskiy Theatre *(see p119)*, Matilda Kshesinskaya (1872–1971) graduated from the Imperial Ballet School *(see p118)* in 1890. She was equally famous for her celebrated affair with the tsarevich, later Tsar Nicholas II, which began soon after she graduated. Kshesinskaya emigrated to Paris in 1920 where she married the Grand Duke Andrey Vladimirovich, another member of the imperial family and the father of her 11-year old son. It was in Paris that she wrote her controver-sial memoirs, *Dancing in St Petersburg*, which tells the tale of her affair with the last Russian tsar.

A von Gogen's elegant recital hall in the Kshesinskaya Mansion

The historic cruiser Aurora (1900), moored in front of the Neo-Baroque Nakhimov Naval Academy (1912)

Cruiser Aurora ⑫
Крейсер Аврора
Kreyser Avrora

Petrogradskaya naberezhnaya 3.
Map 2 F3. *Tel* 230 8440. 🚌 49,
K-30, K-183. 🚋 6, 40. 🕙 10:30am–
4pm Tue–Thu, Sat & Sun. 🗣 English,
German or French, for a fee. Phone
to book.

According to the annals of
the Revolution, at 9:40pm on
25 October 1917, the cruiser
Aurora signalled the storming
of the Winter Palace *(see
p28)*, by firing a single blank
round from its bow gun.
   The ship entered active
service in 1903. It was later
converted into a training ship
and at the start of the Siege
of Leningrad *(see p27)* it was
sunk to protect it from German
forces. The ship was raised in
1944 and has been a museum
since 1956. The famous gun,
bell and the crew's quarters
can be viewed, along with an
exhibition on the ship's history.

Cabin of Peter the Great ⑬
Музей-домик Петра I
Muzey-domik Petra I

Petrovskaya naberezhnaya 6.
Map 2 F3. *Tel* 232 4576, 314 0374.
Ⓜ *Gorkovskaya.* 🕙 10am–5:30pm
Wed–Sun. 🌑 last Mon of month.
📷 ♿

This pine-log cabin was built
for Peter the Great by his
soldier-carpenters in just three
days in 1703. Peter lived here
for six years while overseeing

the construction of his new
city *(see pp20–21)*. Catherine
the Great, ever keen to glorify
Peter, had a protective brick
shell erected around the cabin.
   There are only two rooms,
both with period furnishings,
and a hallway which doubled
as a bedroom. Among Peter's
personal possessions are a
compass, a frock coat and his
rowing boat.
   Adorning the steps outside
are two statues of the Shih Tze
frog-lions, brought from
Manchuria during the Russo-
Japanese War (1904–5).

Trinity Square ⑭
Троицкая площадь
Troitskaya ploshchad

Map 2 E3. Ⓜ *Gorkovskaya.* 🚌 46.
🚋 6, 40.

Throughout the early 18th
century, the whole of Petrogradskaya was known as
Trinity Island. The name was

derived from the Church of
the Trinity (built in 1710;
demolished 1930s) in Trinity
Square, which formed the
nucleus of the city's merchant
quarter. In 2002–3 the Trinity
Chapel was built here to honour the 300th anniversary of
St Petersburg. Despite having
no direct links to the mainland
until the early 20th century, the
area flourished with shops, a
printing house and the city's
first stock exchange.
   In the 1905 Revolution *(see
p26)* the square witnessed the
massacre of 48 workers, killed
by government troops. During
the Communist era, the
square became known as
ploshchad Revolyutsii.
   From the square, across the
widest point of the Neva, the
Style-Moderne Trinity Bridge
(see p35) stretches nearly
600 m (1,970 ft). Its construction led to a building boom on
Petrogradskaya *(see p65)* and
its completion in 1903 coinci-
ded with the city's bicentenary.

The ornate Trinity Bridge, crossing the Neva from Trinity Square

PALACE EMBANKMENT

In terms of sheer scale and grandeur, St Petersburg's magnificent south waterfront has few equals. Its formidable granite quays stretch over 2 km (1 mile) from the Senate building in the west to Peter the Great's Summer Palace in the east, and the surrounding area of stately aristocratic palaces and ornamental canal bridges are justly famous worldwide.

Every aspect of the city's history is juxtaposed in this rich area. Falconet's statue of Peter the Great, the Bronze Horseman, is an eloquent testimony to imperial ambition while the square in which it stands is where the Decembrist rebels rose up against the tsarist regime in 1825.

Alexander Column, Palace Square

In Palace Square, Rastrelli's Winter Palace (part of the Hermitage) evokes the opulence of Imperial Russia while the Eternal Flame, flickering in the Field of Mars, is a more sombre reminder of revolutionary sacrifice.

Dominating St Petersburg's skyline are the magnificent dome of St Isaac's Cathedral and the gilded spire of the Admiralty. Some of the best views can be appreciated by making a boat trip along the waterways *(see pp226–7)*, or by strolling through the Summer Garden.

SIGHTS AT A GLANCE

Palaces and Gardens
Marble Palace ⑭
Summer Garden ⑯
Summer Palace ⑰

Museums
The Hermitage pp84–93 ⑫

Historical Buildings and Monuments
The Admiralty ①
The Bronze Horseman ③
Horseguards' Manège ④
House of Fabergé ⑨

Churches
St Isaac's Cathedral pp80–81 ⑤

Streets and Squares
Field of Mars ⑮
Malaya Morskaya Ulitsa ⑧
Millionaires' Street ⑬
Palace Square ⑪
St Isaac's Square ⑥
Senate Square ②

Hotels and Cafés
Angleterre Hotel ⑦
Literary Café ⑩

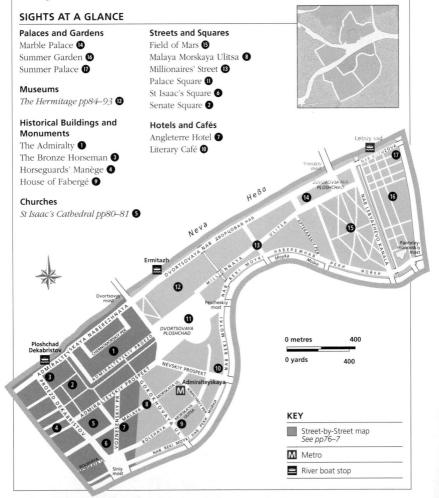

KEY

	Street-by-Street map *See pp76–7*
M	Metro
	River boat stop

Street-by-Street: St Isaac's Square

Detail from the frieze on the Admiralty gate tower

The highlight of St Isaac's Square is the imposing cathedral at its centre, which opened in 1858 and is the fourth church to stand on this site. The cathedral, and subsequently the square, were named after St Isaac of Dalmatia, because Peter the Great's birthday fell on this saint's day. The busy square, used as a market place in the first half of the 19th century, is now at the heart of an area teeming with buildings and statues of historical and architectural interest. Among them are the Admiralty, the Mariinskiy Palace and the Bronze Horseman.

Horseguards' Manège
Built in 1804–7 by Giacomo Quarenghi, this building housed the Life Guards' Mounted Regiment ❹

The Bronze Horseman
Etienne Falconet's magnificent statue of Peter the Great, his horse trampling the serpent of treason, captures the spirit of the city's uncompromising and wilful founder ❸

Senate Square
Dominating the western side of the square are Carlo Rossi's monumental Senate and Synod buildings, linked by a triumphal arch ❷

The Glory Columns, topped by bronze angels, were erected in 1845–6.

Myatlev House

The Former German Embassy was designed by Peter Behrens in 1911–12.

★ St Isaac's Cathedral
The magnificent golden dome of the cathedral is visible all across the city. 100kg (220lb) of gold leaf were needed to cover the dome's surface ❺

0 metres 100

0 yards 100

The Hermitage and Winter Palace

LOCATOR MAP
See Street Finder maps 2, 5 & 6

The Admiralty
Sculptures and reliefs, celebrating the power of Russia's navy, decorate the Admiralty's façade. The archway of the main entrance is framed by nymphs carrying globes on their shoulders ❶

The Former Prince Lobanov-Rostovskiy Mansion is now a design institute. The lions in front of the arcade are by Italian sculptor Paolo Triscorni.

STAR SIGHT

★ St Isaac's Cathedral

ADMIRALTEYSKIY PROSPEKT

GOROKHOVAYA UL

VOZNESENSKIY PROSPEKT

MAL MORSKAYA UL

Nevskiy prospekt

Angleterre Hotel
Originally built in the 1850s, the Angleterre Hotel (see p174) was the site of the first major public protest in the history of the Soviet Union. The hotel has been restored to its 19th-century splendour ❼

The Former Ministry of State Property, designed by Nikolay Yefimov in 1844, is a fine example of Neo-Renaissance architecture.

MORSKAYA UL

REKI MOYKI

Siniy most *(see p79)*

St Isaac's Square
Overlooking the square is Pyotr Klodt's statue of Tsar Nicholas I. The reliefs on the pedestal depict episodes from his reign. Tellingly, two of them show the suppression of rebellions ❻

The Mariinskiy Palace, named in honour of Maria, daughter of Nicholas I, now houses the St Petersburg city hall.

KEY

– – – Suggested route

The Admiralty ❶
Адмиралтейство
Admiralteystvo

Admiralteyskaya naberezhnaya 2.
Map 5 C1. 🚌 *7, 10, 24, 100, 191, K-169, K-209, K-252.* 🚎 *1, 5, 7, 10, 11, 17, 22.*

Having founded a city and built a fortress, Peter the Great's next priority was to create a Russian navy to gua-rantee access to the sea and dominance over Sweden.

The Admiralty began life as a fortified shipyard built on this site between 1704–11. Two years later, some 10,000 men were employed in building the first battleships.

One of Russia's most inspired architects, Andrey Zakharov, began to rebuild the Admiralty in 1806. The remarkable façade is 407 m (1,335 ft) in length and is adorned with an abun-dance of sculptures and reliefs which document the glory of the Russian fleet. Zakharov retained some of the original features, including the central gate tower and spire which he recast in Neo-Classical style with columned porticos and pavilions. The heightened spire was gilded and topped with a model frigate. This has become a symbol of the city, just like the trumpet-blowing pair of angels on the portals of the façade overlooking the Neva.

In the 1840s, shipbuilding was moved downstream and the Admiralty was handed over to the Russian navy. It has been occupied by the Naval Engineering School since 1925.

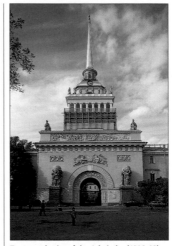

Tower and spire of the Admiralty (1806–23)

Senate Square ❷
Сенатская Площадь
Senatskaya Ploshchad

Map 5 C1. 🚌 *3, 10, 22, 27, 71, 100, K-169, K-187, K-306.* 🚎 *5, 22.*

The momentous Decembrist uprising took place here on 14 December 1825 *(see p23)*. During the inauguration of Nicholas I, Guards officers intent on imposing a constitu-tional monarchy attempted to stage a coup d'état in the square. After a confused stand-off which lasted several hours, the rebel forces were routed with grapeshot by the new tsar and loyalist troops. Five of the ringleaders were later executed and 121 others exiled to Siberia, thus

effectively ending Russia's first revolution.

The imposing Neo-Classical buildings that command the western side of Senate Square were intended to harmonize with the Admiralty. Designed by Carlo Rossi between 1829–34, they were the headquarters of two important institutions which were originally created by Peter the Great: the Supreme Court, or Senate, and the Holy Synod which was responsible for the administration of the Orthodox Church. The two buildings, which now house historical archives, are linked to each other by a triumphal arch supported by Corinthian columns and decorated with a Neo-Classical frieze and a plethora of statuary.

The Bronze Horseman (1766–78)

The Bronze Horseman ❸
Медный Всадник
Mednyy Vsadnik

Senatskaya ploshchad. **Map** 5 C1. 🚌 *3, 10, 22, 27, 71, 100, K-169, K-187, K-306.* 🚎 *5, 22.*

The magnificent equestrian statue of Peter the Great was unveiled in Senate Square in 1782, as a tribute from Catherine the Great. The statue is known as the Bronze Horse-man after Pushkin's famous poem. A French sculptor, Etienne Falconet, spent more than 12 years overseeing this ambitious project. The pedestal

---

THE BRONZE HORSEMAN BY PUSHKIN

1956 stamp of Pushkin and the statue that inspired his poem

The famous statue of Peter the Great is brought to life in Alexander Pushkin's epic poem *The Bronze Horseman* (1833). In this haunting vision of the Great Flood of 1824 *(see p37)*, the hero is pursued through the mist-shrouded streets by the terrifying bronze statue. Pushkin's words evoke the domi-neering and implacable will for which the tsar was renowned: *"How terrible he was in the surrounding gloom! … what strength was in him! And in that steed, what fire!"*

alone weighs 1,625 tonnes and was hewn from a single block of granite, which was hauled from the Gulf of Finland. It bears the simple inscription "To Peter I from Catherine II" in Latin and Russian. A serpent, symbolizing treason, is crushed beneath the horse's hooves.

Horseguards' Manège ❹
Конногвардейский манеж
Konnogvardeyskiy manezh

Isaakievskaya ploshchad 1. **Map** 5 C2. **Tel** 312 2243, 571 4157 *(ticket office).* ⬤ *variable.* 🚌 *3, 22, 27, 71, 100, K-169, K-187, K-306.* 🚎 *5, 22.* 📷 📖

The enormous indoor riding school of the Life Guards' Mounted Regiment was built by Giacomo Quarenghi in 1804–7 to resemble a Roman basilica. Two clues to the building's original function are the dynamic frieze of a horse race beneath the pediment and the statues on either side of the portico. The statues of the unclad twin sons of Zeus reining in wild horses are copies from the Quirinale Palace in Rome. The Holy Synod, scandalized by this display of nakedness so near to St Isaac's Cathedral, ordered their removal. The statues were re-erected in 1954.

Next to the manège, which is now used as an exhibition hall, are two marble pillars surmounted by bronze angels cast in Berlin, which were sent over from Germany as a gift in 1840.

St Isaac's Cathedral ❺

See pp80–81.

St Isaac's Square ❻
Исаакиевская площадь
Issakievskaya ploshchad

Map 5 C2. 🚌 *3, 10, 22, 27, 71, 100, K-169, K-187, K-306.* 🚎 *5, 22.*

Dominated by Auguste de Montferrand's majestic St Isaac's Cathedral, this impressive square was created during the reign of Nicholas I,

St Isaac's Cathedral, statue of St Nicholas I and the Angleterre, St Isaac's Square

although a few of its earlier buildings date from the 18th century. The monument to Nicholas I at its centre was also designed by Montferrand. Erected in 1859 and sculpted by Pyotr Klodt, it depicts the tsar in the uniform of one of Russia's most prestigious regiments, the Kavalergardskiy guards. The pedestal is embellished with allegorical sculptures of his daughters and his wife who represent Faith, Wisdom, Justice and Might.

On the western side of the square, at No. 9, the Myatlev House is a Neo-Classical mansion, dating from the 1760s, which belonged to one of Russia's most illustrious families. The French encyclopedist, Denis Diderot, stayed here in 1773–4 following an invitation from Catherine the Great. In the 1920s it became the premises of the State Institute of Artistic Culture where some of Russia's most influential avant-garde artists, including Kazimir Malevich and Vladimir Tatlin *(see p107)*, worked.

The impressive granite-faced building alongside is the former German embassy, designed in 1911–12 by the German architect, Peter Behrens.

Across the 100-m (330-ft) wide Blue Bridge (Siniy most), which was the site of a serf market until 1861, the Mariinskiy Palace *(see p77)* dominates the southern end of the square.

Angleterre Hotel ❼
Гостиница Астория
Gostinitsa Astoriya

Bolshaya Morskaya ulitsa 39. **Map** 6 D2. **Tel** 494 5757. 🚌 *3, 10, 22, 27, K-169, K-306.* 🚎 *5, 22. See Where to Stay p180.*

Now one of St Petersburg's leading hotels, the seven-storey Angleterre was designed by Fyodor Lidval in the Style Moderne *(see p71)* in 1910–12.

American writer, John Reed, author of the famous eyewitness account of the Revolution *Ten Days that Shook the World*, was staying here when the Bolsheviks seized power.

In 1925, the poet Sergey Yesenin, husband of Isadora Duncan, hanged himself in the annexe, after daubing the walls of his room with a farewell verse in his blood "To die is not new – but neither is it new to be alive".

The hotel's banqueting hall was to be the venue for Hitler's prematurely planned victory celebration, so sure was he that he would conquer the city.

Restored Style-Moderne foyer in the Angleterre Hotel, on the eastern edge of St Isaac's Square

St Isaac's Cathedral ❺

Исаакиевский собор

Isaakievskiy sobor

St Isaac's, one of the world's largest cathedrals, was designed in 1818 by the then unknown architect Auguste de Montferrand. The construction of the colossal building was a major engineering feat. Thousands of wooden piles were sunk into the marshy ground to support its weight of 300,000 tonnes and 48 huge columns were hauled into place. The cathedral opened in 1858 but was deconsecrated and became a museum of atheism during the Soviet era. Officially still a museum today, the church is filled with hundreds of 19th-century works of art.

The Dome

From the dome there are panoramic views over the city which include the Admiralty (see p78) and the Hermitage (see pp84–93). Adorning the gilded dome are angels sculpted by Josef Hermann.

The mosaic icons on the iconostasis are by Bryullov, Neff and Zhivago.

Angels with Torch

Ivan Vitali created many of the cathedral's sculptures, including the pairs of angels supporting gas torches which crown the four attic corners.

This chapel honours Alexander Nevsky who defeated the Swedes in 1240 *(see p17).*

★ Iconostasis

Three rows of icons surround the royal doors through which a stained-glass window (1843) is visible. Above the doors is Pyotr Klodt's gilded sculpture, Christ in Majesty *(1859).*

The north pediment is ornamented with a bronze relief (1842–4) of the Resurrection designed by François Lemaire.

Exit

Malachite and lapis lazuli columns frame the iconostasis. About 16,000 kg (35,280 lbs) of malachite decorate the cathedral.

St Catherine's Chapel has an exquisite white marble iconostasis, crowned by a sculpted Resurrection (1850–4) by Nikolay Pimenov.

The silver dove (1850) hanging in the cupola is a symbol of the Holy Spirit.

★ **Ceiling Painting**
The celestial Virgin in Majesty *by Karl Bryullov (see p105), dating to 1847, covers an area of 816 sq m (8,780 sq ft). It is ringed by exuberant gilded stucco mouldings and white marble.*

Portraits of apostles and evangelists

Statue of St Matthew

The entrance is through the side doors on St Isaac's Square.

South Doors
Three great doors of oak and bronze (1841–6), weighing 20 tonnes, are decorated with carved reliefs by Ivan Vitali. The exteriors of the doors show scenes from the life of Christ and saints, including Alexander Nevsky (see p130).

The relief of St Isaac blessing the Emperor Theodosius and his wife Flaccilla is by Ivan Vitali. On the extreme left, Montferrand is depicted clutching a model of his cathedral.

The walls are adorned with 14 coloured marbles and 43 other types of semi-precious stones and minerals.

The vast interior covers 4,000 sq m (43,000 sq ft).

Red granite columns, each weighing 114 tonnes, were transported from Finland by specially constructed ships.

STAR SIGHTS

★ Iconostasis

★ Ceiling Painting

Malaya Morskaya ulitsa with No. 13 in the middle

Malaya Morskaya Ulitsa ❽

Малая Морская улица

Malaya Morskaya ulitsa

Map 6 D1. ▦ *3, 10, 22, 27, K-306.* ▦ *5, 22.*

Malaya Morskaya Ulitsa used to be referred to as ulitsa Gogolya after the great prose-writer, Nikolai Gogol (1809–52) who lived at No. 17 from 1833–6. It was here that Gogol wrote *The Diary of a Madman* and *The Nose*, two biting satires on the archetypal Petersburg bureaucrat "drowned by the trivial, meaningless labours at which he spends his useless life". Gogol's bitingly humorous, fantastical and grotesque tales reveal a nightmarish and deeply pessimistic view of modern urban life.

The composer, Pyotr Tchaikovsky *(see p42)*, died in the top floor apartment of No. 13 shortly after the completion of his *Pathétique* symphony in November 1893. Officially he was supposed to have died of cholera, but it is commonly believed that he

committed suicide, due to pressure from Conservatory colleagues wishing to avoid a scandal after Tchaikovsky's alleged homosexual affair.

The house at No. 23 was occupied by the novelist Fyodor Dostoevsky *(see p123)* from 1848–9. It was here that he was arrested and charged with political conspiracy for his participation in the socialist Petrashevsky circle *(see p123)*. Today, the street manages to exude a 19th-century feel despite the many busy shops and businesses.

House of Fabergé ❾

Дом Фаберже

Dom Faberzhe

Bolshaya Morskaya ulitsa 24.
Map 6 D1. ◉ *to public.* ▦ *3, 22, 27.* ▦ *5, 22.*

The world-famous Fabergé jeweller's was established in Bolshaya Morskaya ulitsa in 1842 by Gustav Fabergé, of French Huguenot origin. It was not until the 1880s that his sons Carl and Agathon abandoned conventional jewellery-making for intricate and exquisitely crafted *objets d'art* of a highly innovative design. Most famous of all their works are the imaginatively designed Easter eggs made for the tsars.

In 1900 Carl moved the business from No. 16–18 into purpose-built premises at No. 24, where it remained until the Revolution. The exterior, designed by his relative, Karl Schmidt, has striking triangular roof gables and multi-textured stonework. The original show-room, with its squat red granite pillars, was on the ground floor. It is still a jeweller's, but with no connection to Fabergé. In the workshops above, young apprentices were trained by master craftsmen in the arts of enamelling, engraving, stone cutting and jewelling.

In 1996, the 150th anniversary of Carl Fabergé's birth was marked by the unveiling of a memorial plaque at No. 24 and of a monument, designed by the sculptor Leonid Aristov and others, on the corner of Zanevskiy prospekt and prospekt Energetikov.

FABERGE EGGS

In 1885 Alexander III commissioned the Fabergé brothers to create an Easter egg for Tsarina Maria Fyodorovna. Inside the shell of gold and white enamel was a beautifully sculpted golden hen. A tradition was established and, by the Revolution, there were 54 Fabergé Easter eggs, no two of which were alike. The *pièce de résistance* is the Siberian Railway Egg, commissioned by Nicholas II in 1900. The Bonbonnière Egg was commissioned by Kelch, a wealthy industrialist, for his wife Varvara in 1903. Regrettably, the only eggs on public display in Russia today are in the State Armoury of the Kremlin in Moscow.

The Kelch Bonbonnière Egg

DEATH OF A POET

In November 1836 Pushkin received an anonymous letter which awarded him the title of "Grand Master of the Most Serene Order of Cuckolds". It had been sent by Georges d'Anthès, a ne'er-do-well cavalry officer who for some time had been making overtures towards Pushkin's wife, the beauty and socialite Natalya Goncharova. Pushkin challenged d'Anthès to a duel and, on the afternoon of 27

A Naumov's painting of Pushkin, fatally wounded after his duel

January 1837, he met his opponent in snow-bound woodland to the north of the city. D'Anthès fired first and Pushkin was mortally wounded. He died two days later, aged 38. D'Anthès was later reduced to the ranks and banished from Russia.

Sign outside the Literary Café

Literary Café ⑩
Литературное кафе
Literaturnoe kafe

Nevskiy prospekt 18. **Map** 6 E1.
Tel 312 6057. ⬜ *11am–1am.*
Ⓜ *Nevskiy Prospekt.* ♿
See Restaurants and Cafés p187.

Also known as the Café Wulf et Beranger after its original owners, this café is famous for its association with Alexander Pushkin, Russia's greatest poet *(see p43)*. It was here that Pushkin met his second, Konstantin Danzas, before setting out for his ill-fated duel with Baron d'Anthès. The café was a popular haunt for St Petersburg writers from its beginning, frequented by Fyodor Dostoevsky and the poet Mikhail Lermontov (1814–41), among others.

Despite its hallowed literary importance and elegant setting, in Vasiliy Stasov's handsome building of 1815, the café itself does not merit the high prices.

Palace Square ⑪
Дворцовая площадЬ
Dvortsovaya ploshchad

Map 6 D1 🚌 *7, 10, 24, 191, K-209.*
🚎 *1, 7, 10, 11.*

Palace Square has played a unique role in Russian history. Before the Revolution the square was the setting for colourful military parades, often led by the tsar on horseback. In January 1905, it was the scene of the massacre of "Bloody Sunday" *(see p26)* when gathered troops fired on thousands of unarmed demonstrators. Then, on 7 November 1917, Lenin's Bolshevik supporters secured the Revolution by attacking the Winter Palace *(see pp28–9)* from the square, as well as its west side. It is still a favourite venue for political meetings and cultural events such as rock concerts *(see p51)*.

The resplendent square is the work of the inspired architect Carlo Rossi *(see p110)*. Facing the Winter Palace on its southern side is Rossi's magnificent General Staff Building (1819–29), the headquarters for the Russian army. Rossi demolished an entire row of houses to make room for it.

The two graceful, curving wings (the eastern one now a branch of the Hermitage) are connected by a double arch leading to Bolshaya Morskaya ulitsa. The arch is crowned by a sculpture of Victory in her chariot (1829), by Stepan Pimenov and Vasiliy Demut-Malinovskiy. Forming the eastern side of this striking architectural ensemble is the Guards Headquarters, designed by Aleksandr Bryullov in 1837–43. To the west lies the Admiralty *(see p78)*.

The Alexander Column in the centre of the square is dedicated to Tsar Alexander I for his role in the triumph over Napoleon *(see pp22–3)*. On the pedestal are inscribed the words "To Alexander I, from a grateful Russia". The red granite pillar is balanced by its 600-tonne weight, making it the largest free-standing monument in the world. The column was designed by Auguste de Montferrand in 1829 and it took 2,400 soldiers and workmen two years to hew and transport the granite. It was erected in 1830–34. The column is topped by a bronze angel, and together they stand 47 m (154 ft) high.

The Alexander Column and General Staff Building in Palace Square

The Hermitage ⑫

Эрмитаж
Ermitazh

One of the largest museums in the world, the Hermitage occupies a grand ensemble of buildings. The most impressive is the Winter Palace *(see pp92–3)*, to which Catherine the Great added the more intimate Small Hermitage. In 1771–87, she built the Large Hermitage to house her growing collection of art. The Theatre was built in 1785–7, the New Hermitage in 1839–51. The New and Large Hermitages were opened by Nicholas I in 1852 as a public museum. From 1918 to 1939 the Winter Palace was slowly incorporated into the museum ensemble. In the late 1990s the majestic, Neo-Classical General Staff Building was added. It houses the collections of 19th- and 20th-century art.

The New Hermitage
(1839–51) was designed by Leo von Klenze to form a coherent part of the Large Hermitage. It is the only purpose-built museum within the whole complex.

Court ministries
were located here until the 1880s.

Atlantes
Ten 5-m (16-ft) tall granite Atlantes hold up what was the public entrance to the Hermitage museum from 1852 until after the Revolution.

The Winter Canal
(see p36)

A gallery spanning the canal connects the Theatre to the Large Hermitage and forms the theatre foyer.

The Large Hermitage was designed by Yuriy Velten to house Catherine's paintings.

Theatre
During Catherine's reign, there were regular performances held in Quarenghi's theatre. Today it hosts conferences and concerts (see p202).

★ **Raphael Loggias**
Catherine was so impressed by engravings of Raphael's frescoes in the Vatican that in 1787 she commissioned copies to be made on canvas. Small alterations were made, such as replacing the Pope's coat of arms with the Romanov two-headed eagle.

Hanging Gardens
This unusual raised garden is decorated with statues and fountains. During the Siege of Leningrad (see p27) Hermitage curators grew vegetables here.

The Small Hermitage (1764–75), by Vallin de la Mothe and Yuriy Velten, served as Catherine's retreat from the bustle of the court.

VISITORS' CHECKLIST

Dvortsovaya ploshchad 2. **Map** 2 D5. **Tel** 710 9079. 🚌 7, 10, 24, 191, K-209. 🚎 1, 7, 10, 11. ☐ 10:30am–6pm Tue–Sat; 10:30am–5pm Sun. Last adm 1 hr before closing. 🎫 📷 English (571 8446 to book). ♿ 📷 📺 **www.**hermitagemuseum.org

Winter Palace Façade
Rastrelli embellished the palace façades with 400 columns and 16 different window designs.

STAR SIGHTS

★ Winter Palace State Rooms

★ Pavilion Hall

★ Raphael Loggias

Palace Square

Main entrance via courtyard

General Staff Building

River Neva

The Winter Palace (1754–62) was the official residence of the Imperial family until the Revolution.

★ Pavilion Hall (1850–58)
Andrey Stakenschneider's striking white marble and gold hall replaced Catherine's original interior. It houses Englishman James Cox's famous Peacock Clock (1772), which was once owned by Catherine's secret husband, Prince Grigory Potemkin.

★ Winter Palace State Rooms
The tsars spared no expense in decorating rooms such as the Hall of St George. These rooms were not intended for private life, but were used instead for state ceremonies.

The Hermitage Collections

The Knights' Hall (1842–51) is used for displays of armour and weapons from the former Imperial arsenal.

Catherine the Great purchased some of Western Europe's best collections between 1764 and 1774, acquiring over 2,500 paintings, 10,000 carved gems, 10,000 drawings and a vast amount of silver and porcelain with which to adorn her palaces. None of her successors matched the quantity of her remarkable purchases. After the Revolution, the nationalization of both royal and private property brought more paintings and works of applied art, making the Hermitage one of the world's leading museums.

Entrance for tours and guided groups

Stairs to ground floor

First Floor

Raphael Loggias *(see p84)*

The Gallery of Ancient Painting (1842–51) is decorated with scenes from ancient literature. It houses a superb display of 19th-century European sculpture.

Skylight Rooms

★ **Litta Madonna** (c.1491)
One of two works by Leonardo da Vinci in the museum, this masterpiece was admired by his contemporaries and was frequently copied.

Ground Floor

European Gold Collection

STAR EXHIBITS

- ★ Abraham's Sacrifice by Rembrandt
- ★ Ea Haere Ia Oe by Gauguin
- ★ La Danse by Matisse
- ★ Litta Madonna by Leonardo da Vinci

The Hall of Twenty Columns (1842–51) is painted in Etruscan style.

GALLERY GUIDE
Enter via Palace Square, then cross the main courtyard; group tours use other entrances. Start with the interiors of the Winter Palace state rooms on the first floor to get an overview of the museum. For 19th- and 20th-century European Art use either of the staircases on the Palace Square side of the Winter Palace. Note collections may move.

★ **Abraham's Sacrifice** (1635)
In the 1630s Rembrandt was painting religious scenes in a High Baroque style, using dramatic and striking gestures rather than detail to convey his message.

Main entrance

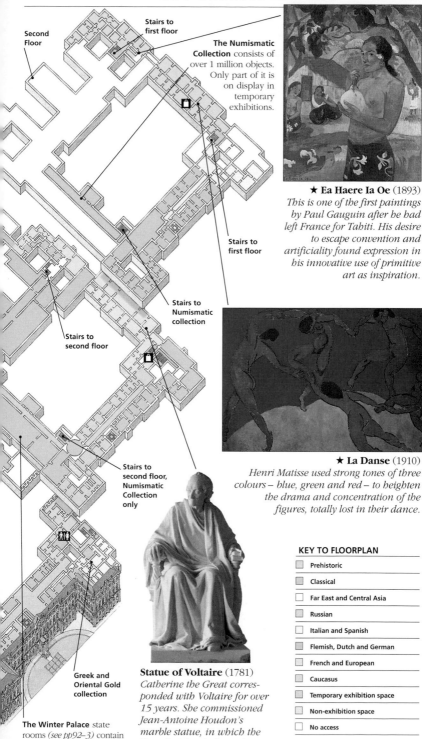

Second Floor

Stairs to first floor

The Numismatic Collection consists of over 1 million objects. Only part of it is on display in temporary exhibitions.

Stairs to first floor

Stairs to Numismatic collection

Stairs to second floor

Stairs to second floor, Numismatic Collection only

Greek and Oriental Gold collection

The Winter Palace state rooms (see pp92–3) contain magnificent Russian and European objets d'art.

★ **Ea Haere Ia Oe** (1893)
This is one of the first paintings by Paul Gauguin after he had left France for Tahiti. His desire to escape convention and artificiality found expression in his innovative use of primitive art as inspiration.

★ **La Danse** (1910)
Henri Matisse used strong tones of three colours – blue, green and red – to heighten the drama and concentration of the figures, totally lost in their dance.

Statue of Voltaire (1781)
Catherine the Great corresponded with Voltaire for over 15 years. She commissioned Jean-Antoine Houdon's marble statue, in which the French writer is dressed as a Greek philosopher.

KEY TO FLOORPLAN

- Prehistoric
- Classical
- Far East and Central Asia
- Russian
- Italian and Spanish
- Flemish, Dutch and German
- French and European
- Caucasus
- Temporary exhibition space
- Non-exhibition space
- No access

Exploring the Hermitage Collections

It is impossible to absorb the Hermitage's vast, encyclo-pedic collection in one or even two visits. Whether it be Scythian gold, antique vases and cameos, or Iranian silver, every room has something to capture the eye. The furniture, applied art, portraits and rich clothing of the imperial family went to make up the Russian section, which also includes the superb state rooms. The collec-tion of European paintings was put together largely according to the personal taste of the imperial family while most of the 19th- and 20th-century European art, notably the Impressionists, Matisse and Picasso, came from private collections after the Revolution.

Scythian gold stag dating from 7th–6th century BC

PREHISTORIC ART

Prehistoric artifacts found all over the former Russian Empire include pots, arrow heads and sculptures from Palaeolithic sites, which date back nearly 24,000 years, and rich gold items from the time of the Scythian nomads living in the 7th–3rd centuries BC.

Peter the Great's famous Siberian collection of delicate gold work includes Scythian animal-style brooches, sword handles and buckles. Objects continued to be discovered in Siberia and in 1897 a large stylized stag, which once deco-rated an iron shield, was found at Kostromskaya. This and other gold pieces are held in the European Gold Collection (for which a separate ticket is required). Copies are on display in the Scythian rooms.

Greek masters also worked for the Scythians, and from the Dnepr region came a late 5th-century comb decorated with amazingly naturalistic figures of Scythians fighting, as well as the late 4th-century Chertomlyk Vase with scenes depicting animal taming.

Excavations in the Altai, notably at Pazyryk in 1927–49, uncovered burials nearly 2,500 years old. Many perishable materials were preserved by the frozen land, including textiles, a burial cart and even a man's heavily tattooed skin.

Gonzaga Cameo (285–246 BC), made in Alexandria

CLASSICAL ART

The large number of Graeco-Roman marble sculptures range from the famous Tauride Venus of the 3rd century BC, acquired by Peter the Great in 1720, to Roman portrait busts. The smaller objects, however, are the real pride and joy of the Classical department.

The collection of red-figured Attic vases of the 6th–4th centuries BC is unequalled any-where in the world. Exquisitely proportioned and with a lustrous shine, they are deco-rated with scenes of libation, episodes from the Trojan War, and in one case a famous image of the sighting of the first swallow (c.510 BC).

In the 4th and 3rd centuries BC, Tanagra was the centre for the production of small, ele-gant terracotta figurines. They were discovered in the 19th century and became so pop-ular that fakes were produced on a grand scale. The Russian ambassador in Athens, Pyotr Saburov, put his collection together in the 1880s before the copies appeared, making it unusually valuable.

Catherine the Great's true passion was for carved gems, which she bought en masse. In just ten years, she purchased some 10,000 pieces. The largest and most stunning gem in the Classical collection, however, is the Gonzaga Cameo, which was presented by Napoleon's ex-wife Josephine Beauharnais to Tsar Alexander I in 1814.

The Greek and Oriental Gold Collection contains some items of 5th-century gold jewellery made by Athenian craftsmen. They used a filigree technique for working gold so finely that the detail can only be seen through a magnifying glass.

FAR EAST AND CENTRAL ASIA

This selection of more than 180,000 artifacts covers a wide range of cultures; from ancient Egypt and Assyria, through Byzantium, India, Iran, China, Japan and the marvels of Uzbekistan and Tajikistan. The most complete sections are those where excavations were conducted by the Hermitage, mainly in China and Mongolia before the Revolution, and in Central Asia during the Soviet period.

Dating back to the 19th century BC, at the time of the

8th-century fresco of a wounded warrior from Tajikistan

Middle Kingdom, is a seated porphyry portrait of Pharaoh Amenemhet III. The star of the Egyptian collection is an extremely rare, small, wooden statue of a standing man from the 15th century BC.

From the Far East – Japan, India, Indonesia, China and Mongolia – comes an array of objects ranging from Buddhist sculptures and fabrics to a display of tiny netsukes (ivory toggles). Excavations at the cave temple of the Thousand Buddhas near Dun Huan in western China revealed 6th–10th-century icons, wall paintings and plaster sculptures, including the lions that once guarded the cave. During the 13th-century Mongol invasion, the town of Khara-Khoto was destroyed and taken over by the surrounding desert. The sand preserved many usually perishable objects, from 12th-century silks to woodcuts.

From Byzantium come early secular items, such as icons, religious utensils and a 5th-century ivory diptych with scenes from a Roman circus.

Iran produced a large number of silver and bronze vessels, many of which were taken by medieval traders to Siberia and the Urals where they were rediscovered by specialists in the 19th century. There is also a large collection of traditional Persian miniatures and a rich display of 19th-century Persian court portraits, of traditional elements with western oil painting, as in the *Portrait of*

Fatkh-Ali Shah (1813–14). Uzbekistan and Tajikistan revealed marvellous frescoes in complexes of 8th-century buildings at Varaksha, Adjina-Tepe and Pendzhikent. Rare Mughal jewelled vessels, Iranian weapons and Chinese gold objects are displayed in the Greek and Oriental Gold Collection. These rooms are undergoing a three-year renovation.

RUSSIAN ART

Although major Russian works of art were transferred to the Russian Museum (*see pp104–107*) in 1898, everything else that belonged to the imperial family was nationalized after the Revolution. This included anything from official portraits and thrones to looking glasses and petticoats. Over 300 items of apparel belonging to Peter the Great alone survive. Later, the museum also began acquiring medieval Russian art, including icons and church utensils.

The tsars from Peter the Great onwards invited foreign

Universal sundial (1714–19) from Peter the Great's collection

craftsmen and artists to train locals. Peter studied with them and his fascination for practical things is reflected in his large collection of sundials, instruments and wood-turning lathes which includes the universal sundial by Master John Rowley. A bust by Bartolomeo Carlo Rastrelli (1723–30), however, portrays Peter as the mighty and cruel emperor.

Russian artists were soon combining traditional art forms with European skills to create such intricate marvels as the openwork walrus ivory vase by Nikolay Vereshchagin (1798), and the large silver sarcophagus and memorial to Alexander Nevsky, truly Russian in scale (1747–52).

The gunsmiths of Tula (south of Moscow) perfected their technique to such an extent that they began producing unique furniture in steel inlaid with gilded bronze, such as the decorative, Empire-style dressing table set (1801).

The state interiors (*see pp92–3*) are the pride of the Russian department, revealing the work of Russian and foreign craftsmen from the mid-18th to the early 20th century. The discovery of large deposits of coloured stones in the Urals inspired Russian artists to decorate whole rooms with malachite and to fill every corner of the Winter Palace with marble vases. It was through these rooms that the imperial family paraded on state occasions, greeting courtiers and ambassadors en route in the Field Marshals' Hall.

Steel dressing table set from Tula dating from 1801

ITALIAN AND SPANISH ART

The display of Italian art contains some fine pieces. A few early works reveal the rise of the Renaissance in the 14th and 15th centuries and the styles then in vogue. Simone Martini's stiff *Madonna* (1340–44) contrasts with Fra Angelico's more humane fresco of the Virgin and Child (1424–30).

In the late 15th and early 16th century, artists disputed the merits of line, as practised by the Florentine school, and the merits of colour, virtue of the Venetians. The former can be seen in the *Litta Madonna* (c.1491) and the *Madonna Benois* (1478) by Leonardo da Vinci, a marble *Crouching Boy* by Michelangelo (c.1530) and two early portraits of the Virgin by Raphael (1502 and 1506). Venice is represented by *Judith* by Giorgione (1478–1510) and an array of works by Titian (c.1490–1576). The Skylight Rooms are packed with vast Baroque canvases, including works by Luca Giordano (1634–1704) and Guido Reni (1575–1642), and even larger 18th-century masterpieces by Tiepolo. The works of the Italian sculptor Antonio Canova (1757–1822) (*Cupid and Psyche, The Three Graces*) stand in the Gallery of Ancient Painting.

The Spanish collection is more modest, but Spain's greatest painters can all be

seen, from El Greco with *The Apostles Peter and Paul* (1587–92), through to Ribera, Murillo, and Zurbarán with *St Lawrence* (1636). The portrait of a courtier, *Count Olivares*, painted c.1640 by Velázquez, contrasts with a much earlier genre scene of a peasant's breakfast (1617–18).

Venus and Cupid (1509) by Lucas Cranach the Elder

FLEMISH, DUTCH AND GERMAN ART

The small collection of early paintings from the Netherlands includes a marvellous, jewel-like *Madonna and Child*

(1430s) by the Master of Flemalle. He is thought to have been the teacher of Rogier van der Weyden, who is represented by *St Luke Painting the Madonna* (c.1435).

Over 40 works by Rubens include religious subjects (*The Descent from the Cross,* 1617–18) and scenes from Classical mythology (*Perseus and Andromeda,* 1620–21), as well as landscapes and an immensely obese *Bacchus* (1636–40). His portraits, such as the *Infanta's Maid* (1625), reveal the link with his famous pupil Van Dyck, whose paintings include a series of formal, full-length portraits and a dashing and romantic self-portrait from the late 1620s.

The Dutch section is rich in Rembrandts. Within a short period of time he produced the dramatic *Abraham's Sacrifice* (1636), the gentle *Flora* (1634) and the brilliant effects of *The Descent from the Cross* (1634). One of his last works was the *Return of the Prodigal Son* (1668–9), with an emotional depth unseen before.

Among the many small-genre paintings is Gerard Terborch's *Glass of Lemonade* from the mid-17th century. All the usual elements of a genre scene are imbued with psychological tension and heavy symbolism.

In the German collection, it is the works of Lucas Cranach the Elder which captivate the viewer. His *Venus and Cupid* (1509), the stylish *Portrait of a Woman in a Hat* (1526) and the tender *Virgin and Child Beneath an Apple Tree* reveal the varied aspects of his talent.

FRENCH AND ENGLISH ART

French art was *de rigueur* for collectors in the 18th century. Major artists of the 17th century, including Louis Le Nain and the two brilliant and contrasting painters Claude Lorrain and Nicolas Poussin, are well represented. Antoine Watteau's elegant *Embarrassing Proposal* (c.1716), *Stolen Kiss* (1780s) by Jean Honoré Fragonard and François Boucher's fleshy and certainly far-from-virtuous

A Young Man Playing a Lute, by Michelangelo Caravaggio (1573–1610)

Still Life with the Attributes of the Arts (1766), by Jean-Baptiste Chardin

heroines represent the more wicked side of 18th-century taste, but Catherine the Great preferred didactic or instructional works. She bought *Still Life with Attributes of the Arts* (1766) by Chardin and, on the advice of Denis Diderot, Jean-Baptiste Greuze's moralizing *The Fruits of a Good Education* (1763). She also patronized sculptors, purchasing works by Etienne-Maurice Falconet (*Winter*, carved 1771) and Jean-Antoine Houdon (*Voltaire*, 1781).

Catherine also acquired English works, including a portrait of the philosopher John Locke (1697) by Sir Godfrey Kneller, who was also author of a portrait of Pyotr Potemkin (1682) in Russian 17th-century court dress. From Sir Joshua Reynolds Catherine commissioned *The Infant Hercules Strangling the Serpents* (1788). Her most daring purchase was of works by the still largely unknown Joseph Wright of Derby. *The Iron Forge* (1773) is a masterpiece of artificial lighting, but *Firework Display at the Castel Sant'Angelo* (1774–5) is a truly romantic fiery spectacle. She provided much work for English cabinet-makers and carvers of cameos. She became one of Josiah Wedgwood's most prestigious clients, ordering the famous Green Frog Service for her Chesma Palace *(see p130)*.

The Green Frog Service, Wedgwood (1773–4)

19TH- & 20TH-CENTURY EUROPEAN ART

Although the royal family did not patronize the new movements in art in the 19th century, there were far-sighted private individuals whose collections were nationalized and entered the Hermitage after the 1917 Revolution. Thanks to them, the Barbizon school is represented by works such as Camille Corot's charming silvery *Landscape with a Lake*, French Romanticism by two richly-coloured Moroccan scenes of the 1850s by Delacroix. But Nicholas I himself did acquire works by the German Romantic painter Caspar David Friedrich, among them *On the Prow of the Ship* (1818–20).

Two collectors, Ivan Morozov and Sergey Shchukin, brought the Hermitage its superb array of Impressionist and Post-Impressionist paintings. Monet's art can be admired both in his early *Woman in a Garden* (1860s) and in the later, more exploratory *Waterloo Bridge, Effect of Mist* (1903). Renoir and Degas perpetually returned to women as subjects, as in Renoir's charming *Portrait of the Actress Jeanne Samary* (1878) and Degas' pastels of women washing (1880s–90s). Pissarro's *Boulevard Montmartre in Paris* (1897) is typical of his urban scenes.

A change in colour and technique appeared as artists investigated new possibilities. Van Gogh used deeper tones in his *Women of Arles* (1888) and stronger brushstrokes in *Cottages* (1890). Gauguin turned to a different culture for inspiration, and his Tahitian period is represented by enigmatic works, such as *Ea Haere Ia Oe* (1893). In *The Smoker* (c.1890–2) and *Mont Ste-Victoire* (1896–8), Cézanne introduced experiments with plane and surface which were to have a strong influence on the next generation.

Matisse played both with colour and surface, in the carpet-like effect of *The Red Room* (1908–9) and the flatness of the panels *La Musique* and *La Danse* (1909–10). His visit to Morocco introduced new light effects, as in *Arab Coffeehouse* (1913), but it was Picasso who took Cézanne's experiments one stage further. In early works such as *Visit* (1902) from his Blue Period, Picasso concentrates on mood, but the surface destruction of the Cubist period of 1907–12, including *L'Homme aux Bras Croisés*, fills a whole room.

L'Homme aux Bras Croisés, painted by Pablo Picasso in 1909

The Winter Palace

Preceded by three earlier versions on this site, the existing Winter Palace (1754–62) is a superb example of Russian Baroque. Built for Tsarina Elizabeth, this opulent winter residence was the finest achievement of Bartolomeo Rastrelli. Though the exterior has changed little, the interiors were altered by a number of architects and then largely restored after a fire gutted the palace in 1837. After the assassination of Alexander II in 1881, the imperial family rarely lived here. During World War I a field hospital was set up in the Nicholas Hall and other state rooms. Then, in July 1917, the Provisional Government took the palace as its headquarters, which led to its storming by the Bolsheviks *(see pp28–9)*.

The 1812 Gallery (1826) has portraits of Russian military heroes of the Napoleonic War, most by English artist George Dawe.

The Armorial Hall (1839), with its vast gilded columns, covers over 800 sq m (8,600 sq ft). Hospital beds were set up here during the First World War.

★ Small Throne Room
Dedicated in 1833 to the memory of Peter the Great, this room houses a silver-gilt English throne, made in 1731.

The Field Marshals' Hall (1833) was the reception room where the devastating fire of 1837 broke out.

The Hall of St George (1795) has monolithic columns and wall facings of Italian Carrara marble.

The Nicholas Hall, the largest room in the palace, was always used for the first ball of the season.

North façade overlooking the Neva

★ Main Staircase
This vast, sweeping staircase (1762) was Rastrelli's master-piece. It was from here that the imperial family watched the Epiphany ceremony of baptism in the Neva, which celebrated Christ's baptism in the Jordan.

★ Malachite Room
Over two tonnes of ornamental stone were used in this sumptuous room (1839) which is decorated with malachite columns and vases, gilded doors and ceiling, and rich parquet flooring.

Alexander Hall
Architect Aleksandr Bryullov employed a mixture of Gothic vaulting and Neo-Classical stucco bas-reliefs of military themes in this reception room of 1837.

BARTOLOMEO RASTRELLI

The Italian architect Rastrelli (1700–71) came to Russia with his father in 1716 to work for Peter the Great. His rich Baroque style became highly fashionable and he was appointed Chief Court Architect in 1738. During Elizabeth's reign, Rastrelli designed several buildings, including the Winter Palace, the Palace of Tsarkoe Selo *(see pp152–7)* and Smolnyy Convent *(see p128).* Unlike Elizabeth, Catherine the Great preferred Classical simplicity and Rastrelli retired in 1763, after she came to power.

The French Rooms, designed by Bryullov in 1839, house a collection of 18th-century French art.

The White Hall was decorated for the wedding of the future Alexander II in 1841.

South façade on Palace Square

Dark Corridor
The French and Flemish tapestries here include The Marriage of Emperor Constantine, *made in Paris in the 17th century to designs by Rubens.*

The Rotunda (1830) connected the private apartments in the west with the state apartments on the palace's north side.

West wing

The Gothic Library and other rooms in the northwest part of the palace were adapted to suit Nicholas II's bourgeois lifestyle. This wood-panelled library was created by Meltzer in 1894.

STAR FEATURES

★ Small Throne Room

★ Malachite Room

★ Main Staircase

The Gold Drawing Room
Created in the 1850s, this room was extravagantly decorated in the 1870s with all-over gilding of walls and ceiling. It houses a display of Western European carved gems.

Millionaires' Street ⑬

Миллионная улица
Millionnaya ulitsa

Map 2 E5.

Millionaires' Street takes its name from the aristocrats and members of the imperial family who once inhabited its opulent residences. Since the main façades and entrances overlook the river, some house numbers correspond to the embankment side.

On the eve of the Revolution, No. 26 (on the embankment) was the home of Grand Duke Vladimir Aleksandrovich who was responsible for firing on peaceful demonstrators on Bloody Sunday *(see p26)*. His consort, Maria Pavlovna, was one of Russia's leading society hostesses who gave soirées and balls that eclipsed even those of the imperial court. The building (1867–72), which was designed by Aleksandr Rezanov in the style of the Florentine Renaissance, is now the House of Scholars.

Putyatin's house, at No. 12 Millionaires' Street, witnessed the end of the Romanov dynasty. It was here that Grand Duke Mikhail Aleksandrovich, Nicholas II's brother, signed the decree of abdication in March 1917. Next door, No. 10, was where French novelist Honoré de Balzac stayed in 1843, while courting his future wife, Countess Eveline Hanska. The mid-19th-century house was designed by Andrey Stakenschneider for his own use.

The delicately sculpted façade of No. 10 Millionaires' Street

Gala staircase of the Marble Palace

Marble Palace ⑭

Мраморный дворец
Mramornyy dvorets

Millionnaya ulitsa 5 (entrance from the Field of Mars). **Map** 2 E4. **Tel** 312 9054. 🚌 46, 49, K-46, K-76. ☐ 10am–6pm Wed–Sun, 10am–5pm Mon. ☒ ☒ *English.* **www.rusmuseum.ru**

The Marble Palace was built as a present from Catherine the Great to her lover Grigoriy Orlov who had been instrumental in bringing her to power in 1762 *(see p22)*. An early example of Neo-Classical architecture, dating from 1768–85, the building is considered one of Antonio Rinaldi's masterpiece.

The palace takes its name from the marbles used in its construction. Most of the interiors were reconstructed in the 1840s by Aleksandr Bryullov, although the gala staircase and the Marble Hall are Rinaldi's work. The latter has marbled walls of grey, green, white, yellow, pink and lapis lazuli, and a ceiling painting, the *Triumph of Venus* (1780s) by Stefano Torelli.

The palace, which housed a Lenin museum for 55 years, is now a branch of the Russian Museum *(see pp104–107)*. On display are temporary exhibitions of work by foreign artists and modern art bequeathed by the German collectors Peter and Irene Ludwig. Their collection includes a Picasso, *Large Heads* (1969), and work by post-war artists Jean-Michel Basquiat, Andy Warhol, Ilya Kabakov and Roy Lichtenstein.

In front of the palace stands a curious equestrian statue of Alexander III by Prince Pavel Trubetskoy. Unveiled on ploshchad Vosstaniya in 1911, the ridiculed statue was removed from its original site in 1937 and its vast pedestal was cut up to create statues of new heroes, such as Lenin.

Field of Mars ⑮

Марсово Поле
Marsovo Pole

Map 2 F5. 🚌 46, 49, K-46, K-76.

Once a vast marshland, this area was drained during the 19th century and utilized for military manoeuvres and parades, fairs and other festivities. It was appropriately named after Mars, the Roman god of war. Between 1917 and 1923 the area, by then a sandy expanse, was nicknamed the "Petersburg Sahara". It was landscaped and transformed into a war memorial. The granite *Monument to Revolutionary Fighters* (1917–19), by Lev Rudnev, and the Eternal Flame (1957) commemorate the victims of the Revolutions of 1917 and the Civil War *(see p27)*.

Eternal Flame, Field of Mars

The west of the square is dominated by an imposing Neo-Classical building erected by Vasiliy Stasov in 1817–19. This was formerly the barracks of the Pavlovskiy Guards which were founded by Tsar Paul I in 1796. The military-obsessed tsar is said to have only recruited guardsmen with snub noses like his own. The Pavlovskiy officers were among the first to turn against the tsarist government in the 1917 Revolution *(see pp28–9)*.

Today the huge square is a popular spot for locals in the summer evenings, when the flowers are in bloom.

Summer Garden 🔟

Летний сад
Letniy sad

Letniy Sad. **Map** 2 F4. 🚌 *46, 49,
K-46, K-76, K-212.* ⬜ *May–Sep:
10am–10pm daily; Oct–Mar:
10am–6pm daily.* ♿ 📷

In 1704 Peter the Great commissioned this beautiful formal garden which was among the first in the city. Designed by a Frenchman in the style of Versailles, the allées were planted with imported elms and oaks and adorned with fountains, pavilions and some 250 Italian statues dating from the 17th and 18th centuries. A flood in 1777 destroyed most of the Summer Garden and the English-style garden which exists today is largely the result of Catherine the Great's more sober tastes. A splendid feature is the fine filigree iron grille (1771–84) along the Neva embankment, created by Yuriy Velten and Pyotr Yegorov.

For a century the Summer Garden was an exclusive preserve of the nobility. When the garden was opened to "respectably dressed members of the public" by Nicholas I, two Neo-Classical pavilions, the Tea House and the Coffee House, were erected overlooking the Fontanka. These are now used for temporary exhibitions of art.

Nearby, the bronze statue of Ivan Krylov, Russia's most famous writer of fables, is a favourite with Russian children. It was sculpted by Pyotr Klodt in 1854 with charming bas-reliefs on the pedestal depicting animals from his fables.

Ivan Krylov's statue amidst autumn foliage in the Summer Garden

Summer Palace 🔟

Летний дворец
Letniy dvorets

Naberezhnaya Kutuzova. **Map** 2 F4.
Tel *314 0374.* ⬜ *May–Nov:
11am–5:30pm Wed–Mon.* ⬤ *last
Mon of each month.* 🚌 *46, 49,
K-46, K-76, K-212.* 📷 📷

Built for Peter the Great, the modest two-storey Summer Palace is the oldest stone building in the city. It was designed in the Dutch style by Domenico Trezzini and was completed in 1714. The Prussian sculptor Andreas Schlüter created the delightful maritime bas-reliefs (1713) as an allegorical commentary on Russia's naval triumphs under Peter the Great's stewardship.

Grander than his wooden cabin *(see p73)*, Peter's second St Petersburg residence is still by no means comparable to the magnificent palaces built by his successors.

On the ground floor, the reception room is hung with portraits of the tsar and his ministers and contains Peter's oak Admiralty Chair. The tsar's bedroom has its original four-poster bed with a coverlet of Chinese silk, and an 18th-century ceiling painting showing the triumph of Morpheus, the god of sleep. Next door is the turnery which contains some original Russian lathes as well as an elaborately carved wooden meteorological instrument, designed in Dresden in 1714.

The palace boasted the city's first plumbing system with water piped directly into the kitchen. The original black marble sink can still be seen, along with the beautifully tiled kitchen stove and an array of early 18th-century cooking utensils. The kitchen opens onto the exquisite dining room, imaginatively refurbished to convey an atmosphere of domesticity. It was used only for small family gatherings since major banquets were held at the Menshikov Palace *(see p62)*.

An original staircase leads up to the first floor and the more lavish suite of Peter's second wife, Catherine. The throne in the aptly named Throne Room is ornamented with Nereides and other sea deities. The glass cupboards in the Green Room once displayed Peter's fascinating collection of curiosa before it was transferred to the Kunstkammer *(see p60)*.

The remarkable stove in the Summer Palace's tiled kitchen

GOSTINYY DVOR

The Great Bazaar, Gostinyy Dvor, was the commercial heart of St Petersburg at the beginning of the 18th century and today it still hums with activity. A profusion of smaller retail outlets soon appeared on and around Nevskiy prospekt. Thriving communities of foreign merchants and businessmen also took up residence in the neighbourhood.

Until the mid-19th century, shops in this area catered almost exclusively for the luxury end of the market, fulfilling the limitless demand, created by the royal and aristocratic households, for gold and silverware, jewellery and

Statues on façade of the Russian Museum

haute couture. Increasing commercial and financial activity created a new middle class of business entrepreneurs. By the Revolution, banks proliferated around Nevskiy prospekt, their imposing new offices introducing diverse architectural styles to a largely Neo-Classical setting. Today the wheels of capitalism are turning again and Nevskiy prospekt still attracts a wealthy clientele. In contrast to the bustling commercial atmosphere of much of the area is the calm oasis of Arts Square, with the Russian Museum and other institutions which act as a reminder of the city's rich cultural life.

SIGHTS AT A GLANCE

Churches
Armenian Church **7**
Cathedral of Our Lady of Kazan **15**
Church on Spilled Blood p100 **1**
Lutheran Church **17**

Museums
Mikhaylovskiy Castle **2**
Pushkin House-Museum **19**
Russian Museum pp104–107 **3**

Streets and Squares
Arts Square **4**
Nevskiy Prospekt **6**
Ostrovskiy Square **11**
Ulitsa Zodchego Rossi **12**

Markets and Shops
Apraksin Market **14**
Gostinyy Dvor **8**
Yeliseev's **9**

Palaces
Anichkov Palace **10**
Stroganov Palace **16**
Vorontsov Palace **13**

Hotels
Grand Hotel Europe **5**

Historic Buildings
Glinka Capella **18**
Imperial Stables **20**

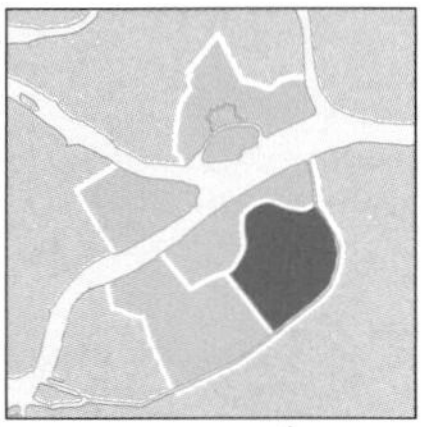

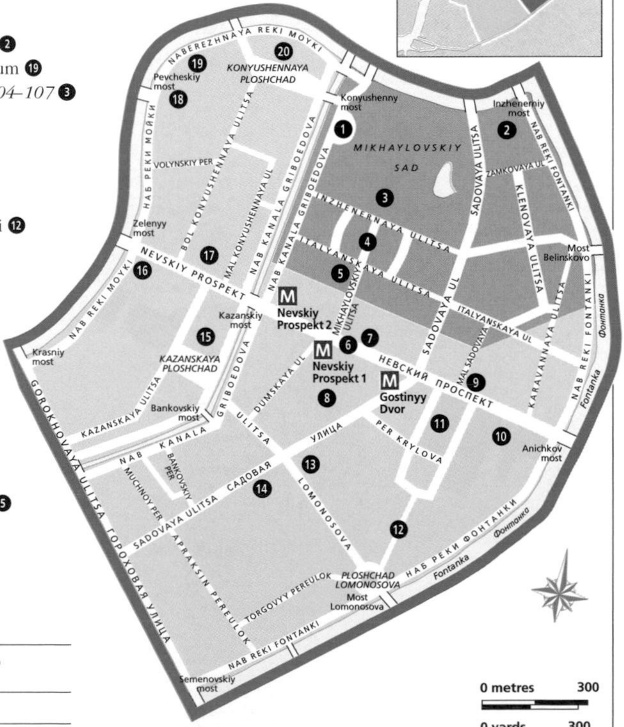

KEY

■ Street-by-Street map
  See pp98–9

Ⓜ Metro

◁ **Side view of the imposing Mikhaylovskiy Castle *(see p101)*, a branch of the Russian Museum**

Street-by-Street: Around Arts Square

Peter the Great statue

The aptly named Arts Square, one of Carlo Rossi's finest creations, is surrounded by buildings revealing the city's impressive cultural heritage. The grand palace housing the Russian Museum is flanked by theatres and the Philharmonia concert hall. Behind it is the leafy Mikhaylovskiy Garden, a haunt of St Petersburg's intellectuals. The gardens stretch down to the beautiful Moyka river which together with two other waterways, the Griboedov and Fontanka, create a shimmering frame for this picturesque area.

★ Church on Spilled Blood
Colourful mosaics and elaborate stone carving are the main features of the church's exterior, which emulates traditional 17th-century Russian style ❶

Mikhaylovskiy Garden

★ Russian Museum
Located in Rossi's Mikhaylovskiy Palace, this famous gallery boasts a fabulous collection of Russian painting, sculpture and applied art. The grand staircase and White Hall are original features ❸

Arts Square
The square's present name derives from the number of cultural institutions situated here. On the western side, the Mikhailovsky Theatre opened in 1833 for opera performances ❹

Statue of Pushkin (1957)

Nevskiy prospekt

The Great Hall of the Philharmonia is one of the major concert venues in St Petersburg *(see p202).*

Grand Hotel Europe
This famous St Petersburg hotel was constructed by Ludwig Fontana in 1873–5. Mighty atlantes adorn its eclectic façade which stretches all the way down to Nevskiy prospekt ❺

The Panteleymon Bridge was rebuilt in 1907–8 to support a new tramway but it retains its original Empire-style decor by Lev Ilyin *(see p37).*

LOCATOR MAP
See Street Finder map 6

GOSTINYY DVOR

SENNAYA
PLOSHCHAD

The bird statue, cast in 1995 by Rezo Gabriadze, refers to a popular rhyme about vodka drinking.

Statue of Peter the Great (1747)

Mikhaylovskiy Castle
Originally built for Paul I in 1797–1801, this castle was acquired by the Guards Corps of Engineers in 1823. Today it forms part of the Russian Museum and displays historical portraits ❷

ZAMKOVAYA ULITSA

NAB REKI FONTANKA

FONTANKA

SADOVAYA ULITSA

INZHENERNAYA ULITSA

KLENOVAYA ALLEYA

KARAVANNAYA ULITSA

PLOSCHAD BELINSKOVO

MANEZHNAYA PLOSCHAD

STAR SIGHTS

★ Russian Museum

★ Church on Spilled Blood

KEY

– – – Suggested route

| 0 metres | 100 |
| 0 yards | 100 |

Nevskiy prospekt

The Museum of Hygiene, with macabre displays of preserved human organs, was set up in 1919 to teach the public about health and hygiene.

The Circus or *"tsirk"* began performing in the 19th century when it was known as the Ciniselli Circus. It still offers traditional performances *(see p201)* in its historic venue by the Fontanka. Its original façade was reinstated in 2003.

Church on Spilled Blood ❶

Храм Спаса-на-Крови

Khram Spasa-na-Krovi

VISITORS' CHECKLIST

Kanala Griboedova 2b. **Map** 2
E5. *Tel* 315 1636. Ⓜ *Gostinyy
Dvor, Nevskiy Prospekt.* ◻ *May–
Sep: 10am–11pm (Oct–Apr:
11am–7pm) Thu–Tue.* 🖼 💷 🎫

The Church on Spilled Blood, also known as the
Resurrection Church of Our Saviour, was built on the
spot where on 1 March 1881 Tsar Alexander II was
assassinated *(see p26)*. In 1883 his successor, Alexander
III, launched a competition for a permanent memorial.
The winning design, in the Russian Revival style
favoured by the tsar himself, was by Alfred
Parland and Ignatiy Malyshev. The foundation
stone was laid in October 1883.

A riot of colour, the overall effect of the
church is created by the imaginative juxtaposition of materials. Inside, more than 20 types of
minerals, including jasper, rhodonite, porphyry
and Italian marble are lavished on the mosaics
of the iconostasis, icon cases, canopy and
floor. The interior reopened in 1998 after
more than 20 years of restoration.

Mosaic Tympanum
*Mosaic panels showing scenes from the
New Testament adorn the exterior. They
were based on designs by artists such as
Viktor Vasnetsov and Mikhail Nesterov.*

**The tent-roofed
steeple** is 81 m
(265 ft) high.

Coat of Arms
*The 144 mosaic coats
of arms on the bell
tower represent the
regions, towns and
provinces of the
Russian empire.
They were intended
to reflect the grief
shared by all
Russians in
the wake of
Alexander's
assassination.*

Jewellers' enamel was
used to cover the
1,000 sq m
(10,760 sq ft) surface
of the five domes.

Glazed ceramic
tiles enliven
the façade.

Twenty dark red
plaques of Norwegian
granite are engraved in
gilt letters with the most
outstanding events of
Alexander II's reign
(1855–81). Among the
historic events recorded
are the emancipation of
the serfs in 1861 and
the conquest of Central
Asia (1860–81).

Intricate Detailing
*The flamboyant
Russian Revival style
of the exterior
provides a dra-
matic contrast to
the Neo-Classical
and Baroque
architecture
which dominates
the centre of
St Petersburg.*

Mosaic portraits
of the saints are
set in tiers of
kokoshniki gables.
Almost 7,000 sq m
(75,300 sq ft) of
mosaics embellish
the church's extra-
vagant exterior.

Window Frames
*The windows are
flanked by carved
columns of ornate
Estonian marble. The
casings are in the form
of double and triple
kokoshniki (tiered
decorative arches).*

South façade of Mikhaylovskiy Castle and statue of Peter the Great

Mikhaylovskiy Castle ❷

Михайловский замок
Mikhaylovskiy zamok

Sadovaya ulitsa 2. **Map** 2 F5. **Tel** 570 5112. 🚌 46, K-46, K-76, K-212. ⬜ 10am–6pm Wed–Sun, 10am–5pm Mon. 📷 📞 book by phone. ♿

The imposing red brick castle overlooking the Moyka and Fontanka rivers is also known as the Engineers' Castle. It was erected in 1797–1801 by Vasiliy Bazhenov and Vincenzo Brenna for Tsar Paul I. The tsar's obsessive fear of being assassinated led him to surround his new residence with moats and drawbridges, and to build a secret underground passage to the barracks on the Field of Mars *(see p94)*. Unfortunately, all these precautions proved futile and, after living in his fortified castle for just 40 days, Paul fell victim to a military conspiracy that resulted in his murder *(see p22)*.

In 1823 the fortress was acquired by the Guards

Corps of Engineers. The school's most famous graduate was the writer Fyodor Dostoevsky *(see p123)*. Today the castle serves as a branch of the nearby Russian Museum. It is used to house temporary exhibitions.

The Church of the Archangel Michael is accessed via the exhibition and is a good example of Brenna's Neo-Classical style.

In front of the castle stands a bronze statue of Peter the Great on horseback, designed by Bartolomeo Carlo Rastrelli and cast in 1747.

Russian Museum ❸

See pp104–107.

Arts Square ❹

Площадь Искусств
Ploshchad Iskusstv

Map 6 F1. Ⓜ *Nevskiy Prospekt, Gostinyy Dvor.*

Several of the city's leading cultural institutions are located on this leafy Neo-Classical square, hence its name. The attractive square was designed by Carlo Rossi in the early 19th century to harmonize with the magnificent Mikhaylovskiy Palace (now the Russian Museum) which stands on its northern side.

On the opposite side of the square is the Great Hall of the St Petersburg Philharmonia, also known as the Shostakovich Hall *(see p43)*. This is where the Philharmonic Orchestra has been based since the 1920s *(see p202)*. Constructed by

Paul Jacot in 1834–9, it started as a Nobles' Club where concerts were held. Among the works premiered here were Beethoven's *Missa Solemnis* in 1824 and Tchaikovsky's *(see p42) Pathétique* in 1893.

On the square's western side is the Mikhailovsky Theatre *(see p202)*, rebuilt by Albert Kavos in the mid-19th century. In the centre of the square is a sculpture of one of Russia's greatest literary figures, Alexander Pushkin *(see p43)*. The statue was executed by leading post-war sculptor, Mikhail Anikushin.

Grand Hotel Europe's elegant Style-Moderne restaurant *(see p188)*

Grand Hotel Europe ❺

Гранд Отель Европа
Grand Otel Evropa

Mikhaylovskaya ulitsa 1/7. **Map** 6 F1. **Tel** 329 6000. Ⓜ *Nevskiy Prospekt, Gostinyy Dvor.* ♿ *See* Where to Stay *p175.*

One of Russia's most famous hotels, the ornate Grand Hotel Europe (1873–5) was designed by Ludwig Fontana. The building owes much of its character to alterations made in the 1910s by Style-Moderne architect Fyodor Lidval.

Before the Revolution, the hotel's magnificent restaurant was a favourite rendezvous for members of the diplomatic corps and secret police. In the 1970s, the hotel café became a popular meeting place for young intellectuals and artists.

Pushkin's statue in front of the Russian Museum, Arts Square

The Church on Spilled Blood, a magical remnant of old Russia ▷

Russian Museum ❸

Русский Музей
Russkiy Muzey

The museum is housed in the Mikhailovsky Palace, one of Carlo Rossi's finest Neo-Classical creations, which was built in 1819–25 for Grand Duke Mikhail Pavlovich. Alexander III's plans to create a public museum were realized by his son, Nicholas II, when the Russian Museum opened here in 1898. Today, the museum holds one of the world's greatest collections of Russian art.

The Benois Wing, named after its main architect Leontiy Benois, was added in 1913–19.

Stairs to ground floor

71 72 70 89 73 90 69 88 68 74 91 92 67 75 93 87 66 76 94 85 77 78 79 84 80 81 83 82

★ **Princess Olga Konstantinovna Orlova** (1911)
By the turn of the 20th century, Valentin Serov was the most successful portrait painter in Russia.

Entrance

Temporary exhibitions of 20th-century art are often displayed.

107 108 109 106 105 104 103 102 101

Stairs to first floor of Benois Wing

A Meal in the Monastery (1865–76)
Vasiliy Perov's canvas exposes the hypocrisy of the Orthodox clergy, with the juxtaposition of good and evil, rich and poor, false piety and true faith.

GALLERY GUIDE

The main entrance on Arts Square leads to the ticket office on the lower ground floor. The exhibition starts on the first floor. It is arranged chronologically, starting with icons in Room 1. It continues on the ground floor of the main building and Rossi Wing, then the first floor of the Benois Wing. Exhibitions are changed regularly.

STAR EXHIBITS

★ Princess Olga Konstantinovna Orlova by Serov

★ The Last Day of Pompeii by Bryullov

★ Barge-Haulers on the Volga by Repin

Folk Art Toy (1930s)
This clay toy from Dykomovo is part of the colourful selection of folk art which also includes lacquer boxes, painted ceramics and textiles.

★ The Last Day of Pompeii (1833)
Karl Bryullov's Classical subject embodies the aesthetic principles of the Academy of Arts. This vivid depiction of the eruption of Vesuvius won him the Grand Prix at the Paris Salon.

VISITORS' CHECKLIST

Inzhenernaya ulitsa 4. **Map** 6 F1.
Tel 595 4248. M Nevskiy Prospekt, Gostinyy Dvor. 3, 7, 22, 24, 27, 191, K-212, K-289. 1, 5, 7, 10, 11, 22. 10am–5pm Mon, 10am–6pm Wed–Sun (last ticket an hour before closing). phone for details. English (tel: 314 3448). English. www.rusmuseum.ru

★ Barge-Haulers on the Volga (1870–73)
Ilya Repin was the most famous member of the Wanderers, a group of artists dedicated to social realism and Russian themes. His powerful indictment of forced labour imbues the oppressed victims with sullen dignity.

Stairs to ground floor

The White Hall contains original Empire-style furniture by Carlo Rossi.

Rossi Wing

Start of exhibition

14, 15, 16, 17, 13, 12, 11, 10, 9, 8, 7, 6, 5, 4, 1, 2, 3

Entrance points from lower ground floor ticket office

Phryne at the Festival of Poseidon in Eleusin (1889)
Henryk Siemiradzki's paintings are fine examples of late European Neo-Classicism. He is renowned for his academic scenes of life in ancient Greece and Rome.

44, 43, 42, 41, 40, 39, 49, 54, 35, 36, 37, 38, 33, 34, 32, 31, 30, 29, 28, 27, 26, 25, 24, 23, 22, 21, 18, 19, 20

The portico of eight Corinthian columns is the central feature of Rossi's façade. Behind is a frieze of Classical figures, designed by Rossi and executed by Demut-Malinovskiy.

Stairs to first floor

The main entrance is through a small door leading to the lower ground floor with a ticket office, a cloakroom, toilets and a café.

KEY

	Old Russian art
	18th-century art
	Early 19th-century art
	Late 19th-century art
	20th-century art
	18th–20th-century sculpture
	Folk art
	Temporary exhibitions
	Non-exhibition space

Exploring the Russian Museum

Housing one of the world's greatest collections of Russian art, the museum originally comprised officially approved works from the Academy of Arts *(see p63)*. When the museum was nationalized after the Revolution, art was transferred from palaces, churches and private collections. By the 1930s, Socialist Realism had become state policy and avant-garde works were stored away, to re-emerge with the advent of *perestroika* in the 1980s.

The Angel with the Golden Hair, an icon from the early 12th century

OLD RUSSIAN ART

The museum's fine collection begins with icons dating from the 12th–17th centuries. Russian icons derive from the Orthodox tradition and thus, just like Byzantine icons, tend to be sombre, marked by an absence of movement and a remote, mystic characterization of the saints. A superb example is one of the earliest icons, *The Angel with the Golden Hair*, in which the large, expressive eyes and delicate modelling of the Archangel Gabriel's face convey a sense of ethereal grace.

The Novgorod School *(see p165)* encouraged a much bolder and brighter style with a greater sense of drama and movement. And yet it is the poetically expressive and technically refined work of Andrey Rublev (c.1340–c.1430) that is considered by many to mark the pinnacle of Russian icon painting.

18TH–19TH-CENTURY ART

The first secular portraits (which owed much to the static quality of the icons) appeared in the second half of the 17th century. It was, however, under Peter the Great that Russian painting fully cast off from its Byzantine moorings. Peter the Great himself was the first patron to send young artists, often serfs, to study abroad. Secular art began to gain momentum in 1757 with the establishment of the Academy of Arts *(see p63)* which placed a heavy emphasis on classical and mythological subjects.

European influence permeates the work of Russia's first important portrait painters, Ivan Nikitin (1688–1741) and Andrey Matveev (1701–39). The art of portraiture matured with Dmitriy Levitskiy (1735–1822), amongst whose best known works is a series of portraits of noble girls from the Smolnyy Institute.

Russian landscape painting was stimulated by the Romantic movement and in particular artists who sought inspiration abroad, including Silvestr Shchedrin (1791–1830) and

Portrait of E I Nelidova (1773), by Dmitriy Levitskiy

Fyodor Matveev (1758–1826). Ivan Aivazovskiy's (1817–1900) vast marine paintings, however, have something purely Russian in their scale and mood. Romanticism also influenced history painters such as Karl Bryullov (1799–1852), as in his depiction of *The Last Day of Pompeii*.

In 1863 a group of students, led by Ivan Kramskoy (1837–87), rebelled against the conservatism of the Academy of Arts. Seven years later they set up the Association of Travelling Art Exhibitions, and came to be known as the Wanderers *(Peredvizhniki)*, or the Itinerants. They demanded that painting should be more socially relevant, and were fundamentally committed to Russian subject matter.

The most versatile of the Wanderers was Ilya Repin *(see p43)* whose bold canvas *Barge-Haulers on the Volga* combines a visually powerful

Knight at the Crossroads (1882), by Viktor Vasnetsov

The Six-Winged Seraph (1904), by Mikhail Vrubel

attack on forced labour with a romantic view of the Russian people. Meanwhile, *A Meal in the Monastery* by Vasiliy Perov (1833–82) is a satirical and equally effective attack on social injustice.

The nationalist element led history painters such as Nikolay Ge (1831–94) and Vasiliy Surikov (1848–1916) to turn to Russian history for inspiration, treating their subjects with a new psychological understanding, as in Ge's canvas of 1871–2, in which Peter the Great interrogates his sullenly resistant son.

The general Slavic revival also breathed new life into landscape painting, concentrating on the beauties of the Russian countryside. The master of the genre was Isaak Levitan (1860–1900), whose *Golden Autumn Village*, dated 1889, is almost Impressionist in style, a sign perhaps that the ascendancy of the Wanderers was coming to an end.

Viktor Vasnetsov (1848–1926) turned to Russia's heroic, and often legendary, pre-European past, in realistically painted canvases such as the *Knight at the Crossroads*. A haunting metaphor for Russia's uncertain future, the painting reveals that Vasnetsov was unable to avoid the fin-de-siècle melancholy and mysticism which was so potently expressed in the work of the next up-and-coming generation of artists, notably the Symbolists.

20TH-CENTURY ART

The dark, brooding canvases of Symbolist Mikhail Vrubel (1856–1910) combine Russian and religious themes with a more international outlook. Vrubel used colour and form to depict emotion and in *The Six-Winged Seraph* he employs a broken, vibrant, surface to express tension.

Another major contribution to 20th-century art was the "World of Art" movement, founded by Alexandre Benois and Sergey Diaghilev in the 1890s *(see p26)*. It rejected the notion of "socially useful art" in favour of a new tenet, "art pure and unfettered", and also opened up Russian painting to Western influences. Many members of the group,

Portrait of the Director Vsevolod Meyerhold (1916), Boris Grigorev

including Benois and Leon Bakst, designed stage sets and costumes for Diaghilev's Ballets Russes *(see p119)*.

The Russian avant-garde grew out of these local influences, plus the art of Cézanne, Picasso and Matisse. Mikhail Larionov (1881–1964) and Natalya Goncharova (1881–1962) both made brilliant use of Russian folk art as inspiration for primitivist works such as Goncharova's *Bleaching Canvas* (1908). They often altered their style in response to changing stimuli and later turned to Futurism's cult of the machine, as in Goncharova's *Cyclist* (1913) *(see p40)*.

The link between innovation in painting and the arts in general at this time is strikingly depicted in Boris Grigorev's angular portrait of Meyerhold, himself renowned for his radical approach to theatre.

Kazimir Malevich's (1878–1935) fascination with the juxtaposition of simple geometric shapes inspired the Suprematist movement. Vasily Kandinsky (1866–1944), a leading member of Munich's Blaue Reiter group, was also a key figure in the growth of Russian abstract art.

Marc Chagall (1887–1985), El Lissitskiy (1890–1941) and Alexander Rodchenko (1891–1956) are also represented.

Due to the high demand for the loan of avant-garde works abroad, the selection on view changes regularly.

FOLK ART

Folk art became a strong influence on the development of modern Russian art in the 1860s when the wealthy industrialist and patron Savva Mamontov established an artists' colony at Abramtsevo, near Moscow. Vasiliy Polenov (1844–1927), Ilya Repin and Viktor Vasnetsov were among the painters encouraged to work alongside, and learn from, the serf craftsmen on the estate. The museum's collection of folk art is wonderfully diverse and includes exquisitely embroidered tapestries, traditional headdresses, painted tiles, porcelain toys, and lacquered spoons and dishes.

Nevskiy Prospekt ❻

Невский проспект

Nevskiy prospekt

Map 6 D1–8 D3. Ⓜ *Nevskiy Prospekt, Gostinyy Dvor. See also pp46–9.*

Russia's most famous street, Nevskiy prospekt, is also St Petersburg's main thoroughfare and artery. In the 1830s, the novelist Nikolai Gogol *(see p42)* declared with great pride: "There is nothing finer than Nevskiy Avenue…in St Petersburg it is everything…is there anything more gay, more brilliant, more resplendent than this beautiful street of our capital?". In this respect very little has actually changed, for Nevskiy prospekt's intrinsic importance still prevails today.

Laid out in the early days of the city, it was first known as the Great Perspective Road, running 4.5 km (3 miles) from the Admiralty *(see p78)* to the Alexander Nevsky Monastery *(see pp130–31)*. In spite of roaming wolves and uncontrollable flooding from the Neva *(see p37)* which made the avenue navigable in 1721, fine mansions, such as the Stroganov Palace *(see p112)* were built. Shops and bazaars, catering for the nobility, and inns for travelling merchants followed. A magnet attracting rich and poor alike, by the mid-18th century the avenue had become the place to see and be seen, to meet for gossip, business and pleasure.

Today, the street still teems with people until late into the night throughout the year. Many of the city's sights are close to the stretch between the Admiralty and Anichkov Bridge *(see pp46–7)*. Some of the best shops *(see pp194–5)* can be found along the stretch between the Fontanka and Vosstaniya. Nevskiy prospekt also offers a wealth of cultural interest: the Small Philharmonia concert hall *(see p202)*, the Russian national library, Beloselskiy-Belozerskiy Palace *(see p49)* and a wide variety of museums, theatres, churches, including the Church of St Catherine *(see p48)*, shops, cinemas and eateries.

View of the bustling Nevskiy prospekt, the spine of St Petersburg

Armenian Church portico (1771–9)

Armenian Church ❼

Армянская церковь

Armyanskaya tserkov

Nevskiy prospekt 40–42. **Map** 6 F1. **Tel** 710 5061. Ⓜ *Gostinyy Dvor.* ⏱ 9am–9pm.

Yuriy Velten designed the beautiful blue and white Armenian Church of St Catherine, with its Neo-Classical portico and single cupola. The church, which opened in 1780, was financed by a wealthy Armenian businessman called Ioakim Lazarev, who acquired the money from the sale of a Persian diamond which Count Grigoriy Orlov purchased for Catherine the Great *(see p22)*.

Closed in 1930, the building has now been returned to the Armenian community and visitors are welcome to attend a service.

Gostinyy Dvor ❽

Гостиный двор

Gostinyy dvor

Nevskiy pr 35. **Map** 6 F2. **Tel** 710 5408. Ⓜ *Gostinyy Dvor.* ⏱ 10am–10pm Fri–Tue, 10am–10:30pm Wed & Thu. **www**.bgd.ru

The term *gostinyy dvor* originally meant a coaching inn, but as trade developed around the inns, with travelling merchants setting up their stalls, it later came to mean "trading rows". The original wooden structure of this *gostinyy dvor* was destroyed by fire in 1736. Twenty years later, Bartolomeo Rastrelli designed a new building but the project proved too costly and ambitious. Building recommenced in 1761 and continued until 1785. Vallin de la Mothe created the striking sequence of columned arcades and massive porticos. The prominent yellow building forms an irregular quadrangle which is bounded on one side by Nevskiy prospekt. The combined length of its façades is nearly 1 km (3,300 ft).

In the 19th century the gallery became a fashionable promenade where more than 5,000 people were employed. Serious damage during the Siege of Leningrad (see p27) led to major reconstruction, making it more like a modern department store. Even now, it has retained its layout of "stalls" of individual trading units. It offers a wide range of products, making it a central supplier of basic goods and souvenirs (see p195).

Style-Moderne stained-glass windows in Yeliseev's

building, designed by Gavriil Baranovskiy in 1901–3, it is adorned with bronzes, heroic sculptures and huge windows. A plaque by the main door honours the grandsons.

Today the second floor of the building is home to the Akimov Comedy Theatre, while the ground floor houses a shop that offers a range of expensive food delicacies.

Columned arcades, Gostinyy dvor

Yeliseev's ❾

Елисеевский гастроном

Yeliseevskiy gastronom

Nevskiy prospekt 56. **Map** 6 F1.
Ⓜ Gostinyy Dvor.

The successful Yeliseev dynasty was founded by Pyotr Yeliseev, an ambitious peasant who, in 1813, opened a wine shop on Nevskiy prospekt. By the turn of the century his grandsons owned a chocolate factory, numerous houses, inns and this famous former food store. The city's most opulent Style-Moderne

Anichkov Palace ❿

Аничков дворец

Anichkov dvorets

Nevskiy prospekt 39.
Map 7 A2. Ⓜ Gostinyy Dvor.
🚌 3, 7, 22, 24, 27, 191. 🚊 1, 5, 7, 10, 11, 22. ⬤ to public except for special events.

In the early days, the broad Fontanka river was lined by palaces accessible mainly by boat. One of them was the Anichkov Palace (1741–50), remodelled in Baroque style in 1754. The palace was a gift from Tsarina Elizabeth to her lover Aleksey Razumovskiy. It was named after Lieutenant Colonel Mikhail Anichkov who set up camp on this site at the time of the founding of the city. Over the years the palace was rebuilt and altered many

times, according to the tastes of each successive owner. After Razumovskiy's death, Catherine the Great in turn gave the building to her lover, Prince Potemkin (see p25). In the early 19th century, Neo-Classical details were added by Carlo Rossi.

The palace then became the traditional winter residence of the heir to the throne. When Alexander III became tsar in 1881, he continued to live here, however, rather than move to the Winter Palace as was customary. After his death, his widow Maria Fyodorovna stayed on until the Revolution.

The palace originally had large gardens to the west but these were curtailed in 1816 when Ostrovskiy Square (see p110) was created and two Neo-Classical pavilions were added. The elegant colonnaded building overlooking the Fontanka to the east was commissioned by Giacomo Quarenghi in 1803–5. It was initially built as an arcade where goods from the imperial factories were stored before being allocated to the palaces. Later it was converted into government offices and now also houses the Cultural Centre of Children's Creative Work.

Quarenghi's addition to the Anichkov Palace from Nevskiy prospekt

Porticoed façade of Alexandrinskiy Theatre (1828–32), Ostrovskiy Square

Ostrovskiy Square ⓫
Площадь Островского
Ploshchad Ostrovskovo

Map 6 F2. Ⓜ *Gostinyy Dvor.* 🚌 *3, 7, 22, 24, 27.* 🚎 *1, 5, 7, 10, 11, 22.* **Russian National Library Tel** *310 7137.* ◯ *9am–9pm.* **Theatre Museum Tel** *571 2195.* ◯ *11am– 6pm Thu–Mon, 1–7pm Wed.* ◉ *last Fri of each month and public hols.* 🎫 www.theatremuseum.ru

One of Russia's most brilliant architects, Carlo Rossi, created this early 19th-century square, which is now named in honour of the dramatist Aleksandr Ostrovskiy (1823–86).

The focal point of the square is the elegant Alexandrinskiy Theatre *(see p202)*, designed in the Neo-Classical style which Rossi favoured. The portico of six Corinthian columns is crowned by a chariot of Apollo, sculpted by Stepan Pimenov.

The building was the new home to Russia's oldest theatre company, set up in 1756. Plays premiered here, and still performed today, include Nikolai Gogol's *The Inspector General* (1836) and Anton Chekhov's *The Seagull* (1901). In Soviet times the theatre was renamed the Pushkin Theatre.

In the garden is a monument to Catherine the Great, the only one in the city. It was designed principally by Mikhail Mikeshin and unveiled in 1873. The statue depicts Catherine surrounded by states-men and other worthies, and includes the female president (1783–96) of the Academy of Sciences, Princess Yekaterina Dashkova.

The benches behind the monument are packed during the summer months with chess players and spectators. On the west side of the square, opposite the Anichkov Palace *(see p109)* is an elegant colonnade decorated with Classical sculptures. This is the extension of the Russian Library, made by Rossi in 1828–34. Founded in 1795, the library currently holds more than 28 million items. A prized possession is the personal library of the French philosopher Voltaire, which Catherine the Great purchased to show her appreciation of her sometime mentor and correspondent.

In the southeast corner of the square, at No. 6, is the Theatre Museum which traces the evolution of the Russian stage from its origins in mid-18th-century serf and imperial theatres. Amid the eclectic array of playbills, photographs, costumes, set designs and other artifacts, there are also some set designs by one of the great innovators of modern theatre, the director Vsevolod Meyerhold (1874–1940).

Ulitsa Zodchego Rossi ⓬
У лица Зодчего Росси
Ulitsa Zodchevo Rossi

Map 6 F2. Ⓜ *Gostinyy Dvor.*

There could be no better memorial to Carlo Rossi than the near perfect architectural ensemble of identical arcades and colonnades forming "Architect Rossi Street". The 22-m (72-ft) high buildings stand precisely 22 m (72 ft) apart and stretch for 220 m (720 ft). In 2008 the street had its 180-year anniversary. Seen from ploshchad Lomonosova, the perspective hypnotically coaxes the eye towards the Alexandriinskiy Theatre.

At No. 2 is the home of the former Imperial School of Ballet, now named after the teacher Agrippina Vaganova (1879–1951), one of the few dancers not to emigrate after the Revolution. The school began in 1738 when Jean-Baptiste Landé began training orphans and palace servants' children to take part in court entertainment. It has produced many of Russia's most celebrated dancers *(see p118)*, including Anna Pavlova and Rudolf Nureyev.

19th-century photograph of ulitsa Zodchego Rossi (1828–34)

ARCHITECT CARLO ROSSI

Carlo Rossi (1775–1849) was one of the last great exponents of Neo-Classicism in St Petersburg. He found an ideal client in Alexander I, who shared his belief in the use of architecture to express the power of the ruling autocracy. By the time of his death, Rossi had created no fewer than 12 of St Petersburg's impressive streets and 13 of its squares, including Palace Square *(see p83)*. Rossi's status as Alexander I's favourite architect encouraged rumours that Rossi was the offspring of an affair between Tsar Paul I and Rossi's Italian ballerina mother.

Central corpus of Vorontsov Palace

Vorontsov Palace ⑬
Воронцовский дворец
Vorontsovskiy dvorets

Sadovaya ulitsa 26. **Map** 6 F2.
⬤ *to public.* Ⓜ *Gostinyy Dvor,
Sennaya Ploshchad.*

The most exclusive military school in the Russian empire, the Corps des Pages, occupied the Vorontsov Palace from 1810–1918. Among those privileged enough to study here were a number of the Decembrists *(see pp22–3)* and Prince Felix Yusupov *(see p121).* Today the palace houses the Suvorov Military Academy.

Designed by Bartolomeo Rastrelli *(see p93),* the handsome palace, which once stood in its own extensive grounds, was built in 1749–57 for Prince Mikhail Vorontsov, one of Tsarina Elizabeth's leading ministers. Rastrelli's graceful wrought-iron railings are among the earliest examples of their kind in Russia.

Apraksin Market ⑭
Апраксин двор
Apraksin dvor

Sadovaya ulitsa. **Map** 6 E2.
Ⓜ *Gostinyy Dvor, Sennaya
Ploshchad, Sadovaya, Spassky.*

Founded in the late 18th century, the market takes its name from the Apraksin family who owned the land it was built on. When fire destroyed the original wooden stalls in 1862, the arcade was erected. By 1900 there were more than 600 outlets selling everything from food, wine and spices to furs, furniture and haberdashery. The large street market has now moved to Rustavelli Street, far from the city centre. The historic Apraksin Market is being reconstructed; in the meantime arcade shops continue to open.

Cathedral of Our Lady of Kazan ⑮
Собор Казанской
Богоматери
Sobor Kazanskoy Bogomateri

Kazanskaya pl 2. **Map** 6 E1. *Tel* 314 4663. Ⓜ *Nevskiy Prospekt.* 🚌 *3, 7, 22, 24, 27, 191.* 🚎 *1, 5, 7, 10, 11, 22.* ◯ *9am–7:30pm daily.* ✦ ✝

One of St Petersburg's most majestic churches, the Cathedral of Our Lady of Kazan was commissioned by Paul I and took over a decade to build (1801–11). The impressive design by serf architect Andrey Voronikhin was inspired by St Peter's in Rome. Its 111-m (364-ft) long, curved colonnade disguises the orientation of the building, which runs parallel to Nevskiy prospekt, conforming to a religious stipulation that the main altar face east. In Voronikhin's original design he intended to duplicate the colonnade on the south side. The cathedral is named after the miracle-working icon of Our Lady of Kazan. The icon is now kept in the cathedral.

The interior decoration is generally subdued. Its most impressive features are the great 80-m (262-ft) high dome and the massive pink Finnish granite columns with bronze capitals and bases. Occupied in the Communist era by a Museum of Atheism, the building was returned to exclusive religious use in 1999.

Completed in 1811, the cathedral is intimately linked with the wars against Napoleon *(see p22)* fought during the same period. In 1813 Field Marshal Mikhail Kutuzov (1745–1813), mastermind of a successful retreat from Moscow following the invasion of Napoleon's Grand Army in 1812, was buried here with full military honours. Kutuzov has been immortalized in Tolstoy's great novel *War and Peace* (1865–9). His statue and that of his comrade-in-arms, Mikhail Barclay de Tolly (1761–1818), both by Boris Orlovskiy, have stood outside the cathedral since 1837.

Pink granite columns and mosaic floor in main nave, Kazan Cathedral

Stroganov Palace ⓰
Строгановский дворец
Stroganovskiy dvorets

Nevskiy prospekt 17. **Map** 6 E1.
Tel 571 8238. Ⓜ *Nevskiy Prospekt.*
▦ 3, 7, 22, 24, 27, 191. ▦ 1, 5, 7,
10, 11, 17. ◯ *10am–6pm Wed–Sun
(10am–5pm Mon).* ▧

This Baroque masterpiece
was designed in 1752–4 by
Bartolomeo Rastrelli *(see
p93).* Commissioned by the
enormously wealthy Count
Sergey Stroganov, the palace
was occupied by his descendants until the 1917 Revolution.
The vast Stroganov fortune
was amassed mainly through
the monopoly the family held
on salt, which they mined
from their territories in the
north of the Russian empire.
   The pink and white palace,
which overlooks both Nevskiy
prospekt and the Moyka river,
was one of the city's most
impressive private residences.
The magnificent river façade is
decorated with Doric columns,
cornices, pediments and inven-
tive window surrounds.
   The Stroganovs were noted
collectors of everything from
Egyptian antiquities and Roman
coins to icons and Old Masters.
The palace was nationalized
after the Revolution and then
preserved for ten years as a
museum of the life of the
decadent aristocracy. When it

**Neo-Romanesque portal of the
Lutheran Church (1832–8)**

was closed, some of the objects
were auctioned in the West,
and the rest were transferred
to the Hermitage *(see pp84–
93).* The building now belongs
to the Russian Museum *(see
pp104–107)* and has temporary exhibitions and a collection
of waxwork figures.

Lutheran Church ⓱
Лютеранская церковь
Lyuteranskaya tserkov

Nevskiy prospekt 22–24. **Map** 6 E1.
Ⓜ *Nevskiy Prospekt.*

Set back a little from Nevskiy
prospekt, the attractive, twin-
towered Lutheran church is
dedicated to St Peter. Built in
its present form during the

1830s, the church served
St Petersburg's ever-growing
German community *(see p57).*
The prize-winning design by
Aleksandr Bryullov is in an unusual, Neo-Romanesque style.
   From 1936 the church was
used as a vegetable store until,
in the late 1950s, it was converted into a swimming pool.
The basin was carved out of
the nave floor, the gallery
lined with spectator benches
and there was a high diving
board under the apse. The
building has now been handed
back to the German-Lutheran
Church of Russia. The church
has been fully restored and
now offers regular services.

The Academic Capella concert hall

Academic Capella ⓲
Академическая капелла
Akademicheskaya kapella

Naberezhnaya reki Moyki 20.
Map 2 E5. **Tel** 314 1058. Ⓜ *Nevskiy
Prospekt.* ◯ *for concerts only.* ▧
▨ *See* Entertainment *p194.*

Enclosed within a courtyard
off the Moyka river is this
ochre-coloured concert hall
with a façade in the French
Classical style of Louis XV.
The Academic Capella was
designed by Leontiy Benois in
1887–9 as the residence of the
Imperial Court choir. Founded
during the reign of Peter the
Great, the choir is as old as
the city itself. Its former
directors have included the
distinguished Russian composers Mikhail Glinka
(1804–57) and Nikolai
Rimsky-Korsakov (1844–1908).
   With its excellent acoustics,
the Academic Capella can
claim to be one of the best
concert halls in the world.
Outside is the aptly named
Singers' Bridge (Pevcheskiy
most), which was designed by
Yegor Adam in 1837–40.

Elaborate west façade of the Stroganov Palace overlooking the Moyka river

Personal effects in Pushkin's study, Pushkin House-Museum

than 4,500 volumes in a staggering 14 European and Oriental languages. Among these are works by the authors whom Pushkin most admired, including Shakespeare, Byron, Heine, Dante and Voltaire.

Pushkin House-Museum ⑲
Музей-квартира
А. С. Пушкина
Muzey-kvartira AS Pushkina

Naberezhnaya reki Moyki 12. **Map** 2 E5. **Tel** 571 3531. ◯ 10:30am–6pm Wed–Mon. ● last Fri of each month and public hols. 🖼 📷

Every year on the anniversary of Alexander Pushkin's death (29 January 1837), loyal devotees of Russia's greatest poet come to lay floral tributes outside his apartment. Pushkin was born in Moscow in 1799, but spent many years of his life in St Petersburg and the museum is one of several places in the city with which the poet is associated.

From the autumn of 1836 until his death, Pushkin lived in this fairly opulent apartment overlooking the Moyka, with his wife Natalya, their four children and Natalya's two sisters. It was here on the couchette in the study that he bled to death after his fateful duel with d'Anthès *(see p83)*.

Some half dozen rooms on the first floor have been refurbished in the Empire style of the period. By far the most evocative is Pushkin's study, which is arranged exactly as it was when he died. On the writing table is an ivory paper knife given to the poet by his sister, a bronze handbell and a treasured inkstand *(see p39)*. Embellished with the figure of an Ethiopian boy, the inkstand is a reminder of Pushkin's great grandfather, Abram Hannibal. Bought by the Russian ambassador in Constantinople as a

slave in 1706, Hannibal served as a general under Peter the Great. He was the inspiration for the unfinished novel *The Negro of Peter the Great* on which Pushkin was working at the time of his death.

On the wall in front of his desk is a Turkish sabre presented to Pushkin in the Caucasus, where he had been exiled in 1820 for his radical views. Ironically it was there that he spent some of his happiest years. It was there too that he began his most famous work, *Eugene Onegin*, a novel in verse written in 1823–30.

The most impressive feature of the apartment is the poet's library which contains more

Imperial Stables ⑳
Конюшенное Ведомство
Konyushennoe Vedomstvo

Konyushennaya ploshchad 1. **Map** 2 E5. **Church** ◯ 10am–7pm daily. ✝ 📷

The long, salmon-coloured building running parallel to the Moyka embankment is the former Imperial stables. Originally built in the first part of the 18th century, the stables were reconstructed by Vasiliy Stasov in 1817–23.

The only part of the building open to the public lies behind the central section of the long south façade, crowned by a silver dome and cross. This is the church where Alexander Pushkin's funeral took place on 1 February 1837. Its Neo-Classical interior is in the form of a basilica and is decorated with yellow marble pillars. It is now a fully functional Orthodox church.

North façade of Imperial Stables (left) and Little Stable Bridge on the Moyka

SENNAYA PLOSHCHAD

The western part of St Petersburg is an area of contrasts, home to some of the city's wealthiest residences and most poverty-stricken dwellings. The palatial architecture along the English Embankment is a world away from the decrepit living quarters around Sennaya ploshchad, which have changed little since Dostoevsky *(see p123)* described them. In between lies the old maritime quarter, once inhabited by Peter the Great's shipwrights, many of whom were English. This area extended all the way from the New Holland ware-

Coat of arms on Yusupov Palace

houses to St Nicholas' Cathedral, which stands on the site of the naval parade ground. Theatre Square has been a hub of entertainment since the mid-18th century. It is dominated by the prestigious Mariinskiy Theatre and the Rimsky-Korsakov Conservatory, where many of Russia's greatest artists began their careers. Before 1917, the streets leading off the square were home to theatre directors, actors, ballerinas, artists and musicians. Today, performing artists are once more returning to live here, attracted by the peace of the tree-lined canals.

SIGHTS AT A GLANCE

Cathedrals
St Nicholas' Cathedral ❷

Historic Buildings and Areas
Choral Synagogue ❺
Main Post Office ❽
New Holland ❻
Rimsky-Korsakov
 Conservatory ❸

Theatres
Mariinskiy Theatre ❶

Palaces
Yusupov Palace ❹

Streets and Squares
Bolshaya Morskaya Ulitsa ❾
The English Embankment ❼
Sennaya Ploshchad ❿

Museums
Railway Museum ⓫

KEY

■ Street-by-Street map
See pp116–17

Ⓜ Metro

0 metres 600
0 yards 600

◁ **Gilded Baroque interior of the upper church of St Nicholas' Cathedral**

Street-by-Street: Theatre Square

Theatre Square was once known as Carousel Square and was frequently used as the site for fairs and festivals. During the 19th century when St Petersburg became the cultural capital of Russia, the Mariinskiy Theatre and Rimsky-Korsakov Conservatory were established, and the neighbourhood became home to many artists. Today, the tradition of entertainment is still thriving and Theatre Square remains a focal point for theatrical and musical life *(see p202)*.

Atlas on prospekt Rimskovo-Korsakova Nearby, the tree-lined canal embankments and the gardens surrounding the beautiful St Nicholas' Cathedral are enchanting places to stroll.

The Monument to Rimsky-Korsakov, who taught at the Conservatory for 37 years, was designed by Veniamin Bogolyubov and Vladimir Ingal and erected in 1952.

Yusupov Palace
Historic site of the gruesome murder of Rasputin (see p121), this grand palace belonged to the wealthy Yusupov family. Its opulent interiors include this Italian marble staircase and a tiny Rococo theatre ❹

Rimsky-Korsakov Conservatory
Tchaikovsky, Prokofiev and Shostakovich (see p43) were among the talents nurtured by Russia's first conservatory, founded in 1862 by pianist and composer Anton Rubinstein ❸

Monument to Mikhail Glinka
(see p44)

★ Mariinskiy Theatre
This theatre has been home to the world-famous Mariinskiy (Kirov) Opera and Ballet Company since 1860. Hidden behind its imposing façade is the sumptuous auditorium where many of Russia's greatest dancers (see p118) have performed ❶

The Lion Bridge *(Lvinyy Most)* is one of a number of quaint and curious suspension bridges on the narrow, tree-lined Griboedov canal *(see p36)*. These bridges are well-known meeting places, notably for romantic trysts.

LOCATOR MAP
See Street Finder, map 5

The House of Mikhail Fokin at No. 109 is where the renowned ballet-master and choreographer lived before the Revolution.

STAR SIGHT

★ Mariinskiy Theatre

The Benois House belonged to an artistic dynasty which included the co-founder of the World of Art movement, Alexandre Benois *(see p107)*.

The Belfry, an elegant four-tiered structure with a gilded spire, was built to mark the main entrance to St Nicholas' Cathedral.

St Nicholas' Cathedral
A fine example of 18th-century Russian Baroque, the lofty upper church is richly decorated with icons, gilding and this carved iconostasis. The lower church, beautifully lit with candles, is also open for worship ❷

KEY

— — — Suggested route

NAB KANALA GRIBOEDOVA

...KOVO-KORSAKOVA

NIKOLSKIY PEREULOK

KANAL GRIBOEDOVA

SADOVAYA ULITSA

0 metres   100

0 yards   100

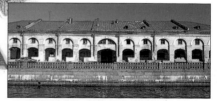

The former Nicholas market, characterized by its long arcade and steep roof, was constructed in 1788–9. In the 19th century it became an unofficial labour exchange as many unemployed workers gathered here.

Ballet in St Petersburg

Admired throughout the world, Russian ballet traces its origins back to 1738 when a French dancing master, Jean-Baptiste Landé, established a school in St Petersburg to train the children of palace employees. The Imperial Ballet School, as it soon became known, flourished under a string of distinguished foreign teachers, culminating in Marius Petipa (1818–1910). Petipa first joined the school in 1847 as a principal dancer and later choreographed over 60 ballets, inspiring such famous dancers as Matilda Kshesinskaya *(see p72)*.

Matilda Kshesinskaya's ballet shoes

Following the 1905 Revolution, a reaction against Classicism led to an increasing number of defections from the Imperial theatres to the new private companies like Sergey Diaghilev's Ballets Russes. The dispersion of talent increased after the Bolsheviks seized power in 1917 and many artists went into exile abroad. Fortunately for Soviet Russia, the distinguished prima ballerina Agrippina Vaganova remained to train the next generation of dancers. St Petersburg's Russian Ballet Academy now bears her name *(see p110)*.

Anna Pavlova's *(1885–1931) most famous role, The Dying Swan, was created especially for her by Mikhail Fokin. In 1912 Pavlova left Russia to form her own touring company, spreading her enthusiasm for ballet across Europe and beyond.*

Vaslaw Nijinsky *(1890–1950) had one of his greatest roles as the golden slave in Schéhérazade which took Paris by storm in 1910. A principal of the Ballets Russes before World War I, he revolutionized male roles. His incomparable technical skills and expressive qualities influenced future generations of dancers.*

Rudolf Nureyev *(1938–93), seen here in Sleeping Beauty at the Mariinskiy, defected to the West in 1961. As both choreographer and dancer, Nureyev continued to enthral audiences for over 30 years until his death in 1993.*

The Mariinskiy Ballet, *usually known abroad as the Kirov, is now reviving some of the original productions of the Ballets Russes, including their version of Giselle, previously not shown in Russia.*

THE BALLETS RUSSES

The legendary touring company which revolutionized ballet between 1909 and 1929 was the brainchild of the impresario and art critic Sergey Diaghilev *(see p43)*. Diaghilev found a kindred spirit in the choreographer Mikhail Fokin, who shared his vision of a spectacle that would fuse music, ballet and decor in a seamless artistic whole.

Diaghilev had the pick of dancers from the Mariinskiy and, in 1909, he brought his Ballets Russes to Paris. The company went from strength to strength with successful tours worldwide.

Diaghilev's new company had a remarkable impact on the contemporary art world. The ballets of Fokine, in particular, prepared audiences for greater innovation and experiment. Exciting contributions from costume and set designers Léon Bakst and Alexandre Benois, the composer Igor Stravinsky and the dancers Vaslaw Nijinsky, Anna Pavlova and Tamara Karsavina all played a part in expanding the artistic horizons. After Diaghilev's death in 1929, the Ballets Russes fragmented but its ethos and traditions have been preserved in many of today's leading companies.

Early 20th-century programme for the Ballets Russes

One of Russia's most important cultural institutions, the Mariinskiy Theatre

Mariinskiy Theatre ❶
Мариинский театр
Mariinskiy teatr

Teatralnaya ploshchad 1 & Dekabristov ulitsa 37. **Map** 5 B3. **Tel** 346 4141. 🚌 2, 3, 6, 22, 27, 71, K-1, K-2, K-62, K-124, K-154, K-169, K-186, K-350. 🚊 5, 22. ⬜ For information on performances see p202. 🎭 📷 🛗 🚭 **www**.mariinsky.ru

Named in honour of Tsarina Maria Alexandrovna, wife of Alexander II, the theatre is known abroad by its Soviet title, the Kirov, while at home it has reverted to its original name, the Mariinskiy Theatre. A concert hall opened here in 2007 with plans to add more stages.

The building was erected in 1860 by the architect Albert Kavos, who designed the Bolshoy Theatre in Moscow. It stands on the site of an earlier theatre which was destroyed by fire. In 1883–96, the Neo-Renaissance façade was re-modelled by Viktor Schröter, who added most of the ornamental detail. The pale blue and gold auditorium, where so many illustrious dancers have made their debut, creates a dazzling impression. Its architectural decoration of twisted columns,

Imperial eagle on the royal box

atlantes, cherubs and cameo medallions has remained unchanged since the theatre's completion, and the imperial eagles have been restored to the royal box. The ceiling painting of dancing girls and cupids by Italian artist Enrico Franchioli dates from c.1856, while the superb stage curtain was added during Russian ballet's golden age in 1914. Equally remarkable is the glittering festive foyer, decorated with fluted pilasters, bas-reliefs of Russian composers and mirrored doors.

Although the Mariinskiy is better known abroad for its ballet company, it is also one of the country's leading opera houses. Most of the great 19th-century Russian operas were premiered here, including Mussorgsky's *Boris Godunov* (1874), Tchaikovsky's *Queen of Spades* (1890), and Shostakovich's controversial opera *Lady Macbeth of Mtsensk* (1934).

The Mariinskiy's luxuriant stage curtain, designed by Aleksandr Golovin in 1914

St Nicholas' Cathedral ❷

Никольский собор
Nikolskiy sobor

Nikolskaya ploshchad 1/3. **Map** 5 C4. **Tel** 714 0862. 🚌 2, 3, 22, 27, 49, 71, 181, K-2, K-154, K-212. ⬤ 7am–7pm daily.

This stunning Baroque cathedral by Savva Chevakinskiy, one of Russia's great 18th-century architects, was built in 1753–62. Founded for sailors and Admiralty employees housed in the neighbourhood, and named after St Nicholas, the patron saint of sailors, the cathedral became known as the "Sailors' Church".

The striking exterior is decorated with white Corinthian pilasters and surmounted by five gilded cupolas. Nearby, within the cathedral's leafy grounds and overlooking the intersection of the Kryukov and Griboedov canals, is a slender four-tiered bell tower crowned by a spire.

Following the Russian tradition, there are two churches within the cathedral. The lower church, intended for daily use, is lit by icon lamps, candles and chandeliers, creating a magical effect. The icons (1755–7) are the work of the brothers Fedot and Menas Kolokolnikov. The upper church, used on Sundays and for weddings, is brighter and has a Baroque exuberance, with gilt and stucco ornamentation and Italianate paintings.

The pale blue and white Baroque façade of St Nicholas' Cathedral

Islamic arches and coffered ceiling in the Moorish Room, Yusupov Palace

The most impressive feature is the magnificent gilded iconostasis dating from 1755–60.

Rimsky-Korsakov Conservatory ❸

Консерватория имени Римского-Корсакова
Konservatoriya imeni Rimskovo-Korsakova

Teatralnaya ploshchad 3. **Map** 5 B3. **Tel** 571 8574. 🚌 2, 3, 6, 22, 27, 71, K-1, K-2, K-62, K-124, K-154, K-169, K-186, K-350. 🚊 5, 22. ⬤ for performances only. 🎫 🎭 by appt (**Tel** 312 2507).

Russia's oldest music school, the conservatory was founded in 1862 by the piano virtuoso Anton Rubinstein (1829–94). The present building was designed in 1896 by Vladimir Nicolas.

Among those to graduate from the school before the Revolution were Tchaikovsky *(see p42)* and Sergey Prokofiev. In the Soviet years, the school continued to flourish, and the greatest musical figure to emerge from this era was composer Dmitriy Shostakovich (1906–75) *(see p43)*.

In the forecourt outside are two statues. On the left, a 1952 memorial honours the school's influential teacher, Nikolai Rimsky-Korsakov. On the right, the statue of Mikhail Glinka (1906) by Robert Bach is a reminder that the conservatory stands on the original site where Russia's first opera, Glinka's *A Life for the Tsar*, was premiered in 1836 in the old Kamennyy (Stone) Theatre.

Yusupov Palace ❹

Юсуповскис дворец
Yusupovskiy dvorets

Naberezhnaya reki Moyki 94. **Map** 5 B3. **Tel** 314 9883. 🚌 3, 22, 27. ⬤ 11am–5pm daily. 🎧 English (audio tours only).

Overlooking the Moyka, this yellow, colonnaded building (1760s) was designed by Vallin de la Mothe. The palace was acquired in 1830 by the aristocratic Yusupov family to house their superb collection of paintings. Major work was then carried out on the interior by Andrey Mikhaylov and Ippolito Monighetti.

The interiors, notable among them the exotic Moorish Room, with its fountain, mosaics and arches, can be viewed by guided or audio tour only. Separate tickets are needed for the tour of the cellars, which house an exhibition on Grigoriy Rasputin, the infamous "holy man" who was murdered here by Prince Felix Yusupov.

The elegant, Rococo-style family theatre seats just 180, and attending a concert *(see p202)* is an experience in itself.

THE GRIM DEATH OF RASPUTIN

The Russian peasant and mystic Grigoriy Rasputin (1869–1916) exercised an extraordinarily powerful influence over the court and government of Russia *(see p26)*. The mysterious circumstances of his dramatic death on 17 December 1916 are legendary. Lured to Yusupov's palace on the pretext of a party, Rasputin was poisoned, then shot by Prince Felix Yusupov and left for dead. Returning to the scene the prince found Rasputin still alive and a struggle ensued before Rasputin disappeared into the courtyard. Pursued by the conspirators he was shot another three times and brutally battered before being dumped in the river. When his corpse was found three days later, clinging to the supports of a bridge, water in his lungs indicated death by drowning.

Choral Synagogue ❺
Хоральная Синагога
Khoralnaya Sinagoga

Lermontovskiy prospekt 2. **Map** 5 B3. *Tel* 713 8186. 🚃 3, 6, 22, 27, K-1, K-169.

In 1826 Tsar Nicholas I decreed that all Jews, save 29 employed on behalf of the Court, be exiled from the city. Further "purifications" took place in the 1830s. However, after Nicholas' death in 1855 the Jewish population grew rapidly and in 1879 a site was approved for a permanent house of prayer.

Designed in Moorish style by architects Ivan Shaposhnikov and Viktor Shreter, the Synagogue opened in 1893, by which time the Jewish community had reached 16,500, nearly 2 per cent of the city's population. Accommodating 1,200 or more, the Synagogue was the only Jewish place of

Vallin de la Mothe's impressive arch on the Moyka, leading into New Holland

prayer to survive the repressions of the 1930s. It continued to function during the Siege of 1941; the community remaining largely intact whilst other Jewish communities in Eastern Europe were decimated. Today, the Synagogue still has an active community.

New Holland ❻
Новая Голландия
Novaya Gollandiya

Naberezhnaya reki Moyki. **Map** 5 B3. 🚃 3, 6, 22, 27, 70, 100, K-169, K-350. ⬤ *for restoration until 2015.*

Created when the Kryukov canal was constructed between the Moyka and Neva rivers in 1719, this triangular island was originally used for storing ship timber. The name is in honour of the Dutch shipbuilders who inspired Peter the Great's naval ambitions.

In 1765, the original wooden warehouses were rebuilt in red brick by Savva Chevakinskiy. At the same time Vallin de la Mothe designed the austere but romantic arch facing onto the

Moyka which creates an atmospheric entrance to the timber yard. Barges would pass through the arch and into a turning basin beyond, then return loaded with timber along the canals towards the Admiralty shipyards. A cultural complex is now being built here, and is partially open during the summer.

The English Embankment ❼
Английская набережная
Angliyskaya naberezhnaya

Map 5 A2. 🚊 6, 11, K-124, K-154, K-350.

English merchants settled here in the 1730s, and were soon followed by craftsmen, architects, artists, innkeepers and factory owners. By 1800 the area was one of the city's most prestigious addresses.

It still boasts impressive buildings. The Neo-Classical mansion at No. 10 was the fictional setting for the debutante ball of Natasha Rostova in Tolstoy's novel *War and Peace*. No. 28 was occupied by the lover of ballet dancer Matilda Kshesinskaya *(see p72)*, and is the former headquarters of the Socialist-Revolutionary Party. On ploshchad Truda, the former palace of Grand Duke Nikolai Nikolaevich (son of Nicholas I) was given in 1917 to the trades unions.

Quarenghi's grand porticoed façade, at No. 32 on the English Embankment

Main Post Office ⑧

Главпочтамт
Glavpochtamt

Pochtamtskaya ulitsa 9. **Map** 5 C2.
Tel 315 8022. 🚌 3, 22, 27, 70, 100,
K-169, K-187, K-306. 🚊 5, 22.
🕐 9am–9pm daily.

The building's main exterior
feature is the arched gallery
spanning Pochtamtskaya
ulitsa. Built as an extension to
Nikolay Lvov's main building,
the gallery was added by
Albert Kavos in 1859. Under
the Pochtamt (Post Office)
sign on the arch is a clock
showing the time in major
cities around the world.

Inside the post office, behind
Lvov's porticoed Neo-Classical
façade of 1782–9, is a splendid
Style-Moderne hall characterized by decorative ironwork
and a glass ceiling. The
hall was created in the early
20th century when a roof
was constructed over what
had originally been the
courtyard stables.

Porticoed façade, Main Post Office

Bolshaya Morskaya Ulitsa ⑨

Большая Морская улица
Bolshaya Morskaya ulitsa

Map 5 C2. 🚌 3, 22, 27, K-187,
K-209. 🚊 5, 22.

Always one of St Petersburg's
most fashionable streets,
shady Bolshaya Morskaya ulitsa
is the choice of the artistic
elite to this day. It has some
exceedingly handsome 19th-
century mansions hidden away
between St Isaac's Square

**Stone atlas at No. 43 Bolshaya
Morskaya ulitsa (1840)**

(see p79) and Post Office
Bridge (Pochtamtskiy most).

The mansion at No. 61 was
built by Albert Kavos in the
1840s for the St Petersburg
Stage Coach Company. No. 52,
nearby, was acquired by the
Russian Union of Architects in
1932. Built by Aleksandr Pel
in 1835–6, it was formerly the
residence of the celebrated
patron of the arts Aleksandr
Polovtsov, who built up the
impressive collection of the
Stieglitz Museum *(see p127)*.
The striking late 19th-century
interiors with mahogany panelling, tapestries and carved
ceilings were designed by
Maximilian Messmacher and
Nikolay Brullov and can be
admired from the Osobnyak
Polovtseva restaurant within.

Just across the street, No. 47
is a particularly fine example

of Style-Moderne architecture
with sculpted stone rosettes
and delicate iron tracery. This
is the work of Mikhail Geisler
and Boris Guslistiy, dating
from 1901–2. It was in this
mansion that the celebrated
émigré novelist Vladimir
Nabokov (1899–1977) grew
up, and there is a small
museum to him on the first
floor. Admired for his linguis-
tic ingenuity in both English
and Russian, Nabokov hit the
headlines across the world
with the publication of *Lolita*,
his *succès de scandale* of 1959.

Next door at No. 45 is the
Union of Composers, the former home of socialite Princess
Gagarina who lived here in
the 1870s. The mansion was
reconstructed in the 1840s by
Auguste-Ricard de Montferrand,
and it retains elements of the
original 18th-century building.

Montferrand also built the
former residence of millionaire
industrialist Pyotr Demidov at
No. 43. A mass of Renaissance
and Baroque elements, the
façade also bears the
Demidov's coat of arms.

Sennaya Ploshchad ⑩

Сенная площадь
Sennaya ploshchad

Map 6 D3. Ⓜ *Sennaya Ploshchad,
Sadovaya, Spasskaya.*

This is one of the oldest
squares in St Petersburg. The
square's name, meaning
Haymarket, derives from the
original market where livestock, fodder and firewood
were sold which opened in
the 1730s. A 10-minute stroll
from Nevskiy, the area around
the square was inhabited by
the poor and the market was
the cheapest and liveliest in
the city (the so-called "belly of
St Petersburg"). The oldest

Style-Moderne mosaic frieze at No. 47 Bolshaya Morskaya ulitsa (1901–2)

FYODOR DOSTOEVSKY

One of Russia's greatest writers, Fyodor Dostoevsky *(see pp43–4)* was born in 1821 in Moscow but spent most of his adult life in St Petersburg, where many of his novels and short stories are set. A defining moment in his life occurred in 1849 when he was arrested and charged with revolutionary conspiracy. After eight months of solitary confinement in the Peter and Paul Fortress *(see pp66–7)*, Dostoevsky and 21 other "conspirators" from the socialist Petrashevsky Circle were subjected to a macabre mock execution before being exiled to hard labour in Siberia until 1859. The sinister experience is recalled in his novel *The Idiot* (1868). He died in 1881.

building, at the centre of the square, is the former guardhouse, a single-storey Neo-Classical building with a columned portico, which dates to 1818–20. The guardsmen's duties ranged from supervising the traders to flogging serfs, mostly for minor misdemeanours. By that time the neighbourhood had become synonymous with dirt, squalor, crime and vice. At No. 3 is the site of "Vyazemskiy's Monastery", the nickname for a notorious tenement overrun with pubs, gambling dens and brothels in the 1850s and '60s.

This was the squalid world so vividly evoked in Fyodor Dostoevsky's masterpiece *Crime and Punishment*. As the

The guardhouse on bustling Sennaya ploshchad

contemptuous hero of the novel, Raskolnikov, wanders around the market, he absorbs the "heat in the street.... the airlessness, the bustle and the plaster, scaffolding, bricks and dust.... that special St Petersburg stench.... and the numerous drunken men" which "completed the revolting misery of the picture". The novel was finished in 1866 while Dostoevsky was living at Alonkin's House, (No. 7 Przhevalskovo ulitsa), to the west of the square.

During the Soviet era the square was given a new image, stallholders were banished, trees were planted and it was optimistically renamed Peace Square (ploshchad Mira). The five-storey, yellow and white apartment blocks that surround the square today were also built then, in Stalin's version of Neo-Classicism. Sadly, in 1961, the square's most attractive monument, the Baroque Church of the Assumption, built in 1765, was pulled down to make way for one of the city's earliest metro stations.

Railway Museum ⓫

Музей железнодорожного транспорта
Muzey zheleznodorozbnovo transporta

Sadovaya ulitsa 50. **Map** 6 D4.
Tel 315 1476. Ⓜ *Sennaya ploshchad, Sadovaya, Spasskaya.*
◯ *11am–5pm Sun–Thu.* ⬤ *last Thu of month.* ▧ *English.*

More than 6,000 fascinating exhibits illustrate the history of the Russian railway system since 1813. The most interesting sections of the museum deal with the earliest railways, including Russia's first from Tsarskoe Selo to St Petersburg which began running in 1837, and the 650-km (404-mile) line from Moscow to St Petersburg (1851).

Exhibits include models of the first Russian steam engine, built by the Cherepanovs in 1834, and of an armoured train used by Trotsky to defend the city during the Civil War *(see p27)*. An insight into luxury travel in the late tsarist period can be gained from the walkthrough section of a first-class sleeping compartment with Style-Moderne decoration.

Model of 1830s engine for the Tsarskoe Selo railway, Railway Museum

FURTHER AFIELD

While the majority of St Petersburg's sights are centrally located, the outlying areas of the city have a number of places of architectural, cultural and historical importance.

To the east is the Smolnyy district, taking its name from the tar yard which supplied the city's ship-building industry in the 18th century. The highlight of this area is Rastrelli's dazzling Baroque Smolnyy Convent. Nearby, the Smolnyy Institute is famed for its historic role as the Bolshevik headquarters during the October Revolution (see pp28–9).

Ceramic tile from 1770s stove, Stieglitz Museum

Southeast of the centre lies the Alexander Nevskiy Monastery where many of Russia's celebrated artists, architects and composers are buried.

The southern suburbs offer a strikingly different perspective of the city, with rows of grandiose 1930s–50s houses, a reminder that Stalin sought to destroy the city's historical heart by relocating the centre to the area around Moskovskaya ploshchad. The south also has the Chesma Church and the 1970s Victory Monument, a memorial to the suffering of St Petersburgers during the Siege of Leningrad.

SIGHTS AT A GLANCE

Palaces
Sheremetev Palace ⑨
Tauride Palace ⑥
Yelagin Palace ①

Museums
Dostoevsky House-Museum ⑩
Stieglitz Museum ④

Churches
Alexander Nevskiy Monastery ⑪
Cathedral of the
  Transfiguration ⑤
Chesma Church ⑫
Smolnyy Convent ⑦

Historic Buildings and Monuments
Finland Station ③
Piskarevskoe Memorial
  Cemetery ②
Smolnyy Institute ⑧
Victory Monument ⑬

KEY

■	Central St Petersburg
■	Greater St Petersburg
✈	Airport
🚉	Railway station
⛴	Ferry port
━	Major road
═	Minor road

0 kilometres 3

0 miles 3

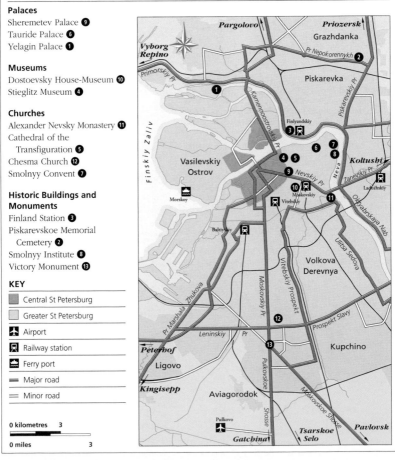

◁ The Baroque Sheremetev Palace on the east bank of the Fontanka river

East façade of Yelagin Palace with Srednaya Nevka river in foreground

Yelagin Palace ❶
Елагин дворец
Yelagin dvorets

Yelagin ostrov 1. **Tel** *430 1131.*
Ⓜ *Krestovskiy ostrov.* ◯ *10am–6pm Tue–Sun.* ◑ *last Tue of month.* 🎟
♿ *to ground floor.* 📷

One of the northernmost islands of St Petersburg, Yelagin Island is named after a court official who built a palace here at the end of the 18th century. Alexander I then bought the island in 1817 for his mother, Maria Fyodorovna, and commissioned Carlo Rossi to rebuild the palace. The magnificent Neo-Classical palace (1818–22), enlivened on the east façade by a half rotunda flanked by Corinthian porticoes, is part of an ensemble which includes an orangery, a horseshoe-shaped stable block and porticoed kitchens.

The palace interior was destroyed by fire during World War II but is now restored to its former glory. The Oval Hall is resplendent with statuary and trompe l'oeils while the rooms leading from it are exquisitely decorated with stucco, *faux marbre* and painted friezes, executed by gifted artists and craftsmen.

Statue of Mother Russia (1956–60), Piskarevskoe Memorial Cemetery

In the Soviet period, the whole of the wooded island became the Central Park of Culture and Rest *(see pp136–7)*. Festivals and public entertainments are held here, and there is an exhibition of decorative art in the palace's former stables.

Piskarevskoe Memorial Cemetery ❷
Пискаревское мемориальное кладбище
Piskarevskoe memorialnoe kladbishche

Prospekt Nepokorennykh 72–74.
Tel *247 5716.* Ⓜ *Akademicheskaya.*
🚌 *80, 123, 138, 178.* ◯ *24 hours daily. Memorial halls 10am–5pm daily.* 📷

This vast, bleak cemetery is a memorial to the two million people who died during the Siege of Leningrad, 1941–4 *(see p27)*. With little food and no electricity, water or heating, the citizens of Leningrad perished in vast numbers from starvation, cold and disease. Corpses were dragged on sledges to collection points from where they were taken for burial to mass cemeteries on the outskirts of town. Piskarevskoe was the largest, with 490,000 burials.

Today the cemetery is a place of pilgrimage for those who lost relatives and friends during those desperate times. The memorial complex, designed by Yevgeniy Levinson and Aleksandr Vasiliev, opened in 1960, on the 15th anniversary of the end of the war. Two memorial halls, one of which contains an exhibition on the Siege, flank the stairs down to a 300-m (984-ft) long avenue, which culminates in a towering, heroic bronze statue of Mother Russia by Vera

Isayeva and Robert Taurit. On the wall behind are verses composed by Olga Bergholts, herself a survivor of the Siege. The funereal music broadcast over the whole cemetery adds to the sombre atmosphere.

On either side of the avenue are 186 grassy mounds, each with a granite slab marking the year and indicating, with a red star or hammer and sickle, whether those interred were soldiers or civilians.

Locomotive 293, Finland Station

Finland Station ❸
Финляндский вокзал
Finlyandskiy vokzal

Ploshchad Lenina 6. **Map** 3 B3.
Ⓜ *Ploshchad Lenina.*
See also p221.

On the night of 3 April 1917, the exiled Vladimir Lenin and his Bolshevik companions arrived at Finland Station after travelling from Switzerland on a sealed train. A triumphant reception awaited their return to Russia and, on leaving the station, Lenin spoke to cheering crowds of soldiers, sailors and workers. A statue erected outside the station in 1926 depicts Lenin delivering his speech.

The modern terminal was opened in the 1960s. On platform 5 there is a huge glass case containing Locomotive 293 which Lenin rode when fleeing the capital for a second time in July 1917. After spending the summer as a fugitive in Russian Finland, Lenin returned on the same train and spurred on the October Revolution *(see pp28–9)*.

Stieglitz Museum ❹

Музей Штиглица

Muzey Shtiglitsa

Solyanoy pereulok 13–15. **Map** 3
A5. **Tel** 273 3258. 🚌 46, K-76,
K-100, K-217. ◯ Sep–Jul: 11am–
4:30pm Tue–Sat. ◉ last Fri of
month. 🖼 🖻

The millionaire industrialist
Baron Aleksandr Stieglitz
founded the
Central School of
Industrial
Design in 1876.
His aim was to
provide
a top quality
collection of
original works for
the use of Russian
students of applied
arts and design.

**19th-century crystal
vase, Stieglitz Museum**

With a large budget and the
good taste of Stieglitz's son-
in-law, Aleksandr Polovtsov
(see p122), the collection,
unusual in covering both
Western European and
Oriental art, soon outgrew the
school and in 1896 a Museum
of Applied Arts opened next
door. This magnificent building, designed by Maximilian
Messmacher, was inspired by
Italian Renaissance palaces.
Inside, the halls and galleries
were decorated in an impressive variety of national and
period styles, echoing French

and German Baroque and,
above all, Italian Renaissance
monuments, such as St Mark's
Library in Venice, the Raphael
Loggias of the Vatican and the
Villa Madama, also in Rome.

After the Revolution the
school was closed and the
museum became a branch of
the Hermitage *(see pp84–93)*.
Serious damage to the building
was inflicted during the Siege
of Leningrad *(see
p27)*. At the end
of the war the
school was
revived to train
gilders and carvers
for the huge res-
toration programme
needed to repair the
damaged city.

Situated on the
ground floor, the
exhibition features opulent
displays of glassware, ceramics
and majolica, as well as
porcelain from all the great
European manufacturers. One
room, decorated in the style
of the medieval Terem Palace
in the Kremlin, provides a
superb backdrop for a collection of embroidered
dresses and headgear made
by Russian peasant women.

Some pieces of decorative
metalwork including locks,
keys and craft tools date back
to the Middle Ages. The work-
manship seen on the wooden

furniture is breathtaking. The
Neo-Gothic cabinet is a
beautiful example. Its finely
inlaid doors, depicting church
naves in perspective, open to
reveal sculpted biblical scenes.

One way to end your visit
is with a look at the stunning
Grand Exhibition Hall with its
curving staircase of Italian marble and magnificent glass roof.

Cathedral of the Transfiguration ❺

Спасо-Преображенский
собор

Spaso-Preobrazhenskiy sobor

Preobrazhenskaya ploshchad 1. **Map**
3 B5. **Tel** 579 6010. Ⓜ *Chernyshevskaya.* 🚌 46, K-46, K-76, K-90, K-177,
K-258. 🚋 3, 8, 15. ◯ 8am–8pm daily.

Despite its monumental
Neo-Classicism, and the
surrounding fence made of
guns captured during the
Russo-Turkish wars *(see p22)*,
Vasiliy Stasov's church has an
intimate air as it nestles in its
leafy square. The original
church on this site was built
by Tsarina Elizabeth to honour
the Preobrazhenskiy Guards,
but it was rebuilt after a fire
in 1825. Today, the church is
famous for its excellent choir,
which is second only to that
in the Alexander Nevsky
Monastery *(see pp130–31)*.

Dolls in 17th–19th century Russian folk costumes, in front of the Terem Room, Stieglitz Museum

Tauride Palace ⑥

Таврический дворец

Tavricheskiy dvorets

Shpalernaya ulitsa 47. **Map** 4 D4.
Ⓜ *Chernyshevskaya.* 🚌 *46, 136.*
⚫ *to public.*

This finely proportioned
palace by Ivan Starov was
built in 1783–9 as a present
from Catherine the Great to
her influential lover Prince
Grigoriy Potemkin *(see p25)*.
Potemkin had successfully
annexed the Crimea (Tauris) to
Russia in 1783 and was given
the title of Prince of Tauris,
hence the palace's name.

Uncompromising in its lack
of external ornamentation, the
long, yellow building with its
distinctive six-columned portico was one of Russia's first
Neo-Classical designs. Sadly,
the magnificent interiors have
been badly damaged both
by Catherine's son, Paul I,
who turned the palace into a
barracks, and by the many
reconstructions undertaken.

The palace played a vital
role in 20th-century cultural
and political life. In 1905, the
impresario Sergey Diaghilev
(see p43) organized the first
ever exhibition of Russian 18th-
century portraiture here. The
following year the palace host-
ed Russia's first parliament, the
State Duma. After the February
Revolution of 1917 it became
the seat of the Provisional
Government, then the Petrograd Soviet of Workers' and
Soldiers' Deputies. Today it is
still a government building.

The lovely gardens, with
winding streams, bridges and
an artificial lake, are among
the city's most popular parks.

Façade of the Smolnyy Cathedral with adjacent convent buildings

Smolnyy Convent ⑦

Смольный монастырь

Smolnyy monastyr

Ploshchad Rastrelli 3/1. **Map** 4 F4.
Tel *710 3159.* 🚌 *46, 136.*
⚪ *May–Sep: 10am–7pm Thu–Tue;*
Sep–Apr: 11am–7pm Thu–Tue. 📷
♿ 📷 *English.*

The crowning glory of this
architectural ensemble is the
stunning cathedral with its
dome and four supporting cupolas topped by golden orbs.

As a symbol of her majesty,
Tsarina Elizabeth founded the
convent where many young
noblewomen were to be
educated. It was designed in
1748 by Bartolomeo Rastrelli
(see p93), who conceived a
brilliant fusion of Russian and
Western Baroque styles. Work
advanced extremely slowly;
50,000 wooden piles were
used to secure the foundations
in the marshy soil and the
architect's model alone, now in
the Academy of Arts *(see p63)*,
took seven years to build.

Catherine the Great disliked
Rastrelli's work and had little
sympathy for the late Elizabeth.
When she came to power in

1762, funding for the project
stopped. It was only in 1835
that Nicholas I commissioned
the Neo-Classical architect
Vasiliy Stasov to complete the
cathedral. His austere white
interior contrasts dramatically
with the luxuriant exterior.

Exhibitions are now held
here, as well as regular weekly
concerts *(see p202)*. There are
spectacular views of the city
from the cathedral tower.

Smolnyy Institute ⑧

Смольный Институт

Smolnyy Institut

Smolnyy proezd 1. **Map** 4 F4.
Tel *710 3159, 710 3143.* 🚌 *46, 54,*
74, 136, K-15, K-76, K-136. 🚎 *5, 7,*
11, 15, 16. **Smolnyy Museum**
⚪ *11am–6pm Mon–Fri by appt only.*
📷 ♿ 📷 *English.*

Built in 1806–8 to house a
school for young noblewomen
which had outgrown its premises at the Smolnyy Convent,
Giacomo Quarenghi
considered this Neo-Classical
building to be his masterpiece.

It was from here, on 25
October 1917, that Lenin directed the Bolshevik *coup d'état*
while the second All-Russian
Congress of Soviets was con-
vening in the Assembly Hall.
The Congress confirmed Lenin
in power and this was his seat
of government until March
1918. With the Germans
advancing and the outbreak
of civil war *(see p27)*, the government left for Moscow. The
Institute was taken over by the
Leningrad Communist Party.
On 1 December 1934, the First
Secretary of the party, Sergey
Kirov *(see p72)*, was murdered
here, an event that was to

View of Tauride Gardens and the Tauride Palace beyond the lake

Isaak Brodskiy's 1927 painting of Lenin, Smolnyy Institute Assembly Hall

provide cover for the purges of the late 1930s *(see p27)*.

The rooms where Lenin lived and worked can be viewed by appointment. The rest of the institute is now the Mayor's Office. The imperial eagle has replaced the hammer and sickle, but the statue of Lenin has survived.

Sheremetev Palace ❾
Шереметевский дворец
Sheremetevskiy dvorets

Naberezhnaya reki Fontanki 34. **Map 7 A1.** M *Mayakovskaya, Gostinyy Dvor.* 15, 22, 27, K-15, K-90, K-187, K-258. 3, 8, 15. **Anna Akhmatova Museum** *Tel 571 7239.* 10:30am–6:30pm Tue–Sun. *English.* **Museum of Musical Life** *Tel 272 4441.* 11am–7pm Wed–Sun. last Wed of each month.

The Sheremetev family lived here from 1712, when the palace was built by Field Marshal Boris Sheremetev, until the Revolution. The palace is also known as the Fountain House, or *Fontannyy dom*, because of the many fountains that once adorned its grounds. The Baroque building dates from the 1750s when it was designed by Savva Chevakinskiy and Fyodor Argunov, although numerous later alterations were made.

Field Marshal Sheremetev's descendants were fabulously wealthy, at one time owning some 200,000 serfs. They were among Russia's leading artistic patrons and the palace is now home to the Museum of Musical Life, which charts the family's contribution to the music of the city. In the 18th and 19th centuries, serf composers, musicians and actors from rural estates owned by the family performed in concerts and plays at the palace. Among those to praise the fine Sheremetev choir was the composer Franz Liszt.

The museum's exhibits include a variety of period instruments and a number of scores, some of which are compositions by the Sheremetevs themselves.

One of Russia's greatest 20th-century poets, Anna Akhmatova, lived in one of the service blocks of the palace from 1933 to 1941 and then between 1944 and 1954. Her flat is open to the public as the Anna Akhmatova Museum *(Muzey Anny Akhmatovoy)* and is reached through the courtyard of No. 53 Liteynyy prospekt. By the time she moved into the palace, it had been divided into dingy communal apartments. The rooms where she lived and worked display some of her personal possessions, tracing her intriguing life. Recordings of the poetess reading her own poems can also be heard.

ANNA AKHMATOVA

By 1914 Anna Akhmatova (1889–1966) was a leading light of Russia's "Silver Age" of poetry *(see p44)*. Tragedy gave her work a new dimension when first her husband was shot by the Bolsheviks, and later, her son and her lover were arrested in Stalin's purges. Anna herself was placed under police surveillance and officially silenced for more than 15 years. Her most famous poem, *Requiem* (1935–61), inspired by her son's arrest, was written in fragments and distributed to friends to memorize. Akhmatova's reputation was partially rehabilitated late in her life and she received honorary awards abroad.

Pilastered façade of Sheremetev Palace on the Fontanka embankment

Dostoevsky House-Museum ❿
Музей Достоевского
Muzey Dostoevskovo

Kuznechnyy pereulok 5/2. **Map** 7 B3.
Tel 571 4031. Ⓜ *Vladimirskaya.*
🚃 3, 8, 15. 🚌 49. ⬤ 11am–6pm
Tue–Sun. 🎫 📷 English.

This evocative museum
was the final home of the
famous Russian writer, Fyodor
Dostoevsky *(see p44)*, who
lived here from 1878 until his
death in 1881. Dostoevsky
was then at the height of his
fame, and it was here that he
completed his last great novel,
The Brothers Karamazov, in
1880. Gambling and debts,
however, confined him to a
fairly modest lifestyle in this
five-roomed apartment.

Although Dostoevsky's
public persona was dour and
humourless, he was a devoted and affectionate husband
and father. The delightful nurs-
ery contains a rocking horse,
silhouettes of his children and
the book of fairy tales which
he read aloud to them. In
Dostoevsky's study are his
writing desk and a reproduction of his favourite painting,
Raphael's *Sistine Madonna*.

Chesma Church (1777–80), a very early
example of Neo-Gothic in Russia

Chesma Church ⓬
Чесменская церковь
Chesmenskaya tserkov

Ulitsa Lensoveta 12. Ⓜ *Moskovskaya.*
🚃 16. 🚌 29, 45. ⬤ 10am–7pm
daily.

There is little Russian about
the highly unusual Chesma
Church, which was designed
by Yuriy Velten in 1777–80.
Its fanciful terracotta-coloured

façade is decorated with
thin vertical stripes of
white moulding which
direct the eye upwards to
its zig-zagged crown and
Neo-Gothic cupolas.

The name commemo-
rates the great Russian
naval victory over the
Turks at Chesma in the
Aegean in 1770. During
the Communist era the
church became a museum
to the battle, but today
the building is once
again used as a church.

On the opposite side
of ulitsa Lensoveta is
the Neo-Gothic Chesma
Palace (1774–77), formerly
Kekerekeksinen, or Frog
Marsh Palace. Also de-
signed by Velten, it served
as a staging post for
Catherine the Great en route to
Tsarskoe Selo *(see pp152–5)*.
Wedgwood's famous dinner
service with its frog emblem,
now in the Hermitage *(see
p91)*, was designed specially
for the Chesma Palace.

The palace achieved noto-
riety when Rasputin's body
lay in state here after his murder in 1916 *(see p121)*. Now
substantially altered, it serves
as a home for the elderly.

Alexander Nevsky Monastery ⓫
Александро-Невская лавра
Aleksandro-Nevskaya lavra

Ploshchad Aleksandra Nevskovo.
Map 8 E4. **Tel** 274 2635. Ⓜ *Ploshchad Aleksandra Nevskovo.* 🚃 8, 24,
27, 46, 55, 58, 191, K-156, K-187,
K-209. 🚌 1, 14, 16, 22. 🚌 7, 65.
Holy Trinity Cathedral ⬤ 6am–
8pm daily. **Church of the
Annunciation Tel** 274 2635.
⬤ 9:30am– 5pm; closes 6pm
in summer. ⬤ Mon & Thu. 🎫
cemeteries & Church of the
Annunciation. 📷

Founded by Peter
the Great in 1710,
this monastery is
named after Alexander
Nevsky, the prince of
Novgorod, who
defeated the Swedes in
1240. Peter defeated
them in 1709 *(see p18)*.

From the entrance, a path
runs between two large,

Dostoevsky's
tombstone

walled cemeteries, then across
a stream and into the main
monastic complex. The oldest
building is the Church of the
Annunciation (1717–22), designed by Domenico Trezzini.
The church, its ground floor
recently opened to the public,
was the burial place for non-
ruling members of the Russian
royal family. A series of red
and white, mid-18th-century
monastic buildings, including the Metropolitan's
House (1755–8), sur-
round the courtyard.
Among the trees in the
courtyard lie the
graves of atheist
Soviet scholars and
leading Communists.
Dominating the
essentially Baroque
complex is the twin-
towered and domed
Neo-Classical Holy
Trinity Cathedral, constructed
by architect Ivan Starov in
1776–90. The wide nave

inside is flanked by Corinthian
columns with statues by
Fedot Shubin. This leads to
the impressive red agate and
white marble iconostasis,
which features copies of
works by Van Dyck, Rubens
and others. To the right of the
iconostasis is a silver reliquary

Reliquary with Alexander Nevsky's
remains, Trinity Cathedral

Victory Monument ⑬

Монумент Защитникам Ленинграда

Monument Zashchitnikam Leningrada

Ploshchad Pobedy. **Tel** 371 2951, 373 6563. **M** *Moskovskaya*. ▦ 3, 11, 13, 39, 59, 90, 150, 187, K-13, K-100, K-350. ▦ 27, 29, 45. **Memorial Hall** ◯ 11am–6pm Thu & Sat–Mon, 11am–5pm Tue & Wed. ◯ last Tue of each month. ▣ book by phone.

Erected in 1975 to coincide with the 30th anniversary of the end of World War II, this is on the site of a temporary triumphal arch built to greet the returning troops. Named the Monument to the Heroic Defenders of Leningrad, it commemorates the victims of the Siege *(see p27)*, and its survivors. It was designed by Sergey Speranskiy and Valentin Kamenskiy and sculpted by Mikhail Anikushin. A 48-m (157-ft) high obelisk of red granite is near a vast, circular enclosure which symbolizes the vice-like grip of the siege. Sculptures of soldiers, sailors and grieving mothers surround the monument.

An underpass on Moskovskiy prospekt leads to the Memorial Hall. Here solemn music gives way to the persistent beat of a metronome, the wartime radio signal, intended to represent the city's defiant heartbeat.

The subdued lighting comprises 900 dim, orange lamps, one for each day of the Siege. Tablets are inscribed with the names of the 650 Heroes of the Soviet Union awarded the title after the war; and a mosaic depicts the women of the city greeting their menfolk at the end of the conflict.

Around the hall a small display of artifacts, including Shostakovich's violin *(see p43)*, records the contribution of different sections of the community to the war effort, while an illuminated relief map illustrates the battle lines. Most disturbing is the tiny piece of bread, which was many people's daily ration.

Heroic partisans facing south towards the enemy during the Siege of Leningrad, detail of Victory Monument

that contains the remains of Alexander Nevsky, transferred to the previous church on this site in 1724. Behind the reliquary hangs a painting of Nevsky, who has been venerated as a saint in Russia since the mid-16th century.

Many of the nation's leading cultural figures are buried in the two monastic cemeteries near the main entrance. The city's oldest graveyard, the Lazarus Cemetery, to the east, contains the graves of the polymath Mikhail Lomonosov *(see p45)* and a number of prominent architects, including Andrey Zakharov, Thomas de Thomon, Giacomo Quarenghi, Carlo Rossi *(see p110)* and Andrey Voronikhin. Clustered together along the northern wall of the Tikhvin Cemetery (to the west) are the tombs of some of Russia's most famous composers. Fyodor Dostoevsky *(see p44)* is also buried here, to the right of the entrance.

TOMBS OF INTEREST AT TIKHVIN CEMETERY

1 Mikhail Glinka (Composer, 1804–57)
2 Ivan Krylov (Poet, 1769–1844)
3 Marius Petipa (Choreographer, 1818–1910)
4 Pyotr Klodt (Sculptor, 1805–67)
5 Ivan Kramskoy (Painter, 1837–87)
6 Pyotr Tchaikovsky (Composer, 1840–93)
7 Modest Mussorgsky (Composer, 1839–81)
8 Nikolai Rimsky-Korsakov (Composer, 1844–1908)
9 Fyodor Dostoevsky (Writer, 1821–81)

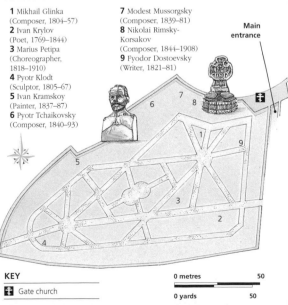

KEY

✠ Gate church

| 0 metres | | 50 |
| 0 yards | | 50 |

THREE GUIDED WALKS

Many of St Petersburg's sights are best appreciated on foot. The three walks chosen present different aspects of the city's character, though water plays a central part in each.

The first walk follows the Moyka river and the Griboedov canal, which criss-cross the heart of the city, and reveals the manificent scale of the buildings erected in the 18th and 19th centuries. It highlights the contrasts between rich palaces and overcrowded apartment blocks, gilded bridges and the dilapidation of the area around Sennaya ploshchad. An alternative way to appreciate the glorious old buildings set on the canals is to take a boat trip *(see pp226–7)*.

19th-century urn on the steps of Yelagin Palace

The second walk explores Yelagin and Kamennyy islands, where Petersburgers traditionally spend much of their free time. The islands to the north of the centre were once the preserve of the rich, who spent the hot summers in the cool of their *dachas*. Now locals come to walk and row boats in summer, to ski and skate in winter, and simply to breathe the fresh spring air.

The third walk follows the river Neva on the Petrograd side, from where there are awe-inspiring views of the city's grand south waterfront and of the river itself. The walk encompasses some significant historic sites including Trinity Square, the Cabin of Peter the Great and the cruiser *Aurora*.

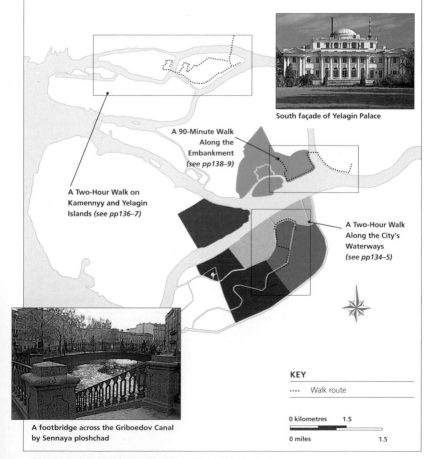

South façade of Yelagin Palace

A 90-Minute Walk Along the Embankment *(see pp138–9)*

A Two-Hour Walk on Kamennyy and Yelagin Islands *(see pp136–7)*

A Two-Hour Walk Along the City's Waterways *(see pp134–5)*

A footbridge across the Griboedov Canal by Sennaya ploshchad

KEY

···· Walk route

0 kilometres   1.5

0 miles   1.5

◁ **Peace and tranquillity enjoyed on one of the lakes of Yelagin Island**

A Two-Hour Walk Along the City's Waterways

A stroll along the embankments of the Moyka river and the Griboedov canal is a chance to appreciate the history and splendid architecture of this beautiful city. The two waterways present interesting contrasts. The Moyka winds past the Imperial Summer and Winter Palaces and the lavish mansions of the aristocracy, while the Griboedov is lined with 19th-century apartments, once home to merchants, civil servants and, towards Sennaya Ploshchad (see p122), the working class. The walk also includes a short stretch of the majestic Nevskiy prospekt.

TIPS FOR WALKERS

Starting point: Church on Spilled Blood.
Length: 5.8 km (3 miles).
Getting there: Nevskiy Prospekt metro. **Stopping-off points:** Bistro Layma, nab kanala Griboedova 16.

View of the Church on Spilled Blood ① and the Griboedov canal

The Moyka River

Begin the walk at the magnificent Church on Spilled Blood ① (see p100), built over the spot where Alexander II was assassinated in 1881 (see p26). From here, walk around the church beside the park, crossing the canal bridge to Konyushennaya ploshchad. The square is embraced by the elongated façade of the former Imperial Stables ② (see p113). Straddling the junction of the Griboedov canal and the Moyka river are two ingeniously linked bridges, the Malo-Konyushennyy most (Small Stable Bridge) and Teatralnyy most (Theatre Bridge) (see p37). Cross over these bridges to the north bank of the Moyka and the expansive façade of the Adamini House ③, designed by Domenico Adamini in 1823–7. Between 1916 and 1919 the basement was used

by artists' and writers' club known as "The Bivouac of the Comedians". Visitors included the avant-garde theatre director Vsevolod Meyerhold and the poets Aleksandr Blok and Anna Akhmatova (see p44).

Turn left onto naberezhnaya reki Moyki and walk past the Round Market ④ built in 1790 by Giacomo Quarenghi, who had shopping arcades as one of his specialities. Continue along the embankment, passing Adam's Bolshoy Konyushennyy most (Great Stables Bridge) to Prince Abamelek-Lazarev's former mansion ⑤ built in 1913–15. The handsome façade, with Corinthian pilasters and graceful reliefs of dancing figures, is by Ivan Fomin. On the opposite bank is the 17th-century apartment block where Pushkin spent the last few months of his life. His flat is now a museum ⑥ (see p113).

At the intersection of Millionaia ulitsa and the beautiful Winter Canal (Zimnaya Kanavka) are the former barracks of the elite First Regiment of the Preobrazhenskiy Life-Guards. This prestigious corps was formed by Peter the Great in the 1690s.

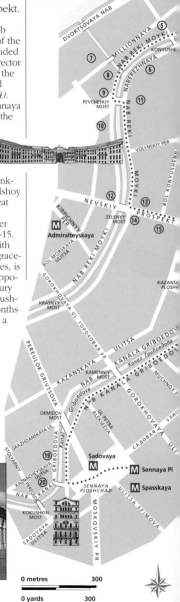

Quarenghi's arcaded Round Market (1790) ④, overlooking the Moyka river

0 metres 300
0 yards 300

KEY

• • • Tour route

Ⓜ Metro station

View of the tree-lined Griboedov canal

Across the Winter Canal is the New Hermitage ⑦ *(see p84)*. Ten granite atlantes bear the weight of the elaborate porch. Returning to the Moyka, the route passes a green, three-storey house ⑧, built by F Demertsov for Alexander I's military advisor and sometime chief minister, Count Aleksey Arakcheev. The Moyka now makes a curve behind the majestic buildings of Palace Square *(see p83)* which includes the Staff of the Guards Corps ⑨ and the huge crescent of Carlo Rossi's imposing yellow General Staff Building ⑩. Cross the Pevcheskiy most (Singers' Bridge) *(see p37)* ⑪ and follow the Moyka down to the Zelenyy most (Green Bridge). The yellow building on the other side of the Moyka is the Literary Café ⑫, renowned as a meeting-place for writers in Pushkin's day *(see p83)*.

Nevskiy Prospekt

Turn left onto St Petersburg's main street, where a range of architectural styles can be seen. On the left, the elegant façade of Paul Jacot's Dutch Church building ⑬ *(see p47)* hides a series of shops. Across

the road, the superb façade of the Baroque Stroganov Palace ⑭ *(see p112)* contrasts starkly with the triple-arched glass frontage of the Style-Moderne Fashion House ⑮ *(see p47)*. The colonnaded forecourt of the Cathedral of Our Lady of Kazan ⑯ *(see p111)* can be seen further along.

The Griboedov Canal

Cross Nevskiy prospekt by the attractive Singer Sewing Machine Building *(see p47)* and follow the Griboedov south. When you reach Georg von Traitteur's Bankovskiy most (Bank Bridge) *(see p35)* ⑰, decorated with golden griffons, cross the canal and continue past the wrought-iron railings to the rear of the former Assignment Bank ⑱ (now occupied by a finance and economics university).

Further south the humped Kamennyy most (Stone Bridge) has survived since 1776 despite an attempt by a revolutionary group to blow it up, as Tsar Alexander II passed in his carriage in 1881. Across the Demidov most, on the corner of Kaznacheyskaya ulitsa ⑲ (No.1),

Griffons on Bank Bridge (1826), Griboedov canal

is the apartment where Dostoevsky wrote *Notes from the House of the Dead* (1861). Also with literary associations, the former Zverkov House ⑳ was where the novelist and dramatist Nikolai Gogol *(see p44)* lived in the 1830s.

The walk ends in Sennaya ploshchad *(see p122)*, where there are three metro stations.

Apartment block where Dostoevsky lived ⑲, on the Griboedov canal

A Two-Hour Walk on Kamennyy and Yelagin Islands

An area of rolling parkland, birch and lime groves and fine river views, the northern islands of the Neva delta offer a retreat from city life. The imperial family built palaces on Kamennyy and Yelagin islands at the end of the 18th century and were soon joined by wealthy aristocratic families. Before the Revolution, many government ministers, industrial magnates and celebrities built themselves a *dacha* here. Today these neglected houses, some intimate, some palatial, in styles ranging from Neo-Gothic to Neo-Classical and Style Moderne, are being returned to their former glory by the business elite.

Wooden façade of Dolgorukov Mansion ③

Continue west, and cross the canal bridge to reach the wooden Kamennoostrovskiy Theatre ⑤ which took only 40 days to erect in 1827. Its Neo-Classical portico, rebuilt by Albert Kavos in 1844, is still impressive. The banks of the Krestovka river, with views across to the boatyards of Krestovskiy Island, offer many ideal spots for a picnic (but bear in mind that admission is charged at weekends). To rejoin the walk, return to the path and cross 1-y Yelagin most to Yelagin Island.

Yelagin Island

This island is an oasis of calm, popular with those wishing to escape the city. A tollgate marks the entrance to the grounds of Carlo Rossi's graceful Yelagin Palace ⑥

South Kamennyy Island

Begin at Chernaya Rechka metro station and head south to Bolshaya Nevka river, then cross Ushakovskiy most (Ushikov Bridge) to Kamennyy Island, an area of recreation and relaxation. Just across the main road is the small redbrick Church of St John the Baptist ①, designed in Neo-Gothic style by Yuriy Velten in 1776–8. Nearby a yellow gateway leads to the grounds of Kamennoostrovskiy Palace ② (which is now a retirement home) from where Alexander I led the 1812 Russian campaign against Napoleon *(see p26)*.

Follow Kamennoostrovskiy prospekt to the Malaya Nevka river, then turn right on to naberezhnaya Maloy Nevki where there is an imposing wooden mansion ③ at No. 11 with a white-columned portico. The Dolgorukov Mansion was built in 1831–2 by Smaragd

Shustov for the Dolgorukovs, one of Russia's oldest aristocratic families.

From this point you can see across to Aptekarskiy or Apothecary's Island, named after the medicinal herb gardens founded by Peter the Great in 1714. St Petersburg's Botanical Gardens are still located there. Continue along the path, which turns into naberezhnaya reki Krestovki. The house on the left, towards the Malo-krestovskiy most (Small Krestovskiy Bridge), is the former home of Sergey Chaev ④, who was the chief engineer of the Trans-Siberian railway. Chaev commissioned the fashionable architect, Vladimir Apyshkov, to build this rather splendid Style-Moderne mansion in 1913–14.

The tower of the Church of St John the Baptist (1776–8) ①

3-Y YELAGIN MOST

2-Y Severnyy prud

4-Y Severnyy prud

5-Y Severnyy prud

YELAGIN OSTROV

⑥

Srednaya Nevka

4-Y Yuzhnyy prud

TSENTRALNIY PARK KULTURIY I OTDYKHA IM KIROVA

Средная Невка

3-Y Yuzhnyy prud

2-Y Yuzhnyy prud

2-Y YELAGIN MOST

2-Y Yuzhnyy prud

1-Y Yuzhnyy prud

Kamennoostrovskiy Theatre's impressive façade (1827) ⑤

(see p126). The western spit of the island is ideal for viewing the spectacular sunsets over the Gulf of Finland, especially during the White Nights *(see p51).* If you want to venture further, head south across 2-y Yelagin most to Krestovskiy Island and the Kirov Stadium, Maritime Victory Park and Primorskiy Park Pobedy. Or, to the north, 3-y Yelagin most leads to Primorskiy prospekt and the Tibetan-inspired Buddhist Temple, erected by Gavriil Baranovskiy in 1909–15.

North Kamennyy Island
Return to Kamennyy Island across 1-y Yelagin most, taking the left fork on to Teatralnaya alleya from where you can see the former mansion of Aleksandr Polovtsov ⑦, minister of foreign affairs under Nicholas II. This splendid Neo-Classical mansion with Style-Moderne touches was built by Ivan Fomin in 1911–13. Leave Teatralnaya alleya and cut through the quiet and restful park, passing between the ponds and the canal. Near the junction with Bolshaya alleya are two more early 20th-century mansions. Follenveider's mansion ⑧ on the left, with its distinctive

Early 20th-century Polovtsov Mansion ⑦

tented tower, was designed by Roman Meltzer in 1904 and now belongs to the Danish consulate. Yevgeniya Gausvald's dacha ⑨ dates from 1898 and stands as one of the earliest Style-Moderne buildings in St Petersburg. It was designed by Vasiliy Schöne and Vladimir Chagin.

Finally, the last stage of the walk leads along the 2-ya Berezovaya alleya, back to the starting point at Ushakovskiy most and Chernaya Rechka metro.

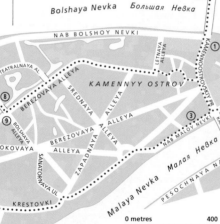

KEY

••• Walk route

Ⓜ Metro station

TIPS FOR WALKERS

Starting point: Chernaya Rechka metro station *(see p215).*
Length: 6 km (3.5 miles).
Stopping-off points: Café in former stables of Yelagin Palace (summer only) and plenty of places to picnic.

The tree-shrouded grassy banks of the Krestovka river

A 90-Minute Walk Along the Embankment

Muscovites envy St Petersburgers their dramatic and open skyline, and this stroll along the northern banks of the Neva offers grand views, not only of the magnificent south waterfront, but also of the Petrograd-skaya Side, as seen from Trinity Bridge where it crosses the river at its widest point. In winter the Neva lies frozen, an expanse of whiteness. In warmer months the water pulses hypnotically through the city. The walk encompasses the best of the city's Style-Moderne architecture, the Cabin of Peter the Great, the cruiser *Aurora*, whose guns began the 1917 Revolution, and the train that brought Lenin to Russia.

Manchurian Lion ⑦

needle-sharp steeple of the Baroque Cathedral of SS Peter and Paul ⑤. The bridge was completed in time for the city's bicentenary in 1903 by the French firm Batignol, which also constructed the Eiffel Tower.

Return to the shore, and stroll east along Petrovskaya Embankment, passing the Cabin of Peter the Great ⑥ *(see p73)*. The tiny cabin was built from pine logs in 3 days

Kamennoostrovskiy Prospekt

From Gorkovskaya metro station, cross the road via the underpass and walk south along Konverskiy prospekt, an avenue noted for its Style-Moderne architecture. Almost immediately, the minarets of the city's only mosque jut up ahead. Sobornaya Mosque ① *(see p70)*, one of Europe's

Trinity Square

Until the fall of the USSR, the square was known as Revolu-tion Square in memory of the 48 workers who were mown down here by government troops. Walk onto Style-Moderne Trinity Bridge ④ *(see p35)*, which spans the Neva at its widest point and affords fine views of the river and the Peter and Paul Fortress *(see pp66–7)*. Look out for the

Interior of the tiny Cabin of Peter the Great ⑥

View of Peter and Paul Fortress with the Cathedral of SS Peter and Paul ⑤

largest, was built in 1913. Slightly further on, at the junction with ulitsa Kuybysheva is the Kshesinskaya Mansion ② *(see p72)*, a delicate, asymmet-rical Style-Moderne building commissioned in 1906 for the ballerina Matilda Kshesinskaya (Nicholas II's former lover). Once the Bolshevik Party HQ, from whose balcony Lenin addressed the crowds, it now houses the Museum of Russian Political History with exhibits from the Revolutionary era.

Take a right down ulitsa Kuy-bysheva and bear left onto Kamennoostrovskiy prospekt *(see p70)*. To your left is Trinity Square ③ *(see p72)*, the heart of the old city's merchant quarter, and site of the "Bloody Sunday" massacre during the 1905 Revolution, and of the relatively new Trinity Chapel.

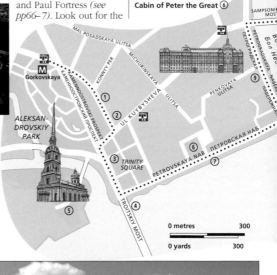

The cruiser *Aurora* (1900) moored in front of the Nakhimov Naval Academy ⑨

View across the frozen River Neva featuring the golden dome of St Isaac's Cathedral on the south embankment

in May 1703, and Peter lived here for 6 years, supervising the building of his city. The brick shell was added later by Catherine the Great. On the steps outside the cabin are the Manchurian Lions ⑦, two odd statues brought from Manchuria during the disastrous (for Russia) Russo-Japanese War of 1904–5.

for firing the shots that signalled the storming of the Winter Palace. This event brought the Bolsheviks to power in 1917. The battleship also contains a museum.

Further along the embankment, the Neo-Baroque building on the left is the Nakhimov Naval Academy ⑨, built in 1910–11.

Now cross Sampsonievskiy most onto Pirogovskaya naberezhnaya. From here you can catch

TIPS FOR WALKERS

Starting point: *Sobornaya Mosque.*
Getting there: *Gorkovskaya metro station (see p223).*
Length: *3.5 km (2 miles).*
Stopping off points: *There are places selling snacks along the north embankment, especially around the cruiser Aurora and the Cabin of Peter the Great.*

Ploshchad Lenina
The majority of statues of Lenin were torn down after the collapse of the USSR. This one was erected in 1926. Note the famous "'taxi-hailing" pose that was so popular among architects of monuments to "Grandfather Lenin", as Soviet children were taught to refer to him. Directly opposite the square, on the other side of the river, looms the "Bolshoy Dom", the gloomy former headquarters of the KGB. Here, death sentences were passed on an estimated 47,000 citizens of St Petersburg, who were then executed by firing squad. It is now the FSB's (the KGB's successors) HQ and a prison. Finally, walk across Ploshchad Lenina to Finland Station ⑫ *(see p126),* home to the train that brought Lenin to Russia to lead the 1917 October Revolution – and to alter the destiny of the largest country on earth. Finland Station also houses the Ploshchad Lenina metro station.

KEY

•••	Walk route
Ⓜ	Metro station
🚊	Tram stop
🚉	Train station
⛴	River boat pier

Statue of Lenin in Ploshchad Lenina ⑪, near Finland Station

The Cruiser *Aurora*
Follow the embankment to Petrogradskaya naberezhnaya and the historic old cruiser *Aurora* ⑧ *(see p73),* famous

tram No. 6 to the end of the walk if you wish.

Continuing on foot, the embankment leads down to Arsenalnaya naberezhnaya, past the Military Medical Academy ⑩ – built in the time of Tsar Paul I in a High-Classical style. Turn left onto Ploshchad Lenina ⑪. In the square is one of the city's few remaining statues of Lenin.

BEYOND
ST PETERSBURG

BEYOND ST PETERSBURG

*T*he countryside around St Petersburg is typical of northwest Russia. Among its flat sweeps of land, pine forests and lakes there are sights of cultural interest, including the imperial palaces and the walled medieval city of Novgorod. Venturing away from St Petersburg allows a richer and deeper insight into this splendid land.

Before St Petersburg was founded in 1703, the surrounding landscape was a marshy and inhospitable wilderness, inhabited by wolves. Nevertheless, the area from the Gulf of Finland to Lake Ladoga was of strategic importance for trading and thus one of the reasons for continuous wars between Sweden and Russia. At the time the only city of importance here was Novgorod, an independent and quite wealthy principality *(see p17)*. It has retained its medieval atmosphere, so different from the imperial palaces adorning the countryside south of St Petersburg. They each reflect the tastes of their owners. Peter the Great's fine residence, Peterhof, is dominated by water; the nearby Gulf and the numerous fountains mirror his maritime interest. Elizabeth wanted vibrant colour and excess to accommodate her extravagant balls, hence the grand Baroque palace at Tsarskoe Selo. Catherine the Great's love of intimacy led her to add private apartments to Tsarskoe Selo, and the exquisite Chinese Palace at Oranienbaum. Paul I's military mania had him turn Gatchina into a castle, while his wife Maria Fyodorovna created a feminine, elegant residence at Pavlovsk. All the palaces except Oranienbaum suffered devastating damage during World War II *(see p27)*. A great deal of effort has been made to restore them over the last 60 years.

Muse of love and poetry, Pavlovsk

While the aristocracy indulged in their extravagances, the middle classes had more modest country houses. The *dacha* of the artist Repin, gives a feel of his more bohemian lifestyle.

The Novgorod Kremlin with the Cathedral of St Sophia and its belfry

◁ **The gilded maze of the main staircase at Peterhof's Grand Palace**

Exploring St Petersburg's Surroundings

Many St Petersburgers leave the city to spend time at their *dacha* or country house for weekends and holidays. But there are several ways of experiencing the countryside around St Petersburg. There are many stunning imperial palaces, spread out like pearls in a necklace south of the city. Each one of them offers splendid interiors as well as beautifully laid out parks and gardens with lakes. Around the artist's studio at Repino is a more typical Baltic landscape, with pine and fir trees stretching down to the pebbly beaches of the Gulf of Finland.

Further away to the south, the medieval town of Novgorod is a great representative of an old Russian city, complete with a walled kremlin and onion-domed churches.

Façade of the Chinese Palace at Oranienbaum

GETTING AROUND

It is relatively easy to get to all of the imperial palaces, and to Repino, by suburban train or by coach *(see p229)*. Driving is less convenient, often taking longer than the train, and driving standards are variable. In summer, a hydrofoil service from the centre offers an alternative way to get to Peterhof *(see pp228–9)*. Each of these sights can easily be visited in a day. Novgorod is situated further away, however, and so it makes sense to spend longer there. Mainline trains depart from Moscow railway station *(see p229)* for Novgorod.

Coastal landscape along the Gulf of Finland

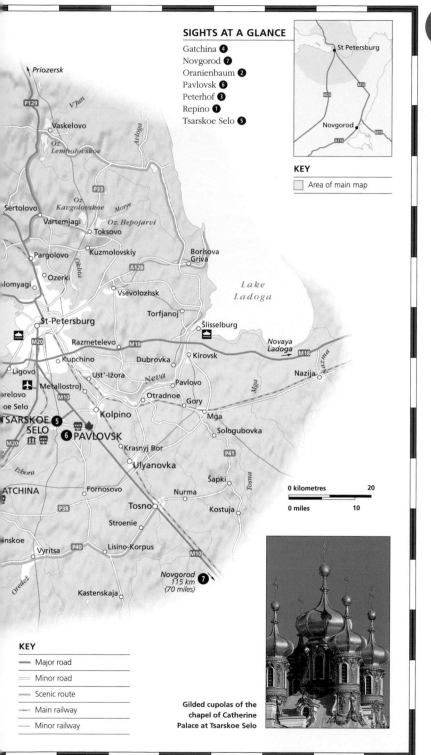

SIGHTS AT A GLANCE

Gatchina ❹
Novgorod ❼
Oranienbaum ❷
Pavlovsk ❻
Peterhof ❸
Repino ❶
Tsarskoe Selo ❺

KEY

☐ Area of main map

KEY

— Major road
═══ Minor road
— Scenic route
⊶ Main railway
— Minor railway

Gilded cupolas of the
chapel of Catherine
Palace at Tsarskoe Selo

Novgorod ❼
115 km
(70 miles)

0 kilometres   20
0 miles   10

Repino ❶

Репино

Repino

47 km (29 miles) NW of St Petersburg.
🚇 *from Finland Station.* 🚌 *211 from
Chernaya Rechka metro.* **Penaty**
Primorskoe shosse 411. **Tel** *432 0834.*
⬤ *10:30am–4pm Wed–Sun.* 📷
🎫 *English.* ♿ *ground floor.*

Only about an hour's drive
from St Petersburg on Primorskoe shosse, the northern
coastal road, is a region of
lakes, pine-scented forests and
sandy beaches. Among the
green-painted *dachas* and
sanatoria is Repino, a resort
named after one of Russia's
greatest artists, Ilya Repin
(see p106–7), who lived here
for over 30 years until his
death in 1930 at the age of 86.
His extraordinary *dacha,* with
its steeply pitched glass roof
and angled windows, was
restored after damage in
World War II and is now open
as a museum.

Named Penaty in honor of
the Roman household gods,
penates, the house was redesigned by Repin himself to
accommodate all that an artist
might need, including a glass-
panelled veranda downstairs,
which was used as a winter
studio. On display in the first
floor studio are the artist's
brushes and a number of his
works, including an unfinished
portrait of Pushkin *(see p44)*
and Repin's last self-portrait.

Works by the artist adorn the
dining room, including portraits
of the singer Fyodor Chalyapin
and writer Maxim Gorky who
were among Repin's many visitors. A revolving dining table
enabled guests to serve themselves and to store away their

Studio of the eminent artist Ilya Repin at his home in Repino

used dishes, since there were
no servants. Anyone failing to
obey this household rule had
to give an impromptu speech
from the lectern in the corner.

In the garden, two small
wooden follies are hidden
among the trees, and Repin's
grave is marked by a simple
cross on the top of a hillock.

Oranienbaum ❷

Ораниенбаум

Oranienbaum

Oranienbaum, 40 km (25 miles) W of
St Petersburg. **Tel** *422 3753,
423 1627 or 422 8016 (excursions).*
🚇 *from Baltic station.* **Grounds**
⬤ *9am–8pm (free after 5pm).* 📷
**Chinese Palace and Palace of St
Peter III** ⬤ *Jun–Sep: 10:30am–6pm
Wed–Mon.* **Sliding Hill Pavilion**
⬤ *temporarily.* 📷 🎫

As the extravagant project of
Peter the Great's closest friend
and main political advisor,
Aleksandr Menshikov *(see p62)*,
Oranienbaum was far more
ambitious in conception than
Peter's palace at Peterhof
(see pp148–51), which lies just
12 km (7 miles) to the west.

The grandiose plan bankrupted
Menshikov and, when he fell
from grace in 1727, the estate
entered the state treasury.

The Baroque appearance of
Oranienbaum's Great Palace
has changed little since it was
constructed in 1710–25. Built
by Gottfried Schädel and
Giovanni-Maria Fontana, its
sweeping wings culminate in
two remarkable pavilions.
Parts of the palace and the
east (Japanese) pavilion are
open to the public.

From 1743 to 1761 the estate
became the residence of the
heir to the throne, the future
Peter III, who built himself a
miniature fortress with a small
lake for his "navy" and a
parade ground where he was
fond of playing war games
with soldiers. Peter also commissioned Antonio Rinaldi to
build him a modest palace.

Peter's wife, Catherine (later
Catherine the Great), abhorred
her isolated existence here,
but after Peter's murder *(see
p22)* she recovered her spirits
and created what she described
as her "personal *dacha*". Built
by Rinaldi in the 1760s and
known as the Chinese Palace,
it is famous for its Rococo
interiors and chinoiserie.

The most unusual building
at Oranienbaum is Rinaldi's
Sliding Hill Pavilion, built in
1762 on Catherine's initiative.
Wooden sledging hills were a
common source of amusement
among the Russian nobility.
Catherine's visitors would climb
the blue and white pavilion
before descending at top
speed by sledge or toboggan
along a roller coaster run. The
track, 500 m (1,640 ft) long,
was originally flanked by a

Façade of Menshikov's Great Palace (1710–25), Oranienbaum

colonnade. Sadly, this structure collapsed in 1813 but there is a model in the pavilion.

A pleasant few hours can be spent in the grounds with their secluded paths, pine woods, ponds and bridges.

Oranienbaum was the only local palace to escape German occupation during World War II *(see p27)*. In 1948, the estate was renamed Lomonosov after the famous 18th-century physicist *(see p45)* who laid many of the foundations of modern Russian science. The complex has now reverted to its original name, an allusion to the exotic orange trees planted here by Menshikov.

Austere central section of Gatchina palace

When Orlov died, two years later, Catherine transferred the estate to her son and heir Paul (later Paul I). Paul asked his favourite architect Vincenzo Brenna to re-fashion the palace. Brenna's large-scale alterations included the construction of an additional storey and a moat with a drawbridge.

The next Romanov to spend any time here was Alexander III who made it his permanent family residence in the late 19th century. The estate provided a safe and remote haven from the sporadic social unrest which was threatening the capital *(see p26)*. The imperial family led a simple and secluded existence here. In keeping with the increasingly bourgeois tastes of the nobility in the whole of Europe, they scorned the state rooms, confining themselves instead to the cosy and more intimate servants' quarters. In 1917, immediately after the

Bolshevik party had seized power, the proclaimed leader of the Provisional Government, Aleksandr Kerensky, fled to Gatchina where he made a last ditch attempt to rally his supporters. After a week, he deserted his troops and slipped away into exile.

After World War II, in which the palace was badly damaged, Gatchina was used for many years as a military academy. The lengthy and thorough restoration process is ongoing. Of the restored rooms, the three most impressive are the Marble Dining Room, Paul I's gloomy bedroom at the top of one of Brenna's towers and the magnificent White Ballroom. There is also a display of weaponry on the ground floor.

The delightful grounds are the wildest of all the palace parks. Among the attractions are the circular Temple of Venus (1792–3) on the secluded Island of Love and the Birch House (1790s). The latter appears to be a pile of logs, but it actually conceals a suite of exquisite rooms.

The lake has boats for hire and its clean water makes it an ideal spot for swimming.

Chinoiserie decorations in Catherine the Great's Chinese Palace, Oranienbaum

Peterhof ❸

See pp148–51.

Gatchina ❹
Гатчина
Gatchina

45 km (28 miles) SW of St Petersburg. 🚉 *from Baltic Station.* 🚌 *431, K-18, K-18a from Moskovskaya metro station.* **Tel** *8 81371 93492.* ⏰ *10am–6pm Tue–Sun.* ⚫ *first Tue of month.* 📷 🎫 *English (phone to book).* 🖥 *www.gatchinapalace.ru*

In 1765, Catherine the Great presented the village of Gatchina to her lover, Prince Grigoriy Orlov. He then commissioned Antonio Rinaldi to build a Neo-Classical palace which was completed in 1781.

Tsarskoe Selo ❺

See pp152–5.

Gatchina's sumptuous White Ballroom with its pseudo-Egyptian statues

Peterhof ❸
Петергоф
Petergof

With its commanding views of the Baltic, Peterhof is a perfect expression of triumphalism. Originally designed by Jean Baptiste Le Blond, the Great Palace (1714–21) was transformed during the reign of Tsarina Elizabeth when Bartolomeo Rastrelli added a third storey and wings with pavilions at either end. He tried to preserve Le Blond's early Baroque exterior, but redesigned the interiors, indulging his love for gilded Baroque decoration. Peterhof stands at the centre of a magnificent landscaped park, with both French and English gardens.

View from palace of Grand Cascade leading down to the Gulf of Finland

Neptune Fountain

Oak Fountain

Mezheumnyy Fountain

The Upper Gardens are framed by borders and hedges and punctuated with ornamental ponds.

The Imperial Suite
The imperial suite lies in the palace's east wing. Peter's Oak Study is one of the few rooms to have survived unaltered from Le Blond's design. Some of the oak panel designs are originals (1718–21) by Nicholas Pineau.

Cottage Palace

Orangery

Roman Fountain

★ **The Grand Cascade**
The dazzling cascade (1715–24) is a sequence of 37 gilded bronze sculptures, 64 fountains and 142 water jets (see p151), descending from the terraces of the Great Palace to the Marine Canal and the sea.

Pyramid Fountain

Monplaisir

Adam Fountain

0 metres   25

0 yards   25

PETER THE GREAT'S PALACE

After his victory over the Swedes at Poltava in 1709, Peter the Great decided to build a palace "befitting to the very highest of monarchs". A visit to Versailles in 1717 furthered Peter's ambitions and he employed more than 5,000 labourers, serfs and soldiers, supported by architects, water-engineers, landscape gardeners and sculptors. Work proceeded at a frenetic pace from 1714 until Peterhof was officially opened in 1723.

Le Blond's Great Palace was completed in 1721 and has changed considerably over the decades. Catherine the Great commissioned Yuriy Velten to redecorate some of Rastrelli's interiors in the 1770s, including the Throne Room and the Chesma Room.

Jean Baptiste Le Blond's original two-storey Great Palace

VISITORS' CHECKLIST

Petrodvorets, 30 km (19 miles) W of St Petersburg. **Tel** 420 0073. from Baltic station (see p220) to Novyy Petergof. Hermitage (May–Oct) (see p220). **Great Palace** 10:30am–6pm Tue–Sun. last Tue of each month. **Other pavilions** May–Sep: 11am–5pm Tue–Sun; Oct–Apr: 11am–5pm Sat & Sun. **Fountains** May–early Oct: 10:30am–5pm.

★ Main Staircase
Caryatids and gilded carvings adorn Rastrelli's glittering staircase. The ceiling fresco depicts Aurora and Genius chasing away the night.

Golden Hill Cascade

Marly and Hermitage

Eve Fountain

Samson Fountain

STAR FEATURES

★ Grand Cascade

★ Main Staircase

★ The State Rooms

Hydrofoil and Gulf of Finland

The Marine Canal enabled the tsars to sail from the Gulf of Finland up to the Great Palace.

★ The State Rooms
The highlight of the State Rooms is the opulent Throne Room, redesigned by Yuriy Velten in 1770. The relatively restrained stucco ornamentation, red velvet hangings and parquet floor provide an exquisite setting for portraits of Russia's imperial family.

Exploring Peterhof Park

The grounds at Peterhof include the Upper, Lower and Alexandria parks, covering an area of around 607 hectares (1,500 acres). As well as the numerous palaces and fountains, there are tree-lined avenues, wooded paths and the Baltic shore. Le Blond designed the grounds next to the Great Palace to be laid out in the formal French style with geometrically arranged flower beds, sculptures, summerhouses and pergolas. The trees and shrubs, including limes, elms, maples and roses, were imported from all over Russia and abroad.

Cottage Palace in Alexandria Park

Monplaisir palace (1714–22), overlooking the Gulf of Finland

Monplaisir

This delightfully unpretentious palace was designed in 1714 by Johann Braunstein. Even after the Great Palace was built, Peter continued to live and entertain at Monplaisir where his guests were usually subjected to a punishing regime of heavy drinking. At breakfast the coffee cups were filled with brandy and by nightfall guests were often discovered wandering drunk in the park.

While not as lavish as those of the Great Palace the interiors are still impressive, in particular the wood-panelled Ceremonial Hall. A painting on its vaulted ceiling depicts Apollo surrounded by characters from a masque. Russian icon painters skilfully carried out the decoration of the exquisite Lacquered Study in the Chinese style then in vogue. Peter's collection of canvases by Dutch and Flemish artists hang in the rooms and there are wonderful views of the gulf from the tsar's Naval Study.

Adjoining Monplaisir is the Catherine Wing, which was built for Tsarina Elizabeth by Rastrelli in 1747–54. Catherine

the Great was staying here in 1762 when her lover, Count Orlov, arrived with news of the coup which was to bring her to the throne *(see p24)*.

Marly Palace

Named after Marly-le-Rois, the king of France's hunting lodge which Peter the Great visited on a tour of Europe in 1717, this beautifully proportioned country residence was built for the tsar's guests. The rooms open to the public

Elaborate tiled kitchen in the Marly Palace (1720–3)

include the Oak and Plane Tree studies, Peter's bedroom and the Dining Room. It is set in its own formal garden with sculptures, fountains, a large pond and Niccolò Michetti's Golden Hill Cascade, which was added in 1731–7.

The Hermitage

Standing in splendid isolation on the shores of the gulf, this elegant pavilion (1721–5), by Braunstein, was conceived as a private dining venue for the tsar and his friends. To highlight the need for solitude, the building was raised on a plinth and surrounded by a moat that was crossed by a small drawbridge. The stuccoed façade is decorated with Corinthian pilasters, elaborate wrought-iron balconies and enlarged windows. All the servants were confined to the ground floor and a mechanical device took meals up from the kitchen.

Cottage Palace

The romantic landscaped grounds of Alexandria Park, named after Alexandra, wife of Nicholas I, provide a perfect setting for the Cottage Palace. The Neo-Gothic house is more imposing than the term cottage suggests. The Scottish architect, Adam Menelaws, designed it in 1826–9 for Nicholas I and his wife, who wanted a domestic environment in keeping with their bourgeois tastes.

The Gothic theme is pursued throughout, most effectively in the Great Drawing Room with the rose window motif in the carpet and the lace-like tracery of the stuccoed ceiling. The exquisite 5,200-piece crystal and porcelain dinner service in the Dining Room was made for the royal couple at the Imperial Porcelain factory.

The Fountains at Peterhof

Jean-Baptiste Le Blond submitted his "water plan" to Peter the Great in 1717, by which time the tsar had begun sketching his own ideas. The centrepiece is the Grand Cascade, fed by the underground springs of the Ropsha Hills about 22 km (14 miles) away. The cascade is a celebration of the triumph of Russia over Sweden *(see p19)*, symbolized by Mikhail Kozlovskiy's glorious

Detail of the Mezheumnyy Fountain

sculpture of Samson rending the jaws of a lion. An imaginative variety of fountains, mostly concentrated in the Lower Park, includes triton and lion fountains, dragon fountains with checker-board steps, and smaller fountains with fish-tailed boys blowing sprays of water through conches. Most playful are trick fountains such as the Umbrella which "rains" on those who come too close.

The Adam Fountain, *sculpted by Giovanni Bonazza, was commissioned by Peter in 1718, along with a similar statue of Eve. The two fountains suggest the earthly paradise the tsar had recreated at Peterhof.*

The Roman Fountains *were designed by Ivan Blank and Ivan Davydov in 1738–9. The two-tiered marble fountains were inspired by one in St Peter's Square in Rome.*

The Neptune Fountain *predates Peterhof by more than 50 years. The Baroque sculpture was erected in 1658 in Nuremberg to mark the end of the Thirty Years War and was sold to Tsar Paul I in 1782 because there was not enough water to make it work.*

The Grand Cascade *was originally adorned with lead statues which weathered badly and were recast in bronze and gilded after 1799. Shubin, Martos and other noted sculptors worked to create this stunning cascade.*

The Pyramid Fountain *(1720s) is one of a number of fountains whose jets create a special shape. Over 500 jets of water rise in seven tiers to create an "obelisk" commemorating the Russian victory over Sweden.*

Tsarskoe Selo ❺

Царское Село
Tsarskoe Selo

The lavish imperial palace at Tsarskoe Selo was designed by Rastrelli *(see p93)* in 1752 for Tsarina Elizabeth. She named it the Catherine Palace in honour of her mother, Catherine I, who originally owned the estate. The next ruler to leave a mark on the palace was Catherine the Great, and during her reign she commissioned the Scotsman Charles Cameron to redesign the Baroque interiors according to her more Neo-Classical taste. Cameron also built an ensemble of buildings for taking traditional Russian cold and warm baths, containing the Agate Rooms, and the Cameron Gallery. Post-war restoration continues and 35 state rooms are now open, as well as the beautiful park.

★ The Great Hall
Light streams into Rastrelli's glittering hall illuminating the mirrors, gilded carvings and the vast ceiling painting, The Triumph of Russia *(c.1755), by Giuseppe Valeriani.*

The Great Staircase (1860), by Ippolito Monighetti, ascends to the state rooms on the first floor.

Entrance

Atlantes
The stunning 300-m (980-ft) long Baroque façade is adorned with a profusion of Atlantes, columns, pilasters and ornamented window framings.

| 0 metres | 25 |
| 0 yards | 25 |

The Agate Rooms (see p154) are part of the imperial baths and faced with semi-precious stones from the Urals. (Temporarily closed.)

The Cameron Gallery (see p154)

The Cavaliers' Dining Room
The table is laid for Tsarina Elizabeth's gentlemen-in-waiting, in the refined gold and white room created by Rastrelli.

The Royal Chapel is richly decorated in dark blue and gold. Built by Chevakinskiy in the 1740s, it contains an elaborate six-tiered iconostasis.

VISITORS' CHECKLIST

Tsarskoe Selo, 25 km (16 miles) S of St Petersburg. 🚊 from Vitebskiy station to Detskoe Selo, then 🚌 371 or 382. **Palace** **Tel** 465 2024. ⏰ 10am–5pm Fri–Wed; open noon–2pm & 4–5pm. 🔒 last Mon of month. 📷 🎫 🚻 🖥 **Agate Rooms** 🔒 temporarily. **Cameron Gallery** ⏰ 10am–5pm Fri–Wed. **Park** ⏰ daily. 🎫 mid-May–Sep. **www**.tzar.ru

★ **Amber Room**
The original amber panels (1709) by Andreas Schlüter were a gift from Friedrich Wilhelm I of Prussia to Peter the Great. The room has been recreated from photos, complete with carved reliefs and panels in Florentine mosaic.

The Blue Drawing Room is characterized by blue floral motifs painted on silk. Among the royal portraits hanging here is a painting of Peter the Great by Ivan Nikitin, dating from around 1720.

To the Lycée and the Church of the Sign *(see p155)*

The Picture Gallery displays canvases by Italian, French, Dutch and Flemish masters of the 17th and 18th centuries.

★ **Green Dining Room**
Cameron's restrained Neo-Classical style contrasts with the Baroque flamboyance of Rastrelli's work. The exquisite stucco bas-reliefs, sculpted by Ivan Martos, were based on motifs from frescoes discovered in Pompeii.

The French-style formal gardens were laid out in the 1740s. Their formality and symmetry contrasts with the naturalistic English-style landscaping of the park *(see p154)*, created in 1768.

Small Enfilade
A varied selection of furniture and objets d'art *make up the exhibition in these unrestored rooms. Chinese lacquer furniture and Oriental rugs were among the treasures used to furnish the palace in the 19th century.*

STAR FEATURES

★ The Great Hall

★ Amber Room

★ Green Dining Room

Exploring Tsarskoe Selo

The magnificent parks and gardens of Tsarskoe Selo (the Tsar's Village) were created out of dense forest by thousands of soldiers and labourers. Work began on the formal gardens in 1744 but later, in 1768, Catherine the Great commissioned one of Russia's first landscaped parks. The 567 hectares (1,400 acres) of grounds are dotted with captivating pavilions set around the central lake. The grounds and the town of Tsarskoe Selo, to the northeast of the palace, are also a delight to explore.

Formal gardens in front of Catherine Palace, Catherine Park

Catherine Park

The formal gardens to the southeast of the palace are laid out geometrically with radiating avenues, parterres and terraces, decorative ponds, hedges, elegant pavilions and Classical statuary. Nearest to the palace are Cameron's **Agate Rooms** (1780–87), which are currently closed. Their heavily rusticated lower storey contrasts with the upper tier, modelled on a Renaissance villa. The building takes its name from the agate, jasper and malachite covering the interior.

The impressive **Cameron Gallery**, built in 1783–7, has a rusticated stone ground floor, surmounted by a Neo-Classical peristyle of 44 Ionic columns. Ranged along the colonnade are bronze busts of ancient philosophers, poets and rulers. In 1792–4 Cameron added a long stone ramp to facilitate access to the gardens for the ageing Catherine the Great. The Neo-Classical **Lower and Upper Baths** were built by Ilya Neyelov in 1777–80. The domed Lower Baths were for the use of courtiers while the exquisite Upper Baths were reserved for members of the imperial family. Construction work on Rastrelli's **Grotto** began in 1749, but the original decoration of the interior with more than 250,000 shells continued well into the 1770s.

The gardens' main avenue leads to the **Hermitage** (1756), a Baroque pavilion built by Rastrelli, where Elizabeth would entertain small groups of guests for dinner.

The romantic landscaped area of the lower park was begun in 1768 by master gardeners such as John Bush, who worked under the overall supervision of the architect, Vasiliy Neyelov. A 16-km (10-mile) waterway was built to feed the numerous canals, cascades and man-made lakes,

Girl with a Pitcher by Pavel Sokolov (1816)

including the *pièce de résistance*, the **Great Pond**. From Giacomo Quarenghi's pavilion (1786) on the island, musicians would serenade Catherine and her courtiers as they floated by in gilded gondolas.

A naval theme links Vasiliy Neyelov's Dutch, Neo-Gothic **Admiralty** (1773–7) with the 25-m (82-ft) high **Chesma Column** which is decorated with ships' prows. The column, designed by Antonio Rinaldi in 1771, commemorates the Russian victory over the Turks in the Aegean.

The reflection of the pink dome and minaret of the **Turkish Bath** shimmers in the placid waters on the far side of the lake. Nearby is Neyelov's colonnaded **Marble Bridge** (1770–76). Perched on a rock overlooking the pond is the **Girl with a Pitcher**, a statue by Pavel Sokolov. The figure inspired Pushkin to write his memorable poem, *Fountain at Tsarskoe Selo,* in which he muses on the girl who has broken her urn and now "sits timelessly sad over the timeless stream".

Evidence of the 18th-century craze for chinoiserie can be found on the border with the wilder Alexander Park where Cameron built his **Chinese Village** in 1782–96. Other examples are Yuriy Velten's **Creaking Pavilion**, designed to creak when visitors entered, and Neyelov's **Great Caprice** (1770s), a hump-backed bridge surmounted by a pagoda-like columned structure.

The Moorish-style Turkish Baths (1852) by Ippolito Monighetti

Creaking Pavilion (1778–86)

The Town of Tsarskoe Selo
This town of 99,000 inhabitants was developed in the 19th century as a summer resort for the aristocracy. In 1937, it was renamed after the poet Alexander Pushkin *(see p43)* who was educated at the local **Lycée** in 1811–17 and is also referred to as Pushkin town. One of Russia's most prestigious schools, it was founded by Alexander I in 1811 to educate members of the nobility.

The attractive **Church of the Sign** (1734) is one of the town's oldest buildings. In a garden next door a statue by Roman Bach depicts Pushkin dressed in the Lycée uniform.

Pushkin and his new bride, Natalya, spent the summer of 1831 in the delightful wooden house, now named **Pushkin's Dacha**. The writer, Nikolai Gogol, was amongst the many friends they entertained here.

On the town's western edge is the **Alexander Palace**, commissioned by Catherine for her grandson, the future Alexander I. Designed in 1792 by Giacomo Quarenghi, the austere, Neo-Classical building has a colonnaded façade and protruding wings. It was the residence of Russia's last tsar, Nicholas II and his family from 1904 until their arrest in 1917 *(see p28)*. There is an exhibition inside.

Lycée Sadovaya 2. *Tel* 476 6411. 10:30am–5pm Wed–Mon. last Fri of month.

Pushkin's Dacha Pushkinskaya 2/19. *Tel* 476 6990. 10:30am–5:30pm Wed–Sun. last Fri of month. **Alexander Palace** Dvortsovaya 2. *Tel* 466 6669. 10am–6pm Wed–Mon. last Wed of month. www.tzar.ru

Alexander Pushkin's statue (1900), by Roman Bach

TSARSKOE SELO PARK

0 metres   500
0 yards   500
Key to Symbols *see back flap*

Imperial standard of the Romanovs flying at the Catherine Palace ▷

Pavlovsk ⑥

Павловск
Pavlovsk

To celebrate the birth of his heir, Catherine the Great presented her son, the Grand Duke Paul, with these lands in 1777. She also "gave" him her favourite architect, Charles Cameron, to design both palace and park. Work at Pavlovsk (from "Pavel" or Paul) began in 1780 and was continued by Paul's grieving widow, Maria Fyodorovna, long after his death. "English gardens" were at the height of fashion and inspired Cameron's design of a seemingly natural landscape dotted with pavilions (used for informal parties), romantic ruins and attractive vistas around the Slavyanka river.

Cold Baths
This austere pavilion was built by Cameron in 1799 as a summer swimming pool, complete with elegant vestibule, paintings, furniture and rich wall upholstery.

The Apollo Colonnade
Cameron's colonnade (1782–83) encircles a copy of the Apollo Belvedere, above a romantically dilapidated cascade.

Three Graces Pavilion

The Centaur Bridge by Voronikhin (1805) nestles on a bend of the Slavyanka river.

Aviary

Cameron's Dairy (1782) housed both a milking shed and a stylish salon.

★ Pavlovsk Palace
Cameron's elegant Palladian mansion (1782–6) forms the central block of today's palace (see pp160–1), with wings added in 1789 by Paul's favoured architect, Vincenzo Brenna.

★ Temple of Friendship
This Doric temple (1780) was the first use of Greek forms in Russia.

Green Woman Alley

Pavlovsk Railway Station

Visconti Bridge
One of the most famous bridges which cross the winding Slavyanka, it was designed by Andrey Voronikhin in 1807.

VISITORS' CHECKLIST

Pavlovsk. **Tel** 452 1536. 🚃 from Vitebskiy, Kupchino or Moscovskay stations, then bus 370, 383, 493, K-286, K-299, K-513 (see p228). **Grounds** ⬚ daily. 🎫 May–Nov 10am–5pm. **Palace** ⬚ 10am–5pm Sat–Thu. ⬤ winter: first Mon of month. 🅿 🍴 🛍 🚻 🎧 English. www.pavlovskmuseum.ru

The Étoile
The Étoile, the earliest landscaped area in the park, was laid out by Cameron in 1780. The circle of statues represents the nine Muses, protectresses of the arts and sciences.

The Beautiful Valley was the favourite spot of Elizabeth, wife of Alexander I.

| 0 metres | 200 |
| 0 yards | 200 |

Paul's Mausoleum (1808–9) bears the inscription "To my beneficent consort".

The Rose Pavilion was the favourite haunt of Maria Fyodorovna from 1812. She held many concerts and literary evenings in this cottage.

STAR FEATURES

★ Temple of Friendship

★ Great Palace

Pil Tower and Bridge
Brenna's tower (1795–7) contained a spiral staircase, lounge and library. The bridge was a later addition made in 1808.

Exploring Pavlovsk Palace

Late 18th-century clock, Grecian Hall

Catherine commissioned Charles Cameron to build the Great Palace (1782–6) whilst Paul and his wife Maria Fyodorovna travelled around Europe incognito as the Comte and Comtesse du Nord. They, meanwhile, bought up everything they saw including French clocks, Sèvres porcelain, tapestries and furniture, to fill their new home. Once back in Russia, they brought in Brenna to add taller, more elaborate wings to Cameron's elegant Palladian mansion, turning it into a true palace.

West façade of the Palladian mansion

PLAN OF PAVLOVSK PALACE, FIRST FLOOR

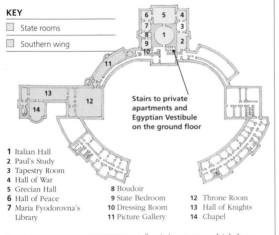

KEY

☐ State rooms

☐ Southern wing

Stairs to private apartments and Egyptian Vestibule on the ground floor

1 Italian Hall
2 Paul's Study
3 Tapestry Room
4 Hall of War
5 Grecian Hall
6 Hall of Peace
7 Maria Fyodorovna's Library
8 Boudoir
9 State Bedroom
10 Dressing Room
11 Picture Gallery
12 Throne Room
13 Hall of Knights
14 Chapel

STATE ROOMS

The Italian Hall, originally by Cameron and Brenna, 1789

Nearly all of the palace apartments at Pavlovsk, including the official ones, are relatively modest in scale. They reflect Maria Fyodorovna's intensely feminine tastes which have given Pavlovsk a distinct charm rather than grandeur.

A fire in 1803 necessitated some remodelling of the palace interiors by Andrey Voronikhin. The entrance hall, or Egyptian Vestibule, gained its present appearance after he added the painted bronze figures and zodiac medallions. At the top of the stairs is Brenna's State Vestibule, where the bas-reliefs reflected Paul's passion for all things military. It leads onto the Italian Hall, situated beneath the central cupola, with lantern windows and heavy doors of rosewood and mahogany.

The northern row of rooms on this floor were for Paul, the southern ones for Maria. Paul's Study is dominated by Johann Lampi's fine portrait of Maria (1794), who holds a drawing of six of their children. Beneath it is a model temple of amber, ivory and gilded bronze, made by Maria herself. Next door, the Tapestry Room is named after the Don Quixote tapestries made by Gobelin and presented to Paul by Louis XVI. The mahogany writing table was actually made for Mikhaylovskiy Castle (*see p101*) but, after Paul's murder there in 1801 (*see p22*), Maria moved much of the specially designed furniture to Pavlovsk Palace.

The corner rooms are a Hall of War for Paul and Maria's contrasting Hall of Peace, both richly adorned with bas-reliefs and heavy gilding. Between the two lies the magnificent Grecian Hall, Cameron's Neo-Classical masterpiece.

Maria Fyodorovna's rooms commence with a small, comfortable library. The chair at the desk was designed for her by Voronikhin; note the pots built into the spine for flowers. Her Boudoir has pilasters painted with motifs copied from the Raphael Loggias in the Vatican, and a porphyry fireplace. The State Bedroom was reputedly never slept in, but was part of court ceremony. Opposite the

Maria Fyodorovna's Boudoir, designed by Brenna, 1789

Brenna's Picture Gallery (1789), with chandeliers by Johann Zeck

bed is a 64-piece Sèvres toilet set, complete with a coffee cup and an eye bath, which was a gift from Marie Antoinette.

Another present dominates the Dressing Room, a superb set of steel furniture including dressing table, chair, vases and ink stand made by the renowned gun-makers of Tula (1789). This was presented to Maria by Catherine the Great.

SOUTHERN WING

From the elegantly curved picture gallery, built in 1798, there are excellent views. Only a few of the paintings, mostly purchased during the young couple's trip to France, are worthy of special notice, as their taste was for applied art.

The largest room in the palace is the Throne Room, designed by Brenna (1797) after Paul became tsar. Despite its name it was generally used for balls and state dinners. The tables are now laid with part of a 606-piece gilded dinner service. Vast blue Sèvres vases

stand on plinths, bought directly from the factory (Paul and Maria spent huge sums on porcelain there alone). The ceiling was painted during restoration after World War II *(see p26)*, and is taken from an original design which was never used.

The Knights of St John chose Paul as Grand Master when they fled Napoleon's occupation of Malta in 1798. This suited Paul's military taste and he commissioned vast lamps, thrones and decorative items (now in the Hermitage), as well as the Hall of Knights, for ceremonies of the Order. The pale green room is adorned with Classical statues, saved from the Germans in World War II by being buried in the grounds.

The suite of rooms ends with the Imperial Chapel of SS Peter and Paul, a very un-Orthodox church by Brenna (1797–8), decorated with copies of European paintings.

PRIVATE APARTMENTS

Located on the ground floor are the private apartments. The Pilaster Room (1800), with its golden pilasters, is furnished with a dark mahogany suite. The Lantern Study, designed a few years later by Voronikhin, is named after its apsed bay window forming the "lantern".

Maria Fyodorovna's Dressing Room leads into the Bedroom (1805) she actually used (as opposed to the State Bedroom upstairs). Pieces of the original silk were saved in the war and used to edge the new curtains.

The small pink and blue Ballroom was for private parties and hung with paintings by the most fashionable artist of the day, Hubert Robert. The General Study, used as a family sitting room, is decorated with portraits of the family. The Raspberry Room, Paul's private study, contains paintings with views of Gatchina Palace, made for Mikhaylovskiy Castle.

The Lantern Study, one of Voronikhin's most successfully designed interiors, 1804

MARIA FYODOROVNA (1759–1828)

Paul's wife, Maria Fyodorovna, bore 10 children, and Pavlovsk was considered her 11th child. Paul himself preferred Gatchina *(see p147)* and in 1788 Maria was given Pavlovsk entirely. She devoted all her energy to adorning both palace and park, giving precise directions to designers and architects, who bemoaned their lack of independence. Born Sophia of Württemberg-Stuttgart, Maria had a practical German upbringing which she put to good use. Pieces of her own work, from furniture to family portraits, are throughout the palace.

Inkstand (1795) created from an initial design by Maria Fyodorovna

Novgorod ❼

Detail of bronze door on Cathedral of St Sophia

The ancient town of Novgorod (New Town) was founded in 859 by the Varangian (Viking) Prince Rurik *(see p17)*. The city's proud tradition of self-government began in the 11th century and lasted until 1478, when Ivan III subjugated the city. Favourably sited on the River Volkhov with convenient connections from Scandinavia to the Aegean, the city of Novgorod became a powerful trading community during this period. In 1570, Ivan the Terrible put Novgorod to the sword, torturing and massacring thousands of its inhabitants when the city plotted against him. It was, however, the rise of St Petersburg which finally set the seal on Novgorod's decline. Much of the city's splendid cultural heritage, damaged in World War II, has been restored and can be appreciated in the many medieval churches and picturesque streets of the old town.

The Kremlin

Situated on the left bank, or Sofiskaya Storona (Sophia side), of the River Volkhov, the formidable red-brick walls and cone-topped towers of the oval-shaped Detinets, or Kremlin, date from the 11th to the 17th centuries. According to the prevailing practice at the time, the first stone of the original walls was laid on the body of a living child.

Of the many towers, the 17th-century Kukui is the most remarkable, and also the tallest at 32m (105ft). The lower floors once contained a wine cellar and treasury chamber, while the octagonal room beneath the cupola was used, according to chronicles, "for surveying the whole town".

Kremlin walls, with the silver dome of St Sophia's Belfry (15th century)

At the heart of the fortress is Novgorod's oldest and largest church, the strongly Byzantine **Cathedral of St Sophia** (1045–62). It was modelled on the cathedral of the same name in Kiev, but the tendencies of the Novgorod school already appear in the lack of ornament and the scarcity of windows,

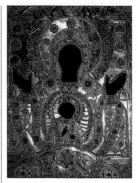

Bejewelled metal icon cover on display in the Chamber of Facets

necessary because of the cold. On the north wall a section of whitewash has been removed to reveal the original mosaic effect of the grey-yellow stone and brick façade.

The exquisitely sculpted and extremely rare bronze doors adorning the west side were seized as booty in 1187 from the Swedish town of Sigtuna. In the lower left hand corner there are portraits of the craftsmen, named in the Latin inscription as Riquin and Weissmut. The interior is divided by piers into five aisles, three ending in altar apses. Fragments of early frescoes survive, but the icon-ostasis is one of the oldest in Russia and contains icons from the 11th–17th centuries.

East of the cathedral is **St Sophia's Belfry**, much altered since it was first built in 1439. The bells, now displayed below, were cast in the late 16th and early 17th centuries.

The northwest corner of the Kremlin is occupied by the **Archbishops' Court**, in its heyday a powerful body with its own treasury, police force and military guard. Beneath the 15th-century clock tower an attractive staircase leads to the **Library**, housing magnificent medieval religious manuscripts. Backing onto the cathedral, the **Chamber of Facets** is the most famous part of this ensemble. A superb reception hall with star-shaped vaulting dates from 1433 and displays treasures from the cathedral, including jewelled mitres and icon covers in precious metals.

The 11th-century Cathedral of St Sophia, the landmark of Novgorod

Within the Kremlin is the **Museum of History, Architecture and Art**, which houses a magnificent collection of 12th–17th-century icons of the Novgorod school. One of the most remarkable is the 12th-century portable icon of the Virgin of the Sign, whose miraculous image is said to have saved Novgorod from the armies of Prince Andrey Bogolyubskiy of Suzdal in 1169. Scenes from the battle are depicted on a vibrant 15th-century icon *(see p165)*. There are also works by leading 18th- and 19th-century artists, including Dmitriy Levitskiy, Karl Bryullov and Vasiliy Serov *(see p106)*. The museum has a number of precious public documents and private letters written on birch bark, some of which date from the 11th century. These give details of ordinary, everyday life and are evidence of the unusually widespread literacy among the city's inhabitants.

In the Kremlin's central square, the huge, bell-shaped **Millennium Monument** was sculpted by Mikhail Mikeshin. The monument was unveiled in 1862, a thousand years after Rurik's arrival in Novgorod. The figure kneeling before the Orthodox cross personifies Mother Russia while, below, the decorative frieze depicts Rurik, Ivan III, Mikhail (the first Romanov tsar), Peter the Great and many others. The frieze around the base shows over 100 figures: heroes, statesmen, artists, composers, princes and chroniclers.

The carved Royal Gates of an iconostasis in the Museum of History, Architecture and Art

Yaroslav's Court

Across the River Volkhov was the official seat of the princes, known as Yaroslav's Court. The palace of Yaroslav the Wise (1019–54) has since disappeared but several churches have survived. The area adjacent to the Court is Novgorod's

VISITORS' CHECKLIST

190 km (118 miles) S of St Petersburg. 🏘 240,000. 🚇 *from Moscow Station.* 🚌 *from Coach Station (see p221).* 🛈 *Intourist Hotel, ul Velikaya 16, (8162) 775089.*

commercial centre, once the site of the medieval market, part of whose wall still stands.

The oldest church on this side of the river, **St Nicholas' Cathedral** (1113–36), was built by Prince Mstislav. It dominates the area and once symbolized the prince's power.

Novgorod's merchants were keen to show their recognition of God's hand in their prosperity, and so funded many of the city's churches. **St Paraskeva Pyatnitsa**, erected in 1207 and then rebuilt in 1345, was dedicated to the patron saint of commerce. The more decorative **Church of the Holy Women** and **Church of St Procopius**, both 16th century, were financed by wealthy Moscow merchants. The fanciful tastes of the Muscovite patrons mark a departure from Novgorod's austere style.

🟥 Cathedral of St Sophia
Tel (8162) 773556.
◯ 10am–6pm daily.
🏛 Chamber of Facets
Tel (8162) 773608. ◯ 10am–6pm Thu–Tue. 🗟 🖅 English by appt.

🏛 Museum of History, Architecture and Art
Tel (8162) 773770. ◯ 10am–6pm Wed–Mon. 🗟 🖅 English by appt.

Millennium Monument, celebrating Novgorod's 1,000 years of history

Yuriev Monastery walls and bell tower with the silvery domes of the Cathedral of St George in the background

Beyond Yaroslav's Court

In the 12th century, Novgorod boasted over 200 churches, while there are only 30 today. Many of these are hidden away in the quiet hinterland of 19th-century streets to the east of Yaroslav's Court. On Ilyina ulitsa, the arrangement of windows, niches and inset crosses on the **Church of the Saviour of the Transfiguration** façade (1374) is almost whimsical. Inside, there are original frescoes by one of Russia's greatest medieval artists, Theophanes the Greek (1335–c.1410), who came from Constantinople and decorated 40 Russian churches. Andrey Rublev (1360–1430), Russia's most famous icon painter, worked under Theophanes at the beginning of his career.

On the same street, the five-domed **Znamenskiy Cathedral**, or Cathedral of the Sign (1682–8), has an attractive gateway and faded frescoes on the outer walls. The beautiful interior was decorated in 1702 by Ivan Bakhmatov.

The **Church of Theodore Stratilates** on Mstinskaya ulitsa to the north was built in 1360–61 by the widow of a wealthy Novgorod merchant. The delicate purple and pink

Fresco inside Znamenskiy Cathedral

frescoes contrast with the harsher colours found in most 14th-century Novgorod frescoes. *The Annunciation,* for example, combines sensitivity and charm with religious intensity.

Further Afield

A pleasant stroll 3 km (2 miles) south along the river bank leads to the **Yuriev Monastery**. This is the area's largest and most important monastery, founded in 1030 and built on the orders of Prince Vsevolod. Its imposing Cathedral of St George was built in 1119–30 by "Master Peter", the first named architect in Russian chronicles. This beautifully proportioned church with its

three asymmetrical cupolas was restored in the 19th century, and unfortunately most of the interior murals were lost. There were once 20 monastic buildings in the complex, dating mainly from the 19th century.

In the woods across the road lies the fascinating open-air **Museum of Wooden Architecture**, which displays churches and peasant huts moved from local villages. Of particular interest are the 17th-century two-tiered Kuritsko Church of the Dormition and the tiny wooden church of St Nicholas from Tukhel village.

🏛 Yuriev Monastery
Yurevskaya nab. *Tel* (8162) 773020. ⏱ 10am–6pm daily.

🏛 Museum of Wooden Architecture (Vitoslavlitsi)
Yurevo. *Tel* (8162) 773770. ⏱ May–Sep: 10am–8pm daily; Oct–Apr: 10am–6pm daily. 🖼 📷

A 19th-century peasant hut *(izba),* Museum of Wooden Architecture

Russian Icon Painting

The Russian Orthodox Church uses icons for both worship and teaching, but never for mere ornament, and there are strict rules for the creation of each image. Icons were believed to be imbued with the force of the saint depicted, and were therefore invoked for protection during wars. Because the content was considered more important than the style, old, revered icons were often repainted again and again.

Early stone icon found in Novgorod

The first icons were brought to Russia from Byzantium. Greek masters came too, to train local painters. The northern schools which developed during the 13th–15th centuries were less restricted by Byzantine canons and have an earthy style linked to Russian peasant life. Novgorod, never under the Mongol yoke and with a thriving economy, was the source of many of the finest icons made for the northern monasteries.

Virgin of Vladimir
The most venerated icon in Russia, this 12th-century work was made in Constantinople. Its huge influence on Russian icon painting cannot be overstated.

Battle of Novgorod and Suzdal
This mid-15th century work of the Novgorod School is thought to be Russia's earliest historical painting. Icons could have a political purpose – in this case to use Novgorod's great past as a justification for its independence from Moscow. Note the multiple touches of red – a colour central to everyday Russian life and typical for icons of the Novgorod School.

THE ICONOSTASIS

The iconostasis screens off the sanctuary from the main part of the church, as if it were a boundary between heaven and earth. In Russian practice it is covered with icons strictly arranged in up to six tiers, each with its own dogmatic purpose.

The Festival Tier shows the 12 major church festivals, such as the Entry into Jerusalem and the Crucifixion. Such pictorial representation aided the faith of the illiterate.

Christ Enthroned

The Deesis Tier, above the Royal Gates, contains Christ Enthroned, flanked by the Virgin and St John interceding on behalf of mortal sinners.

The Royal Gates represent the entrance from the temporal world to the spiritual, between which the priests pass during the service.

The Local Tier is for local saints, those the church is dedicated to and patron saints of major donors.

Old Testament Trinity by Rublev
Andrey Rublev was one of the greatest artists of the Moscow School. He was strongly influenced by recent developments in Byzantine painting, brought to Russia by Greek masters in the late 14th century. His Trinity icon dates from the early 15th century.

TRAVELLERS' NEEDS

WHERE TO STAY

With space in the historic centre of the city at a premium, new hotels nontheless continue to open. The city has sprouted many "mini-hotels" (privately run establishments in or near the centre with anything from 4 to 15 rooms), and investors have opened large, luxury hotels in outstanding locations. The quality of service in the larger hotels is as good as that on offer in Western Europe. Many tourists visiting in the summer with a package tour, however, are still housed in large, somewhat anonymous hotels outside the

Doorman at Hotel Europe

centre. These provide reasonable service and full amenities such as restaurants, bars and fitness facilities. Travelling outside the White Nights period cuts costs and opens up the opportunity for booking one of the many excellent deals available at more central hotels. Bookings can be made independently or via an agency. For the summer months, particularly during the White Nights, reservations should be made well in advance for accommodation at all price levels. There is a selection of hotels on *pp174–7*.

Park Inn Pribaltiyskaya, a popular hotel for package tours (see p177)

WHERE TO LOOK

There are few large, inexpensive hotels in central St Petersburg. Many of those listed in this chapter are scattered around the city. Visitors on a package tour usually find themselves staying in a former Intourist hotel such as the Park Inn Pribaliyskaya or Pulkovskaya, situated in modern high-rise areas on the city's outskirts. Mini hotels and bed-and-breakfast establishments, by contrast, are frequently found in quiet streets near the centre. Independent travellers should consider their priorities from the start: is it location, price or facilities?

HOW TO BOOK

Hotel reservations for the White Nights *(see p51)* should be made several months in advance, and as early as possible for the more popular

establishments. Nearly all hotels can now be booked online or by fax. The larger hotels will require travellers to supply a credit card number, and money will be debited if a cancellation is made less than 72 hours in advance. Some of the smaller hotels can be booked through one of the agencies listed on page 171. All hotels and agencies recommended can provide visa support *(see p208)*, unless stated otherwise.

FACILITIES

Rooms in all the hotels listed include at least a shower, a television and a telephone. Most have air conditioning. Large hotels have a luggage room for storing baggage after the midday check-out time. Bars frequently work at night, and extensive fitness and sauna facilities are more or less standard features in bigger establishments.

PRICE

The most important thing to remember in St Petersburg is that prices in big hotels more than double for the six weeks or so of the White Nights and for the World Economic Forum in early June. These higher prices are quoted throughout the hotel listings *(see pp174–7)*. Normal prices return during the "mid-season", usually April–May and late July–late September. Outside that period, particularly during the "White Days" of winter, there are frequently excellent deals to be had.

Large central hotels, it should be noted, nearly all fall into the luxury category, and offer everything from exclusive single rooms to imperial suites costing several thousand dollars a day. By opting for a smaller hotel

Fitness centre at the Grand Hotel Europe (see p175)

◁ **Floating bars on the Moyka river**

with fewer facilities or a bed and breakfast (usually a small, basic hotel rather than a family home), you can be just as central for much less money. Many smaller hotels have only shower cabins, not full baths.

Note that prices are not displayed in hotels, and that only some small hotels and hostels take credit cards. To avoid upset, it is important to be prepared to pay in cash.

Entrance to the luxurious, modern Corinthia Nevskij Palace *(see p176)*

HIDDEN EXTRAS

Large hotels, which provide visa support and obligatory passport registration *(see p208)* for free, often do not include local taxes or breakfast in the prices they quote. Both of these can be a significant addition to the final bill. (The price categories used in the hotel listings on pages 174–7 include both breakfast and taxes.) Be warned that the cost of making international or even local phone calls from your room in the large hotels is likely to be prohibitive. On the other hand, phones which use the local network are relatively cheap and phone-cards can be purchased to make international calls from street booths or fixed phones *(see p216)*. In smaller hotels, breakfast tends to be included in the price, but you should expect to pay extra for the initial visa support. Calls from phones in small hotels and hostels may be free or very cheap if they use the local telephone system. Phonecards can be used to make interna-tional calls from such phones.

SECURITY

Some top-range establishments have metal detectors and selec-tive bag searches at entrances. Smaller hotels have a door-man, who may ask to see a visitor's card or identification. Since this is simply a precau-tion for guests' protection, there is no reason to object.

Most hotels have safes in the rooms and/or security deposit boxes at the front desk. Large sums of money and valuables should always be left in one of these places.

DISABLED TRAVELLERS

Due to the thick snow in winter, most buildings in St Petersburg have steps up to their entrances, making access extremely difficult for disabled visitors. Only a few of the élite hotels are fully wheelchair accessible, with staff trained to be of assistance, although other hotels are increasingly adding ramps, widening doors and trying to adapt to meet the needs of disabled travellers.

Room in the Grand Hotel Europe *(see p175)*

Those with special require-ments should contact their preferred hotel before booking.

CHILDREN

St Petersburg has never been vaunted as a great children's destination, and few hotels cater specifically for families. It is, however, possible to arrange babysitters in all the large hotels, and increasingly in some of the smaller hotels. It is worth checking the situation before you book.

The elegant Winter Garden restaurant in the Astoria Hotel *(see p174)*

MINI-HOTELS

St Petersburg has a very good range of mini-hotels available; far too many to list in full. The best, however, are included in this guide's hotel listings (see pp174–7).

Not necessarily a truly budget option – because some are extremely luxurious – the city's extensive range of mini-hotels, with anything from 4 to 15 or 20 rooms, offer some of the most comfortable and pleasant accommodation available. And the personalized service on offer is often hard to beat.

Many mini-hotels can be booked through agencies, notably **Ostwest**, **City Realty** and **Eridan Travel Company**, which include a selection on their websites.

Interior of the Petro Palace hotel
(see p174)

BUDGET ACCOMMODATION

Truly cheap accommodation is hard to find in St Petersburg. If hostels are not for you but your budget is tight, choose one of the more modest mini-hotels, which usually describe themselves as "bed and breakfast". This usually means they offer a small number of rooms in a converted flat in an ordinary building, with a housekeeper who makes breakfast in the apartment's kitchen. There may be a shared toilet rather than separate facilities.

Accommodation agencies such as Ostwest, **STN** and City Realty also offer short-term apartment rental, which can be very cheap for a group of friends who are sharing. The apartments are refurbished and central, with anything from one to five rooms, usually with satellite TV.

Efficient and helpful Sindbad Travel Centre at the St Petersburg International Youth Hostel

In many cases, although the apartment has been refurbished, the communal staircase to the building may be a little on the grubby side. This grittiness can be off-putting at first, but it does offer the feel of living in the true St Petersburg.

The best way to cut costs is, of course, to give up hopes of seeing the White Nights, and travel in the off season. Mini-hotels and short-let apartments can be extremely cheap at this time of year, and even the big hotels offer excellent deals. April can be dry and sunny, if still cold, and October can be beautiful, particularly if you catch the brief northern autumn. Travelling in February more or less guarantees the vision of a Russia covered in snow.

HOSTELS

For the budget traveller seeking comfortable accommodation in a reasonably central location, there are now several centrally located hostels to choose from. All offer visa support and registration and are extremely friendly. **St Petersburg International**

Youth Hostel, with its attached budget travel company, **Sindbad Travel Centre**, is best known and is often booked up well in advance. The inexpensive but clean and comfortable **Nord Hostel**, on the other hand, is unmatched for location. You could also try **CubaHostel Backpackers**, which offers a wide selection of cheap accommodation.

None of these are "youth" hostels as such, although young people do tend to dominate in the summer months. In the off season, however, 50 per cent of hostel guests tend to be over-forty.

STAYING WITH FAMILIES

For a really good insight into Russian life, staying with a family can be an interesting and cheap option. The system works very much like any bed and breakfast in Europe, with prices including breakfast but no other meals. Extra meals can usually be provided at a small cost.

HOFA (Host Families Association) and Ostwest have a wide range of families on their books and a particularly good reputation in this area. Your hosts are likely to be extremely hospitable and will tend to overfeed you rather than otherwise. Many of HOFA's hosts are academics, well educated and speak several languages. As a general rule,

Impressive façade of the Oktiabrskaya Hotel, dating from 1847 *(see p176)*

hosts will be keen to talk to you about their life in Russia and Western perceptions of their country.

Many Russian apartments are reached through scruffy entrance halls or decrepit courtyards, but do not let this put you off, as it gives little indication of the quality of the accommodation inside.

CAMPING AND OUTDOOR LIVING

Russians love getting out of town for walks, swimming and mushroom gathering. All are possible on day trips from the city, but staying out of town is more complicated.

St Petersburg's cold winter weather does not make it ideal for camping, though the forests along the north side of the Gulf of Finland are excellent in milder seasons.

Those thinking of renting a *dacha* or small house in the country will find this difficult. Most people with modest

dachas let them to people they know. None of the firms specializing in lets to foreigners deal in *dachas*, and demand within 100 km (62 miles) of the city far outstrips properties available. As a result, rental costs can be exorbitant (about US$5,000 per week). In order to find anything at all, book as early as February. The best range of *dachas* (from around US$500 per week) is available through **Alexander**, but you will need to speak Russian or use a

Dacha in pine forest near Repino on the Gulf of Finland *(see p146)*

travel company that does to make a booking. The best option for cheaper living with modern facilities is to rent a chalet attached to a motel. **Retur Camping** offers chalets, camp sites, a swimming pool, sauna, tennis courts and riding.

EXTENDED STAYS

Those intending to stay in St Petersburg for a month or more will find the cost of renting apartments much cheaper. While hostels do not offer long-term reductions, companies such as City Realty have plenty of flats that are available at more modest rates than those advertised for short lets. Be aware, however, that tourist visas cannot usually be registered *(see p208)* for more than three months, and that a longer stay will require a non-tourist visa arranged through a company that can legally register you for the period you will be in the country.

DIRECTORY

ACCOMMODATION AGENCIES

Alexander
Potemkinskaya ul 13.
Map 3 C4.
Tel 327 1616.
www.anspb.ru

City Realty
Muchnoi per 2.
Map 6 E2.
Tel 570 6342.
Fax 315 9151.
www.cityrealtyrussia.com

Eridan Travel Company
Ul Artilleriyskaya 1,
Business Centre Europa
House, Office 619.
Map 3 B5.
Tel 324 23 05.
Fax 322 57 38.
www.rus-tours.com

HOFA Host Families Association
Tavricheskaya ul 5,
Apartment 25.
Map 4 D5.
Tel 7911 7665464.
Fax 275 1992.
www.hofa.ru

MIR Travel Company
Nevskiy pr 11/2.
Map 6 D1. *Tel* 325 2595.
Fax 315 3001.
www.mir-travel.com

Ostwest
Ligovskiy pr 10.
Map 7 C2. *Tel* 327 3416.
Fax 327 3417.
www.ostwest.com

Sindbad Travel Centre
2-ya Sovetskaya ulitsa 12.
Map 7 C2. *Tel* 332 2020.

STN
Nevisky pr 66/29.
Map 7 A2.
Tel 337 1223.
Fax 310 6717.
www.2piter.com

MINI-HOTEL NETWORKS

Anabel
Tel 717 0800.
www.mini-hotel.com

Filippov Hotels
Tel 274 5363.
Fax 274 9084.
www.filippovhotel.ru

Hotels on Nevsky
Tel 703 3860.
Fax 703 3861.
www.hon.ru

Rinaldi Bed & Breakfast
Tel 325 4188.
Fax 325 4189.
www.rinaldi.ru

HOSTELS

CubaHostel Backpackers
Kazanskaya ul 5.
Map 6 E2. *Tel* 921 7115.
www.cubahostel.ru

Hostel All Seasons
Yakovlevskiy per 11.
Tel 327 1070.
Fax 327 1033.
www.hostel.ru

Na Muchnom
Sadovaya ul 25.
Map 6 E2.
Tel/Fax 310 0412.
www.namuchnom.ru

Nord Hostel
Bolshaya Morskaya ul 10.
Map 6 D1.
Tel/Fax 571 0342.
www.nordhostel.com

Prima Sport Hotel
Nevskiy prospekt 5.
Map 6 D1.
Tel/Fax 346 5049.
www.comfitelhotel.com

St Petersburg International Youth Hostel
3-ya Sovetskaya ul 28.
Map 7 C2.
Tel 717 0569.
Fax 329 8018.
www.ryh.ru

Useful Website
www.russia-hostelling.ru

CAMPING

Retur Camping
Bolshaya Kupalnaya str.
28, Sestroretsk.
26 km (16 miles)
NW of St Petersburg.
Tel 434 5022.
Fax 437 7533.
www.retur-motel.ru

Popular Hotels in St Petersburg

Accommodation in St Petersburg is extremely varied and there are many hotels from which to choose. Unfortunately few of the most affordable are conveniently situated for the city centre and it is important to decide on your priorities, be it location, price, character, service or amenities. This selection represents the city's most popular hotels.

Prestige Hotel
This hotel (see p174) is tucked away on a small residential street. Stay here and feel like a local, but with all modern comforts.

Rennaisance St Petersburg Baltic
Central and prestigious, yet set apart from the hurly-burly of Nevskiy prospekt, the Baltic feels like a small hotel while offering "big" hotel service (see p174).

Azimut Hotel St Petersburg
This 1970s hotel (see p176) offers wonderful views of the city centre from its bar. At sunset or during White Nights the vista is particularly magical.

Astoria Hotel
One of the city's most luxurious and centrally located hotels, the Astoria (see p174) is perfect for exploring St Petersburg on foot. The attractive building overlooks St Isaac's Square and Cathedral.

St Petersburg
The package-holiday tourists who usually stay here get a wonderful, sweeping view across the broad expanse of the River Neva, towards Palace Embankment, from the bel-étage (see p177).

Grand Hotel Europe
Situated in the heart of the city, this historic hotel (see p175) *is one of the finest in St Petersburg. Elegant decor and refined service are complemented by many facilities.*

Hotel Dostoevsky
Located just a stone's throw from the tourist heart of St Petersburg, the Dostoevsky (see p176) *combines old and new, historical and modern, in both its design and its service.*

Park Inn Pulkovskaya
Comfortable and clean, this vast modern hotel (see p176) *has many business facilities, including an auditorium. The hotel's main advantage is its proximity to the airport.*

| 0 kilometres | 2 |
| 0 miles | 2 |

Choosing a Hotel

Hotels have been selected across a wide price range for facilities, good value and location. All rooms have a shower, TV, telephone and Wi-Fi. The chart lists the hotels by area. Within each area, entries are organized alpha-betically within each price category, from the least to the most expensive. For map references, *see pp238–45.*

PRICE CATEGORIES
The following price ranges are for a double room per night, including taxes and breakfast, during the high season. In the low season, prices can halve.
Ⓡ Under 3,000 roubles
ⓇⓇ 3,000–5,200 roubles
ⓇⓇⓇ 5,200–7,500 roubles
ⓇⓇⓇⓇ 7,500–9,700 roubles
ⓇⓇⓇⓇⓇ over 9,700 roubles

CITY CENTRE

VASILEVSKIY ISLAND Prestige Hotel Престиж отель   ⓇⓇ
Malyy prospekt 27, Vasilevskiy ostrov **Tel** 328 5011 **Fax** 328 5011 **Rooms** 10   **Map** 1 A4

This is a modern hotel, set in a restored 19th-century building on a residential street on Vasilevskiy Island, just a short walk away from the Strelka and the sights, and the shops and bustling atmosphere around Vasileostrovskaya metro station. There is no lift, but there are few floors. **www.prestige-hotels.com**

VASILEVSKIY ISLAND Shelfort Шелфорт   ⓇⓇⓇ
3-ya liniya 26, Vasilevskiy ostrov **Tel** 328 0555 **Fax** 323 5154 **Rooms** 15   **Map** 1 A5

Set on a quiet residential street a short walk from the Strelka, the Shelfort has good, plain interiors with beautifully restored tiled stoves. Two luxury suites have fireplaces; one also has a balcony. The hotel does not have a lift, but consists of ground and first floors only (wheelchair users can request a room on the ground floor). **www.shelfort.ru**

PALACE EMBANKMENT Prestige Hotel Centre Престиж отель центр   🗐🖺   ⓇⓇ
Gorokhovaya ulitsa 5 **Tel** 312 0405 **Fax** 315 9357 **Rooms** 45   **Map** 6 D1

A modest hotel in a plain building, tucked away by the Admiralty Gardens. Rooms are furnished with simple, inexpensive metal and plastic furniture; most have a shower but not a bath. The on-site bistro and café serve a variety of Russian dishes. The friendly concierge can book cars. **www.prestige-hotels.com**

PALACE EMBANKMENT Comfort Комфорт   🗔🗐🗖   ⓇⓇⓇ
Bolshaya Morskaya ulitsa 25 **Tel** 570 6700 **Fax** 570 6700 **Rooms** 18   **Map** 6 D2

Despite limited facilities, the Comfort offers excellent value for money by virtue of its helpful staff and unbeatable location at the heart of the historic centre, which is packed with restaurants. Rooms are unfussy and airy. Cots are available. One suite is adapted for use as an office by those visiting on business. **www.comfort-hotel.org**

PALACE EMBANKMENT Casa Leto   🗐   ⓇⓇⓇⓇ
Bolshaya Morskaya ulitsa 34 **Tel** 600 1096 **Fax** 3146639 **Rooms** 5   **Map** 6 D2

Run by an Italian-Russian couple, this tiny establishment is arguably the best of the "mini hotels". It boasts light-filled rooms, many complimentary extras and a superb central location. Personal service includes business support, and tour and ticket booking. The Trezzini Suite has a shower only; others also have a bath. **www.casaleto.com**

PALACE EMBANKMENT Petro Palace Отель Петро палас   🗔🍴🖺🗐🗖   ⓇⓇⓇ
Malaya Morskaya ulitsa 14 **Tel** 571 2880 **Fax** 571 1686 **Rooms** 193   **Map** 6 D1

An elegant hotel that attracts many wealthy Russians as well as tourists. Its extensive facilities are unmatched at this price, particularly in the centre, and include a fitness suite, pool and massage services. The renovated and extended 19th-century building offers good views from the seventh floor. **www.petropalacehotel.com**

PALACE EMBANKMENT Angleterre Отель Англетер   🗔🍴🎢🖺🗐🗖   ⓇⓇⓇⓇ
Malaya Morskaya ulitsa 24 **Tel** 494 5666 **Fax** 494 5125 **Rooms** 193   **Map** 6 D2

The Angleterre is the stylishly refurbished, Western-run sister hotel to the slightly superior Astoria next door, whose facilities it shares. There is a rather good lunchtime brasserie. The superb central location on St Isaac's Square is within easy walking distance of the Hermitage and Nevskiy prospekt. **www.angleterrehotel.com**

PALACE EMBANKMENT Astoria Отель Астория   🗔🍴🎢🖺🗐🗖   ⓇⓇⓇⓇⓇ
Isaakievskaya ploshchad, Bolshaya Morskaya ulitsa 39 **Tel** 494 5750 **Fax** 494 5059 **Rooms** 188   **Map** 6 D2

The Astoria's historic interior has the calm and grace of a hotel with a history. Rooms at the front offer outstanding views over St Isaac's Cathedral and Square, and along the river Moyka. You don't have to be staying here to visit for tea in the downstairs lounge. **www.thehotelastoria.com**

PALACE EMBANKMENT Renaissance St Petersburg Baltic   🗔🍴🖺🗐🗖   ⓇⓇⓇⓇ
Pochtamtskaya ulitsa 4a **Tel** 380 4000 **Fax** 380 4001 **Rooms** 102   **Map** 5 C2

An elegant establishment, decorated on the theme of "historic St Petersburg", using old-fashioned materials and modern design. Some rooms offer views over St Isaac's Square, and the area is very quiet. Despite its luxury status, with one of the best fitness suites in the city, the hotel feels cosy. **www.marriot.com/ledbr**

Key to Symbols *see back cover flap*

PALACE EMBANKMENT Taleon Imperial Hotel Талион империал отель

 ⓇⓇⓇⓇⓇ

Naberezhnaya reki Moyki 59 **Tel** *324 9911* **Fax** *324 9957* **Rooms** *89* **Map** *6 D1*

Part of the Taleon Club, this is a luxury hotel, restaurant and fitness complex with benefits for members. There is a wide range of inclusive services, and a personal valet for every guest. Events for children are held. Rooms overlook the river Moyka. **www.taleonimperialhotel.com**

GOSTINYY DVOR Polikoff

ⓇⓇⓇ

Karavannaya 11/64, apt 24–26 **Tel** *995 3488* **Fax** *314 7925* **Rooms** *15* **Map** *7 A2*

The interior is clean and unadorned – all blond wood and metal – and very light, even though most rooms overlook a courtyard. Some rooms have air conditioning. The main drawback is the absence of a lift, as all rooms are on the second or third floors (known as the third and fourth in Russia). Service is efficient and friendly. **www.polikoff.ru**

GOSTINYY DVOR Pushka Inn

ⓇⓇⓇ

Naberezhnaya reki Moyki 14 **Tel** *312 0913* **Fax** *314 1055* **Rooms** *33* **Map** *2 E5*

This historic building, right on the river Moyka and next door to the Pushkin Museum, has been transformed into a comfortable, modern hotel. Simple furniture and interiors make no false allusions to wealth or grandeur. It is almost impossible to stay closer to the Hermitage! There are four "apartments" or family suites. **www.pushkainn.ru**

GOSTINYY DVOR Grand Hotel Europe Гранд отель Европа

ⓇⓇⓇⓇⓇ

Mikhaylovskaya ulitsa 1/7 **Tel** *329 6000* **Fax** *329 6001* **Rooms** *301* **Map** *6 F1*

The Europe's facilities may no longer be unique in St Petersburg, but its location just off Nevskiy prospekt is close both to the main sights and to daily city life. There are historic interiors, and a wonderful, airy mezzanine café for coffee and cakes after an exhausting day's sightseeing. **www.grandhoteleurope.com**

GOSTINYY DVOR Kempinski Hotel Moika 22

ⓇⓇⓇⓇⓇ

Naberezhnaya reki Moyki 22 **Tel** *335 9111* **Fax** *3359190* **Rooms** *197* **Map** *2 E5*

Pamper yourself here: take a room with a view over the Hermitage, take lunch in the restaurant with views right across the city, then, maybe, take a Turkish bath to relax after sightseeing, before attending a concert at the Capella next door. A concierge service will help arrange reservations. **www.kempinski.com**

SENNAYA PLOSHCHAD Alexander House Club

ⓇⓇⓇⓇⓇ

Naberezhnaya Kryukova kanala 27 **Tel** *575 3877* **Fax** *575 3879* **Rooms** *19* **Map** *5 C4*

In this family guest house, run as a boutique hotel, each room is named after and decorated in the style of a capital city. Most have views, and the common areas have working fireplaces. Breakfast can be taken in the rooms. Although there is no lift, rooms on the ground floor are accessible by wheelchair. **www.a-house.ru**

SENNAYA PLOSHCHAD Ambassador Hotel

ⓇⓇⓇⓇⓇ

Rimskovo-Korsakova prospekt 5–7 **Tel** *331 8844* **Fax** *331 9300* **Rooms** *251* **Map** *6 D3*

The luxurious rooms at the Ambassador are decorated in pastel shades and all have good views of the city. The hotel is close to several historic sights, including St Nicholas' Cathedral, the Mariinskiy Theatre and the Yusupov Palace. Some rooms are accessible by wheelchair. The fitness centre has a swimming pool. **www.ambassador-hotel.ru**

FURTHER AFIELD

EAST OF THE FONTANKA Arbat Nord Арбат Норд

ⓇⓇⓇ

Artilleriyskaya ulitsa 4 **Tel** *703 1899* **Fax** *703 1898* **Rooms** *33* **Map** *3 B5*

The Arbat Nord is located close to the Summer Gardens and Field of Mars, in the residential and business district, and was built originally for business guests. Today it also caters for tourist groups and individual travellers. Rooms are modern with dark wood and pale walls; some are reserved for non-smokers. Free parking. **www.arbat-nord.ru**

EAST OF THE FONTANKA Brothers Karamazov Братья Карамазовы

ⓇⓇⓇ

Sotsialisticheskaya ulitsa 11a **Tel** *335 1185* **Fax** *335 1186* **Rooms** *28* **Map** *7 A4*

At the heart of Dostoyevsky country, close by the apartment (now a museum, *see p130*) where he wrote *The Brothers Karamazov*. Each room is named after a heroine of one of the author's works. The hotel is airy, decorated mainly in white and cream – no Dostoyevskian tragedy here! **www.karamazovhotel.ru**

EAST OF THE FONTANKA Fifth Corner Business Hotel Пятый угол

ⓇⓇⓇ

Zagorodnyy pr 13 **Tel** *380 8181* **Fax** *380 8181* **Rooms** *34* **Map** *7 A3*

Specifically marketed as a business hotel, with many Russian clients, Fifth Corner emphasizes business-related services. The hotel none the less provides visa and all other support for tourists, including excursions. All rooms are uncluttered and overlook the street, although some only have showers rather than a full bathroom suite. **www.5ugol.ru**

EAST OF THE FONTANKA Moskva Москва

ⓇⓇⓇ

Aleksandra Nevskogo ploshchad 2 **Tel** *274 0022* **Fax** *274 2130* **Rooms** *825* **Map** *8 E3*

The Moskva is the most centrally located of the package-tour establishments, next door to the metro station and bus stops, and opposite the Alexander Nevsky Monastery. It has a lobby bar with 24-hour service, a buffet restaurant and a more formal restaurant on the 8th floor with views of the city. **www.hotel-moscow.ru**

EAST OF THE FONTANKA Oktiabrskaya Октябрьская ®®®®

Ligovskiy prospekt 10 **Tel** *578 1144* **Fax** *3157501* **Rooms** *484*
Map *7 C2*

An expensive hotel, if judged on its facilities, but the location is grand. The extension opposite Moscow Station has been renovated, so all rooms are now of a decent standard. In the main block, there is a glorious rabbit-warren of corridors, and a sense of faded grandeur. **www.oktober-hotel.spb.ru**

EAST OF THE FONTANKA Hotel Dostoevsky Отель достоевский ®®®®®

Vladimirskiy prospekt 19 **Tel** *331 3203* **Fax** *331 3203* **Rooms** *218*
Map *7 A3*

Part of the 24-hour Vladimirskiy Passazh shopping mall, but an élite, very modern hotel with its own entrance. Most rooms overlook courtyards, some offer views over the Vladimir Cathedral. The location is good for sightseeing, being near Nevskiy prospekt, and for shopping at and around Kuznechnyy Market. **www.dostoevsky-hotel.ru**

EAST OF THE FONTANKA Novotel Новотель ®®®®®

Mayakovskovo ulitsa 3a **Tel** *335 1188* **Fax** *335 1180* **Rooms** *233*
Map *7 B2*

Ultra-modern block tucked away a stone's throw from Nevskiy prospekt. Executive suites on the ninth floor offer superb views, and the Côte Jardin restaurant offers a Russian take on Mediterranean cooking. Business facilities are excellent and, unusually for this city, three rooms have been specially adapted for disabled visitors. **www.novotel.spb.ru**

EAST OF THE FONTANKA Radisson Royal Hotel ®®®®®

Nevskiy prospekt 49/2 **Tel** *322 5000* **Fax** *322 5001* **Rooms** *164*
Map *7 A2*

The Radisson is a modern hotel set inside a historic building right on the busy Nevskiy prospekt. A short walk from the Fontanka, its rooms and ground-floor Cannelle Bar and Café offer views of the main street, bustling with shoppers and promenaders throughout the year. **www.radissonblu.com**

EAST OF THE FONTANKA Corinthia Nevskij Palace ®®®®®

Nevskiy prospekt 57 **Tel** *380 2001* **Fax** *380 1937* **Rooms** *380*
Map *7 B2*

This sleek, modern hotel is where visiting dignitaries and Russian pop stars often stay, making it the place to see and be seen. With three bars and a DJ in the lobby at weekends, it is worth a visit even if you are not staying here. Meeting rooms and a central location make this a good spot to combine business and pleasure. **www.corinthia.com**

EAST OF THE FONTANKA Grand Hotel Emerald ®®®®®

Suvorovskiy prospekt 18 **Tel** *740 5000* **Fax** *740 5001* **Rooms** *90*
Map *8 D2*

A post-modern exterior hides a pseudo-historic interior filled with soft piano music and pot plants. There is a superb fitness centre with a large sauna and Turkish bath. Afternoon tea is served in the atrium café in a glass-roofed courtyard. The location is not absolutely central, but public transport links are excellent. **www.grandhotelemerald.com**

SOUTH OF THE CENTRE Azimut Hotel St Petersburg ®®

Lermontovskiy prospekt 43/1 **Tel** *740 2640* **Fax** *740 2688* **Rooms** *1,026*
Map *5 B5*

Formerly Sovetskaya hotel, Azimut Hotel St Petersburg offers plenty of facilities with low rates and stunning views along the river. It is popular with tourists looking for standard accommodation. Despite rebranding, service remains quite "Soviet" and can leave much to be desired. **www.azimuthotels.com**

SOUTH OF THE CENTRE German Club Немецкий клуб ®®

Gastello ulitsa 20 **Tel** *371 5104* **Fax** *371 5690* **Rooms** *16*

One of the city's first "mini-hotels", the German Club is modest but cosy, and set in a quiet location a short walk from Moskovskaya metro station. Staff are very friendly and offer numerous extra, personalized services, from arranging guided tours and tickets, to simple advice on where to go and what to do. **www.hotelgermanclub.com**

SOUTH OF THE CENTRE Rossiya Россия ®®

Chernyshevskovo ploschad 11 **Tel** *329 3932* **Fax** *329 3902* **Rooms** *413*

Set somewhat apart amidst the Stalinist buildings of Moskovskiy prospekt, and refurbished to European standards, the Rossiya remains unpretentious. It has 10 storeys, and rooms offer sweeping views of the southern part of town. Guests comprise both Russians and tourists, and there is a lively atmosphere in the restaurant. **www.rossiya-hotel.ru**

SOUTH OF THE CENTRE Neptun Нептун ®®®

Naberezhnaya Obvodnovo kanala 93a **Tel** *324 4610* **Fax** *324 4611* **Rooms** *150*
Map *7 A5*

A reliable, no-frills Best Western hotel attached to St Petersburg's first business centre. Set in a modern building in a business district, Neptun offers rooms that are smart but without pretension, and efficient service. It is a 15-minute walk from the nearest metro, and has a superb sports and leisure complex. **www.neptun.spb.ru**

SOUTH OF THE CENTRE Holiday Inn St Petersburg ®®®®

Moskovskiy prospekt 97a **Tel** *448 7171* **Fax** *448 7172* **Rooms** *557*

This modern, high-rise hotel is situated mid-way between Pulkovo airport and the city centre. The hotel is popular with business travellers, but good transport links also make it a handy base for exploring the city. Guest rooms are minimalist in style and well equipped. Breakfast is available and a restaurant serves hearty grills. **www.holidayinn.com**

SOUTH OF THE CENTRE Park Inn Pulkovskaya Парк Инн Пулковская ®®®®®

Pobedy ploschad 1 **Tel** *740 3900* **Fax** *740 3948* **Rooms** *840*

This hotel is close to the airport and conveniently located for trips to the palaces of Tsarskoe Selo, Pavlovsk and Gatchina. It is popular therefore with package tourists and business guests. The hotel has a selection of bars and restaurants, one of which is popular with local wedding parties. **www.rezidorparkinn.com**

Key to Price Guide *see p174* **Key to Symbols** *see back cover flap*

WEST OF THE CENTRE Park Inn Pribaltiyskaya Парк Инн Прибалтийская 🖼 🍴 📋 🛗 ®®®

*Korablestroiteley ulitsa 14 **Tel** 329 2626 **Fax** 356 6094 **Rooms** 1200*

The Park Inn Pribaltiyskaya is a huge, 1980s package-tour hotel, set right on the Gulf of Finland. It boasts superb views across the water, and a water-park with pool and sports facilities. It is a long walk to the metro from here – and in the winter it can be very windy – but buses and taxis are available. **www.rezidorparkinn.com**

NORTH OF THE NEVA Kronverk Кронверк 🖼 🍴 📋 🛗 ®®

*Blokhina ulitsa 9 **Tel** 703 3663 **Fax** 449 6701 **Rooms** 26* **Map** 1 C3

This hotel is in an unusual and extremely attractive location on Petrogradskaya, right by the Peter and Paul Fortress, a scenic walk across two bridges from the Hermitage. It is located in a high-tech business centre, and popular therefore with business people as well as tourists. Apartments are available for longer stays. No visa support. **www.kronverk.com**

NORTH OF THE NEVA Andersen Hotel 🖼 🍴 📋 🛗 ®®®

*Chapygina ulitsa 4A **Tel** 740 5140 **Fax** 740 5142 **Rooms** 140*

With pleasantly furnished rooms, the Andersen hotel offers well-priced accommodation which is favourably set on the Petrogradskaya Side, allowing good access to all St Petersburg's sights. The hotel also organizes tours of the city centre and suburbs. A restaurant and lobby bar are open until late evening. **www.andersenhotel.ru**

NORTH OF THE NEVA St Petersburg Санкт-Петербург 🖼 🍴 🛗 ®®®

*Pirogovskaya naberezhnaya 5/2 **Tel** 380 1919 **Fax** 380 1920 **Rooms** 401* **Map** 3 A2

A modern package-tour hotel, in a central location, but a little cut off from public transport. Its main attraction lies in the stunning views that can be had from rooms along the south side and the breakfast room on the bel-étage. In summer, however, when the sun hardly sets, guests may wish to trade the views for the restful dark. **www.hotel-spb.ru**

NORTH OF THE NEVA Stony Island Hotel 🖼 🍴 📋 ®®®

*Kamennoostrovskiy prospekt 45 **Tel** 337 2434 **Fax** 346 1920 **Rooms** 50* **Map** 2 D1

The historical building that houses the Stony Island Hotel has been renovated to a minimalist design, with straight lines and plain colours. It is located on the elegant main street of the Petrograd Side, near Petrogradskaya metro, and is aimed at regular visitors and those who dislike the busy city centre, rather than tourists. **www.stonyisland.ru**

EAST OF THE NEVA Okhtinskaya Охтинская 🖼 🍴 🛗 ®®

*Bolsheokhtinskiy prospekt 4 **Tel** 318 0038 **Fax** 227 2514 **Rooms** 294* **Map** 4 F3

Rooms in this hotel overlook the river near the Smolny Cathedral, somewhat compensating for its out-of-town location. Public transport is widely available, but in summer the bridges are raised at 2am, so guests need to allow plenty of time to get back after a night out. The building is modern, with airy rooms and public spaces. **www.okhtinskaya.com**

BEYOND ST PETERSBURG

NOVGOROD Volkhov Волхов 🖼 🍴 🛗 ®

*Predtechenskaya ulitsa 24 **Tel** (8162) 225548 **Fax** (8162) 229067 **Rooms** 127*

Volkhov has by far the best location of all the Novgorod hotels, in the historical centre by the Detinets or Kremlin. The building is five storeys tall, with plain interiors. Rooms have showers rather than baths, and facilities are only modest, though there is a sauna. There is also rather a lot of nylon in the decor. **www.hotel-volkhov.ru**

NOVGOROD Park Inn by Radisson Veliky Novgorod Hotel 🖼 🍴 🖼 🛗 ®®

*Studencheskaya ulitsa 2 **Tel** (8162) 940910 **Fax** (8162) 940925 **Rooms** 226*

The best equipped hotel in Novgorod, the Beresta Palace comprises a large, modern complex with huge conference halls, tennis courts and a rather smart pool. Many rooms have views over the river Volkhov, and even the semi-luxurious apartments are not very expensive. **www.parkinn.com**

PUSHKIN Natali Натали 🅿 🖼 🍸 ®®

*Malaya ulitsa 56a **Tel** 466 2768 **Fax** 466 0277 **Rooms** 47*

A privately run hotel on a quiet residential street in the leafy town of Pushkin, not far from Tsarskoe Selo palace. The building is modern in style. Although there is no lift, the Natali only has three storeys and some rooms are on the ground floor. There are "romantic" rooms under the eaves. Visa support is not offered. **www.hotelnatali.ru**

STRELNA Baltic Star Hotel Отель Балтийская звезда 🖼 🍴 🖼 📋 🛗 ®®®

*Berezovaya alleya 3 **Tel** 438 5700 **Fax** 438 5888 **Rooms** 106 and 20 cottages*

Set in the country between St Petersburg and Peterhof, beside the "re-created" presidential Constantine Palace, which is used for state events and receptions, the Baltic Star is popular with official delegations. The main building has historic-style interiors, and 20 "cottages" for guests who prefer greater privacy. **www.balticstar-hotel.ru**

ZELENOGORSK Gelios Гелиос отель 🖼 🍴 🖼 🖼 🛗 ®®

*Primorskoe shosse 593 **Tel** 702 2626 **Fax** 702 2622 **Rooms** 195 and 3 cottages*

About 50km north of the city on the shore of the Gulf of Finland, this modern hotel surrounded by trees offers healthy walks, skiing in winter and a spa centre with mud and mineral water treatments, hydromassage and a gym. Cottages in the grounds must be booked well in advance. **www.gelios-otel.ru**

RESTAURANTS AND CAFES

Sign for Noble Nest

A huge variety of restaurants serving international cuisine line almost every block in the centre of St Petersburg. Most serve simple set menus at lunch and dinner, offering visitors a risk-free opportunity to try out more expensive places. Russian cuisine is still popular, and is available at numerous traditional-style restaurants.

Ethnic food from the former Soviet republics and abroad provides a wide selection of vegetarian dishes. Small cafés offer a chance to escape the more garish tourist traps found near some sights. And, though getting a plain green salad may still pose a problem, other fresh salads are offered by most restaurants and good-quality cafés. For a list of recommended restaurants and cafés, see pp184–91.

Podvorie restaurant, a re-creation of a 17th-century wooden house (see p191)

WHERE TO EAT

Restaurants on Nevskiy prospekt tend to be more expensive than those in other streets. A few steps off Nevskiy, however, a variety of eateries line the streets – Bolshaya Konyushennaya, Rubinshteyna, Vladimirskiy prospekt and ulitsa Vosstaniya – offering something to suit most pockets and tastes. Venture out a little further, and the short ulitsa Belinskovo, for instance, offers at least five highly recommended options.

TYPES OF RESTAURANT

All large hotels offer good eating opportunities, but hotel restaurants are included in the guide only if they are out-standing or found in places that are short on other options.

Style and fashion now dominate in some restaurants, so the food often suffers and prices can be unjustifiably high. Other establishments, however, manage to combine food, decor and service in fine

Russian style. Dining trends include "imperial Russian" amidst sumptuous interiors (Old Customs House see p184), and exotic Caucuse restaurant (Baky, see p188). Top-range restaurants serve a mix of European and Russian dishes, with some Asian elements.

The former Soviet republics Georgia and Armenia have left their mark on Russian cuisine.

Outdoor café in the arcade of Gostinyy dvor (see p108)

Try Salkhino (see p185) or Lagidze Waters (see p189) for Georgian food, Erivan (see p187) for Armenian cuisine, and Apsheron (see p188) for an Azeri experience. Asian restaurants are numerous if generally uninspiring; sushi restaurant Yakitoriya (see p185) is a rare exception.

READING THE MENU

Large restaurants and some cafés have menus in English. Any restaurant that accepts credit cards will usually have English-speaking waiters, and, in those places that do not, most waiters try to overcome language difficulties.

PAYMENT AND TIPPING

All restaurants and cafés show meal prices in roubles. The listings in the guide give an indication of price ranges in roubles as restaurants cannot by law accept foreign currency (see pp214–15). Guests must pay with either cash or a credit card.

Major restaurants accept most credit cards, but it is advisable to check before-hand. Amex and Diners Club cards are almost never accepted. Credit card payment is still limited in Russia, especially in smaller establishments, so it is advisable to carry some cash with you at all times.

Tips are usually 10–15 per cent unless service is already included in the bill. To ensure the waiter receives the tip, it is best to give it in cash, rather than as part of a credit card payment.

OPENING TIMES

Most restaurants in St Petersburg open at noon and stay open until around 11pm or midnight. Increasingly, the more expensive restaurants, and particularly those that are attached to a casino or nightclub *(see pp204–5)*, may stay open well into the early morning hours. Cafés close early, usually around 10pm.

For those who wish to eat after an evening event, many restaurants stay open until the last customer leaves. A number of bars, for example Jili-bili *(see p193)*, offer food into the small hours. In addition, if all else fails, the lights of many fast-food outlets, such as Layma *(see p193)*, are often to be found burning after midnight.

The beautifully decorated interior of the Russian Room in the Demidoff *(see p190)*

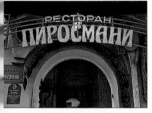

Street sign for Pirosmani *(see p191)*

MAKING A RESERVATION

It is always advisable to book ahead, especially during the White Nights *(see p51)* when upmarket restaurants may take bookings weeks in advance. Your hotel concierge can help. Smaller restaurants and cafés do not require reservations, but as they rely on special events such as weddings and birthdays they sometimes close unexpectedly.

CHILDREN

Russians are acquiring the habit of taking their children out to dine with them. On the whole Russians love children, few restaurants will refuse them entry, and staff will often adjust dishes to meet

their needs. A number of city eateries, such as Tres Amigos *(see p189)*, Botanica and Il Patio *(see p193)*, have children's parties and even nannies at weekends. A cosy room at Botanica is equipped with a play area, books, and a TV showing cartoons. Some places advertised to foreigners – but none in this guide – have "entertainment" that is not suitable for children.

LIVE MUSIC

Most restaurants and cafés have some kind of music on Fridays or Saturdays – DJs spinning disks or live acts. The listings that follow on pages 184 to 191 note only those which have live music on other days as well.

VEGETARIANS

Traditional Russian food is meat oriented, but the increasing number of eateries aimed at a more Westernized crowd, such as Krokodil *(see p186)*, include vegetarian options, and Georgian and Armenian cuisines offer a wide range of vegetable and bean dishes. At the time of writing, there are just a few vegetarian restaurants in St Petersburg, and a small number of vegetarian cafés.

For those who eat fish, however, there is always plenty of choice.

SMOKING

Most restaurants still allow smoking, but ever more places either have non-smoking areas or – albeit more rarely – ban smoking altogether. A few have a small, separate room that can be booked in advance for any occasion and declared a "no smoking" zone. The disadvantage is that such rooms are cut off from the atmosphere of the main restaurant.

DRESS CODE

Formal dress is *de rigueur* only in large and very fashionable restaurants, but guests should always be neatly and cleanly dressed. Trainers and tracksuits are acceptable in the less expensive cafés.

DISABLED ACCESS

Only a few restaurants have ramps or no stairs at all, but waiters and doormen are used to intrepid Europeans in wheelchairs (Russians in wheelchairs rarely venture outside the home) and are usually very helpful.

Cafés and bars prove more problematic, with stairs and narrow doors, and certainly no disabled toilets. People with disabilities may find themselves confined to hotel dining or the more expensive eateries and bars.

WEBSITES

Most restaurant websites are in Russian only, or are poorly maintained. Many places do not run independent websites, but appear on the St Petersburg restaurant site, which has an English-language version at: **www**.restoran.ru For Russian speakers, there are now many listings and reviews online. Try: **www**.allcafe.info, which has many listings; **www**.menu.ru; or the excellent archive of reviews at the Time Out site, **www**.spb.timeout.ru

The Flavours of St Petersburg

Russia's culinary reputation centres on warming stews, full of wintery vegetables such as cabbage, beetroot and potatoes. Yet St Petersburg was once the capital of a vast empire stretching from Poland to the Pacific and this is reflected in the variety of food on offer there. Aubergine (eggplant) and tomatoes, from the Caucasus in the south, bring in the flavours of the Mediterranean, while spices from Central Asia lend an exotic touch. On the stalls of the city's Kuznechniy Market, caviar and crayfish sit alongside honey from Siberia and melons and peaches from Georgia.

Wild Mushrooms

Caviar, the roe of sturgeon from Russia's warm southern waters

RUSSIAN COUNTRYSIDE

Many St Petersburgers have small country houses within easy reach of the city, and spend weekends from spring to early winter tending their immaculate vegetable gardens, or combing the countryside for wild berries and mushrooms. Much of this bountiful harvest is made into preserves and pickles. There is a refreshing soup, *solianka*, in which pickled cucumbers impart an unusual salty taste. Pickled mushrooms in sour cream make a regular appearance on restaurant menus, as do a variety of fresh berry juices.

In a country where food shortages are a fairly recent memory, very little is wasted. *Kvas*, a popular, mildly alcoholic drink is frequently made at home by fermenting stale bread with sugar and a scattering of fruit. Summer visitors should make a point of trying the seasonal cold soup *okroshka*, which is based on *kvas*.

Russia is also a land with hundreds of rivers and lakes, and has a long tradition of fish cookery. Dishes range from simple soups, such as *ukha*, to caviar and sturgeon, and salmon cooked in a bewildering variety of ways.

Blinis　　**Pickled mushrooms**　　**Spiced cheese**　　**Rye bread**　　**Gherkins**　　**Salted fish**　　**Soured cream**　　**Pickled herring**

A typical spread of *zakuski* (cold appertizers)

LOCAL DISHES AND SPECIALITIES

Borsch (beetroot soup) and *blinis* (buttery pancakes) with caviar are perhaps two of the most famous Russian dishes – one a peasant dish which varies with the availability of ingredients and the other a staple for the week leading up to Lent, when rich food would be eaten to fatten up before the fast. Much of Russia's cuisine is designed to make use of what is readily to hand or is warming and filling. A popular main course is *kulebiaka*, a hearty fish pie, larded with eggs, rice, dill and onion and encased in a buttery crust. Another is beef stroganoff with its creamy mushroom sauce, created in 18th-century St Petersburg by the chef of the wealthy Stroganoff family.

Beetroot

Borsch *Made with meat or vegetable stock, this beetroot soup is usually served with dill and soured cream.*

Market vegetable stall in St Petersburg

THE CAUCASUS

The former Soviet states of the Caucasus – Georgia, Azerbaijan and Armenia – are renowned for their legendary banquets, where the tables are laden with an enormous quantity and variety of food and drink. They still supply Russia's cities with a tempting range of fine subtropical produce. Limes, lemons, oranges, walnuts, figs, pomegranates, peaches, beans, salty cheeses and herbs are all shipped in season to St Petersburg's markets and its many Georgian restaurants. The cuisine of Georgia, with its focus on freshly grilled meats, pulses, vegetables, yogurt, herbs and nut sauces – including the hallmark walnut sauce, *satsivi* – is famously healthy and makes a delicious, unusual-tasting treat.

CENTRAL ASIA

From the Central Asian republics of the old Soviet Union come a range of

Freshly picked lingonberries from Russia's bumper autumn harvest

culinary traditions based on the nomadic lifestyles of Russia's one-time overlords, the Mongol or Tartar Hordes. The meat of fat-tailed sheep, which thrive in the dry desert air, is used to make communal piles of *plov* (pilaf) around which guests sit, eating in the traditional manner with their hands.

Served in St Petersburg's Uzbek restaurants, it shares the menu with warm flat breads, spicy noodle soups, *manti* (tasty dumplings reminiscent of Chinese cuisine) and a variety of melons and grapes, which proliferate in the desert oases, and apricots and nuts, grown in the mountains.

ZAKUSKI

A traditional Russian meal generally begins with *zakuski*, a selection of cold appetizers. These may include pickled mushrooms (*gribi*), gherkins (*ogurtsi*), salted herrings (*seliodka*), an assortment of smoked fish, blinis topped with caviar, various vegetable pâtés (sometimes known as vegetable caviars), stuffed eggs (*yaitsa farshirovanniye*), spiced cheese (*brinza*), beetroot salad (*salat iz svyokly*) and small meat pies (*pirozhki*), accompanied by fried rye bread and washed down with shots of vodka. A bowl of steaming soup often follows, before the main course reaches the table.

Kulebiaka *Rich, buttery puff pastry is wrapped around a mix of fish, hard-boiled eggs, rice, onion and chopped dill.*

Pelmeni *These meat-stuffed dumplings may be served in a clear broth, or with tomato sauce or soured cream.*

Kissel *A mix of red berries is used to make this soft, fruity jelly, which is served topped with a swirl of fresh cream.*

What to Drink in St Petersburg

Flavoured vodka

Russian vodka is famous throughout the world and the Liviz distillery in St Petersburg is Russia's second largest distillery, the largest being in Moscow. Vodka first appeared in Russia sometime in the 14th or 15th century. Peter the Great *(see p18)* was particularly fond of anise- or pepper-flavoured vodkas and devised modifications to the distillation process which greatly improved the quality of the finished drink.

Tea is Russia's other national drink. Traditionally made using a samovar and served black, tea has been popular in Russia since the end of the 18th century, when it was first imported from China.

A 19th-century Russian peasant family drinking vodka and tea

CLEAR VODKA

Diplomat   **Russian Standard**   **Five Star**

Vodka is produced from grain, usually wheat, although some rye is also used in Russia. Local Liviz vodkas dominate in St Petersburg, the best of which are Diplomat, Five Star and Russian Standard. Moscow's Kristall company, which produces Kristall and Gzhelka vodka, is increasingly popular, while Flagman distillery proudly proclaims that it is the official purveyor of vodka to the Kremlin. The range of vodkas available these days is over-whelming. There is one golden rule: if it is under $3 or $4 for half a litre, do not drink it.

Kubanskaya

Vodka is always served with food, often with a range of richly flavoured accompaniments called *zakuski (see p181)*, particularly black bread, pickled cucumbers and herring. Vodka is not always served ice cold, but it should be chilled.

FLAVOURED VODKA

The practice of flavouring vodka has entirely practical origins. When vodka was first produced commercially in the Middle Ages, the techniques and equipment were so primitive that it was

Pepper vodka

impossible to remove all the impurities. This left unpleasant aromas and flavours, which were disguised by adding honey together with aromatic oils and spices. As distillation techniques improved, flavoured vodkas became a speciality in their own right. Limonnaya, its taste deriving from lemon zest, is one of the most traditional, as is Pertsovka, flavoured with red chilli pepper pods. Klukvennaya (cranberry) and Oblepikha (sea buckthorn, an orange Siberian berry) are also favourites. Some of the best flavoured vodkas are made at home by soaking peach stones or whole berries in alcohol for months.

Limonnaya   **Klukvennaya**   **Oblepikha**

MAJOR WINE REGIONS

■	Wine growing region	■	Russia
■	Moldova	■	Georgia
■	Ukraine	■	Armenia
		■	Azerbaijan
		—	International boundaries

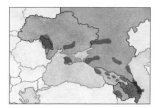

White and red Georgian wine

Shampanskoe

WINE

The Soviet Union was one of the world's largest producers of wine (*vino*), but many of the major wine regions are now republics in their own right. Several indigenous types of grape are cultivated in the different regions, along with many of the more familiar international varieties.

Georgia is considered the best wine-making area. Its wines include those made from the Rkatsiteli grape, characterized by a floral aroma and subtle, fruity flavour, and the Gurdzhaani which gives a unique, slightly bitter touch. Among its best red wines is the smooth Mukuzani. Moldova produces white, sparkling wines in the south and central regions, while the south is also known for its red wines. Since 1799, Moldova also produces a sweet, champagne-like wine called Shampanskoe.

OTHER ALCOHOLIC DRINKS

Brandy (konyak) was originally a by-product of wine-making and commercial production only began in Russia in the 19th century. Armenian brandy is one of the finest with a distinctive vanilla fragrance, resulting from its ageing in 70–100-year-old oak barrels. Georgia and Daghestan also produce good brandies. St Petersburg beer (*pivo*) is amongst the best in Russia. Baltika, Vena and Stepan Razin make a full range of beers in bottles and on draught. In addition, Tver beers such as Afanasy are well worth trying. Various imported beers are also available.

Baltika Beer   **Armenian brandy**

OTHER DRINKS

Kvas is a lightly fermented drink made from rye and barley, consumed by adults and children alike. Russia's vast range of mineral waters (*mineralnaya voda*) includes many with unusually high mineral contents. Mineral waters from the Caucasus are particularly prized. Also widely available are fruit juices (*sok, mors* or *kompot*), including cranberry (*klyukva*). Look out for traditional Russian *shiten*, made from honey and herbs.

Mineral water   Kvas   Cranberry juice

TEA

Russian tea is served black with a slice of lemon and may be drunk from tall glasses or cups. Sweetened with jam or sugar, tea (*chay*) is an ideal accompaniment to rich cakes and pastries. The boiling water for tea traditionally comes from a samovar. The water is used to brew a pot of tea, from which a little is poured into a cup and is then diluted with more hot water.

A glass of tea, with jam (varenye) to sweeten it

THE SAMOVAR

Made from brass or copper and heated by coals in the central chimney, samovars traditionally provided boiling water for a wide variety of domestic purposes and were an essential wedding gift. Modern electric ones are made of stainless steel and are used mainly for boiling water to make tea. The word samovar comes from *samo* meaning "itself" and *varit* meaning "to boil".

Choosing a Restaurant

The restaurants in this section have been selected across a wide price range for their good value and exceptional food. Within each area, entries are listed alphabetically within each price category, from the least to the most expensive. For details of *Light Meals and Snacks*, see pages 192–3. For map references, *see pp238–45*.

PRICE CATEGORIES
The following price ranges are for a three-course meal for one including a glass of house wine, all unavoidable charges and a modest service charge (tip).
® Under 750 roubles
®® 750–1,200 roubles
®®® 1,200–1,800 roubles
®®®® 1,800–2,400 roubles
®®®®® over 2,400 roubles

VASILEVSKIY ISLAND

Troitskiy Most Троицкий мост ®

6-ya Vasilevskiy ostrov 27 **Tel** *327 4622*   **Map** *1 A5*

A no-smoking, vegetarian café-restaurant that does not serve coffee. The emphasis is on fresh vegetables in this rare establishment; one of the few non-fusion restaurants in the city that serves asparagus and spinach – and knows what to do with them. Try cheese and spinach salad or *tagliatelli* with mushroom sauce.

Imperator Император ®®

Tamozhennyy pereulok 2 **Tel** *323 3031*   **Map** *1 C5*

The Strelka has a number of restaurants but none of them can match Imperator for price. Tucked away in the basement of the Academy of Sciences, next to the Kunstkammer, it serves the usual mix of European and Caucasian cuisine, with the slightly odd addition of Mexican dishes. The small non-smoking room should be booked ahead.

Ketino Кэтино ®®

8-ya liniya 23, Vasilevskiy ostrov **Tel** *326 0196*   **Map** *1 A5*

Ketino is the sister Georgian restaurant to Salkhino on Petrogradskaya, with a larger, slightly less intimate though none the less friendly setting. Take their advice on what to order, but not in great quantities: once you have tried one dish, you may want everything else on the menu. (*Llobio* with green beans and spices, for example.) Wine can be expensive.

Casa del Мясо ®®®

Birzhevoy proezd 6 **Tel** *320 9746*   **Map** *1 C5*

This is in a very convenient location, just a short walk from the Rostral Columns and the Strelka in the historic part of the city. The restaurant is unusual in offering a wide variety of different meat dishes on the menu. The Kunstkammer and Zoological Museum are also close by.

Russian Kitsch Русский китч ®®®

Universitetskaya naberezhnaya 25 **Tel** *325 1122*   **Map** *5 B1*

A slightly ironic, grand venue with luxurious, if not always tasteful, trappings from the period of *Perestroika* – painted ceilings, green marble and gilt. The menu consists of a mix of fusion and sushi rather than *pelmeni* and cabbage, but the popular dance floor is very Russian. Glass galleries give views across the Neva. **www.concord-catering.ru**

New Island ®®®®®

Rumyantsevskiy spusk, Universitetskaya naberezhnaya **Tel** *320 2100*   **Map** *5 B1*

This floating restaurant, much loved by the powerful, has played host to Bush, Putin and Chirac. In winter the boat is reserved for banquets, but from late spring to autumn it sails four times daily (at 2pm, 4pm, 8pm and 10:30pm). Eat caviar and *blini* as the boat sails past the Winter Palace towards Smolnyy, where it turns back to its moorings.

Old Customs House Старая таможня ®®®®

Tamozhennyy pereulok 1 **Tel** *327 8980*   **Map** *1 C5*

Conveniently located behind the Kunstkammer at the tip of the Strelka, the House is a good, reliable establishment with a general air of bonhomie. It has a strongly French orientation in its wines and menu, and serves plenty of meat. The vaulted interior is of unplastered brick, and there is an open kitchen, a balcony and a private room.

PETROGRADSKAYA

Demyanova Ukha Демьянова уха ®®

Kronverkskiy prospekt 53 **Tel** *232 8090*   **Map** *1 C3*

The city's first specialist fish restaurant retains its premier position over the competition by dint of hard work and unpretentious, traditional, hearty cooking. Fittingly, the name Demyanova Ukha ("Demyanov's Fish Soup") is a reference to a Russian tale about an over-zealous host forcing ever more food on his guests.

Key to Symbols *see back cover flap*

Na zdorovye! На здоровье!

Bolshoy prospekt 13, Petrogradskaya **Tel** 232 4039

Map 1 B3 ®®

Those who have seen and liked Boris Kustodiev's colourful pictures of buxom Russian beauties in the Russian Museum will love the garish interior of Na zdorovye. The name translates as "Your health!", and guests who practise the toast here will soon find themselves clinking glasses, in a whirl of Russian hospitality, to the sound of gypsy songs.

Tbiliso Тбилисо

Sytninskaya ulitsa 10 **Tel** 232 9391

Map 2 D2 ®®

A Georgian eaterie. The waiters wear Georgian dress and suitably impressive moustaches, and the authentic menu includes such dishes as *mamalyga* (ground corn with salted cheese), which will turn a true Georgian's knees weak with joy. Tables are arranged to create booths for privacy – a "true" Georgian man dines only with his lady love and close friends.

Yakitoriya

Petrovskaya naberezhnaya 4, Petrogradskaya **Tel** 970 4858

Map 2 F3 ®®

One of the best sushi restaurants in St Petersburg, Yakitoriya is favourably located near the Cabin of Peter the Great, just a five-minute walk from Peter and Paul Fortress. It's difficult to find good sushi in the city but this restaurant offers not only high quality food but very attractive prices, too.

Okean Океан

Prospekt Dobrolyubova 14a **Tel** 986 8600

Map 1 C4 ®®®

With floor-to-ceiling windows and views across the River Neva, this light-filled barge offers St Petersburg's glitterati a place to rest their heels with a cocktail on the terrace, or a chance to sample modern interpretations of traditional seafood dishes. The location and view make this an enjoyable place to dine.

Salkhino Салхино

Kronverkskiy prospekt 25 **Tel** 232 7891

Map 2 D2 ®®®

Generous home cooking is offered at this sister restaurant to Ketino on Vasilevskiy Island, by two Georgian women who know how to tempt. Their *khachapuri* (cheese-filled bread) is arguably the best in town. Try the aubergine (eggplant) stuffed with walnuts. Be wary of allowing the staff to order for you: it is easy to end up with more than you can eat.

Volna Волна

Petrovskaya naberezhnaya 4 **Tel** 322 5383

Map 2 F3 ®®®

One of the cheaper fusion restaurants in town, with an Asian accent on the menu. The Japanese-style minimalist interior complements the cuisine. Try the Italian lettuce with salmon tempura or the grilled white salmon with mint and prawn sauce. Volna is found just behind the Cabin of Peter the Great.

Austeria Аустерия

Peter and Paul Fortress **Tel** 230 0369

Map 2 E3 ®®®®

Location is Austeria's strong point – right by Peter and Paul Fortress – and those who plan to see all the sights hereabouts will certainly need refreshment. The interior re-creates Peter the Great's favourite Dutch style, as does the Fortress Cathedral, while the menu comprises traditional Russian dishes.

Magnolia Магнолия

Petrovskaya Naberezhnaya 4 **Tel** 232 4529

Map 2 F3 ®®®®

Located on the embankment across from the Hermitage, this two-story Georgian eatery serves classic cuisine, including traditional baked turkey served with baked apples and cottage cheese, Georgian cheeses and the chef's speciality matsoni – a blend of yoghurt and herbs. The restaurant also boasts impressive views of the River Neva.

Zver Зверь

Aleksandrovskiy park 5b **Tel** 232 2062

Map 2 E3 ®®®®

Zver means "wild animal" and every hunter's catch imaginable is available here, from wild boar to hare. The place resembles a huge steak house, with long wooden tables and hearty portions, and has a good children's menu. It is set deep among trees; avoid the garish pavilions opposite the Fortress, and plunge further into the park to find it.

Terrace Терраса

Flying Dutchman, Mytninskaya naberezhnaya, Birzhevoy most **Tel** 336 3737

Map 1 C4 ®®®®®

On board the frigate *Flying Dutchman*, this modern restaurant boasts a fireplace and broad views across the Neva to the Winter Palace. European and Latin American dishes are on the menu; there are sushi and salad bars, and a selection of elegant pastries. A nanny is available, and you can halve your bill by dining in the Zebra Bar.

PALACE EMBANKMENT

1913

Voznesenskiy prospekt 13 **Tel** 315 5148

Map 5 C2 ®®

Named after the last year of Russian imperial greatness, 1913 prides itself on generous portions and outstanding regional dishes such as *draniki* (potato pancakes) with bacon, and sorrel soup, as well as "fine" dishes such as lobster. A warm atmosphere and excellent service compensate for a bland interior. A singer and guitarist perform Russian songs from 8pm.

Baltika Brew
 ®®
Bolshaya Morskaya ulitsa 3/5 **Tel** *921 0912* **Map** *6 D1*

Under an impressive arched passageway opposite the Hermitage Museum, this brewery and restaurant serves a selection of international dishes. The menu includes an Indian selection, with the chef preparing meals from Cashmere, Goa and Delhi, to accompany nearly a dozen home-made beers in addition to imported and local brands.

Krokodil Крокодил
®®
Galernaya ulitsa 18 **Tel** *314 9437* **Map** *5 B2*

Krokodil offers easily the best value for money in the St Isaac's area. Small, dark and intimate, it was one of the first restaurants to introduce fresh salads, plentiful vegetarian options and a non-smoking room. A selection of board games is available for diners to play.

Da Albertone
®®®
Millionnaya ulitsa 23 **Tel** *315 8673* **Map** *2 E5*

Just behind the Hermitage, this plain Italian restaurant is an oustanding option for those with children. The kids' menu offers animal-shaped pizzas, there is a richly equipped children's room, and a nanny is available every day from noon until late. For added adult indulgence, there are 40 types of pizza and a variety of pasta dishes.

Gastronom Гастроном
®®®
Marsovo Pole 7 **Tel** *314 3849* **Map** *2 F5*

With its fashionable mixture of Italian and Japanese cuisine – plus a dash of Russian in its jellied meats with horseradish and mustard – the menu is aimed at a young crowd. But with a location like this, and tables on the pavement in summer, Gastronom is always going to be popular with tourists of all ages, even just for a beer.

Gosti Гости
®®®
Malaya Morskaya ulitsa 13 **Tel** *312 5820* **Map** *6 D1*

Casual and cozy, this restaurant serves Italian classics alongside Serbian specialities, including a wide selection of pies with sweet and savoury fillings. Spread over several floors it offers a separate play area for children, making for an enjoyable and relaxed atmosphere.

Park Giuseppe Парк Джузеппе
®®®
Naberezhnaya kanala Griboedova 2b **Tel** *571 7309* **Map** *2 F5*

On the corner of the Mikhaylovskiy Garden, with views across the Moyka to the Field of Mars, this is an ideal White Nights location; a place for eating late and sipping Italian wine as the sun gently dips, but never sets. The menu is Italian, with Neapolitan pizza baked in a wood-burning stove. A terrace is open for summer dining al fresco.

Russkaya Ryumochnaya No.1 Русскя Рюмочная №1
®®®
Konnogvardeiskiy Bulvar 4 **Tel** *570 6420* **Map** *5 B2*

Offering an old-world style dining room serving modern interpretations of Russian classics, this restaurant also has more than 100 different vodkas on its menu, many of them flavoured. In addition, the restaurant also houses a gallery with rotating exhibitions.

T-Lounge
®®®
Renaissance Hotel, Pochtamtskaya ulitsa 4 **Tel** *380 4000* **Map** *5 C2*

The T-Lounge offers delicious sandwiches, salads and pastries throughout the day, with live music in the evenings. Located within the Renaissance St Petersburg Baltic hotel, alongside the Canvas restaurant, it is close to all the sights and is justifiably popular with locals as well as hotel guests.

Borsalino борсалино
®®®
Bolshaya Morskaya ulitsa 39 **Tel** *494 5115* **Map** *6 D2*

Borsalino offers an authentic Italian menu of high quality food within the historic Angleterre hotel *(see p174)*. The great food and fabulous interiors attract locals as well as hotel guests and visitors. The restaurant is an especially good place to relax after a day's sightseeing, offering live jazz in the bar most evenings.

Canvas
®®®
Renaissance Hotel, Pochtamtskaya ulitsa 4 **Tel** *380 4000* **Map** *5 C2*

The breakfast room in this modern hotel in the quiet area beyond St Isaac's turns into a restaurant later in the day. In an area that is rather deprived of quality restaurants – most emphasise historic interiors to the detriment of the cooking – Canvas concentrates on food and service, and offers fine, traditional European cuisine.

Bellevue
®®®®
Kempinski Hotel Moika 22, Naberezhnaya reki Moyki 22 **Tel** *335 9111* **Map** *2 E5*

On the 9th floor, Bellevue offers such superlative views over the city centre, of Palace Square and the Winter Palace, that diners may be tempted to ignore the food. But the modern European menu is good, if not cheap. This place charges for the food itself, and not for a merely stylish veneer, the way some other St Petersburg restaurants do.

Tsar
®®®®®
Sadovaya ulitsa 12 **Tel** *930 0444* **Map** *2 F1*

Housed within a former palace, Tsar occupies a suite of painstakingly restored rooms that offer diners a sumptuous setting in which to enjoy first-rate Russian classics. With its nostalgia for Imperial Russia, the service is suitably subdued and every detail, down to the cut crystal glassware and portraits of Russian nobility, exudes opulent indulgence.

Key to Price Guide *see p184* **Key to Symbols** *see back cover flap*

GOSTINYY DVOR

Aragvi
Nab Reki Fontanki 9 **Tel** *570 5643*
⬛️🔳 ®®
Map *2 F5*

Aragvi features light, elegant interiors and large windows which offer enchanting views on to the Fontanka river. The restaurant serves authentic Georgian cuisine and you can try almost all the traditional Georgian dishes here, including *satsivi* (walnut sauce), *khachapuri* (baked bread filled with cheese) and pork *shashlyk* (kebabs).

Fartuk Фартук
Ulitsa Rubinshteyna 15–17 **Tel** *764 5256*
🔳🎵🔳🔳🔳 ®®
Map *1 A2*

In the warmer months, this restaurant offers some of the city centre's most relaxed outdoor dining. The menu has European influences with a focus on the Mediterranean and the home-made lemonades provide excellent refreshment. The communal country-kitchen style dining table means that reservations must be made in advance.

Fasol Фасоль
Gorokhovaya ulitsa 17 **Tel** *571 0907*
🔳🔳🔳 ®®
Map *6 D2*

Fasol means haricot bean, but this is not a vegetarian restaurant. It does, however, have plenty of healthy, relatively low-fat dishes on its restaurant-scale menu. Service is speedy, and the interior is modern, café-style. By virtue of its superb location on the corner of the Moyka, there is nowhere better for filling up while walking the canals.

Kvartirka Квартирка
Nevskiy prospekt 51 **Tel** *315 5561*
🔳🔳🔳 ®®
Map *7 A2*

This Soviet-era themed café packs in locals hungry for rustic cooking, as well as tourists in the know, for hearty portions of traditional Russian food at reasonable prices. All dishes use freshly prepared ingredients. The service is mock brusque, carrying the Soviet theme through the entire dining experience.

Literary Café Литературное кафе
Nevskiy prospekt 18 **Tel** *312 6057*
🔳🔳🎵🔳🔳 ®®
Map *6 E1*

This is the former Wolff and Beranger Café, from where the idolized Russian poet Alexander Pushkin set off for his fatal duel. The venue retains its popularity with tourists and lovers of Russian literature, though the experience of eating here is more exciting historically than gastronomically. Traditional, rather heavy dishes are served, with lots of meat in rich sauces.

Mama Roma Мама Рома
Karavannaya ulitsa 3 **Tel** *314 0347*
🔳🔳🔳 ®®
Map *7 A1*

One of the city's first authentic Italian restaurants, Mama Roma attracts many middle-class Russians. Like any good Italian restaurant, the interior is light and airy, and children are welcome. There is a junior menu and toys. The excellent Vinarium downstairs is a good place to buy wine for a boat trip.

Suliko Сулико
Kazanskaya ulitsa 6 **Tel** *314 7373*
🔳🎵🔳🔳 ®®
Map *6 E2*

Most central of all the truly Georgian restaurants, tucked away behind the Kazan Cathedral, Suliko is a lot cheaper than the Kavkaz-Bar and popular with Georgians themselves. More meat- than vegetable-oriented, there is no pandering to European tastes here.

Erivan Еривань
Naberezhnaya reki Fontanki 51 **Tel** *703 3820*
🔳🔳🔳🎵🔳🔳 ®®®
Map *6 F2*

All three rooms are furnished in Armenian style, with rugs and brightly coloured tablecloths and crockery. Ignore the VIP room and head for the Rural Room. All dishes are traditional, with lots of mutton and veal – which are hard to find in Europe today – and rarities such as brains in olive oil.

Kalinka-Malinka Калинка-Малинка
Italyanskaya ulitsa 5 **Tel** *314 2681*
🎵🔳 ®®®
Map *6 F1*

"Kalinka-Malinka" is the Russian folk song that is played whenever a Russian appears in a Hollywood film or on TV. Kalinka-Malinka the restaurant has a rustic, wooden-hut interior and serves traditional Russian meals, with romantic songs and folk music most evenings. It attracts lots of tourists and groups, but is none the worse for that.

Kavkaz-Bar Кавказ-бар
Karavannaya ulitsa 18 **Tel** *312 1665*
🔳🔳🎵🔳🔳 ®®®
Map *7 A1*

Caucasian (Georgian and Armenian) cuisine, and excellent wines and brandies are on offer here – at a price. Kavkaz-Bar has a superb location close to Nevskiy prospekt, and an intimate atmosphere. It also serves the best vegetarian kebabs in town. A selection of dishes is available in the less formal outer café, overlooking a quiet square.

Ket Кэт
Karavannaya ulitsa 24 **Tel** *315 3800*
🔳🎵🔳🔳 ®®®
Map *7 A1*

A small and comfortable basement restaurant, Ket specializes in Georgian dishes; the owner prides himself on being descended from Georgian princes. Rare for the city centre in attracting mainly local customers, and remarkable for its lack of pretension, this is a good place to mix with "old-style" Russians.

Ruskaya Charka Русская Чарка

 ®®®

Naberezhnaya reki Fontanki 92 **Tel** 495 5558 **Map** 6 E3

Traditional decor with expertly painted murals and woven textiles set the scene for one of the city's most authentic Russian restaurants. Ruskaya Charka goes the extra step to provide a memorable dining experience, with specialities from across the country and a selection of old-fashioned game dishes such as Siberian venison.

St Petersburg Санкт-Петербург

®®®

Naberezhnaya kanala Griboedova 5 **Tel** 314 4947 **Map** 6 E2

The cost of a meal here is high considering the standard Russian fare on offer (albeit served in abundant portions), but it does include a popular "folk" floor show at 9pm every night except Sunday. Live music begins at 8pm, after which there are Russian dancers and *balalaikas*. It may not be authentic, but it is extremely lively and loud, and great fun.

Baky Баку

®®®®

Sadovaya ulitsa 12/23 **Tel** 941 3756 **Map** 6 F1

Baky transports diners to an exotic Central Asian oasis filled with colour and light. The menu includes a mix of Continental and Caucuses cuisine; the kitchen also prepares complete banquets for as few as four diners. Nightly entertainment completes the vibrant atmosphere.

Barbaresco

®®®

Konyushennaya ploschad 2 **Tel** 647 8282 **Map** 2 E5

The two levels of this intimate and popular Italian restaurant attract the city's older arty crowd, sampling the simple but high-end Italian food. Hearty portions of classic dishes are served accompanied by wine produced in the north of Italy. A speciality is the fresh seafood. Try the multi-course tasting menu.

Caviar Bar and Restaurant

®®®®

Grand Hotel Europe, Mikhaylovskaya ulitsa 1/7 **Tel** 329 6000 **Map** 6 F1

Open in the evenings only, this bar-restaurant has the most elegant and varied ways of serving caviar and fish in town. Try caviar on a delicate blini or one of the special Russian regional dishes. The interior is tiny with a small fountain, rather like a grotto in an 18th-century park.

L'Europe Европа

 ®®®®®

Grand Hotel Europe, Mikhaylovskaya ulitsa 1/7 **Tel** 329 6000 **Map** 6 F1

This cavernous, Art-Nouveau (Style-Moderne) hall with stained-glass ceiling is not a re-creation of St Petersburg's glorious past, but the real thing, beautifully restored. The food is first-class European – lobster soup, steak tartare – but there are regular special events and celebrations of Russian cuisine. Sunday brunch attracts many Russian and ex-pat locals.

SENNAYA PLOSHCHAD

Apsheron Апшерон

®®

Kazanskaya ulitsa 39 **Tel** 312 7253 **Map** 6 D2

The meat-oriented cuisine at Apsheron comes from Azerbaijan in Central Asia, and is cooked by an Azeri chef brought in from Baku. There are plenty of vegetarian dishes on the menu, too, and even Azeri wine. To suit the Azeris who flock here, each of the three dining rooms is comfortably warm and colourful. No fashionable minimalism here.

Wasabi Васаби

®®

Ulitsa Yefimova 3 **Tel** 244 7303 **Map** 6 E3

This chain restaurant, located inside a shopping mall, has a wide selection of freshly prepared sushi and hot meals. It offers an excellent location for refreshment between sightseeing and shopping. Tea ceremonies can also be arranged with advanced planning.

Entrée Антрэ

®®®

Nikolskaya ploschad 6 **Tel** 572 5201 **Map** 5 C4

Located between the Mariinskiy Theatre and Senaya Ploschad, this French bistro is not in a central location, but it's worth a visit. Serving well-prepared food such as beef, duck and salmon *carpaccio* as well as traditional dishes at reasonable prices. There is also a separate café/patisserie area serving delicious pastries, noted as the best in town.

Mozzarella Bar Моццарелла Бар

®®®

Naberezhnaya kanala Griboedova 64 **Tel** 310 6454 **Map** 6 D3

Located in the city centre, Mozzarella bar attracts a young and casual crowd for an unusual mix of Italian and Japanese food. The friendly young waiting staff are obliging and courteous, and the menu offers something for everyone, making it the perfect spot for a group of diners that have different tastes.

Bella Vista Белла Виста

®®®®®

Angliyskaya naberezhnaya 26 **Tel** 312 3238 **Map** 5 B1

Bella Vista is the perfect place for a romantic pre- or post-theatre dinner. Serving upscale Italian food in an elegant, country-chic atmosphere. Impeccable service and a summer-only terrace adds to the restaurant's delights. Stunning views across the River Neva and in walking distance of a number of theatres, including the Mariinskiy.

Key to Price Guide *see p184* **Key to Symbols** *see back cover flap*

FURTHER AFIELD

EAST OF THE FONTANKA Lagidze Лагидзе   ®
Ulitsa Belinskovo 3 **Tel** *579 1104*   **Map** *7 A1*

Excellently located a short walk from the centre, on one of the city's shortest and best restaurant-lined streets, Lagidze serves Georgian food and wine in a modest but modern interior, at modest prices. Try the *lodka* (hot cheese-filled bread with egg) and the *satsivi* (chicken in walnut sauce), and finish the meal with Georgian vodka.

EAST OF THE FONTANKA Staryy Dom Старый дом   ®
Ulitsa Nekrasova 25 **Tel** *579 8343*   **Map** *7 B1*

Azerbaijanian and Russian food is served in this simple basement café-restaurant furnished with pine benches and tables. Real home cooking is on offer, including meaty *kharcho* soup and vegetarian *chebureki* filled with herbs and grasses rather than meat, as well as excellent wine served in faience jugs. Very popular with Georgians.

EAST OF THE FONTANKA Bufet Буфет   ®®
Pushkinskaya ulitsa 7 **Tel** *764 7888*   **Map** *7 B2*

Close to Nevskiy prospekt, Bufet's charming interior is made to look like a good, old-fashioned St Petersburg apartment. With only 20 place settings, framed photographs and mementos on the walls, it almost feels like one. The cuisine is Russian and plain, the atmosphere is warm and prices are moderate. A special place.

EAST OF THE FONTANKA Imbir   ®®
Zagorodnyy prospekt 15 **Tel** *713 3215*   **Map** *7 A3*

Originally an oriental restaurant (Imbir means "ginger"), this eaterie now offers an eclectic mix of noodles, sushi, lighter Russian meat and fish dishes (try the poached salmon), and simple but good wines. Its unpretentious, café style attracts a quiet, relatively young crowd, and it is a good place for people-watching. There's a new dish every month.

EAST OF THE FONTANKA Jean-Jacques Rousseau Жан-Жак Руссо   ®®
Ulitsa Marata 10 **Tel** *315 4903*   **Map** *7 B2*

A French bistro with friendly staff and a classic menu at affordable prices, Jean-Jacques serves breakfast, lunch and dinner and caters mostly to a relaxed crowd of young professionals. The wine list is extensive and all the classic tipples can be found at the bar. They also schedule regular events for families with children at their Nevskiy branch.

EAST OF THE FONTANKA Kompot   ®®
Ulitsa Zhukovskovo 10 **Tel** *719 6542*   **Map** *7 B1*

Amongst the city's *haute cuisine* establishments, Kompot has been doing especially well. The restuarant has a stylish modern interior and offers a mixture of Italian, European and Asian cuisine, with seafood delicacies and an extensive wine list. Watch out for the slippery metal stairs at the entrance.

EAST OF THE FONTANKA Palermo   ®®
Naberezhnaya reki Fontanki 50 **Tel** *764 3764*   **Map** *7 A2*

Pictures of Sicilian landscapes hang in the windows, the walls are painted in sand yellow and olive green, even the chef comes from Sicily. But there is no need to fear the Mafia here: this is simply a good Italian family restaurant, offering a classic Sicilian menu with the addition of a few European favourites – mainly heavy meat dishes.

EAST OF THE FONTANKA Sunduk Сундук   ®®
Furshtatskaya ulitsa 42 **Tel** *272 3100*   **Map** *3 C4*

Technically an art café, Sunduk is too good a restaurant to be hidden in the Nightlife section of this guide. It boasts an extensive wine list, a filling Russian and European menu, and good live jazz (for which there is a $3 surcharge after 8:30pm). The back room is the quietest. A clown entertains children every Sunday from noon to 5pm.

EAST OF THE FONTANKA Tres Amigos   ®®
Ulitsa Rubinshteyna 25 **Tel** *572 2685*   **Map** *7 A3*

A range of Latin American dishes is on offer, together with a bizarre mix of decor inspired by Aztecs and beer halls. Tres Amigos deserves a mention mainly for its excellent children's room with slide and swings, its children's menu, and the professional nanny it employs at weekends to entertain the kids while adults down tequila.

EAST OF THE FONTANKA Xren   ®®
Zagorodnyy prospekt 13 **Tel** *347 8850*   **Map** *7 A3*

Guests choose which of four rooms they want to eat in (each has a different look), order stylishly designed food, and sit and watch the world bustling by through windows overlooking the "Five Corners" (an intersection not far from Nevskiy prospekt). The menu includes marbled beef steaks, a house speciality. DJs perform every weekend.

EAST OF THE FONTANKA Baklazhan Баклажан   ®®®
Ligovskiy prospekt 30 **Tel** *677 7372*   **Map** *7 C3*

Set on top of a shopping complex next to the city's main railway station, this Georgian-inspired restaurant couldn't feel more relaxed. The menu offers expertly prepared renditions of Asian classics at reasonable prices, and the service is professional and warm. The home-made noodles and baked goods come highly recommended.

EAST OF THE FONTANKA Demidoff Демидов

Naberezhnyaya reki Fontanki 14 **Tel** *272 9181*

Map *3 A5*

There are two rooms in this touristy but adequate restaurant, one for elegant 19th-century dining, one for dining in a pseudo "Old Russian" interior (with brightly coloured, painted vaults). However, the pan-Russian menus are the same and include everything from quail's eggs to pancakes and caviar. There is Gypsy music every evening from 8pm.

EAST OF THE FONTANKA Marcelli's Марчелли's

Ulitsa Vosstaniya 15 **Tel** *702 8010*

Map *7 C1*

This combination of restaurant/café and delicatessen is a well-loved destination for Italian food lovers in the city centre. Founded on a philosophy of providing the best possible food at the most reasonable prices, lunch specials are exceedingly affordable, while dinner is an extravagant, yet refined, affair. The interior is casual and spacious.

EAST OF THE FONTANKA Novaya Istoriya Новая история

Ulitsa Belinskogo 8 **Tel** *579 8550*

Map *7 A1*

With a menu weighted heavily towards hearty meat dishes, this shabby chic restaurant looks a bit like a country cottage. Homely, comfortable and within easy walking distance of the circus, it makes just as good a venue for a family outing as for a romantic dinner for two.

EAST OF THE FONTANKA Povari Повари

Bolshoy prospekt 38/40, Petrogradskaya **Tel** *233 7042*

Map *1 C2*

Look, no pizza! This Italian restaurant specializes in all kinds of freshly made pasta, such as *fettuccini* with mushrooms and truffle sauce. In winter, tables are tucked away inside the building, but in warmer weather the covered terrace on the square outside sprouts comfortable wicker chairs. This is the perfect place to watch shoppers on bustling Petrogradskaya.

EAST OF THE FONTANKA Probka

Ulitsa Belinskovo 5 **Tel** *273 4904*

Map *7 A1*

This elegant Italian wine bar has the same management as more expensive Il Grappolo next door. Minimalist decor complements minimalist Italian cuisine – with fine sauces rather than the heavy, creamy pastas served in some of the city's other Italian restaurants. On warm days, huge windows open to embrace the outdoors.

EAST OF THE FONTANKA Sherbet Шербет

Ulitsa Vosstaniya 26 **Tel** *716 0874*

Map *7 C1*

Uzbekistan meets 21st-century cool at Sherbet. The ambience is very laid back, with elegant, candlelit tables and sofas scattered with silk cushions. The menu is not entirely Uzbek (though the *plov* or pilau is definitely worth tasting), but combines the best "Oriental" cooking with some Turkish dishes.

EAST OF THE FONTANKA Shinok Шинок

Zagorodnyy prospekt 13 **Tel** *571 8262*

Map *7 A3*

This restaurant offers food and folk music from the former Slavic Soviet republic of Ukraine. The elegant minimalism of St Petersburg's coolest restaurants is forsaken here in favour of good, stout food with three kinds of *salo* (salted pork belly), and Ukrainian vodka to drink. There is a Ukrainian folk show every evening at 8:30pm, and lots of jollity.

EAST OF THE FONTANKA Troika Тройка

Zagorodnyy prospekt 27 **Tel** *407 5343*

Map *6 F3*

Troika is not just a restaurant, but a remainder from the good old Soviet days of floorshows, with circus acrobatics (slender girls doing strange things with hoops), folk songs, Russian dancing, glitz and glamour. There is no erotica, unlike in some of the other locations. The menu is unremarkable, but the show is the star.

EAST OF THE FONTANKA Dickens Restaurant

Naberezhnaya reki Fontanki 108, 2nd floor **Tel** *702 6263*

Map *6 E3*

This cosy restaurant above the ever-popular Dickens Pub serves a rich menu specializing in steaks and game dishes. A small but respectable wine list, old-world style décor with sofas imported from England, and fantastic views onto the Fontanka make Dickens a special place for celebrations. A selection of fine cigars are also offered in the lounge.

EAST OF THE FONTANKA Matrosskaya Tishina Матросская тишина

Ulitsa Marata 54/34 **Tel** *764 4413*

Map *7 B4*

The advertisement for this restaurant reads "fish fashion", and so it is. Inside there is a real trawler cut into pieces, aquariums stuffed with live lobsters, oysters and crayfish; and tiger prawns and sea scallops, and just the right wines to wash them down. None of the fish or seafood is frozen – everything is delivered fresh and kept cool on ice.

WEST OF THE CENTRE Karl & Friedrich Карл и Фридрих

Yuzhnaya doroga 15, Krestovskiy ostrov **Tel** *320 7978*

Map *®®®*

A taxi is needed to get to and from this restaurant-brewery on Krestovskiy Island near the Gulf of Finland. The venue is aimed at families and employs a nanny from 7pm to 10pm during the week, and two nannies and a clown from 2pm to 10pm at weekends. There is a strong meat orientation to the menu, and great beer.

WEST OF THE CENTRE Krestovskiy sad Крестовский сад

Yuzhnaya doroga 15, Krestovskiy ostrov **Tel** *320 7978*

Another eaterie in the Karl & Friedrich brewery complex, Krestovskiy sad serves roast lamb cooked on an open spit in the grounds in summer – perfect for the White Nights. Sit at a table outside and watch the sun sink slowly over the Gulf of Finland, or eat at the smaller, seasonal café on the nearby beach.

WEST OF THE CENTRE Russian Fishing Русская рыбалка   🔣 V 🔣   ®®®
Yuzhnaya doroga 11, Krestovskiy ostrov **Tel** *323 9813*

This is a stylized fisherman's hut with a pond in which guests can catch their own fish – trout, sturgeon, beluga sterlet – and watch it cooked. The concept is masculine, but the restaurant tends to attract families during the day because of the playground outside and children's room inside. The place is more adult at night, and can get rowdy in the early hours.

NORTH OF THE NEVA Staraya Derevnya Старая деревня   🔣🔣V🔣   ®®
Ulitsa Savushkina 72 **Tel** *431 0000*

One of St Petersburg's first independent restaurants, Staraya Derevnya is still one of the friendliest places in town. A long way from the centre, it is nevertheless perfect for those driving back into town from the Gulf of Finland. Service is personal, the interior informal – like an old-fashioned apartment. Russian and Gypsy songs are performed in the evening.

NORTH OF THE NEVA 7:40   🔣🔣🔣V🔣   ®®®
Bolshoy Sampsonievskiy prospekt 108 **Tel** *492 3444*

The best known Jewish restaurant in town. Its name (*sem-sorok* in Russian) refers to the well-known Jewish song and dance that gets faster and faster until participants are whirling, which is just the kind of exuberant spirit this friendly establishment aims to emulate. Staff serve a wide range of traditional Jewish dishes in a colourful interior.

NORTH OF THE NEVA Pirosmani Пиросмани   🔣🔣V   ®®®
Bolshoy prospekt 14, Petrogradskaya **Tel** *235 4666*   **Map** *1 B3*

This colourful Georgian restaurant is set out like a Georgian hill village, with wattle and daub houses, a stained-glass window and even real ponds (when booking, ask to sit on a raft). Walls are hung with works by Pirosmani, arguably the best Georgian painter of the 20th century. Try the *lobio* – beans in spicy sauce – washed down with Old Tbilisi wine.

NORTH OF THE NEVA Ryba Рыба   🔣🔣🔣V🔣   ®®®®
Ulitsa Akademika Pavlova 5 **Tel** *234 5060*

Diners can choose between traditional Italian fare including a range of pasta dishes and a wide selection of pizzas or Asian wok based dishes at one of the highest restaurants in the city. Ryba occupies the top floor of a business centre and visitors dine here for the breathtaking views over the rooftops.

BEYOND ST PETERSBURG

NOVGOROD Yuryevskoye Podvorie Юрьевское подворье   🔣🔣🔣V🔣   ®®
Yuryevskoye shosse 6a **Tel** *(8162) 946066*

Especially attractive in summer, this restaurant is the ideal place if you want to avoid the crowds and noisy venues closer to the city. It has two large dining halls serving Russian cuisine, such as salads, mushrooms, pancakes with caviar, *borsch* and *ukha* (fish soup).

PAVLOVSK Podvorie Подворье   🔣🔣🔣V🔣   ®®®®
Filtrovskoe shossee 16, Pavlovsk **Tel** *4668544*

It is worth making a special trip to this re-creation of a 17th-century wooden house, situated by the grounds of Pavlovsk Palace, a short walk from Pavlovsk railway station. The restaurant is kitsch and great fun, with folk songs at lunchtime, and a traditional Russian menu with *pelmeni*, plenty of meaty soups and vodka. In the snow, it is magical.

NOVGOROD Volkhov Гостиница Волхов   🔣🔣🔣V🔣   ®®
Predtechenskaya ulitsa 24 **Tel** *(8162) 225 509*

This restaurant, at one of Novgord's most popular hotels, serves tourists visiting the nearby Kremlin. Volkhov serves provincial Russian fare and is also a popular evening venue. Book ahead as banquets can sometimes occupy the entire restaurant at weekends. An adjacent café offers lighter meals at reasonable prices.

PUSHKIN Staraya Bashnya Старая башня   🔣🔣V   ®®®
Akademicheskiy prospekt 14 **Tel** *466 6698*

With its huge menu and wine list, this is something of a find in provincial Pushkin: prices are half what they would be in St Petersburg itself. The restaurant is near the famous district of Fyodorovskiy gorodok, which was built in 1913 to mark the 300th anniversary of the Romanovs.

REPINO Chaliapin Шаляпин   🔣V🔣   ®®®
Ulitsa Nagornaya 1 **Tel** *432 0775*

In summer the Gulf is rich in cafés offering *shashlyk* (kebabs), but year round the best place to eat out here is Chaliapin. Do not be put off by the unattractive concrete exterior, and the location over a supermarket (though surrounded by trees), because inside it is charming, with a vast fireplace in winter. In summer, there is a roof terrace.

SHUVALOVKA Krapiva   🔣🔣V🔣   ®®
Sankt-Peterburgskoe shosse 111, between Strelna and Petrodvorets **Tel** *450 5393*

Set in a stylized Russian tower at the heart of the Shuvalovka Russian Village (a sort of Russian Disneyland on the road to Peterhof), Krapiva is a good place to try traditional Russian rural dishes and listen to folk songs – even for those who have not been sliding down snowhills and riding in a *troika* in the Village.

Light Meals and Snacks

Despite their plastic chairs and metal tables, Russian and ethnic cafés often serve very tasty food – from simple sandwiches to hefty meat dishes. Look out for the word кафе (café) and try one. Cautious travellers can experiment in one of the restaurants listed opposite, which frequently offer moderately priced meals between noon and 4pm. A number of bars and "art cafés" with live music *(see p205)* also have excellent kitchens. (In the evening these may be filled with people and noise, but at lunchtime they are calmer.) During the summer many cafés add tables outside – which is great for people-watching. In colder weather, the ground-floor cafés of the Moika or Radisson SAS hotels, Jili-bili or Il Patio are almost as good.

RUSSIAN

Traditional Russian dishes such as *borsch* and *draniki* (potato pancakes) are widely offered. *Pelmeni* (dumplings filled with meat) and *vareniki* (dumplings filled with fruit or vegetables) are in a class of their own. Specialist *pelmeni* establishments are truly "local", with no flashy decor or tourists. Try the **Pelmeni Bar** behind the Peter and Paul Fortress. Russian *bliny* and *blinchiki* (flat pancakes) come in both sweet and savoury varieties at the outstandingly cheap **Cherdak**.

Some places listed are quite plain, notable mainly for their location. **Priboy** is behind the Hermitage *(see pp84–93)*, **Sadko** is next to the Mariinskiy Theatre, **Café de Clie** is next to the Peter and Paul Fortress. **Gloss Café** serves Asian food and is located in the courtyard of the Stroganov Palace. Near St Isaac's Square *(see p79)* is **Idiot**, a vegetarian café popular with ex-pats. **Luna** is cheap, cheerful and busy. **Botanica** is known for its vegetarian dishes and generous portions.

ETHNIC FOOD

Georgian and Armenian foods are popular in St Petersburg. The **Kavkaz-Bar** restaurant *(see p187)* also has an informal café, and other small cafés offer Caucasian dishes. **Mops** is the city's only Thai restaurant. Filling Uzbek food is on offer at **Asia**, a tiny, bustling and cheap café in the heart of the residential and consulate area.

FAST FOOD, PIZZA AND PASTA

The first Russian fast food was an open sandwich with cheese or salami, or *pirozhki* (small buns) filled with rice, cabbage or something sweet like apple. The best *pirozhki* come from **Stolle**. A slightly cheaper version is available from the **Bulochnaya** on Bolshaya Konyushennaya ulitsa. Always avoid fried *pirozhki* with meat. Never buy them on the street.

In addition to the well-known fast-food chains, local options include the 24-hour **Layma** and **NyamBurg**, where customers can choose by pointing. **Teremok** specializes in pancakes. **Troitskiy Most** is a popular and inexpensive vegetarian option. Pizza and pasta houses are popular. (**Il Patio** caters for children.)

PASTRIES AND SWEETS

Russians are sweet-toothed, and in private homes tea is never offered without biscuits or cakes. Ice cream – best bought from one of the many street sellers – is enjoyed all year round. **Sladkoezhka** sells a wide range of fresh cream desserts and pastries, and is probably the city's favourite spot for a hit of sugar. Coffee shops, such as **Bushe Byuie** and the **Idealnaya Chashka** chain, also offer a variety of cheesecakes and cakes. At **Stirka 40°** customers drink tea while doing their washing (it doubles as the city's only launderette).

PUBS AND BARS

Most bars serve a good range of food. In addition to the standard English and Irish pubs, where food is unadventurous, expensive and the clientele is composed mostly of ex-pats, there are now a number of Russian "pubs", such as **Pivnaya 0.5** and **Vdali ot zhen**, that offer a range of excellent local beers. **Tinkoff** make their own beer on the premises.

One of the joys of summer is to drink beer sitting on one of the pontoons that appear with the warm weather on the canals and rivers, particularly around Nevskiy prospekt. Whilst such places do not usually offer food, they do allow customers to linger and watch the sunset.

SUSHI

An enduring craze for sushi bars – which tend to be quite good – means that there are plenty of good alternatives for quick, healthy lunches in St Petersburg. Menus are easy to understand because they include pictures of each dish. Try **Dve Palochki** or **Planet Sushi**.

EATING OUT ON DAY TRIPS

More effort is required when seeking a place for a modest lunch outside the city. Pavlovsk *(see pp158–61)* and Peterhof *(see pp148–51)* have reasonable cafés in the palaces, although space is limited in summer. Peterhof's tiny **Trapeza** is always a favourite. At Tsarskoe Selo *(see pp152–5)*, there are several cafés along and around Oranzhereynaya ulitsa, leading off the park. Gatchina Palace *(see p147)* has cafés in the grounds and even Oranienbaum *(see p146)* has a tiny café, too. In general, however, the best option is to take a picnic to Gatchina or Oranienbaum. (Delicious take-away pies can be bought from **Stolle**.) In Novgorod *(see pp162–5)*, the **Golden Ladle** serves many kinds of beer and snacks.

DIRECTORY

RUSSIAN

Barberry
Kamennoostrovskiy 10.
Map 2 E2.
Tel 954 0022.

Botanica
Ботаника
Ulitsa Pestelya 7.
Map 3 A5.
Tel 272 7091.

Café de Clie
Kronverkskiy prospekt 27.
Map 2 D2.
Tel 232 3606.

Carusel
Карусель
Ulitsa Kirochnaya 8.
Map 3 B5.
Tel 272 1778.

Chaynaya Khizhina
Чайная хижина
Bolshaya Konyushennaya
ulitsa 19 (entrance from
Volynskiy pereulok).
Map 6 E1.
Tel 570 1947.

Cherdak
Чердак
Ligovskiy prospekt 17.
Map 7 C1.
Tel 272 5564.

Idiot
Идиот
Naberezhnaya reki
Moyki 82. **Map** 5 C2.
Tel 315 1675.

Jili-bili
Жили-были
Nevskiy prospekt 52.
Map 6 F1.
Tel 314 6230.

Luna
Луна
Bolshaya Konyushennaya
ulitsa 5. **Map** 2 E5.
Tel 312 4260.

Pelmeni Bar
Пельмени-бар
Kronverkskiy prospekt 53a
(entry from ulitsa Markina).
Map 1 C3.
Tel 498 0977.

Priboy
Прибой
Naberezhnaya reki
Moyki 19. **Map** 2 E5.
Tel 571 8285.

Sadko

Садко
Ulitsa Glinki 2.
Map 5 B3.
Tel 903 2373.

Soiree
Суаре
Ulitsa Zhukovskovo 28.
Map 7 B1. *Tel 272 3512.*

Troitskiy Most
Kamenoostrovskiy
prospect 9/2.
Map 2 E4.
Tel 232 6693.

ETHNIC FOOD

Asia
Азия
Ulitsa Ryleeva 23.
Map 3 B5. *Tel 272 0168.*

Gloss Café
Nevskiy prospekt 17.
Map 6 E1. *Tel 315 2315.*

Mops
Мопс
Ulitsa Rubinshteyna 12.
Map 7 A2. *Tel 572 3834.*

FAST FOOD, PIZZA AND PASTA

Bulochnaya
Булочная
Bolshaya Konyushennaya
ulitsa 15. **Map** 2 E5.
Nevskiy prospekt 66.
Map 7 A2. *Tel 314 8559.*

Il Patio
Nevskiy prospekt 30.
Map 6 E1. *Tel 314 3215.*
Nevskiy prospekt 182.
Map 8 E3. *Tel 271 3177.*

Layma
Лайма
Naberezhnaya kanala
Griboedova 16. **Map** 6 E1.
Tel 315 5545.

NyamBurg
Нямбург
Nevskiy 78.
Map 6 E1.
Tel 272 7573.

Pelmenia
Пельмения
Nab reki Fontanka 25.
Map 7 A1.
Tel 571 8082.

Stolle

Штолле
Ulitsa Dekabristov 33.
Map 5 C3.
Tel 714 2571.
Konyushennyy pereulok 1/6.
Map 2 E5.
Tel 312 1862.

Teremok (pancakes)
Теремок
Nevskiy prospekt 60.
Map 7 A2.
Tel 314 2701.

Troitskiy Most
Троицкий мост
Kronverkskiy prospekt 35.
Map 2 D2. *Tel 326 8221.*
6-ya liniya 27,
Vasilevskiy ostrov.
Map 1 A5.
Tel 327 4622.

COFFEE, PASTRIES AND SWEETS

Bushe Byuie
Буше
Ulitsa Vosstaniya 10.
Map 7 B1.
Tel 273 7459.

Café Singer
Кафе Зингер
Nevskiy 28.
Map 6 E1.
Tel 571 8223.

Denisov-Nikolaev Confectionery
Денисов и Николаев
Naberezhnaya kanala
Griboedova 77.
Map 6 D3. *Tel 571 9495.*

Idealnaya Chashka
Идеальная чашка
Kamennoostrovskiy
prospekt 2.
Map 2 E2. *Tel 233 4953.*

Sladkoezhka
Сладкоежка
Marata ulitsa 2.
Map 7 B2.
Tel 571 1420.
Sadovaya ulitsa 60.
Map 5 C4.
Tel 310 8144.
Gorokhovaya 44.
Map 6 E3.
Tel 310 8005.

Stirka 40°
Стирка 40°
Kazanskaya ulitsa 26.
Map 6 D2.
Tel 314 5371.

PUBS AND BARS

Pivnaya 0.5
Пивная 0.5
44/2 Zagorodnyy prospekt.
Map 6 E4.
Tel 315 1038.

Tinkoff
Тинькофф
Kazanskaya ulitsa 7.
Map 6 E2.
Tel 718 5566.

Vdali ot zhen
Вдали от жен
Bolshaya Konyushennaya
ulitsa 15.
Map 6 E1.
Tel 571 0154.

SUSHI

Dve Palochki
Две палочки
Ulitsa Vosstaniya 15.
Map 7 C1.
Tel 335 0222.

Eurasia
Евразия
Nevskiy prospekt 13.
Map 6 D1.
Tel 315 1858.

Planet Sushi
Планета Суши
Nevskiy prospekt 94.
Map 7 B2.
Tel 275 7533.

DAY TRIPS

Golden Ladle
Золотой Ковш
Novo-Luchanskaya ulitsa
14, Novgorod.
Tel (8162) 73 05 99.

Linea
Sankt-Peterburgskiy
prospekt 46,
Petrodvorets
(Peterhof).
Tel 450 7878.

Podvorie
Подворье
Filtrovskoye 16.
Tel 466 8544.

Trapeza
Трапеза
Kalininskaya ulitsa 9,
Petrodvorets (Peterhof).
Tel 450 6393.

SHOPS AND MARKETS

A trip round St Petersburg's shops and markets provides an insight into local life. Even today, shopping in the city requires flexibility and even a sense of adventure: you can never depend on finding what you set out to find, but may confidently expect to end up buying something you never guessed you needed. Imported goods have pushed out many local products. Even so, Russian linen,

Matryoshka doll

the city's celebrated Krupsksaya chocolates, vodka, caviar, and Russian crafts and toys all make wonderful gifts. Larger shops are concentrated around main streets such as Nevskiy and Bolshoy prospekts, and metro stations, notably Sennaya Ploshchad and Vasilievskiy Ostrov. However, most buildings are occupied by shops or restaurants at ground level. Do venture in.

Ladies' fashion at one of the numerous up-scale boutiques along Nevskiy prospekt

OPENING HOURS

Hours vary, but shops usually open from 10am until at least 7pm, though "fashionable" outlets may stay open later. A few, mainly cheap food shops, close for lunch. On Sundays department stores remain open, as do other large shops. During the summer, smaller places may reduce their hours and close at weekends. There are 24-hour food shops all over town.

HOW TO PAY

Shops no longer express prices in "y.e." or "conditional units", but a few restaurants still do so. One y.e. is usually worth about one US dollar or one Euro (check at the restaurant for their exchange rate), but the customer must still pay in roubles. Accepting payment in non-Russian currency is a criminal offence. The only place you might be able to pay in foreign currency is at a tourist market.

There are numerous, reliable exchange offices and ATMs inside metro stations and outside banks

Russian box-camera (1920s)

(see p214). Moreover, many stores now accept credit cards. In some shops, customers are forced to peer at goods stacked behind the counter. If you would like a closer look, point to what you want and say "*mozhno*" ("may I?").

To purchase something, pay for it at the cash desk and then return to collect the item from the counter with your receipt. Shop assistants will usually realise if you do not speak Russian, and will write down the prices for you to hand to the cashier. Defective goods can generally be returned provided they are accompanied by a receipt.

BARGAINING ETIQUETTE

If a set price is displayed at markets, this indicates no bargaining. In all other cases you can usually get some reduction if you haggle, especially since visitors (and prosperous-looking Russians) are likely to be quoted a higher price. Haggling in Russia, however, is a serious matter, so do not bother unless you genuinely intend to buy.

BUYING ART AND ANTIQUES

Under Russian law, all objects made before 1956, and all objects made from valuable materials such as gold, silver, precious stones and fur, are subject to strict export controls. Works of art, including contemporary watercolours, also fall under this ruling, likewise books published before 1946.

Be aware that, although there are green and red channels at the airport customs, and not all suitcases are x-rayed, there are random checks. In practice, customs officials

Second-hand bookshop sign

may turn a blind eye to prints and watercolours without frames, and unless a book is extremely rare you are likely to be able to export it without authorization. In all other cases, strict rules are applied.

Permission to export both books and art objects can be obtained from a department of the **Ministry of Culture**. This process is relatively speedy. The gallery from which or the artist from

EXPORT PERMISSIONS

Ministry of Culture
Министерство культуры
Ministerstvo kultury
Malaya Morskaya Ulitsa 17.
Map 6 D1. **Tel** 571 0302.
◐ Mon–Fri 11am–5pm.

Tertia *(see p198)* has exportable antiques to suit all budgets

whom the item is purchased should always assist with the paperwork.

If you have not obviously tried to cheat customs, any objects not allowed through can simply be handed over to someone who is remaining in St Petersburg. If, however, there is any hint of foul play, the item will be placed in storage at the airport, for which, if you wish to reclaim it later, there will be a charge. Any objects that remain unclaimed after a year will be confiscated, as will objects which have obviously been hidden to avoid detection. Valuable pieces may be donated to a museum.

DEPARTMENT STORES

Known as a "univermag" or universal shop, Russian department stores evolved from the old trading rows, which were literally rows of kiosks owned by different traders. Present-day department stores have altered a great deal and now operate as a complex of boutiques and distinct sections. Even though the goods on sale do not differ much from those that are available in European shops, every visitor to St Petersburg should explore **Gostinyy Dvor** *(see p108)*, the oldest shopping centre in the city, and **Passazh** *(see p48)*, a smaller department store. Despite the glitzy goods, however, the narrow

passages and layout speak of a different age.

The newer shopping centre such as the **Nevsky Centre** *(see p199)* and **Galeria** are more like Western European and American shopping malls, with up-scale boutiques and food outlets.

MARKETS AND BAZAARS

Food can be bought in one of the 11 markets (*rynoks*) dotted around the city. The most centrally located is **Kuznechnyy** *(see p199)*, just off Nevskiy prospekt, which sells flowers, fruit, vegetables, delicious home-made cream cheese and wonderful natural honey which you can sample. Note that prices at markets tend to be higher than at the supermarkets, but buyers do have the option of haggling.

Apraksin Dvor has been the site of a thriving market since the mid-18th century. Today it sells everything from cigars to CDs. While the market is undergoing reconstruction, only the shops that have a roof over them remain open. Another famous market is **Unona**, which is at Avtovo metro station. Keep your valuables well hidden – pickpockets are active here.

Flea markets are perpetually being moved on, though some sellers continue to pop up at the city's main markets. The true seeker of unusual finds amid the trash will set off on a Friday or Saturday morning for Udelnaya metro, where a vast unofficial market sprawls along the railway line.

Souvenir watercolours and prints of varying quality are

Souvenirs sold at the tourist market opposite the Church on Spilled Blood

sold throughout the year at the open-air market, **Vernisazh** *(see p199)*, outside the Church of St Catherine *(see p48)* on Nevskiy prospekt. The official **Souvenir Market** *(see p199)* near the Church on Spilled Blood *(see p100)*, sells a wide selection of *matryoshka* dolls *(see p197)*. You are also likely to find handmade chess sets, watches, fur hats, old cameras and military paraphernalia.

Visitors browse the shelves at the Hermitage Museum Shop

MUSEUM SHOPS

The best museum shop is found inside the **Hermitage** *(see pp84–93)* and sells reproduction prints and objects, books on the city and its art, jewellery and silk scarves, both inside the museum and online: www.hermitagemuseum.org

The **Russian Museum** *(see pp104–7)* has several outlets, though these are not run by the museum itself. The best is in the Stroganov Palace *(see p112)*.

Of the other shops attached to museums, the best are found in the **Peter and Paul Fortress** *(see pp66–7)* and in the palaces at **Pavlovsk, Peterhof** and **Tsarskoe Selo** *(see pp148–61)*. These tend to sell souvenirs (rather than reproductions of exhibits and other related objects): amber and semi-precious stone jewellery, dolls, lacquered boxes and books on the city.

What to Buy in St Petersburg

It is easy to find interesting and beautiful souvenirs in St Petersburg. They range in price from small, enamelled badges, which sell for very little, through to hand-painted Palekh boxes and samovars which can be very expensive. Traditional crafts were encouraged

Decorative box

by the state in the old Soviet Union and many items, such as lacquered boxes and bowls, matryoshka dolls, wooden toys and chess sets, are still made by craftsmen and women using age-old methods. Memorabilia from the Soviet era also make good souvenirs and Russia is definitely the best place to buy the national specialities, vodka and caviar.

Samovar
Used to boil water to make tea, samovars come in all shapes and sizes (see p183). A permit is needed to export a pre-1945 samovar.

Vodka and Caviar
An enormous variety of both clear and flavoured vodkas (such as lemon and pepper) is available (see p182). They make excellent accompaniments to black and red caviar (ikra), which are often served with blini (see p180).

Clear vodka

Flavoured vodka

Red caviar

Black caviar

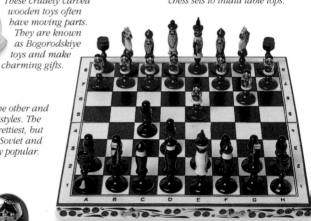

Malachite egg

Amber ring

Semi-precious Stones
Malachite, amber, jasper and a variety of marbles from the Ural mountains are used to make a wide range of items – everything from jewellery and chess sets to inlaid table tops.

Wooden Toy
These crudely carved wooden toys often have moving parts. They are known as Bogorodskiye toys and make charming gifts.

Matryoshka Dolls
These dolls fit one inside the other and come in a huge variety of styles. The traditional dolls are the prettiest, but those painted as Russian, Soviet and world leaders are also very popular.

Chess Sets
Attractive chess sets made from all kinds of beautiful materials, including malachite, are widely available. This wooden chess set is painted in the same style as the matryoshka dolls.

LACQUERED ARTIFACTS

Painted wooden or papier-mâché artifacts make popular souvenirs and are sold all over the city. The exquisite hand-painted, lacquered Palekh boxes can be very costly, but the eggs decorated with icons and the typical red, black and gold bowls are more affordable.

Palekh Box

The art of miniature painting on papier-mâché items origin-ated in the late 18th century. Artists in the four villages of Palekh, Fedoskino, Mstera and Kholui still produce these hand-painted marvels. The images are based on Russian fairytales and legends.

Painted wooden egg

Bowl with Spoon
The brightly painted bowls and spoons, usually known as "Khokhloma", have a lacquer coating, forming a surface which is durable, but not resistant to boiling liquids.

Russian hand-painted tray

Tuners

Strings

Musical Instruments
Russian folk music uses a wide range of musical instruments. This gusli *is similar to the Western psaltery and is played by plucking the strings with both hands. Also available are the brightly painted balalaika and the* bayan *(accordion).*

Russian Scarf
These brilliantly coloured traditional woollen shawls are good for keeping out the cold of a Russian winter. Mass-produced polyester versions are also available, mostly in big department stores, but these are not as warm.

Soviet Memorabilia
An eclectic array of memorabilia from the Soviet era is on sale. Old banknotes, coins, pocket watches and Red Army kits, including belt buckles, badges and other items of uniform, can be found along-side watches with cartoons of KGB agents on their faces.

Pocket watch

Gzhel Vase
Ceramics with a distinctive blue and white pattern are produced in Gzhel, an area near Moscow. Ranging from figurines to household crockery, they are popular with Russians and visitors alike.

Badge with Soviet symbols

Red Army leather belt

Where to Shop in St Petersburg

The main department stores in the city centre stock everything from souvenirs to vodka and furs, all of a high quality. For some local products, however, it is best to visit specialist shops, most of which are conveniently located in or near the centre. In a city which prides itself on its intellectuals, books and art are appropriately St Petersburg's other main exports. Soviet memorabilia has also become very popular souvenirs.

FOOD AND DRINK

Good vodka is to be had everywhere. Avoid cheaper brands in "amusing" packaging, they are invariably of poor quality. Diplomat and Gzhelka are good, standard brands.

Caviar should be bought only from a food shop or department store. **Gostinyy Dvor** department store and the Supermarket in **Passazh** department store are the most central, reliable places for both vodka and caviar. The many **Liviz** outlets also stock a wide range of alcoholic drinks. All kinds of food shopping can be done at **Kuznechnyy Market**, stacked high with Russian specialities. All kinds of meats and cheeses are on sale at the **Stockmann Delicatessen**.

St Petersburg's **Krupskaya Fabrika** chocolate factory has long been famous in the Soviet Union. The **Chocolate Museum** sells novelties such as famous buildings crafted in chocolate.

SOUVENIRS AND CRAFTS

In summer, when traders set up stalls by tourist spots, the city is flooded with *matryoshka* dolls, music boxes shaped like a church, painted lacquerware and chess sets. In winter, it can be quiet on the retail front. The **Souvenir Market** and **Vernisazh** market, however, operate all year, and there are good gifts to be found in Gostinyy Dvor and Passazh department stores. Shops in or near museums also stock souvenirs – notably those in the Stroganov Palace *(see p112)* and Tsarskoe Selo *(see pp152–5)*. The shop inside the Hermitage *(see pp84–5)* sells higher range goods and excellent art books. Local porcelain from the **Imperial**

Porcelain Factory is much prized. The factory makes everything from gaily painted rustic cups to reproduction revolutionary-era porcelain.

Unona at Avtovo is a real local market – a must for cheap clothing and electronics.

SOVIET MEMORABILIA

Artifacts from the Soviet era are now produced specifically for the tourist market. Be careful when buying on the street: many apparently genuine articles are modern reproductions. Original pieces can be picked up at the **Souvenir Market**, though **Nado Zhe** and **Sobiratel** antiques shops are more reliable. Or you could try one of the smaller second-hand shops. Soviet badges are easily transportable. DIY models of Soviet military hardware are available from the top floor of **D.V.K.**

ANTIQUES AND ART

Although older antiques and many works of art need to be cleared with customs, some pieces, such as small water-colours, may be exempt. Many shops are extortionately expensive, but **Tertia** is an exception, with readily expor-table items to suit all pockets, and **Larusse** is a veritable treasure trove. Only buy an expensive object if you are sure the relevant paperwork and export applications can be obtained *(see p194)*. **Antikvariat** should be able to provide the paperwork for purchases made in the centre.

Paintings all require export licences, but as galleries can provide these themselves it is worth dropping in to **Anna Nova**, **S.P.A.S.** or **Borey** to see

what they have. The **Union of Artists** has exhibitions by traditional local artists. The **Pushkinskaya 10** art centre stages shows at weekends, some with works for sale.

BOOKS, FILM AND MUSIC

St Petersburgers perceive their city as an intellectual focal point, with a great literary and artistic past. The centre has been taken over by book chains such as **Bookvoed**, but there are some smaller new and second-hand bookshops. The best are still **Dom Knigi** *(see p47)* and the **Writers' Bookshop**. If you need a holiday novel in English, try **Anglia**, Dom Knigi or Bookvoed. More unusual, second-hand English books – usually donated by tourists – can sometimes be found in **Akademkniga** and **Na Liteynom**. **Severnaya Lira** sells sheet music – everything from classical to folk songs – as well as instruments, CDs and books on music. Art books can be bought in Dom knigi, or second-hand in **Staraya Kniga**.

DVDs of English-language films and CDs can be purchased in shops such as **Porpornyy Legion**.

FURS AND FASHION

Clothes and other accessories are mainly imported. Elegant boutiques occupy part of Gostinyy Dvor and run along streets such as naberezhnaya kanala Griboedova and ulitsa Zhukovskovo. Some local designers have their own boutiques; notably **Tatyana Parfyonova**, whose garments have been purchased by the Russian Museum.

Paloma and the **Hat Shop** offer hats in everything from straw to fur. Furs are sold in **Lena**, Paloma and on the top floor of Gostinyy Dvor. Russian linen is also a good buy. Elegant shift dresses and the traditional *kosovorotka* (peasant shirt) are found in **Slavyanskiy Stil**. Fashion pieces are sold at **Toto**. Locally made jewellery of semi-precious stones from the Urals and amber from the Baltic is available in jewellers such as Samotsvety.

DIRECTORY

DEPARTMENT STORES

Galeria
Галерея
Ligovskiy prospekt 30.
Map 7 C3.

Gostinyy Dvor
Гостиный двор
Nevskiy prospekt 35.
Map 6 F2.

Nevsky Centre
Nevskiy prospekt
114–116. **Map** 7 B2. **Tel** *313 9319.*

Passazh
Пассаж
Nevskiy prospekt 48.
Map 6 F1.

MARKETS

Apraksin Dvor
Sadovaya ulitsa 30.
Map 6 E2.

Kuznechnyy Market
Кузнечный рынок
Kuznechnyy pereulok 3.
Map 7 A3.

Souvenir Market
Рынок сувениров
Naberezhnaya kanala
Griboedova, by Church on
Spilled Blood. **Map** 2 E5.

Unona
Юнона
Ulitsa Marshala
Kazakova 35.
Buses K-60, K-80 from
Avtovo metro station.
Tel *747 0200.*

Vernisazh
Вернисаж
Nevskiy prospekt 32–4.
Map 6 E1.

FOOD AND DRINK

Chocolate Museum
Музей шоколада
Nevskiy prospekt 17.
Map 6 E1. **Tel** *315 1348.*

Krupskaya Fabrika
Кондитерская фабрика
им. Н.К. Крупской
Ulitsa Pravdy 6.
Map 7 A3.

Liviz
ЛИВИЗ
ulitsa Zhukovskovo 27.
Map 7 B1. **Tel** *272 1969.*

Stockmann Delicatessen
Гастроном Стокманн
Nevskiy prospekt 114–
116. **Map** 7 B2.
Tel *313 6000.*

Supermarket at Passazh
Nevskiy prospekt 48.
Map 6 F1. **Tel** *315 5257.*

SOUVENIRS AND CRAFTS

Imperial Porcelain
Императорский
фарфоровый завод
Obukhovskoy oborony
prospekt 151.
Map 8 F4. **Tel** *560 8544.*
Vladimirskiy prospekt 7.
Map 7 A2. **Tel** *713 1513.*
Nevskiy prospekt 160.
Map 8 D3. **Tel** *717 4838.*

SOVIET MEMORABILIA

D.V.K. (Dom Voyennoy Knigi)
Д.В.К. (Дом военной книги)
Nevskiy prospekt 20.
Map 6 E1. **Tel** *312 0563.*

Nado Zhe
Надо же
Rubinsteina 11.
Map 7 A2. **Tel** *314 3247.*

Sobiratel
Собиратель
Sadovaya ulitsa 13.
Map 6 F1. **Tel** *960 6186.*

ANTIQUES AND ART

Anna Nova
ulitsa Zhukovskovo 28.
Map 7 B1. **Tel** *275 9762.*

Antikvariat
Антиквариат
Malaya Morskaya ulitsa 21.
Map 6 D1. **Tel** *571 2643.*

Borey
Борей
Liteynyy prospekt 58.
Map 7 A1. **Tel** *275 3837.*

Larusse
Stremyannaya 3.
Map 7 C2. **Tel** *572 2043.*

Marina Gisich Gallery
Fontanka 121.
Map 6 D3. **Tel** *314 4380.*

Pushkinskaya 10
Пушкинская 10
(The Door Gallery,
Naviuila Artis, Art-Liga,
New Academy of Fine
Arts, Nonconformists'
Museum) Ligovskiy
prospekt 53. **Map** 7 B3.
Tel *764 5371.*

Renaissance Antiques
Pestela 8. **Map** 3 A5.
Tel *272 2894.*

Russkaya Starina
Русская Старина
Nekrasova 6.
Map 6 E1. **Tel** *273 2603.*

S.P.A.S.
С. П.А.С.
Naberezhnaya reki
Moyki 93.
Map 5 C2.
Tel *571 4260.*

Tertia
Терция
Italyanskaya ulitsa 5.
Map 6 E1. **Tel** *710 5568.*

Union of Artists
Союз художников
Bolshaya Morskaya
ulitsa 38. **Map** 6 D2.
Tel *314 7721.*

BOOKS, FILM AND MUSIC

Akademkniga
Академкнига
Liteynyy prospekt 57.
Map 7 A1.
Tel *273 1398.*

Anglia
Англия
Naberezhnaya reki
Fontanki 38.
Map 7 A2.
Tel *579 8007.*

Bookvoed
Буквоед
Ligovskiy prospekt 10.
Map 7 C2.
Tel *346 5327.*

Dom Knigi
Дом книги
Nevskiy prospekt 28.
Map 6 E1.
Tel *448 2355.*

Na Liteynom
На Литейном
(Books and antiques)
Liteynyy prospekt 61.
Map 7 A2.
Tel *275 3874.*

Porpornyy Legion
Пурпурный Легион
Bolshaya Moskovskaya
ulitsa 6. **Map** 7 A3.
Tel *710 8080.*

Severnaya Lira
Северная лира
Nevskiy prospekt 26.
Map 6 E1. **Tel** *312 0796.*

Staraya Kniga
Старая книга
Nevskiy prospekt 3.
Map 6 D1. **Tel** *312 1620.*

Writers' Bookshop
Лавка писателя
Nevskiy prospekt 66.
Map 7 A2. **Tel** *314 4858.*

FURS AND FASHION

Hat Shop
Шляпный магазин
ulitsa Zhukovskovo 11.
Map 7 B1.

Lena
Лена
Kronverkskaya 7.
Map 6 F1. **Tel** *244 7246.*

Paloma
Палома
Nevskiy prospekt 19
Map 6 E1. **Tel** *571 6091.*

Russkiye Samotsvety
Русские Самоцветы
Bolshoi prospekt
Petrogradskaya 45.
Map 1 C2.
Tel *232 7856.*

Slavyanskiy Stil
Славянский стиль
Pushkinskaya ulitsa 3.
Map 7 B2.
Tel *325 8599.*

Tatyana Parfyonova
Татьяна Парфенова
модный дом
Nevskiy prospekt 51.
Map 7 B2.
Tel *713 3669.*

Toto
Nevskiy prospekt 74.
Map 6 E1.
Tel *579 3590.*

ENTERTAINMENT IN ST PETERSBURG

St Petersburg has an impressive and varied choice of entertainment. Its ballet, opera, classical music and theatre are among the best in the world. In addition to the high culture, a thriving and vibrant nightlife is made up of numerous rock and jazz clubs, bars, art cafés, discos, nightclubs and casinos.

Increasingly, international artists are adding St Petersburg to their tours, and mainstream now exists harmoniously alongside underground in music, theatre and cinema. The St Petersburg Philharmonia and the Mariinskiy (Kirov) ballet and opera *(see p119)* deserve their impressive international reputations, though this does mean that they are often away on tour.

St Petersburg's entertainment changes with the seasons. In winter there are concerts and other traditional indoor events. Summer starts with the White Nights, followed by a mass of festivals and outdoor events.

Folk dancer

The magnificent, gilded interior of the Yusupov Theatre

ENTERTAINMENT INFORMATION

St Petersburg can be quite a difficult city to keep up with, as both official and unofficial events are organized at short notice. For example, theatre programmes are not announced more than a couple of months in advance, so it's important to keep alert in order not to miss the fun.

The best listings in English for local events can be found in *The St Petersburg Times*. This weekly newspaper *(see p217)* is distributed free of charge on Wednesdays to hotels, foreign bars, most fast-food chains and museums. A much broader range of information is provided in Russian in two bi-weekly listings magazines: *Afisha* (www.spb.afisha.com) and *Time Out* (www.spb. timeout.ru).

Mariinskiy poster pillar

Tickets for a wide range of events can be booked on the Russian-language website www.bileter.ru.

Most traditional theatres and concert halls close down for July, August and part of September because their troupes go on tour. Whilst this may deprive visitors of local performers, some theatres bring in guest troupes from Moscow and abroad. In addition, other venues such as the Hermitage *(see p84)* and Alexandrinsky *(see p203)* theatres launch summer programmes that are aimed at tourists. It is worth noting that, although they are fun, their opera and ballet shows are sometimes not of the highest quality.

Matinees start at noon and most evening performances at 7pm. To avoid disappointment check tickets carefully so you know when to arrive.

BUYING TICKETS

Most people buy their tickets with cash and in person. Theatre ticket offices and kiosks can be found all over town, offering tickets up to a month in advance. They display a full programme (in Russian) of all theatre and classical music performances for the next 20 days and are generally open daily from 10am–1pm and 4–7pm. Offices within theatres usually work from 11am–3pm and 4–7pm and sell tickets for all advertised concerts. Non-Russian speakers should not be nervous: most ticket cashiers will be helpful and patient while you point to the date you want. Tickets can also be booked by your hotel concierge. The Mariinskiy Theatre has an excellent English-language website on which tickets can be bought (www.mariinsky.ru). Similar services for other theatres are offered on www.artis.spb.ru.

A few venues, notably the Mariinskiy Theatre *(see p119)*, have price bands, with some tickets set aside at a cheaper rate and available only to Russian citizens. Non-Russians trying to use these may be refused entry or asked to pay the difference in price. Visitors, however, may obtain tickets for sold-out performances at the Mariinskiy Theatre if they go on the day.

As in most cities, touts sell tickets for major events, but beware of possible fakes and inflated prices.

Spectacular performance of the famous *Sleeping Beauty* ballet

LATE-NIGHT TRANSPORT

The metro closes its doors soon after midnight and buses run until 12:15am (infrequently after 11pm). There is no all-night public transport, so expect to take a taxi late at night. Avoid any taxis which wait outside foreign hotels and bars as they charge extortionate prices *(see pp222–3)*.

CHILDREN'S ENTERTAINMENT

Many theatres put on plays in Russian especially for children. See the children's section of *Afisha* or *Time Out*. Unfortunately, few give English-language performances except at New Year. No language problems occur at the **Circus**, however, or at the **Dolphinarium** on Krestovskiy Island.

Some of the best shows and concerts for children are held at **Zazerkalye**, while the puppet theatres usually have several productions based on well-known fairytales.

For the "real" Russian winter experience, try a *troika* (sleigh) ride. These are offered at Pavlosk *(see pp158–61)* and at

Shuvalovka, a reproduction Russian village. Located 30 km (19 miles) out of town, Shuvalovka is open throughout the year and includes wooden houses in 17th-century Russian style, a skating rink, ice slides, a working smithy and a museum of peasant life. Take any minibus to Peterhof from Avtovo metro and ask the driver to stop at Shuvalovka.

FESTIVALS

The several White Nights festivals *(see p51)* draw some of the big names of pop and classical music, and ticket prices go up accordingly – as do accommodation rates – during this time. But there are plenty of other worthwhile seasonal festivals. The White Days (taking in Russian Christmas on 7 January, when the city is shrouded in snow) and Shrovetide festivals place the accent on Russian culture.

Numerous jazz festivals (look out for SKIF in April), the long-standing Early Music Festival (Sep and Oct), along with feature and documentary cinema festivals ensure that the city entertainment scene thrives all year round.

THE RUSSIAN CIRCUS

Circuses first appeared in Russia in the early 19th century, but it was not until 1876–7 that Russia's first permanent circus building was erected for Gaetano Ciniselli's Italian circus. St Petersburg's circus is still based at this historic site, which was modernized in 1963, and continues to practise the traditional training, skills and animal acts which have made the Russian circus famous throughout the world.

Acrobatic performers, St Petersburg's circus

The Arts

For a city renowned worldwide for its rich tradition of ballet and classical music, it is not surprising that St Petersburg has a wide range of cultural events on offer. An evening at the Mariinskiy Theatre, along with its Concert Hall, is a highlight of any visit. It is also well worth venturing into the many other theatres, music halls and churches to absorb the city's cultural diversity. Classical music is vastly popular and local orchestras are much in demand the world over. In addition, there are the evocative sounds of church choirs, the lively ambience of folk cabarets, and numerous festivals (see pp50–53) held to encourage young musicians, composers, film-makers and dancers.

MARIINSKIY THEATRE

The **Mariinskiy Theatre** (see p119), the epitome of the best in Russian ballet and opera, is still waiting for its second theatre. However, the original venue is open to the public and gives performances regularly. Its Concert Hall is one of the principal venues for the stars of the White Nights festival. For the most up-to-date information on the theatre's plans and to see the current programme, check the website and keep an eye on the listings.

BALLET

Some of the best dancers in the world come from the **Mariinskiy** (see p119). Tickets for performances by leading ballerinas Ulyana Lopatkina and Diana Vishneva are hard to come by. One of the highlights of the year is the Christmas performance of *The Nutcracker*, danced by children from the Vaganova Ballet School (see p110). Ballet at the **Mussorgsky Opera and Ballet Theatre** and the **Conservatory Opera and Ballet Theatre** (see p120) are of more varied quality but still provide good entertainment.

In summer, many troupes perform for tourists in various theatres, but with inconsistent levels of skill. Boris Eifmann's modern ballet company and Valery Mikhaylovskiy's all-male Muzhskoy Ballet are popular with locals, and play at venues like the **October Concert Hall**.

OPERA

Tchaikovsky's opera *Eugene Onegin* and Mussorgsky's *Boris Godunov* remain stalwarts in any repertory. Operas are performed (usually in their original language) at the **Mikhailovsky Theatre** and at the **Mariinskiy**. Look out for local stars Anna Netrebko and Olga Borodina, or the tenor Vladimir Galuzin. Less common works, including 18th-century chamber operas, are performed by **St Petersburg Opera** on their own stage, and at the **Hermitage** and tiny **Yusupov Theatres**. Look out for sparkling productions at the children's theatre **Zazerkalye** (see p201).

CLASSICAL MUSIC

The city's classical repertoire is huge. Tchaikovsky, Shostakovich, Mussorgsky and Rimsky-Korsakov lived in St Petersburg and their music is performed here frequently. **The Great Hall of the Philharmonia** (see p98), the **Small Hall of the Philharmonia** (see p48) and the **Academic Capella** (see p112) are historic venues for classical concerts. The former is the home of the St Petersburg Philharmonic Orchestra. Other historic locations used for concerts include the Hermitage (see p84), and the palaces of Tsarskoe Selo (see p150) and Sheremetev (see p129). By contrast, **Dom Kochnevoy** and **Beloselskiy-Belozerskiy** are intimate spaces for chamber music.

CHURCH MUSIC

The music of an Orthodox choir is one of the most evocative sounds in Russia. The best are heard on Saturday evenings and Sunday mornings at the **Holy Trinity Cathedral** in Alexander Nevskiy Monastery (see p130) and at the **Cathedral of the Transfiguration** (see p127). Services in the **Cathedral of our Lady of Kazan** (see p111) are also of a high standard. More formal religious music is performed in the **Smolnyy Cathedral** (see p128).

FOLK MUSIC

The tourist industry encourages visits to concerts of Russian folk music and dancing, some of which are very good, especially those at the **Nikolaevskiy Palace**. Many restaurants, such as **St Petersburg** (see p188), have a folk cabaret, though these can be kitsch and loud. **Podvoryie** restaurant (see p191) in the grounds of Pavlovsk Palace, however, has an excellent, small ensemble.

STREET MUSIC

Democracy had the unexpected effect of allowing many informal activities such as busking, which brought some highly talented musicians onto the streets. Today, as skilled players stake their pitches, the sound of music fills the city's streets. The two underpasses beneath Nevskiy prospekt by Gostinyy Dvor are busy busking spots, while other metro stations are popular sites for old ladies singing Russian love ballads.

THEATRE

All performances are in Russian. For non-Russian speakers, productions of classic plays such as *The Cherry Orchard* may be interesting to experience, but more obscure works can be difficult.

Since the days of the Soviet Union, the leading light in the drama world has been the **Bolshoy Drama Theatre** (BDT). The **Alexandrinskiy Theatre** (see p110) is the oldest in Russia; one of the newest is the **Molodyozhnyy (Youth) Theatre**. Lev Dodin's direction of the **Malyy Drama Theatre (MDT)** has brought it international fame as the "Theatre of Europe", despite all performances being in Russian (though some are performed in English).

CINEMA

Most cinemas now show Hollywood blockbusters, but the majority of foreign films are dubbed into Russian rather than subtitled. **Mirage** sometimes holds showings of undubbed films, as do a few Russian cinemas such as **Dom**

Kino and **Avrora**. A large number of film festivals are held in the city every year, and these frequently include films in their original language.

The *St Petersburg Times*, *Afisha* and *Time Out* give full coverage of all festivals, including the main **Festival of Festivals** *(see p51)*.

DIRECTORY

TICKETS

Tickets are sold in city kiosks and at individual theatres unless stated otherwise.

BALLET AND OPERA

Conservatory Opera and Ballet Theatre
Театр оперы и балета Консерватории
Teatr opery i baleta Konservatorii
Teatralnaya pl 3.
Map 5 C3. **Tel** 312 2519.

Hermitage Theatre
Эрмитажный театр
Ermitazhnyy teatr
Dvortsovaya nab 34.
Map 2 E5. **Tel** 571 5059.
(Tickets from city kiosks and hotels only.)

Mariinskiy Theatre
Мариинский театр
Mariinskiy teatr
Teatralnaya pl 1.
Map 5 B3.
Tel 326 4141.
www.mariinsky.ru

Mikhailovsky Theatre
Михайловский Театр
Teatr Mikhailovsky
Pl Iskusstv 1.
Map 6 E1.
Tel 595 4305.
🔲 *late Jul–Aug.*
www.mikhailovsky.ru

October Concert Hall
Большой концертный зал Октябрьский
Bolshoy kontsertnyy zal Oktyabrskiy
Ligovskiy pr 6.
Map 7 C1. **Tel** 275 1273.

St Petersburg Opera
Санкт-Петербург опера
Sankt-Petersburg opera
Galernaya ul 33.
Map 5 B2. **Tel** 312 3982.

Yusupov Theatre
Юсуповский театр
Yusupovskiy teatr
Yusupov Palace, nab reki Moyki 94. **Map** 5 B3.
Tel 314 9883, 314 1991.

CLASSICAL MUSIC

Academic Capella
Академическая Капелла
Akademicheskaya Kapella
Nab reki Moyki 20.
Map 2 E5.
Tel 314 1058.

Beloselskiy-Belozerskiy Palace
Дворец Белосельских-Белозерских
Dvorets Beloselskikh-Belozerskikh
Nevskiy pr 41.
Map 7 A2.
Tel 315 5236.

Dom Kochnevoy
Лом Кочневой
Nab reki Fontanki 41.
Map 6 F2.
Tel 310 2987.

Great Hall of the Philharmonia
Большой зал филармонии
Bolshoy zal Filarmonii
Mikhaylovskaya ul 2.
Map 6 F1.
Tel 710 4257.

Small Hall of the Philharmonia
Малый зал филармонии
Malyy zal Filarmonii
Nevskiy pr 30.
Map 6 F1.
Tel 571 8333.

CHURCH MUSIC

Cathedral of Our Lady of Kazan
Собор Казанской Богоматери
Sobor Kazanskoy Bogomateri
Kazanskaya ploshchad 2.
Map 6 E1.
🕑 *9am & 7:30pm daily.*

Cathedral of the Transfiguration
Спасо-Преображенский собор
Spaso-Preobrazhenskiy sobor
Preobrazhenskaya pl 1.
Map 3 B5.
🕑 *10am & 6pm daily.*

Holy Trinity Cathedral
Свято-Троицкий собор
Svyato-Troitskiy sobor
Alexander Nevsky Monastery, pl Aleksandra-Nevskovo.
Map 8 E4.
🕑 *10am & 6pm daily.*

Smolnyy Cathedral
Смольный собор
Smolnyy sobor
Ploshchad Rastrelli 3.
Map 4 F4.
Tel 577 1421.

FOLK MUSIC

Nikolaevskiy Palace
Николаевский дворец
Nikolaevskiy dvorets
Pl Truda 4. **Map** 5 B2.
Tel 312 5500.

THEATRE

Alexandrinskiy Theatre
Александринский театр
Aleksandrinskiy teatr
Ploshchad Ostrovskovo 6.
Map 6 F2. **Tel** 312 1545.

Bolshoy Drama Theatre (BDT)
Большой драматический театр
Bolshoy dramaticheskiy teatr
Nab reki Fontanki 65.
Map 6 F2.
Tel 310 9242.

Malyy Drama Theatre (MDT)
МДТ – Театр Евролы
MDT – Teatr Evropy
Ul Rubinshteyna 18.
Map 7 A2.
Tel 713 2078.

Molodyozhnyy Theatre
Молодёжный театр на фонтанке
Molodyozhnyy teatr na Fontanke
Nab reki Fontanki 114.
Map 6 D4.
Tel 316 6564.

CINEMA

Avrora Cinema
Аврора
Nevskiy pr 60.
Map 7 A2.
Tel 315 5254.

Crystal Palace
Кристал Палас
Kristal-Palace
Nevskiy pr 72.
Map 7 A2.
Tel 272 2382.

Dom Kino
Дом Кино
Karavannaya ulitsa 12.
Map 7 A1.
Tel 314 0638.

Mirage
Мираж
Bolshoy pr 35,
Petrogradskaya.
Map 1 C2.
Tel 232 4838.

Live Music and Nightlife

St Petersburg was at the heart of the underground Soviet rock scene and many of the best Russian sounds originate here. The nightclub scene offers mostly techno music and mainstream pop, in vast complexes with strobe lights, and attracts the well-paid young and *nouveaux riches*. Some smaller clubs featuring an eclectic mix describe themselves as "art" clubs or cafés, and host live music one night and *avant-garde* fashion shows or films the next. Some large clubs and casinos accept credit cards. Where hours are not given, check programmes before heading out. Avoid places that admit foreigners or females free.

ART AND CAFE CLUBS

Fish Fabrique is probably the oldest art café in town, having survived the ups and downs of recent Russian history. **Brodyachaya Sobaka** has been frequented by poets such as Anna Akhmatova since the Silver Age, and other major poets still come here to perform their works in arts events. **GEZ-21** even manages to fit poetry and philosophy readings in amongst rock concerts.

ROCK VENUES

Under the Soviet regime, Leningrad rock was rebellious without being overtly political. Though there is now less emphasis on poetical lyrics that express a spirit of freedom from control and repression, Russian rock still owes much to its rebellious past, while also managing to incorporate the latest in Western music trends.

Kosmonavt hosts international bands and **Pyatnitsa**, rowdy punk bands. Rockabilly gave birth to **Money Honey** and to the **City Club** upstairs (for older rockers), which in turn led to an explosion of rockabilly groups in the city.

Big-name, massed audience rock and pop concerts are usually held in one of the big concert halls such as the **Oktyabrskiy Bolshoy Kontsertnyy Zal**, or the largest of them all, the **Ledovyy Dvorets**. When major international stars come to town, however, they usually perform on a specially erected stage in Palace Square.

JAZZ VENUES

The father of Petersburg jazz is David Goloshchokin, who set up the **Jazz Philharmonic Hall**. As the name suggests, the jazz played in the hall is mainly very traditional, and, sadly, dancing or talking are prohibited. **JFC** has led the way for improvisation and innovative jazz. Guests here are often musicians with an international reputation. **Jimi Hendrix Blues Club** comes a close second to JFC by virtue of its mixture of blues and rock, and its good food.

Restaurants such as **Sunduk** (*see p189*) often bring in good live performers. **48 Chairs** is a classy, intimate restaurant-club that puts on nightly performances.

BARS WITH MUSIC

Live music is played in many bars around town, but on the whole a lot of the music in such places is awful. It is best to stick with the established, more reliable clubs. **Liverpool**, for example, hosts live bands, not all of whom play Beatles cover versions. In addition, **Manhattan** sometimes has good jazz acts. **Hallelujah Bar** is a small bar hosting regular theme nights. Live music comes courtesy of up and coming student bands.

NIGHTCLUBS AND DISCOS

Big entertainment complexes such as **Metro** (with three floors) cater mainly to the young and upwardly mobile, playing house, techno and Russian dance music. **Barrel**

is an upscale nightclub with guest DJs, karaoke and a restaurant. Despite its out-of-town location, **Efir** is one of the best places to see international musicians and local DJs.

Tribunal has a policy of playing only mainstream music, and thus manges to attract a huge crowd during summer months, when young tourists stream in.

Smaller, more diverse clubs, such as the underground **Griboedov**, are still very much of the alternative culture trend, playing a variety of the latest hits from Europe, and hosting fashion shows and other cultural events. **Begemot** has different music in each room and also serves as a restaurant. Live DJs and food served all night make this a popular venue. **Typographia** offers music to suit all tastes, from tango to house music. It is also renowned for its wide selection of vodka.

GAY CLUBS

For some reason, few gay clubs in St Petersburg manage to last more than four or five years. **Cabaret** is, however, an exception, remaining popular while other venues come and go; and **Central Station** seems to have made a go of it, too. Gay culture in the city is strongly tied into the art world, and events are advertised at Saturday exhibitions in the New Academy of Fine Arts at Pushkinskaya ulitsa 10.

BILLIARDS AND BOWLING

Along with bars and nightclubs, a popular night out in St Petersburg is billiards and bowling.

Billiard halls and bowling alleys are casual but upscale affairs and always serve a full selection of alcohol as well as offering respectable restaurants with extensive menus. Many locals go to these places without ever lifting a pool cue or a bowling ball, instead preferring to enjoy the atmosphere.

DIRECTORY

ART AND CAFE CLUBS

Brodyachaya Sobaka
Бродячая Собака
Italianskaya ulitsa 4.
Map 6 F1.
Tel 312 8047.
www.vsobaka.ru

Fish Fabrique
Ligovskiy pr 53.
Map 7 B3.
Tel 764 4857.
⬚ *3pm–6am daily.*
www.fishfabrique.ru

GEZ-21
ГЕЗ-21
Ligovskiy pr 58.
Map 7 B3.
Tel 764 5263.
www.gez21.ru

ROCK VENUES

Arctica
Арктика
Ul Beringa 38.
Tel 337 3277.

Kosmonavt
Космонавт
Bronnitskaya ulitsa 24.
Map 6 E5.
Tel 922 1300.
www.kosmonavt.su

Ledovyy Dvorets
Ледовый дврец
Pr Pyatiletok 1.
Tel 718 6620.

Money Honey / City Club
Apraksin dvor block 13,
Sadovaya ul 28–30.
Map 6 E2.
Tel 310 0549.

Oktyabrskiy Bolshoy Kontsertnyy Zal
БКЗ Октябрьский
Ligovskiy prospekt 6.
Map 7 C1.
Tel 275 1300.

Pyatnitsa
Пятница
Moskovskiy pr 10–12.
Map 6 D3.
Tel 310 2317.
www.clubfriday.ru

Yubileynyy Dvorets Sporta
Дворец спорта
юбилейный
Pr Dobrolyubova 18.
Map 1 B3.
Tel 702 3622.

JAZZ VENUES

48 Chairs
Ulitsa Rubinshteyna 5.
Map 7 A2.
Tel 315 7775.
www.48chairs.com

Jazz Philharmonic Hall
Филармония Джазовой
музыки
Zagorodnyy prospekt 27.
Tel 764 8565.
⬚ *8–11pm Tue–Sun.*
www.jazz-hall.spb.ru

JFC
Shpalernaya ulitsa 33.
Map 3 C4.
Tel 272 9850.
⬚ *7–11pm daily.*
www.jfc-club.spb.ru

Jimi Hendrix Blues Club
Джими Хендрикс
блюз-клуб
Liteynyy prospekt 33.
Map 3 A5.
Tel 579 8813.
⬚ *noon–midnight daily.*
Concerts 8:30pm.

BARS WITH MUSIC

Datscha
Дача
Dumskaya ul 9.
Map 6 E2.
⬚ *6pm–6am daily.*

Hallelujah Bar
Inzhenernaya ulitsa 7/8.
Map 6 F1.
Tel 940 510.
www.hallebar.ru

Liverpool
Ливерпуль
Ul Mayakovskovo 16.
Map 7 B1.
Tel 579 2054.

Manhattan
Nab reki Fontanki 90.
Map 6 E3.
Tel 713 1945.
⬚ *1pm–midnight daily.*
www.manhattanclub.ru

NIGHTCLUBS AND DISCOS

Barrel
Kazanskaya ulitsa 5.
Map 6 E2.
Tel 929 8298
www.project-barrel.ru

Begemot
Бегемот
Sadovaya ulitsa 12
Map 6 F1.
Tel 925 4000.
www.bar-bergemot.ru

Coyote Ugly
Liteynyy prospekt 57.
Map 7 A1.
Tel 272 0790.
www.coyoteugly.ru

Efir
Ефир
Malyy prospekt
Petrogradskaya 54.
Map 1 B2.
Tel 940 0548.
www.efirclub.ru

Griboedov
Грибоедов
Voronezhskaya ul 2A.
Map 7 B4.
Tel 764 4355.
⬚ *6pm–6am.*
www.griboedovclub.ru

Jakata
Ul Bakunina 5.
Map 8 D2.
Tel 346 7462.

Metro
Метро
Ligovskiy pr 174.
Tel 766 0204.
⬚ *10pm–6am daily.*
www.metroclub.ru

Revolution
Ul Sadovaya 28/30.
Map 6 E2.
Tel 717 5915, 571 2391.
⬚ *1pm–6am daily.*

Tribunal
Karavannaya 26.
Map 5 C1. *Tel 314 2423.*
⬚ *9pm–6am daily.*

Tunnel
Тоннель
Corner of Zverinskaya ul
and Lyubanskiy per.
Map 1 C3. *Tel 233 4015.*

Typographia
Типография
Ulitsa Mira 3
Map 2 D2.
Tel 600 4448.
www.typograf-club.ru

GAY CLUBS

Cabaret (A.K.A. Matrosskaya Tishina)
Кабаре
Razezzhaya 43.
Tel 764 0901.
www.cabarespb.ru

Central Station
Ulitsa Lomonosova 1.
Map 6 E2.
Tel 312 3600.
www.centralstation.ru

BILLIARDS AND BOWLING

Art Billiard
Арт-Бильярд
Bolshaya Morskaya ulitsa 52.
Map 5 C2.
Tel 312 3077.
www.art-billiard.ru.

Bowling City Senaya
Боулинг Сити Сенная
Ulitsa Yefimova 3.
Map 6 E3.
Tel 380 3005.
www.bowlingpark.ru.

The Cellar
Birzhevoi proyezd 2/24.
Map 1 C5.
Tel 335 2207.

Sapsan
Сапсан
Galeria Mall,
Ligovskiy 300.
Map 7 C3.
Tel 600 0331.
www.sapsan-bowling.ru

SURVIVAL
GUIDE

PRACTICAL INFORMATION

VISIT RUSSIA

Russian National
Tourist Office logo

The street signs and maps of St Petersburg are not as difficult to negotiate as it may first appear when confronted with daunting Cyrillic letters. Not only do hotels, restaurants and all service sectors attempt to compensate by being helpful to foreigners, but the city has English signage pointing out major sights and shops. There are also several tourist information offices located near popular places of interest. On the street, many things will seem unfamiliar, but with patience and determination everything is possible, from making international telephone calls and exchanging money to finding emergency medical treatment. The city has developed at an astonishing pace during the last decade, and as quality improves, prices now often outstrip Western equivalents.

The Grand Cascade of Peterhof Palace during the White Nights

WHEN TO GO

The height of the tourist season in St Petersburg is during the famed White Nights *(see p51 and p201)*, from mid-May to mid-July, when the sun barely sets for an hour due to the city's northern location. Prices at this time are at their highest. Fewer tourists visit during the winter.

VISAS AND PASSPORTS

Visas are required for all visitors to Russia. Package tour companies will organize visas for you, but independent travellers need to arrange their own. Document requirements change regularly and it is essential to check these in advance (http://ru.vfsglobal. co.uk). You will need to show proof of an invitation (visa support) from a hotel, tour company or business in Russia. Invitations can be purchased online at **visaable.com** or from **Go Russia**. The easiest option is to pay your travel agency to process the visa for you.

Alternatively, fill in the application yourself and either post it or deliver it in person to the **Russian Visa Centre** in London.

CUSTOMS INFORMATION

Passports and visas are checked thoroughly at immigration. Visitors must fill out an immigration card, which is available in Russian and English. Part of the completed card is retained by travellers for presentation on departure.

There are no limitations on the amount of money you can bring into Russia; Russian money to the value of 326,000 roubles may be exported. Any items of considerable value, such as diamond jewellery, should be noted on a customs form on entry.

All foreigners must register with **OVIR** (visa registration) within seven working days before travelling and obtain a stamp of registration on their migration card or in their passport. Tourists spending less than seven working days in the country do not need to register.

TOURIST INFORMATION

Hotels are a good source of tourist information, as are Tourist information offices. **Sindbad Travel Centre** runs a reliable tourist information service, as well as booking accommodation and entertainment. Also try www.saint-petersburg.com, which is a useful English-language website. The bimonthly free guide *St Petersburg In Your Pocket* and English-language newspapers *(see p217)* give up-to-the-minute information.

Tourist information kiosks can be found all over the city centre: Palace Square Ploshchad Vosstaniya, Smolny Cathedral, Sadovaya Ulitsa and St Isaac's Square. Main offices are at the airport.

Tourists consulting guide books

ADMISSION PRICES

Many museums and theatres, notably the Hermitage *(see pp84–93)*, the Russian Museum *(see pp104–107)* and the Mariinskiy *(see p119)* charge foreigners a higher entry fee than Russians. Students and schoolchildren are entitled to discounts.

The ticket office is often positioned away from the entrance, so look for the "КАССА" sign. Ticket prices vary from about 50 roubles for small state museums to 400 roubles for entrance to the Hermitage. A good value option is to buy a Tourist Card from tourist information offices. Cards are valid for two days (1,950 roubles) to seven days (3,950 roubles), and offer free entry to many state museums, as well as discounts in some restaurants.

OPENING HOURS

Most sights are open from 10:30am to 6pm, with no break for lunch, and close one day a week. They also close one day each month for cleaning; see individual museum entries for this information. Last tickets are sold about 1 hour before closing. Parks are usually open from 10am to 10pm, later during White Nights.

Sign for open *(otkryto)*

Sign for closed *(zakryto)*

VISITING CHURCHES

Attending an Orthodox service is a fascinating experience. Since services tend to run for several hours, it is generally fine simply to drop in. Certain dress codes must be observed: no shorts; men should remove hats; ladies should cover their shoulders and chest and preferably wear a hat or headscarf. Women in trousers are accepted in town churches, but small monasteries outside of the city will strictly enforce the no trousers rule. The most important services are held on Saturday evening, Sunday morning and on major religious holidays.

Most major faiths are represented in the city. Churches

St Isaac's Cathedral, open to visitors

tend to be open all day from early morning until late. Service times at Catholic and Protestant churches are published in *The St Petersburg Times (see p217)*.

LANGUAGE

Cyrillic, the alphabet used in the Russian language, is named after the 9th-century monks Cyril and Methodius who invented it. The apparent similarity between Cyrillic and roman letters can be misleading. Some letters are common to both alphabets, others look similar but represent totally different sounds. Various systems of transliteration are in usage, but they do not differ enough to cause serious confusion.

Most people who come into contact with tourists speak some English and passers-by on the street will do their best if asked directions. Knowledge of a few Russian words *(see pp260–4)* is appreciated.

ETIQUETTE AND SMOKING

On public transport, it is expected that young men should offer their seats to women with young children or the elderly.

Greetings amongst friends involve a handshake (between men) or a kiss, or simply saying – *"privet"* (hi).

Photographic restrictions have more or less disappeared. In museums expect to buy a ticket for the right to photograph or film inside. Tripods and flashes are not to be used. Photography in the

metro is prohibited as it is seen as a threat to national security. If you do wish to take a photo in the metro, approach a police officer, who may allow you to for a fee, which is unlikely to exceed 100 roubles.

Smoking is prohibited in cinemas, museums, theatres and on public transport. Special areas are usually allocated for smoking in restaurants and on long-distance trains. Drinking alcohol is prohibited in the street. Russians take great pleasure in smoking and drinking and frequent toasts are required to justify the filling and draining of glasses. At a private home, always toast the hostess *(za khozyayku)* or the host *(za khozyayina)*.

PUBLIC CONVENIENCES

The situation is improving, but most public toilets are quite basic, and a few cafés do not have any toilet facilities at all. In such cases, go to the nearest hotel or use the pay toilets located in department stores. The person who takes the money also hands out toilet paper. There are portaloos with attendants situated near several of the major tourist attractions. The fee ranges from 10 to 30 roubles. Baby-changing facilities are an extremely rare amenity in Russia and can be found only in upscale hotels, the biggest shopping malls and Western-owned stores such as IKEA, where they are usually free of charge.

TAXES AND TIPPING

Roubles are the sole valid currency in Russia *(see p215)*. All cash payments must be made in roubles only and all prices are given in roubles. Credit cards are accepted in most restaurants and hotels, as well as larger shops, though there are some places that will not accept them so it is best to carry cash with you.

Tipping is a matter of choice. Simply pay what you feel is right; 50 or 100 roubles is usually sufficient.

The Hermitage museum offers disabled access to visitors

TRAVELLERS WITH SPECIAL NEEDS

While just a few years ago, St Petersburg had almost no facilities for disabled visitors, the situation is gradually improving, though services remain far from ideal and transport in particular is a problem. Of the museums, only the Hermitage and the Russian Museum have disabled access. Many 4- and 5-star hotels are now equipped for disabled guests, with ramps, lifts, wider doorways, handrails and showers with removable sides. **Liberty** specializes in tours around St Petersburg and its suburbs for disabled travellers. The company uses minibuses equipped with a lift or folding ramp to transport wheelchair-users around the city, and can also advise on hotels and restaurants with disabled access and facilities.

TRAVELLING WITH CHILDREN

Russians adore children, and travellers in the company of under-tens are likely to attract a good deal of attention and many compliments. Russian *babushki* (grannies) also think nothing of telling parents of their failings.

The city has many parks and during school holidays temporary playgrounds are sometimes set up around town. There are several playgrounds in the Tauride Gardens (*see p128*), as well as a playground in the gardens next to the Bronze Horseman (*see pp78–9*).

Museums and public transport are free for under-sevens. Schoolchildren pay the full fare on transport, but pay a reduced price at museums (proof of being under 18 may be required).

Attractions guaranteed to delight younger travellers are listed in the Children's Entertainment section (*see p201*).

Young visitors enjoying the view

SENIOR TRAVELLERS

St Petersburg is popular with senior travellers and many hotels offer guided coach trips around the city. Concierges can arrange tickets and transport to ballet and opera performances, as well as to the city's museums and the former imperial estates located outside St Petersburg.

Discounts for pensioners are often available at museums and for other activities such as boat trips, but not for single tickets on transport.

The hotels on St Isaac's Square, such as the Astoria and Angleterre (*see p174*), are quiet and in convenient locations, as is the Grand Hotel Europe (*see p175*), located just off Nevsky Prospekt, close to many sights.

GAY AND LESBIAN TRAVELLERS

Russian society is not in general very tolerant of homosexuality, and males in particular should be aware that public displays of affection may attract unwanted attention. The city does however have a thriving gay and lesbian scene, with several gay clubs (*see p204*).

The **Russian LGBT Network** provides general information on gay and lesbian life in the city. Local organizations **Coming Out** and Gay.ru provide information orientated to gay and lesbian visitors. *The St Petersburg Times* includes gay clubs and bars in its club guide, but there are no English-language listings of daily events.

TRAVELLING ON A BUDGET

St Petersburg is no longer a cheap city to visit, and it is increasingly difficult to find things to do on a budget. There are, however, many *stolovayas* (canteens) around the city, where travellers can enjoy traditional Russian food at bargain prices.

There is an increasing number of hostels in the city (*see p170*), such as Life Hostel on Nevsky prospect, from where some of **Peter's Walking Tours** leave. Free English-language walking tours are also available. Several bike rental offices in the city offer an affordable way to get around, and public transport is inexpensive compared to many Western European cities.

An ISIC (international student card) entitles its holder to discounts in museums, and on rail and air travel if it is booked through Sindbad Travel Centre (*see p170*). A visit to the Hermitage is free upon presentation of an ISIC card, and for all visitors on the first Thursday of every month.

Entrance to all parks inside the city is free, as well as to the grounds of the Peter and Paul Fortress (*see pp66–7*). The Field of Mars (*see p94*) is popular with young people in warmer months.

TIME

St Petersburg follows Moscow time, which is 4 hours ahead of Greenwich Mean Time (GMT), and 9 hours ahead of Eastern Standard Time. As of 2011, Russia decided to remain on permanent summertime and abandon the practice of changing the clocks. This decision has proved unpopular, however, and may change.

ELECTRICITY

The electrical current is 220 V. Two-pin plugs are required, but some of the old Soviet two-pin sockets do not take modern European plugs, which have slightly thicker pins. American appliances require a 220:110 current adaptor. Travellers are advised to bring adaptors with them because they can be difficult to find in St Petersburg.

RESPONSIBLE TRAVEL

While St Petersburg, and Russia as a whole, have a regrettably poor record in environmental issues, it is easy to travel about the city using green transport, such as trolleybuses and trams. Bikes can be rented from companies such as **Skat Prokat** and Velotour *(see p223)*, although it is best to stick to quieter side roads.

It is possible to visit most of the city's major attractions on foot, either independently or on a walking tour *(see p222)*.

At **Sennoi Market**, a small part of the outdoor area is devoted to fruit and vegetables that have been locally grown in the Leningrad Oblast area.

CONVERSION TABLE

Imperial to Metric
1 inch = 2.54 centimetres
1 foot = 30 centimetres
1 mile = 1.6 kilometres
1 ounce = 28 grams
1 pound = 454 grams
1 pint = 0.6 litres
1 UK gallon = 4.6 litres

Metric to Imperial
1 centimetre = 0.4 inches
1 metre = 3 feet, 3 inches
1 kilometre = 0.6 miles
1 gram = 0.04 ounces
1 kilogram = 2.2 pounds
1 litre = 1.8 UK pints

DIRECTORY

EMBASSIES AND CONSULATES

Australia
11 Moika Embankment
Tel (495) 315 1100.
http://www.dfat.gov.au/
missions/countries/rupe.
html

Canada
Moscow, Starokonju-
shenny per 23.
Tel (495) 925 6000.

Ireland
30 Kuznetsovskaya Ulitsa.
Tel (495) 326 9057 or
(495) 937 0233.

New Zealand
Moscow, Povorskaya
ul 44.
Tel (495) 956 3579.
http://www.nzembassy.
com/russia

UK
Pl Proletarskoy Diktatury 5.
Map 4 E4.
Tel 320 3200.

US
Furshtatskaya ul 15.
Map 3 B4.
Tel 331 2600.
Fax 331 2852.

VISAS AND PASSPORTS

Go Russia
Boundary House, Boston
Road, London, W7 2QE.
Tel (020) 3355 7717.
www.justgorussia.co.uk

Russian Visa Center
15–27 Gee Street,
London EC1V 3RD.
Tel 0905 889 0149.
http://ru.vfsglobal.co.uk

Visaable.com
Tel +7 921 369 3412.
www.visaable.com

CUSTOMS INFORMATION

OVIR
Овир
(Tsentralnyy district)
Foreign department,
Pereulok Krylova 5.
Map 6 F2.
Tel 315 7936.
(Central) Ul Kirochnaya 4.
Map 3 B5.
Tel 278 3486.
www.visatorussia.com

TOURIST INFORMATION OFFICES

Main Office
14 Sadovaya Ulitsa.
Tel 310 2822.

Information Pavilions

Ploshchad Rastrelli (in front
of Smolny Cathedral)
⏱ *8am–6pm Mon–Fri.*
Palace Square
⏱ *10am–7pm daily.*
St Isaac's Square
⏱ *10am–7pm daily.*
Ploshchad Vosstaniya
⏱ *10am–7pm daily.*
Marine Facade passenger
terminal
⏱ *10am–7pm daily
(May–Sep).*
Kronverkskaya
Embankment (opposite
Peter and Paul Fortress)
⏱ *10am–7pm daily.*
Pulkovo airport, terminals
1 and 2
⏱ *10am–7pm daily.*

Sindbad Travel Centre
12 2-ya Sovietskaya Ulitsa.
Tel 655 0775.
http://edu.sindbad.ru

Visit Russia
257 West 39th St, Studio
39, New York, NY 10018.
Tel (1800) 755 3080.

TRAVELLERS WITH SPECIAL NEEDS

Liberty
12 Ulitsa Polozova.
Tel 232 8163.
www.libertytour.ru

GAY AND LESBIAN TRAVELLERS

Coming Out
Tel (812) 313 9369.
www.comingoutspb.ru

Gay.ru
www.gay.ru

Russian LGBT Network
191040, St Petersburg,
Ligovsky prospekt 87,
office 528.
Tel (812) 454 6452.
http://lgbtnet.ru

TRAVELLNG ON A BUDGET

Peter's Walking Tours
Tel 943 1229.
www.peterswalk.com

RESPONSIBLE TRAVEL

Sennoi Rynok (Sennoi Market)
4a Moskovsky prospekt.
Tel 310 1209.
⏱ *8am–7pm daily.*

Skat Prokat
7 Goncharnaya Ulitsa.
Tel 717 6838.

Personal Security and Health

St Petersburg is a relatively safe city. Petty crime should be the only concern for tourists, and even this can generally be avoided if the usual precautions are taken. Make copies of your passport and visa, note traveller's cheque and credit card numbers and, for language reasons, keep a card with the address you are staying at in Russia. A multilingual tourist helpline (300 3333) can assist with any issue and is a free number from a mobile phone on the Megafon network by dialling 0333. Medical insurance is essential, as local healthcare compares poorly with Western standards, and English-speaking services or medical evacuation via Finland are very expensive. Many medicines are readily available, but it is best to bring specific medication needed.

Police officer *(politsiya)*

POLICE

Several kinds of police officer operate on St Petersburg's streets. Their uniforms change according to the weather, with the very necessary addition of fur hats and big overcoats in the winter. The street officers *(politsiya)* wear dark grey uniforms and many carry guns. The riot police or OMON wear blue camouflage fatigues.

Separate from both these are the traffic police, whose uniforms carry the logo ДПС (DPS) on the chest and shoulder. They have the authority to stop any vehicle to check documents.

Both the street police and traffic police supplement their income by fining people for minor infringements of the law, and have been known to stop tourists for document checks and then "forget" to return wallets or mobile phones. This is far more likely to happen to drunk tourists. Avoid the police if possible and stay alert if stopped.

WHAT TO BE AWARE OF

Every visitor to Russia is seriously advised to take out travel insurance. Once in St Petersburg, simple rules should be observed, such as not displaying large sums of money; carrying cash in a concealed money belt; and keeping passports, tickets and all valuables in the hotel whenever possible. Security in Western-run hotels is very high, but in all hotels it is advisable to place valuables in the safe. Travellers' cheques *(see p214)* may have an insurance policy but are expensive to use and are easily laundered in Russia.

Avoid the "gypsies" who occasionally group on Nevskiy prospekt, apparently begging. If they do approach, do not stop for them and keep a firm hold of your possessions. Also watch out for pick-pockets on the metro and buses. A common tactic is for the culprit to (seemingly accidentally) block your exit from the metro car or bus while another goes through your pockets. Avoid the back doors on buses, which are narrower than those in the centre, and be on guard for people employing these tactics.

Women on their own are unlikely to encounter sexual harassment, though they should ignore kerbcrawlers and avoid taking a cab alone at night. When travelling around as with any city, always be alert and safety-conscious. On the streets be aware of local drivers, who see all pedestrians as a nuisance. Avoid walking on manhole covers, which tend to rock or even collapse under your feet.

IN AN EMERGENCY

In the event of a fire, call 01. For police, call 02 and for an ambulance, call 03. There is also a combined emergency number, 112.

LOST AND STOLEN PROPERTY

The greatest danger faced by foreigners is that posed by pickpockets and petty thieves. If threatened in the streets it is advisable to hand over belongings on demand.

Police car

Fire engine

Ambulance

If you have property stolen, report it to the local police station for insurance purposes. They are unlikely to have an interpreter, so ask your hotel for assistance or call the **Tourist Helpline**. The central place to go to for lost property is on Suvorovsky prospekt. You should take all your documents with you: passport, visa and migration card. You will be required to write a statement, so it is important to call the tourist helpline first for an interpreter to be present. If you lose something on the public transport system, call the main tourist helpline. They will hold items for a limited time, so contact them immediately. If you lose your passport, inform your embassy *(see p211)*. Lost credit or debit cards should be reported to the card issuer *(see p214)*.

HOSPITALS AND PHARMACIES

There are pharmacies *(apteka)* located throughout the city, and many are open 24 hours. Some stronger medications can be bought over the counter, so prescriptions are not necessary. Every assistant is a trained pharmacist and can advise alternative drugs. If you have specific requirements, particularly insulin, bring sufficient supplies for your stay.

If you fall ill, seek advice at your hotel, which should have its own doctor. Several companies, notably the **Medem International Clinic** and **Euromed**, specialize in dealing with foreigners. They cover everything from minor emergencies, dental care, X-rays and pre-natal care to medical evacuation. Their charges are high, but they are used to dealing with foreign insurance policies.

For those in need of immediate attention, the casualty department of the **Trauma Clinic of the Central District** is just off Nevskiy prospekt. Basic care involving stitches or injections can be given. If you are taken to a local hospital and require further treatment, contact either your consulate or

Sign for pharmacy (apteka)

one of the above medical centres. They can either have you moved or they can oversee your care in the hospital.

Dentists can be expensive. The medical clinics listed opposite are covered by insurance policies. **Dental Palace** will offer dental care, but costs will not be reimbursed.

HEALTH PRECAUTIONS

Neither visitors nor residents should drink tap water, which contains heavy metals and *giardia*, a parasite causing stomach problems. To be safe drink bottled water only. If you do pick up *giardia*, it can be treated with metronidazole.

Russian food is unlikely to do much harm, but avoid the meat pies sold on the streets.

Sexually transmitted diseases are on the rise, so all due caution should be exercised.

Mosquitoes *(komari)* are rife between June and late September. Burning oils or using plugs that heat chemical tablets are recommended for use at night time.

TRAVEL AND HEALTH INSURANCE

Visitors to St Petersburg are advised to take out travel insurance. Check the conditions of your cover before you travel – if possessions are stolen, you will need a copy of the police report to make an insurance claim. Make a note of the 24-hour emergency medical assistance telephone number that comes with your policy – the company can give advice if you need urgent medical attention. Keep any receipts or prescriptions so that you can claim the expenses on your insurance.

Banking and Local Currency

Major European debit and credit cards can be used in hotels, as well as in most restaurants and shops in St Petersburg. It is advisable to carry some cash, as there are still places that do not accept credit or debit cards. Roubles are the only legal currency and the city is well equipped with exchange offices and ATMs where visitors can turn their currency into roubles. It is advisable to visit a few exchange points before exchanging money, as commission rates offered do vary.

BANKS AND BUREAU DE CHANGE

Roubles can be obtained outside Russia, but rates are better once in the country. There are numerous exchange offices throughout St Petersburg, including at the airport.

Many exchange offices are open for 24 hours a day. A passport has to be shown when changing money. Any visible defect on foreign bank notes, especially vertical tears or ink or water stains, can make them difficult to exchange. Travellers should make sure that all the bank notes they bring into Russia are in good condition, and that any US dollars were issued after 1990.

As bank rates are so good in St Petersburg, visitors should never be tempted to change their money on the streets, however appealing the rates on offer appear to be. The unpleasant truth is that street-changers will try to cheat anyone willing to take the risk.

A few of the foreign banks in St Petersburg offer over-the-counter services. The most reliable Russian bank is **Sberbank**.

Banks are plentiful in St Petersburg. There are often branches offering both cash currency exchange, and cash advances on credit or debit cards. Some of the larger branches also cash travellers' cheques. Sberbank exchange rates are generally among the best available, and there are branches conveniently located all over the city. **Alfa-Bank**, **Citibank** and **Raiffeisen** also offer currency exchange.

A fast and safe, but also one of the more expensive, ways of transferring cash from abroad to Russia is through wiring via Western Union , which has offices in most major banks located in the city centre.

ATMS

There are ATMs located in major hotels such as the Grand Hotel Europe and Astoria, as well as in Dom Knigi and Gostiny Dvor, and at regular intervals along Nevsky Prospekt and other main streets. All VISA/Maestro cards are accepted, though a fee of about 150 roubles per transaction is levied. As always, it is advisable to be alert to the people around you when withdrawing cash, and to cover the keypad when entering your PIN to avoid becoming the victim of credit card fraud.

CREDIT AND DEBIT CARDS

It is possible to obtain both roubles with a credit card through the larger banks and from ATMs located all over the city.

The local commission is between 2 and 5 per cent, plus credit card charges. (This can work out as cheap or cheaper than bringing cash to change.)

The most accepted cards are VISA, MasterCard and Eurocard. Diners Club and American Express are less widely recognized. Less

ATMs at a branch of Alfa-Bank

commission is charged for cash in roubles.

If your credit card is lost or stolen, you should report it immediately to the credit card company so make sure you keep the relevant telephone number to hand.

It can be difficult to find places to cash travellers' cheques, and banks charge at least 2 per cent to do so.

Only the larger banks, such as Alfa-Bank and Sberbank, offer this service. Travellers' cheques can only be used as payment for goods or services in a few of the large hotels, and are acceptable only in US dollars and euros. You will need to present your passport whenever exchanging or paying with travellers' cheques.

CURRENCY

The Russian currency is the rouble (or ruble), written рубль or abbreviated to р or руб. The higher denominations are available in banknotes, which bear images of Russian cities, the lower denominations in coins. The kopek, of which there are 100 in a rouble, is issued in coins.

Banknotes

There are 6 denominations of notes, with values of 10, 50, 100, 500, 1,000 and 5,000 roubles. When changing money check that the notes correspond to those shown here.

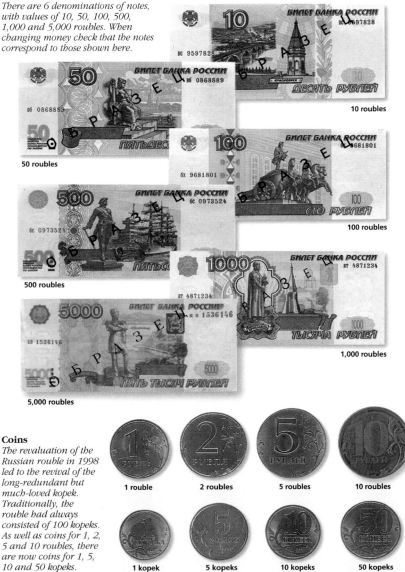

10 roubles

50 roubles

100 roubles

500 roubles

1,000 roubles

5,000 roubles

Coins

The revaluation of the Russian rouble in 1998 led to the revival of the long-redundant but much-loved kopek. Traditionally, the rouble had always consisted of 100 kopeks. As well as coins for 1, 2, 5 and 10 roubles, there are now coins for 1, 5, 10 and 50 kopeks.

1 rouble

2 roubles

5 roubles

10 roubles

1 kopek

5 kopeks

10 kopeks

50 kopeks

Communications and Media

MTS mobile logo

St Petersburg is home to many tech-savvy people and most cafés and restaurants have a Wi-Fi connection, which is usually free. There are dozens of mobile phone shops on and around Nevsky prospekt, where a local SIM card can be purchased cheaply (for about 150 roubles) upon presentation of a passport. Unfortunately, the everyday postal service remains notoriously slow and unreliable, but St Petersburg offers several more efficient alternatives. The abundance of newspapers, magazines and TV channels on offer includes some in English.

Visitors using mobile phones

INTERNATIONAL AND LOCAL TELEPHONE CALLS

The local system, Petersburg Telephone Network (PTS or, in Cyrillic, "ПТС") is reliable and relatively cheap. PTS phone boxes are green and located on the streets and in some metro stations. Most phoneboxes have instructions in Russian only.

Local calls made from private phones are usually free of charge. International calls are much cheaper with a pre-paid phone card such as the Zebra card; these are available to buy from kiosks and branches of Sberbank (see p214) and also serve as Internet pay-as-you-go cards. A more efficient alternative is to buy a Russian SIM card for your mobile phone (see opposite).

From a payphone, the Emergency Services can be reached by dialling a two-digit numbers free of charge: for the fire service dial 01, for the police dial 02 and for the ambulance service dial 03.

MOBILE PHONES

To find out if a mobile phone will work on Russian networks, check with your local service provider before travelling. If you want to ensure your phone will work while you are away you should have a quad-band phone. Tri-band phones from the EU will usually work in Russia, but US mobile phones may not. Visitors should be aware that "roaming" in Russia is very expensive. It is also more expensive to make and receive calls while abroad.

A cheaper option is to buy a Russian SIM card from any of the mobile phone chains, such as Evroset or Svyaznoi. A SIM card costs about 150 roubles and includes the same sum in credit. A passport must be shown when you buy a SIM card.

The four networks – **MTS**, **Megafon**, Beeline and Tele2 all have sufficient coverage and similar charges. Calls within St Petersburg are much cheaper than rates in Western Europe.

REACHING THE RIGHT NUMBER

- To phone **Russia** from abroad, dial 007 followed by the local area code and individual number.
- To phone **St Petersburg**, dial 812 followed by the individual number.
- To phone **Moscow**, dial 495 followed by the individual number.
- St Petersburg directory enquiries, dial 09.
- There is no international directory enquiries.
- Inter-city call booking, dial 07.
- International call booking, dial 315 0012.
- To phone the **UK**, dial 8 (tone) 1044 followed by the number, omitting first 0 from area code.
- To phone **Canada** or the **US**, dial 8 (tone) 101 followed by the number.
- To phone the **Irish Republic**, dial 8 (tone) 10353 followed by the number.
- To phone **Australia**, dial 8 (tone) 1061 then the number.
- To phone **New Zealand**, dial 8 (tone) 1064 followed by the number.
- To phone **South Africa**, dial 8 (tone) 1027 followed by the number.

INTERNET

Internet access is available at cafés and clubs throughout St Petersburg such as **Cafe Max** and **5.3 GHz**. Free Wi-Fi access is available both inside the Hermitage museum and within its grounds (see p84).

The interior and grounds of the Hermitage offer free Wi-Fi access

Wi-Fi coverage is widely available in hotels, as well as at the airport. It is generally free, though some hotels may charge where Internet is only available in a specific area.

POSTAL SERVICES

The state-run, international postal system is generally slow and unreliable. A more efficient and expensive, service is run by **Westpost**, who also offer door-to-door next-day delivery to Moscow. Anything other than papers must go through customs, which can add an extra day. **DHL** and **Fedex** also have offices in the city and take three days to deliver to Europe and four to Australia and the US. The Grand Hotel Europe *(see p176)* runs a quick postal service, taking three days to the UK via Finland, which costs about 130 roubles per letter.

Ordinary post offices, such as the **Main Post Office** *(see p122)*, which is open daily, and those in hotels, sell normal and commemorative Russian stamps, postcards, envelopes and local phonecards. Russian postboxes are marked Почта *(Pochta)* and are plentiful in the city centre. Tourists should use the small pale blue post boxes. The yellow post boxes are used for local delivery services only.

ADDRESSES

After 1917, when the city was renamed Leningrad, many streets and sights were renamed to avoid imperial connotations or in order to commemorate new Soviet heroes. Since the city resumed its original name after a referendum in 1991, most streets in the centre have officially reverted to their pre-1917 names. The area surrounding the city, however, is still the Leningrad Region. Many people use both the original and Soviet names; no offence is caused when one is used in preference to another. Some useful words to recognise are ула (street) and роспект (Nevsky Prospekt).

St Petersburg local newspaper

NEWSPAPERS AND MAGAZINES

There are three English-language newspapers and magazines available in the city, which are distributed free to all hotels, major restaurants and most fast-food chains. *The St Petersburg Times* comes out every Wednesday and provides coverage of local events, as well as national Russian news and politics and detailed culture listings and reviews. Church opening times are listed on its website. A useful source of city information is *St Petersburg In Your Pocket*, a free guidebook aimed at tourists and expats that comes out every two months and can be found in hotels, restaurants and bars.

Foreign papers can be picked up at highly inflated prices from major hotels.

TELEVISION AND RADIO

Russian-language television is dominated by soap operas, detective shows and talk-shows. The two St Petersburg-based channels are Channel 5 and 100TV. Russia Today, the state-run English-language channel widely viewed as a mouthpiece for the Kremlin, is available in most hotels. Its hourly weather forecasts are useful. Most hotels in St Petersburg have satellite television and receive many other Western programmes.

The best English-language radio broadcast to the city on shortwave is still the BBC World Service.

TRAVEL INFORMATION

St Petersburg is growing in popularity as a tourist destination, with the local government making concerted efforts to attract foreign tourists. As the number of business travellers increases, the number of flights and alternative means of transport is on the rise. Flying remains the most popular way of travelling to St Petersburg, both for individuals and groups, with the train from Moscow or Helsinki a close second. There is a ferry link with Helsinki and Stockholm, while the

Aeroflot plane

Baltic capitals can be reached by coach. Independent travel in Russia is difficult for those who don't speak Russian, and for this reason it is worth considering a package tour. British companies run a variety of tours with specialist guides, which often incorporate St Petersburg and Moscow. Package tours can be expensive, but shopping around can uncover some good deals, particularly on flights with stop-overs in Europe or low-season package deals.

Exterior of Pulkovo 1 airport

ARRIVING BY AIR

Direct flights from the UK to St Petersburg run seven days a week on **British Airways** and four days on **Rossiya**, the local airline. **Lufthansa**, **SAS**, **Finnair** and British Airways all serve St Petersburg. There are connecting flights on other airlines departing daily and these can often be a cheaper option. **Scott's Tours** in London are particularly good for budget fares and package deals. The journey from London takes around 3 hours, or about 6 hours with a stopover in a European city.

Direct flights to St Petersburg from Ireland, US, Canada, South Africa and Australia are either very limited or simply do not exist. The usual route from these destinations is to fly via a European city or via Moscow, from where you can transfer to another flight or continue by road or rail.

It is worth noting that travelling from Australia can

be fairly complicated. The most usual route is to pick up a European carrier in Singapore, with a stopover in Europe. On landing, passengers are sometimes required to confirm onward flights. You can do this through the airline you are travelling with or through the **Central Air Communication Agency** on Nevskiy prospekt.

International flights arrive at **Pulkovo 2** which, although modernized, is still small and relatively primitive. Its arrival and departure buildings each have a small duty-free shop. Departures also has a café, a restaurant, snack machines and several expensive souvenir shops. Arrivals has a foreign exchange office and a small tourist information stand, as well as counters where taxis can be ordered for cheaper rates than those outside the exit doors. On arrival, the longest wait is likely to be for passport control. Departures on the weekend can be hectic

and it is best to arrive at least 90 minutes before a flight in high season.

Pulkovo 1 mostly serves domestic flights, although selected international flights may also arrive here. All commercial flights to and from Moscow have a separate arrivals and departure lounge, with various amenities located on the first floor. This has its own entrance, which cannot be reached from inside the main terminal building.

Aeroflot company logo

TRANSPORT TO AND FROM THE AIRPORT

Both airports are located 17 km (11 miles) south of the city centre. The major hotels operate cars to pick up individual tourists for a cost of around 1,500 roubles, but this service is no longer as essential as it once was as there is now a regulated taxi system in the arrivals halls of both airports. Look for the stand near the exit door marked *Taxi*, and tell the attendant where you want to go. The dispatcher will state how much the journey will cost (this price will be fixed), provide you with a printed receipt and radio in a driver. You should expect to pay about 1,000 roubles to get to the city centre.

A cheaper option for those who have already changed money at the airport, is to take the No. 13 bus (from Pulkovo 2) or No. 39 (from Pulkovo 1) to Moskovskaya metro station. Minibuses, travel the same route and charge about twice as much *(see p221)*.

ARRIVING BY RAIL

Rail is a convenient way to travel from Finland to Moscow and within Russia in general, although European student discount passes provide little or no reduction in fares.

More than 10 trains a day run in each direction between Moscow and **Moscow Station** and **Ladozhskiy Station**. Twice daily trains connect Helsinki and **Finlyandskiy Station**. For those with time and some sense of adventure, it is possible to travel by train between London and St Petersburg via Central Europe (Warsaw, Prague, Berlin). It takes about three days and is almost always more costly than flying. Trains are comfortable and usually run on time, but carriages can be overcrowded and thefts are not uncommon. A costly transit visa is also necessary to travel through Belarus. All visitors to Russia need a visa and obtaining one can be a complicated procedure *(see p208)*.

Trains travelling from Eastern Europe arrive and depart from **Vitebskiy Station**. Tickets for train journeys from St Petersburg should be bought from kiosks at the **Central Train Ticket Office** or **Moscow Station**, or from an agent such as Sindbad Travel Centre *(see p211)*.

An overnight sleeper compartment

TRAVELLING BETWEEN MOSCOW AND ST PETERSBURG

Many visitors fly in to Moscow and out of St Petersburg, or vice versa. The most popular form of transport between the two cities is the train, of which there are ten or more a day. The fastest option is the **Sapsan** train, which takes less than 4 hours to travel between the cities, while night-time trains take from 8 to 12 hours.

Prices vary according to the class of the train – the Sapsan being most expensive – and the type of seat. Most trains have a choice of *coupé* (four-person compartment), *platzkart* (dormitory-style carriages), or *sidyachyy* (open seating). For daytime travel *sidyachyy* is more comfortable and cheaper than *platzkarte*. One-way prices for standard trains range from 600 roubles for *sidyachyy* to 2,100 roubles for *coupé*. Sapsan tickets start at 4,200 roubles. Food may be available but it is best to take your own.

Regular commercial flights connecting the two cities take 50–90 minutes. These are run by Aeroflot and independent companies such as Rossiya and Transaero. Prices range from 2,700 roubles for an economy class one-way ticket

to 4,200 roubles for business class. Tickets are sold online, at the airport, or at the **Central Air Communication Agency**. In summer, travelling by boat to and from Moscow is possible *(see p220)*.

RAIL TICKETS AND RESERVATIONS

Tickets can be bought both at **Moscow Station** and at the ticket office on the Canal Griboedov. Long queues are the norm, unless you are prepared to pay about 300 roubles commission to buy tickets (*coupé* class only) from the Service Centre at Moscow train station. E-tickets can be bought online, at www.russianrail.com and www.russiantrains.com. International rail passes are not usually valid on Russian trains and foreigners are not eligible for discounts.

ARRIVING BY COACH

Comfortable coaches run to and from Helsinki in Finland, offering a cheaper alternative to the train. **Finnord** runs one daytime coach and one overnight in each direction; the journey takes around 8 hours. Coach companies do not always use the city's inconvenient coach station, but will drop off instead at various locations in St Petersburg. Dozens of coaches depart for Finland at 6 or 7am every morning and 10 or 11pm every evening from outside the Bukvoyed bookstore on Ploshchad Vosstaniya. The Baltic states can also all be reached by coach. Journey times vary from 8 to 13 hours.

COACH TICKETS AND RESERVATIONS

Timetables, prices and tickets to the Baltic states can all be found at www.ecolines.net and www.luxexpress.eu/ru. They are also sold at the **Eurolines** and **Ecolines** offices. It is best to book ahead as tickets regularly sell out. Students can claim a 10 per cent discount, with an ISIC card. The **Finnord** office also sell tickets.

Sapsan train travelling between Moscow and St Petersburg

ARRIVING BY SEA

Arriving by boat can be one of the most exciting and novel ways to approach St Petersburg. Cruises are an increasingly popular way to visit the city, and there are regular ferry services to Helsinki and Stockholm.

Cruise ships and ferries dock at the **Marine Facade Passenger Terminal** on the north side of Vasilievskiy Island. Trolleybus No. 10 and bus No. 7 run from here to the centre.

In summer, river cruises between Moscow and St Petersburg run along the Volga and across to Lake Ladoga. The trips last about two weeks and make a very pleasurable way to see more of Russia. The cruises are bookable in the UK through **Noble Caledonia** or **Voyages Jules Verne**, and in the US through **Visit Russia**. Ships

St Peter Line cruise ship visiting St Petersburg

dock at St Petersburg's **River Terminal**, a 10 minutes' walk from Proletarskaya metro. Cruise companies run buses to and from the city centre.

FERRY TICKETS AND RESERVATIONS

Tickets for the ferry to and from Stockholm and Helsinki can be bought online at www.stpeterline.com. The Princess Maria ferry travels between St Petersburg and Helsinki three to four times a

week. The journey takes about 12 hours and costs for a one-way ticket range from 1,200 roubles for a berth in a four-person cabin midweek to 18,000 roubles for a spacious deluxe cabin for two at the weekend. The Princess Anastasia ferry travels once or twice a week to Helsinki, Stockholm and Tallinn before returning to St Petersburg. Ticket prices range from 600 to 20,000 roubles, depending on the timing and type of package booked.

DIRECTORY

TOUR COMPANIES

Noble Caledonia
2 Chester Close,
London SW1X 7BE.
Tel (0207) 409 0376.

Scott's Tours
141 Whitfield Street,
London W1T 5EW.
Tel (0207) 383 5353.

Visit Russia
257 West 39th St, Studio 39, New York, NY 10018.
Tel (1800) 755 3080.

Voyages Jules Verne
21 Dorset Square, London NW1 6QG.
Tel (0207) 616 1000.

ARRIVING BY AIR

Pulkovo 1
Пулково 1
Tel 704 3822.

Pulkovo 2
Пулково 2
Tel 704 3444.

British Airways
Malaya Konyushennaya ulitsa 1/3A. **Map** 6 E1.
Tel 380 0206.
Tel 346 8146 (Pulkovo 2).

Central Air Communication Agency
Nevskiy pr 7/9. **Map** 6 D1.
Tel 315 0072 (inter).
Tel 571 8093 (dom & CIS).

Finnair
Malaya Konyushennaya ul. 1/3A. **Map** 6 E1.
Tel 303 9898.
Tel 324 3249 (Pulkovo 2).

KLM
Malaya Morskaya ul 23.
Map 6 D1. **Tel** 346 6864.

Lufthansa
Nevskiy pr. 32. **Map** 6 F2.
Tel 320 1000.
Tel 325 9140 (Pulkovo 2).

Rossiya
Pulkovo-Express, 1-ya Krasnoarmeyskaya ul 4.
Map 6 D5. **Tel** 777 0550.

SAS
Nevskiy pr 22.
Map 6 F2. **Tel** 326 2600.
Tel 324 3244 (Pulkovo 2).

ARRIVING BY RAIL

All Train Enquiries
Tel 055.

Central Train Ticket Office
Центральные железно-дорожные кассы
Tsentralnye zhelezno-dorozhnye kassy
Nab kanala Griboedova 24.
Map 6 E2. **Tel** 067.

Finlyandskiy Station
финляндский вокзал
Finlyandskiy vokzal
Pl Lenina 6. **Map** 3 B3.

Ladozhskiy Station
Ладожский вокзал
Ladozskniy vokzal
Zanevskiy pr 73.

Moscow Station
Московский вокзал
Moskovskiy vokzal
Pl Vosstaniya. **Map** 7 C2.

Vitebskiy Station
Витебский вокзал
Vitebskiy vokzal
Zagorodnyy prospekt 52.
Map 6 E4.

TRAVELLING BETWEEN MOSCOW AND ST PETERSBURG

Sapsan
www.russiantrains.com

ARRIVING BY COACH

Ecolines
3 Podezdnoi pereulok.
Tel 314 2550.
www.ecolines.ru

Eurolines/Lux Express
2 Mitrofanyevskoe shosse.
Tel 441 3757.
www.eurolines.com

Finnord
Italyanskaya ulitsa 37.
Map 6 F1.
Tel 314 8951.

ARRIVING BY SEA

Marine Facade Passenger Terminal
Морской фасад пассажирский терминал
Morskoy Fasad passazhirskiy terminal
Morskaya Naberezhnaya.
Tel 499 0988.
www.portspb.ru

River Terminal
Речной вокзал
Rechnoy vokzal
Prospekt Obukhovskoy Oborony 195.
Tel 262 0239.

GETTING AROUND ST PETERSBURG

Although public transport in the city is abundant, efficient and very cheap, the most enjoyable way to get around and fully appreciate St Petersburg is on foot. A glance at a map shows the city has a rational, organized layout, which makes it easier to negotiate. A boat cruise along the waterways can also be a wonderful way to become acquainted with the city. Nevskiy prospekt is where many of the city's transport routes and main roads meet.

Sign indicating a pedestrian area

Metro lines, tram, bus and trolleybus routes radiate out from here. It is possible to travel without too much difficulty to almost anywhere in town from this main avenue. Driving is not recommended due to the combination of poor road conditions, aggressive Russian driving and over-enthusiastic traffic police. Cyclists, once virtually unheard of in St Petersburg, are now becoming a common sight, and the city has several bike rental companies.

GREEN TRAVEL

The greenest ways to get around St Petersburg are on foot or by bike, both of which are perfectly viable options given the compact size of the historical centre. The public transport system is good enough to make using a car unnecessary and many forms of the transport network are also environmentally friendly, such as the extensive trolleybus and metro routes.

BUSES AND MINIBUSES

All services run every 10 minutes, sometimes less often. Bus stops in the city centre are marked either by white and yellow signs with a black letter "A" for *avtobus*, or by blue signs depicting a bus. Signs are placed by the side of the road or attached to lamp posts. Some routes are duplicated by commercial buses, marked with a "k" before the number, or minibuses (though there are no minibus routes along Nevskiy prospekt).

Fares on these buses are 50 per cent higher than those on non-commercial equivalents, and are paid to the driver when getting on or off – if in doubt just follow what other passengers do. Buses can be hailed or requested to stop anywhere along the route.

Useful routes include the No. 22 bus from the Smolnyy Institute *(see p128)* via St Isaac's Square *(see p79)* to the

Mariinskiy Theatre *(see p119)*. Bus numbers 3, 7, 22 and 27 run along most of Nevsky prospekt between Ploshchad Vosstaniya and the Admiralty.

Open-top **City Tour** red buses offer sightseeing excursions from 9am to 8pm daily. Tickets can be bought on board and are valid for one day, costing 450 roubles for an adult ticket.

TROLLEYBUSES

Trolleybuses offer convenient routes and stops around the city. Stops are marked by small blue-and-white signs suspended from wires or lamp posts, indicating the trolleybus numbers. These signs show a Cyrillic "T" for trolleybus, on a white background. Trolleybuses can be boarded at the front, middle or back doors. The front eight seats are reserved for the disabled, the elderly and passengers with children. All fares are collected on board by a conductor.

TRAMS

Trams are disappearing from many roads in the city centre, but some remain. Stops are marked by red and white signs suspended on wires above the rails. Trams can be boarded via any of the doors and tickets bought in cash from the conductor. Trams will automatically stop along the route.

TICKETS AND TRAVEL CARDS

A flat fare is payable on all forms of transport, whatever the length of the journey. Tickets are bought from the conductor or, on commercial transport, from the driver.

The cheapest way to travel, if you are staying a few weeks or more, is to buy a monthly or half-monthly travel card for all forms of transport, including the metro *(see pp222–3)*. Prices range from 790 to 1,580 roubles. Separate monthly cards are also sold for each form of transport.

A city Trolleybus on Nevskiy prospekt

WALKING

In some areas, particularly around Palace Embankment, sights are situated so close together that using public transport from place to place is unecessary. A few of the more scattered sights are at some distance (20 minutes on foot) from the nearest transport and walking the last stretch is often the most practical option. Apart from the ease, getting around on foot can be a most rewarding way to explore the city, allowing you to soak up the atmosphere and appreciate the fascinating architectural and sculptural detail on many of St Petersburg's buildings.

As soon as the sun appears, in winter as well as in summer, people of all ages emerge onto the streets and into the parks. Locals are very fond of walking, whether it be promenading up and down Nevskiy prospekt, or ambling around the Neva at 2am during the White Nights *(see p51)*. The Summer Gardens *(see p95)* and Mikhaylovskiy Gardens have long been popular with local residents. For longer walks mixed with some architectural interest, two good areas to try are Kamenniy and Yelagin islands *(see pp136–7)*, with their official residences and *dachas*, many of them dating from the early years of the 20th century.

For a romantic stroll around the city away from the traffic, walk along the Moyka or Griboedov canals *(see pp134–5)*. To the south of Nevskiy prospekt, majestic buildings give way to smaller,

Visitors on a walking tour of St Petersburg

19th-century residential blocks, with trees by the waterside and leafy squares and courtyards.

Drivers have little respect for pedestrians and traffic is the main hindrance to walking. Cars drive on the right-hand side, so look left first when crossing the road. If there is a pedestrian underpass, use it and, if not, look for a light-controlled crossing with red and green figures indicating pedestrian right of way. Crossings without lights are marked by a blue sign showing a pedestrian, but although drivers are obliged by law to stop for pedestrians, this does not mean they will, so the greatest care should be taken when crossing the road.

On the main city streets, dark blue sponsored nameplates give street names in Russian and English. Elsewhere, black-on-white street names are in Cyrillic only.

GUIDED TOURS

Walking tours in English can be booked through **Peter's Walking Tours**, which offers themed excursions such as

Rasputin, Dostoevsky, World War II and Style-Moderne architecture. They also offer guided cycling tours, popular during the White Nights. Liberty offer tours for disabled travellers *(see p210)*. Many bike hire companies provide their own tours *(see p223)*. Other English-language excursions are available from **Anglotourismo**, who offer free daily walking tours lasting 3 hours as well as guided boat tours *(see p226)*.

One of the taxi styles

TAXIS

St Petersburg does not have a coordinated official taxi system, and private cabs come in a variety of colours. There is no uniform taxi style, but a taxi will have an orange chequered light on the top or an illuminated green light on the windscreen when it is available. The more expensive taxis have a yellow *"taksi"* sign on the roof.

Taxis can be found outside metro stations, major sights and hotels. It is usually cheaper and easier to ask hotel or restaurant staff to order you a private taxi rather

A pedestrian crossing, one of the safer places to cross Russian roads

than attempting to hail one on the street. Taxis can carry four people. There are no official taxi ranks in the city, but plenty on the streets to hail. Private cars and taxis that have not been pre-booked are best avoided if you are travelling alone at night.

Taxis in Russia rarely have meters, so if you book in advance, agree the price with the driver before you get in. It is best to agree the price with the dispatcher at the time of booking and this will be fixed. Journeys in the city center should cost no more than 400 roubles. After 1am some taxi companies will offer a 10 per cent discount. A journey from the airport to the city centre will cost 1,000 roubles. There may be an extra charge for passengers with large luggage.

DRIVING

Driving is not recommended but if you do choose to drive, be aware that local drivers tend to ignore rules of the road and do more or less as they like, so be on your guard. Drive on the right and make no left turns on main roads unless a road sign indicates that it is permitted.

In winter conditions, driving requires studded tyres as chains can be damaged on tram lines and vice versa.

There is no charge for street parking in most parts of the city centre. The Nevskij Palace and some hotels have 24-hour secured parking, some with an extra charge for non-guests. There are few public car parks in the city centre, with the exception of two at Ploshchad Vosstaniya and one outside **Moscow Train Station**. Car parks are identified by a white letter "P" on a blue sign. These are short-stay car parks and cost 100 roubles for one hour. Car parks are often open 24 hours.

Be aware that the traffic police can pull over drivers at any time in order to check documents and will more often than not find something wrong with your car and may ask for a bribe. Tourists are required by law to have a notarized translation of their driving license, as producing just an international driving license will not suffice.

CYCLING

St Petersburg is flat and compact and should be a haven for cyclists. Unfortunately, it is also a city of reckless drivers. If you choose to cycle, wear a helmet and stick to quieter side roads or take part in a led cycle tour. Parts of the Neva embankment with wider pavements, such as the area near Smolny Cathedral (see p203), is a popular route with cyclists.

Bikes can be rented from **Skat Prokat** and **Velotour**, who also conduct cycling tours. Bike rental costs 150 roubles per hour or 600–800 roubles per day, plus a refundable deposit. Collect your bike from the office or have it delivered for 500 roubles. This delivery service is offered free of charge when you rent a bike with **Rentbike**.

Cycling, an increasingly popular means of transport

DIRECTORY

<table>
<tr><td colspan="4"></td></tr>
</table>

BUSES

City Tours
Pirogovskaya naberezhnaya 7.
Map 5 C2.
Tel 718 4769.
www.citytourspb.ru

Eurolines/Lux Express
2 Mitrofanyevskoe shosse.
Tel 441 3757.
www.eurolines.com

St. Petersburg Bus Station
Naberegnaya Obvodnogo Kanala, #36
Tel 756 5777.

TRAMS AND TROLLEYBUSES

GorElectroTrans
Syzranskaya 15.
Tel 610 2088.
http://electrotrans.spb.ru

GUIDED TOURS

Anglotourismo
Tel 921 989 4722.
www.anglotourismo.com

Peter's Walking Tours
Tel 943 1229.
www.peterswalk.com

TAXIS

St Petersburg Taxi
Tel 068.

Seven Million
Tel 7 000 000.

Six Million
Tel 6 000 000.

DRIVING

Moscow Train Station
Московский вокзал
Moskovskiy vokzal
Pl Vosstaniya.
Map 7 C2.

CYCLING

Rentbike
Griboedova naberezhnaya kanala 57.
Map 5 A4.
Tel 981 0155.
www.rentbike.org

Skat Prokat
Goncharnaya ulitsa 7.
Map 7 C2.
Tel 717 6838.
www.skatprokat.ru

Velotour
Tel 952 351 8883.
www.velotour-spb.ru.

Travelling by Metro

Since overland transport is the most efficient means of getting around the city centre, the metro is used mainly to get to and from the outskirts of the city. As a tourist attraction, however, the metro's stunning stations, intended by Stalin to be "palaces for the people", should be high on your itinerary. The metro

Blue neon metro sign

runs until just after midnight. Travelling in the daytime or late evening will avoid most of the two million people estimated to use the metro each day. With just five lines, negotiating the network is fairly straightforward, especially since there are now basic signs in English. Do watch out for pickpockets on the metro – gangs have been known to target travellers getting off particularly at Nevsky prospekt metro station.

Sculpture in Pushkinskaya metro

THE METRO AS A TOURIST ATTRACTION

Thousands of tonnes of marble, granite and limestone were used to face the walls and sculptures, mosaics and chandeliers were commissioned from leading artists for the St Petersburg metro. The first line – the red line – opened in 1955, and is one of the most fascinating, being the supreme embodiment of Stalinist style and ideals. The line's crowning glory has to be Avtovo, incorporating a wealth of style and detail, even down to the moulded glass columns.

The metro now has 63 stations, ranging in style and ambience from the dim lighting and memorial atmosphere of Ploshchad Muzhestva (Courage Square, 1975) near

Piskarovskoe Memorial Cemetery *(see p126)*, to the 1980s vulgarity of Udelnaya and the cool of Komendantskiy Prospekt (2005).

THE NETWORK

The metro is vital for getting to and from hotels outside the city centre and the airport.

The five lines run from the outskirts through the centre, where they intersect at one of six main stations.

Trains run every few minutes during the day and every 5 minutes late at night. The last train leaves the station of origin at midnight. There is no rush hour as such but the metro tends to be full at most times of day, which makes it generally safe at it is always busy. Platforms are not staffed, but there is an

attendant in a booth at the bottom of each escalator who can call for assistance.

Because of the many waterways in the city, stations are buried deep underground and long escalators lead down to the platforms.

New stations are still being added to the St Petersburg metro to increase efficiency and link the centre to more areas around the city, reducing travel time.

FINDING YOUR WAY

Before setting foot in St Petersburg's metro, ensure you have a network map with the Cyrillic and transliterated names to hand. There are English and Russian signs in the metro, but knowledge of the Cyrillic station names will be useful. When getting to the train turnstiles are located at the top of the escalators, where you can touch in with a magnetic card or pay with a metro token *(see Tickets and Travel Cards)*. Follow the signs in the metro to the platform. Once on the platform, the direction of the trains and a list of all stops along the route are marked on the wall, routes are also displayed inside the carriage.

Busy stations may have safety doors between the platform and the trains. When the train stops, these doors open, and only then do the train doors open.

Before the train doors close, an automatic announcement is made: *"Ostorozhno. Dveri zakryvayutsya"* (Be careful

Signs in both Cyrillic and English in the metro system

the doors are closing). As the train approaches a stop, the name of the station is announced, this will be in Russian only. Announcements will be if the station you are approacahing is an inter-connecting one, allowing you to change lines. Keep count of the stops, in case you do not catch the announcements.

To change to another line, follow the interchange signs for переход (*perekhod* – crossing). The exception is at Tekhnologicheskiy Institut, where the two southbound lines are on parallel platforms, as are the two northbound lines: thus to continue in the same direction on another line you simply cross the central concourse.

Exits are marked выход (*vykhod*). Some stations, such as Moskovskaya (for the airport) and Gostinyy Dvor, have two or more exits.

ST PETERSBURG'S METRO

Magnetic metro card

TICKETS AND TRAVEL CARDS

The most common means of paying for the metro is the token (*zheton*), available to buy from metro stations only. Magnetic cards, which can be topped up with as many trips as needed, are also available. There are no zones in the metro, so as with other forms of transport in the city, there is a flat charge for each journey, regardless of the distance.

Barrier machines are installed at the top of the escalators; most take both cards and tokens. Cards must be touched to the illuminated sensor on top. If you try to go through a machine without paying, an automatic barrier closes in front of you. If you have a large bag or suitcase, you must buy a special luggage token, which allows

Metro token

you to pass through a wider gate at the metro barrier. At the far right an attendant checks passes and allows you to put your token in a machine which does not have automatic barriers. Those with magnetic cards cannot pass through this machine. Monthly magnetic cards for the metro or for all forms of public transport are valid for 70 metro journeys and an infinite number of journeys on overground transport during a calendar month. Cards are valid for 35 metro journeys and unlimited overground transport during a two-week period can also be bought between the 16th to the 5th of each month. Cards can be bought at any

time during the month but are valid only from 1st to 15th of each month.

Visitors who plan to stay in the city for a while may find it worthwhile to purchase a personal "smart" card bearing their photograph, to which they can transfer credit to fund future journeys at any metro station. Such cards are not inserted into the barrier machines that check tickets and tokens, but placed briefly onto a sensor marked with a white circle. There are no further ticket checks once you have past through the barriers inside the metro station.

DIRECTORY

St Petersburg Metro
Tel 301 9700.
www.metro.spb.ru

Canal and River Cruises

St Petersburg's numerous natural waterways were adapted and extended, to make it resemble Peter the Great's beloved Amsterdam *(see pp20–21)*. Indeed, it would be true to say the city vies with Amsterdam for the title "Venice of the North".

A wide selection of cruises, for small and large groups, in open and closed boats, depart from bridges along Nevskiy prospekt and other parts of the city. They offer marvellous opportunities to see more of the city, especially for those unable to walk long distances. Forming part of any cruise are the broad Fontanka river with its Neo-Classical palaces, the leafy Moyka river with its ironwork bridges, and the Griboedov Canal which twists and turns its way through southwest St Petersburg. Bring a bottle of champagne, a picnic, a warm jumper and just relax.

A river cruise passing the Rostral Columns

GENERAL INFORMATION

The weather plays a vital role in determining the exact time of year canal cruises start and finish. Most boats operate daily from mid-May to late September. Their routes also vary because regular construction work such as reinforcing the granite embankments, sometimes prevents movement along parts of the canals.

The Gulf of Finland is tidal and this affects the Neva and inland waterways. Strong winds can cause the water level to rise significantly and boat trips may be cancelled under these conditions.

GUIDED RIVER AND CANAL TRIPS

Large, covered cruise boats depart every 30 minutes, between 11:30am and 8pm, from the Anichkov Bridge on Nevskiy prospekt *(see p49)*. Tickets for the next available boat should be purchased from the kiosk on the embankment, or on board. Trips last 60 minutes and take in the Moyka and Fontanka rivers, and sometimes the Griboedov Canal. Some routes go out onto the Neva, from where there are superb views of the whole city.

Trips usually cost about 500 roubles. Guided tours are available in English from companies such as **Anglotourismo**, **Neptun-boat** and **Astra Marine**. Large groups are advised to book in advance, either at a kiosk or by phone, especially during school holidays. Boat trips providing guided tours in English can be booked through any of the major hotels, though this is a more expensive option.

A popular option are the night-time boat trips along the Neva to watch the bridges opening. No commentary is usually provided on these tours, which depart from the Anichkov bridge pier next to the Anichkov Palace at 1:30am and last for about an hour. Blankets are usually provided, but take your own food and drink, as these are rarely available.

NEVA CRUISES

A variety of boats cruise up and down the Neva. The trips, operating hourly between 10am and 10pm, last an hour. Tickets can be bought on the landing stage or on board for about 500 roubles. The boats leave from in front of the Admiralty *(see p78)* and from near the main entrance of the Hermitage *(see p75)*, as well as from the pier of the Peter and Paul Fortress *(see pp66–7)*, from where tickets can be bought for as little as 300 roubles.

Luxury catered cruises can be booked in advance. **MIR** and **Russkiye Kruizy** offer a variety of routes along the Neva and the city's other rivers and canals. Trips along the Neva are a good way to see all the majestic façades that line the river's embankment. Most trips start by going to the Blagoveshchensky Bridge before turning around. Heading back towards Palace Bridge, sights on the left-hand side include the Academy of Arts *(see p63)*, which is easily identifed by the two Egyptian sphinxes in front of it.

The next building to come into view is the yellow Menshikov Palace *(see p62)*, built by Peter the Great's friend Alexander Menshikov. Peter lived in the relatively humble Summer Palace, which can be seen later on the right hand side in the Summer Gardens.

Shortly after the Menshikov Palace, the side façade of St Petersburg State University comes into view *(see p61)*. The striking turqoise-and-white building soon after is the Kunstkammer *(see p60)*.

On the other side of the river, the Bronze Horseman monument to Peter the Great *(see pp78–9)*, St Isaac's Cathedral *(see pp80–81)* and the Admiralty *(see p78)* can be seen in all their glory.

A cruise along the Neva river

Back on the left, the spit of Vasilyevsky Island is crowned by the stately Stock Exchange building, and completed by the two large red Rostral Columns. Across the Neva is the spectacular Winter Palace *(see pp92–3)*. The next sight on the left is the Peter and Paul Fortress, while shortly afterwards, the enormous blue dome of the city's first mosque can be seen.

On the right, the stunning façade of the Marble Palace *(see p94)* with the onion domes of the Church on Spilled Blood *(see p100)* peeping out above it. After the palace, the iconic intricate railings of the Summer Gardens can be admired.

Most sightseeing boats cruise up to Liteiny Bridge or beyond before doubling back to their original starting point.

DEPARTURE POINTS ALONG RIVERS AND CANALS

Boats depart at regular intervals from the Moika River, Griboedov Canal and Fontanka River at their intersections with Nevsky prospekt *(see pp46–9)*, on both sides of the street. Boats departing from the northern side may be about 50 roubles more expensive as they attract more passers-by. Boats also leave from the eastern side of St Isaac's Square, heading in the direction of Nevsky prospekt. Other boats leave from across from the Field of Mars on the Moika, and from many other points along all of the waterways where there are steps leading down the embankment.

RESTAURANT CRUISES

There are several restaurant boats that sail up and down the Neva, allowing passengers to enjoy views of the city's embankments over dinner.

New Island, the city's oldest restaurant-ship takes passengers from its mooring point at the Rumyantsevsky Dock (near the Blagoveshchensky Bridge) along the Neva as far as Smolny Cathedral and back again. Both an à la carte menu and a set menu are available on this 90-minute trip *(see p184)*.

Those who like the idea of restaurants on water but fear the onset of seasickness might prefer the city's stationary floating restaurants, such as the eccentric **Flying Dutchman**, which combines several restaurants serving Russian, Japanese, French and Italian cuisine. There is also a fitness centre and beauty salon on board.

The more romantically named **Korabl Lyubvi** (Ship of Love), moored next to the two lion sculptures in front of the Admiralty, serves European food. It is more of a café than a restaurant, but its location cannot be beaten in terms of convenience.

Water buses on the Griboedov

WATER BUSES

Water buses operate in St Petersburg during the summer months. They carry up to 12 passengers and are meant to run from 8am to 9pm at 15-minute intervals, but are in fact highly irregular.

The central line has stops at Universitetskaya Naberezhnaya, the Bronze Horseman, the Summer Gardens, Finland Station and Smolny Cathedral. There is also a service from Finland Station to the island of Kronshtadt.

In theory, the boats are a great way to see the city for a bargain price, but the service is sadly highly erratic and so cannot be relied on as a form of transport.

TICKETS

Tickets for all boats can be bought on board. For Neva cruises, they are sold at kiosks on the piers in front of the Admiralty and the Hermitage. Hour-long sightseeing tours along the rivers and canals usually cost about 500 roubles. Children under seven may be allowed to travel for free, while older children may be given a discount. Tickets for the water buses are much cheaper, costing about 40 roubles.

Travelling Beyond St Petersburg

Every weekend during the summer, and even in winter, many locals leave the city. They head for their *dacha* or for the woods, to gather seasonal fruits and vegetables, go cross-country skiing or visit one of the former imperial summer residences. Buses and suburban trains operate frequently throughout the year and are the usual means of transport to sites out of town. Peterhof and Kronshtadt are the exceptions in being accessible by hydrofoil across the Gulf of Finland. Foreigners tend to take coach excursions out of town but, with planning, travelling independently can be part of the fun.

Hydrofoil arriving at the Hermitage landing stage

Interior view of one of St Petersburg's suburban trains

SUBURBAN TRAINS

Train travel is the most comfortable way to visit most of the outlying sights. Tickets can be bought from the local cash desks *(prigorodnyye kassy)* at each station, where a timetable (in Russian) is displayed. Return tickets are no cheaper than two singles. Note that smoking is prohibited and that between the hours of 10am and midday, there is often a break in the timetable.

GETTING TO TSARSKOE SELO AND PAVLOVSK

Trains for Tsarskoe Selo (Pushkin) *(see pp152–5)* and Pavlovsk *(see pp159–61)* depart every 20 minutes from **Vitebskiy Station**. The line was originally built for the royal family to reach their summer residences and the station is a marvellous example of Style-Moderne architecture. The ticket office is on the right of the main building. All local trains take about 30 minutes, stopping

first at Tsarskoe Selo (Detskoe Selo), then Pavlovsk.

At Detskoe Selo station, the 382 and 371 buses go to Tsarskoe Selo, stopping near the palace. On foot, it is about a 20-minute walk from the station to the estate.

At Pavlovsk, the train station is opposite the entrance to the park, through which it is a pleasant 30-minute walk to the palace.

A host of minibuses run to Tsarskoe Selo (Pushkin) and Pavlovsk from Moskovskaya metro station in St Petersburg. They provide a reliable and convenient alternative means of transport to the train.

Passengers boarding suburban train at Vitebskiy Station

GETTING TO PETERHOF AND ORANIENBAUM

The most enjoyable and by far the most scenic way to reach the imperial summer palace of Peterhof is the 45-minute trip across the Gulf of Finland by hydrofoil. The service runs from early June until early October and sets off from the second landing stage outside the Hermitage *(see p75)* where a weekly timetable is posted. Generally hydrofoils operate every hour from 9:30am with the last boat returning at 6pm. It is cheaper to buy a return ticket (for about 700 roubles) than two singles. While it is much more expensive than the train or bus, it is worth the extra cost for the comfort and the view.

On arrival, a fee is charged to enter the lower park and this ticket is needed to get back into the park to return by hydrofoil.

The hydrofoils to Kronshtadt and then Oranienbaum (Lomonosov) are actually part of the water bus network and are used by commuters in these suburbs. Accordingly, it costs about 100 roubles one-way to Kronshtadt, and another 30 roubles from there to Lomonosov. Hydrofoils to Kronshtadt depart from a boat pier in front of **Finland Station**, and from Kronshtadt pier another boat goes to Lomonosov.

There are suburban trains for Peterhof *(see pp148–51)* and Oranienbaum *(see pp148–51)* departing every 20 minutes from **Baltic Station**. The trains that reach Oranienbaum are those destined for Kalishche, or Oranienbaum itself.

For Peterhof, get off the train at Novyy Petergof (40 minutes from town), from where it is 10 minutes to the palace on bus 348, 350, 351, 352 or 356.

At Oranienbaum, turn right out of the station and walk about 200 m (650 ft) to the main road. Almost directly opposite is the entrance to the park, and from here it is only a 5-minute walk to the Great Palace or into the heart of the park.

An efficient minibus service runs passengers to both Peterhof and Oranienbaum located outside Avtovo metro station in the city.

GETTING TO REPINO AND THE GULF OF FINLAND

For Repino *(see p146)* and the Gulf of Finland, trains depart every 20 minutes or so from **Finland Station**. Tickets should be bought at cash desks within the main building. Avoid any train marked Beloostrov or Krugovoy.

At Repino, cross the main road, head down the hill towards the Gulf of Finland and turn left onto the asphalt road until you reach Penaty.

Bus No. 211 also runs to Repino and stops right outside Penaty. Buses to Repino leave from Chernaya Rechka metro and tickets are bought on board.

GETTING TO NOVGOROD

Coaches leave for Novgorod *(see pp162–5)* every 2 hours from the **Coach Station**. The journey takes 4 hours. There are also at least two daily trains from **Moscow Station** that take 3 hours (be warned that there is no toilet on the train). An alternative is to book a guided tour *(see p208)*.

DRIVING OUT OF ST PETERSBURG

Car hire is available from companies such as **Hertz** and **Europcar**, but driving is not recommended. Firstly, there is no need, as the public transport network is excellent and inexpensive, and secondly, the local driving culture and suspicious traffic

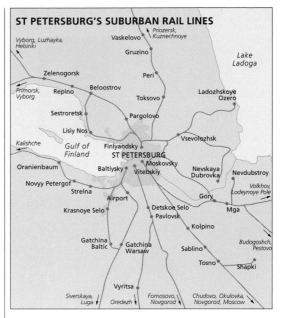

ST PETERSBURG'S SUBURBAN RAIL LINES

police does not make for an enjoyable time on the road.

To drive in Russia, a notarized translation of a foreign licence is obligatory, as well as international insurance and documents proving you have the right to be driving the car: for example, registration documents or a hire agreement bearing your name.

Traffic police *(see p213)* have the right to stop you and check your documents. If a policeman points his baton at your vehicle and signals for you to pull over, you must do so immediately, regardless of whether you have committed any violations. The police may not issue on-the-spot fines for minor infringements – such as having a dirty number plate, not having a first-aid kit, or more serious offences such as drink-driving. (Drivers are not allowed to drink any alcohol.) The proper procedure is to issue a ticket requiring payment within a month at any branch of Sberbank, though the traffic police are notorious for preferring to receive bribes than to issue official fines. For a minor infringement, such as not wearing a seatbelt, a fine may be around 500–1,000 roubles.

DIRECTORY

TRAIN AND COACH STATIONS

All train enquiries
Tel 055.

Baltic Station
Балтийский вокзал
Baltiyskiy vokzal
Nab Obvodnovo kanala 120.

Coach Station
Автобусный вокзал
Avtobusnyy vokzal
Nab Obvodnovo kanala 36.
Map 7 C5. *Tel* 766 5777.

Finland Station
Финляндский вокзал
Finlyandskiy vokzal
Pl Lenina 6. **Map** 3 B3.

Moscow Station
Московский вокзал
Moskovskiy vokzal
Pl Vosstaniya. **Map** 7 C2.

Vitebskiy Station
Витебский вокзал
Vitebskiy vokzal
Zagorodnyy pr 52. **Map** 6 E4.

CAR HIRE

Europcar
Pulkovo 2 Arrivals. *Tel* 7 (911) 987 2956.

Hertz
Pulkovo 1 Arrivals. *Tel* 326 4505.

ST PETERSBURG STREET FINDER

The key map below shows the areas of St Petersburg covered by the *Street Finder*. The map references given throughout the guide for sights, restaurants, hotels, shops or entertainment venues refer to the maps in this section. All the major sights have been clearly marked so they are easy to locate. The key below shows other features marked on the

Pausing on the steps of Kazan Cathedral

maps, such as post offices, metro stations, ferry stops and churches. The *Street Finder* index lists street names in transliteration, followed by the Cyrillic (on the maps, Cyrillic is only given for major roads). This guide uses the now reinstated old Russian street names, rather than the Soviet versions *(see p217)*. Places of interest are listed by their English name.

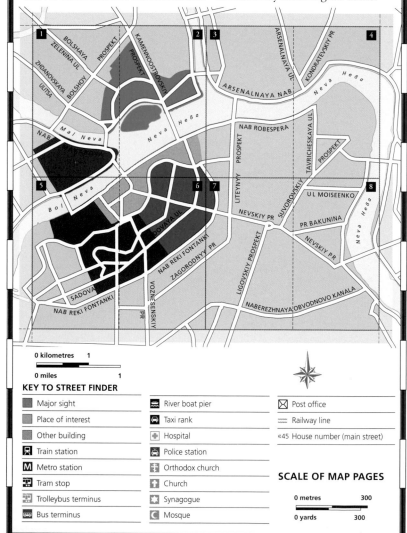

0 kilometres 1
0 miles 1

KEY TO STREET FINDER

■ Major sight	🚢 River boat pier	⊠ Post office
■ Place of interest	🚕 Taxi rank	═ Railway line
■ Other building	✚ Hospital	«45 House number (main street)
🚆 Train station	🚓 Police station	
Ⓜ Metro station	✚ Orthodox church	
🚊 Tram stop	✝ Church	**SCALE OF MAP PAGES**
🚎 Trolleybus terminus	✡ Synagogue	**0 metres** 300
🚌 Bus terminus	☪ Mosque	**0 yards** 300

Street Finder Index

ABBREVIATIONS & USEFUL WORDS

ul	**ulitsa**	street
pl	**ploshchad**	square
pr	**prospekt**	avenue
per	**pereulok**	lane
nab	**naberezhnaya**	embankment
	most	bridge
	sad	garden
	shosse	road

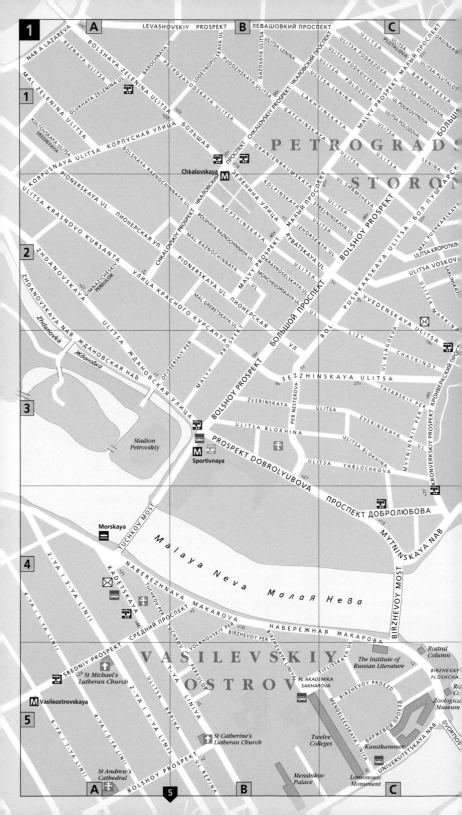

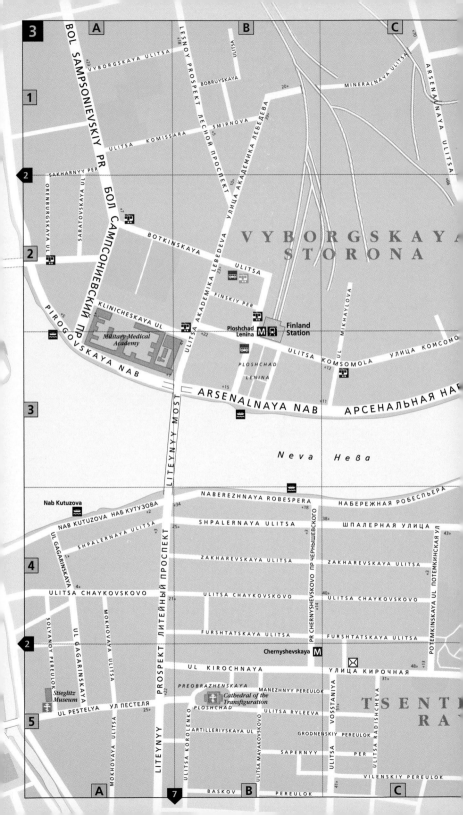

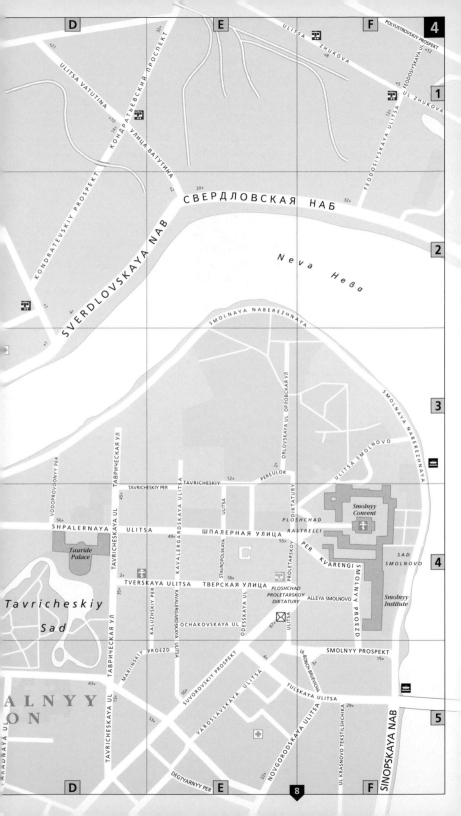

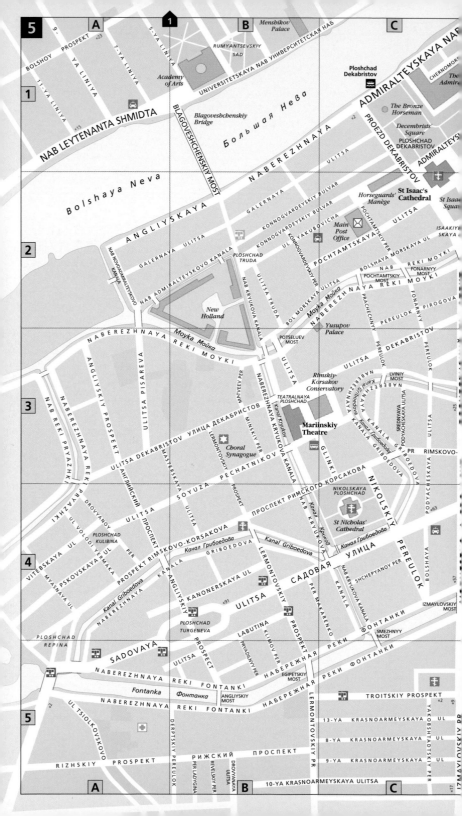

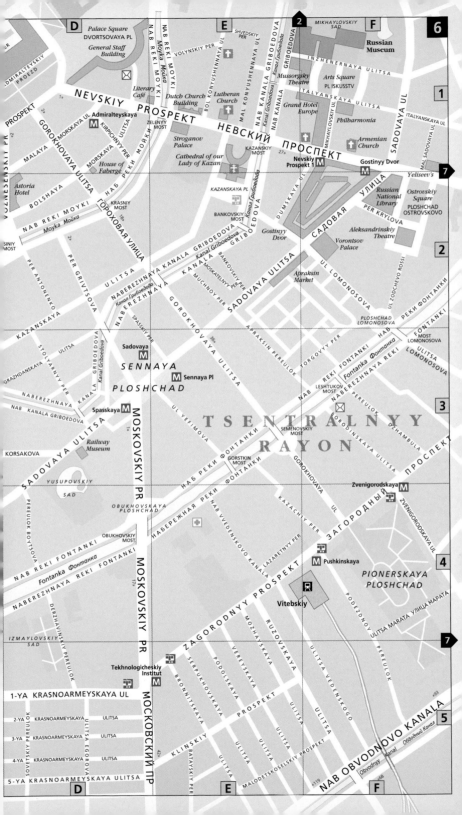

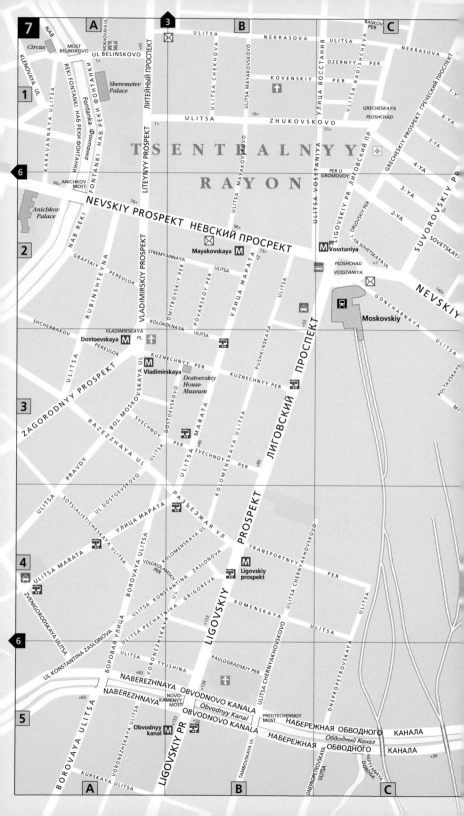

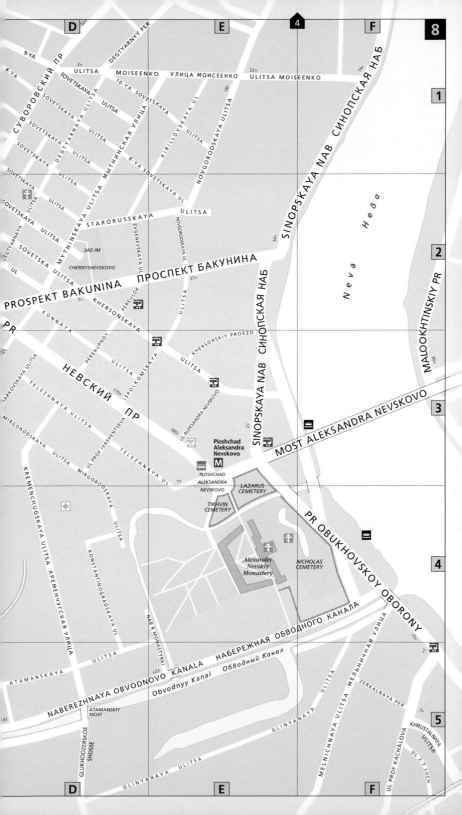

General Index

Acknowledgments

Dorling Kindersley would like to thank the following people whose contributions and assistance have made the preparation of this book possible.

Main Contributor

Christopher Rice holds a PhD in Russian history from the University of Birmingham. He and his wife Melanie, also a writer, first visited Russia in 1978 and have been returning regularly ever since. Together they have written numerous travel guides to the city, and to a variety of other destinations, including Prague, Berlin and Istanbul, as well as the *Eyewitness Travel Guide to Moscow*.

Catherine Phillips is an art historian who arrived in Russia in 1985 and has lived there ever since, moving to St Petersburg in 1989. She covered major events for British and American TV and radio during the early years of *perestroika* and authored and contributed to some of the first guides to the new Russia. Today she concentrates on translating and editing scholarly texts and writing for works of reference.

Additional Contributor

Rose Baring began to study Russian at the age of 12. She has an MA in Modern History and divided her time between London, Moscow and St Petersburg for much of the early 1990s. She has written guides to St Petersburg, Moscow and other destinations, including the *Eyewitness Travel Guide to Istanbul*.

Special Assistance

Dorling Kindersley would like to thank Marc Bennetts (walks writer), Anastasia Makarova (factchecker), Hilary Bird (indexer), Ian Wizniewski (food and drink consultant), Valera Katsuba (photo permissions), Marina Maydanyuk (researcher), Oleksiy Nesnov (language consultant), Victoria Rachevskaya (language consultant), Agency Information Resources for helping with research, Yuliya Motovilova (St Petersburg Tourist Company) and the staff of Peter TiPS.

Proofreader

Stewart J Wild.

Revisions Team

Namrata Adhwaryu, Emma Anacootee, Gillian Allan, Douglas Amrine, Liz Atherton, Andrei Bogdanov, Laurence Broers, Shura Collinson, Lucinda Cooke, Vivien Crump, Dawn Davies-Cook, Hannah Dolan, Alexandra Farrell, Claire Folkard, Chris Gordon, Freddy Hamilton, Paul Hines, Leanne Hogbin, Vicki Ingle, Kathryn Lane, Sam Merrell, Fiona Morgan, Jane Oliver, Helen Partington, Marianne Petrou, Pure Content, Amir Reuveni, Ellen Root, Luke Rozkowski, Alison Stace, Ingrid Vienings, Veronica Wood.

Additional Illustrations

Claire Littlejohn, John Woodcock.

Additional Photography

Valentin Baranovsky, Andrei Bogdanov, Victoria Buyvid, Shura Collinson, Andy Crawford, Erich Crichton, Neil Fletcher, Steve Gorton, Paul Miller, Ian O'Leary, Jon Spaull, Clive Streeter; KOMMERSANT Photo Agency: Yevgeny Pavlenko, Sergey Semyenov.

Photography Permissions

The publisher would like to thank all those who gave permission to photograph at their establishments, including hotels, museums, churches, shops and other sights, too numerous to thank individually.

Picture Credits

Key: a-above; b-below/bottom; c-centre; f-far; l-left; r-right; t-top.

The publisher would like to thank the following individuals, companies and picture libraries for their kind permission to reproduce their photographs:

Aeroflot: 218tc, 218cr; Aisa, Barcelona: 18t, 44t, 55 (insert), 106tr; AKG, London: 16, 17t, 20bl/cl, 20–21c, 25tl, 26cl, 27c, 28br, Erich Lessing 28bl, 29c, 37b, 42cl/bl/br, 43br, State Russian Museum, St Petersburg 105crb; Alamy Images: Art Directors & TRIP/Vladimir Sidropolev 208cl; PE Forsberg 212crb; Frans Lemmens 216cla; Dov Makabaw 221br; Dmitry Mikhaevich 59crb; RIA Novosti 60bl; studio204 216br; Art Kowalsky 10cl; brt Russia 81tc; Medioimages 10br; Robert Harding Picture Library Ltd 10tc, 138cr; Robert Harding

Picture Library Ltd/ Sylvain Grandadam 180cl, 181tl; Peter Titmuss 138br, 210tl; Ancient Art & Architecture Collection: 45cr; APA: Jim Holmes 93tl; Axiom: Jim Holmes 153b; Valentin Baranovsky: 84bl, 85tl, 201t; Ian Bavington-Jones: 130t; Yuri Belinsky: 31t; Bridgeman Art Library, London/New York: 153c; Forbes Magazine Collection 28–9c; State Hermitage, St Petersburg 21cb, 24–5c, 25cl, 86t/b, 87t/b, 88b, 89tr/b, 90t/b, 91t/c, *La Danse,* Henri Matisse (1910) © Succession Henri Matisse/DACS 2011 87c; Private Collection *20th Century Propaganda Poster 1920,* D Moor © DACS 2011 29tr; State Russian Museum, St Petersburg *The Cyclist,* Natalya Goncharova (1913) © ADAGP, Paris and DACS, London 2011 40b, *Portrait of Princess Olga Konstantinovna Orlova,* Valentin Alexandrovich Serov (1911) 104clb; Tretyakov Gallery, Moscow 19t, *The Circus,* Marc Chagall, 1919 © ADAGP, Paris and DACS, London 2011 45tl. ALFA-BANK: 214bl; ANGLOTOURISM.COM: 222tr.

CAMERA PRESS: Roxana Artacho 85bl; DEMETRIO CARRASCO: 2–3, 6b, 15b, 36t, 53bl, 80bl, 93cr/br, 102–103; CENTRAL STATE ARCHIVE OF PHOTOGRAPHS AND FILM DOCUMENTS, ST PETERSBURG: 42t, 72c, 110c, 118bl; JEAN-LOUP CHARMET: 23t; CHRISTIE'S IMAGES: 82b; CORBIS: Dean Conger 52tr, Antoine Gyori 139t; E. O Hoppe/ Bettmann 118cr; Rob Howard 181c; Bob Krist 201b; Library of Congress 28tl; Michael Nicholson 152t; Gianni Dagli Orti 8–9, 119bl; Jose Fuste Raga 222bl; Steve Raymer 31crb, 118br, 138cl; Gregor M. Schmid 138tl; State Hermitage, St Petersburg 24bl; State Russian Museum 25bl; E T ARCHIVE: Bibliotheque Nationale, Paris 17cl; Hermitage, St Petersburg 88t, 89tl. DREAMSTIME.COM: Paha_i 210c. FOTOLIA: Dmitry Vereshchagin 227tl.

GETTY IMAGES: Hulton Archive 43tr, 118cl, 121c, 182tr; The Image Bank/Harald Sund 11br; GIRAUDON: State Russian Museum 43cr, 105cr; Tretyakov Gallery, Moscow 165cr.

MICHAEL HOLFORD: 18c, 19c, 21bl; HOTEL DOSTOEVSKY: 173cb; INTERIOR ARCHIVE: Fritz von der Schulenburg

161c; KATZ PICTURES: 167 (insert); KEA PUBLISHING SERVICES: Francesco Venturi 92 (all three); DAVID KING COLLECTION: 29tl, 30t, 45b, 69b, 129c; LONELY PLANET IMAGES: Jonathan Smith 11tr, 139crb; MARY EVANS PICTURE LIBRARY: 9 (insert), 19b, 21br, 22c, 23c, 24cl/br, 25br, 26t, 29br, 62b, 141 (insert), 161bl, 207 (insert); PAUL MILLER: 51cr; MIR TRAVEL COMPANY: 208tc; MTS: 216tl; NEPTUN-BOATS: 226cl; NOVOSTI (LONDON): 20br, 21tl, 26b, 27t, 30cl, 31c, 43tl, 50c, 51b, 78b, 165t/l; ORONOZ, MADRID: 22t, 43bl.

PARK INN PRIBALTIYSKAYA: 168cl; PLODIMEX AUSSENHANDELS GMBH, HAMBURG: 178cr/bl; NATASHA RAZINA: 152b, 153t; RENAISSANCE ST PETERSBURG BALTIC HOTEL: 172c; REX FEATURES: V. Sichov/SIPA Press 30cr; ROBERT HARDING PICTURE LIBRARY: 84br; ROCCO FORTE HOTELS, ST PETERSBURG: 169br; ELLEN ROONEY: 53t, 79t, 83b, 140–41; RUSSIAN NATIONAL TOURIST OFFICE: 208tc; RUSSIAN RAILWAYS: 219tc, 219bl; GREGOR M SCHMID: 50br; SCIENCE PHOTO LIBRARY: CNES, 1989 Distribution Spot Image 11cr; VLADIMIR SIDOROPOLEV: 182br; SKAT PROKAT: 223cr; STATE RUSSIAN MUSEUM: 7cr; *Blue Crest,* Wassily Kandinsky (1917) © ADAGP, Paris and DACS, London 2011 39br; 93tr, 104bl/br, 105tl, 106tl/b, 107 (all three), 110b; TRAVEL LIBRARY: Stuart Black 85br; VISUAL ARTS LIBRARY: 44b; State Hermitage, St Petersburg *L'Homme aux bras croisés,* Pablo Picasso (1905) © Succession Picasso/DACS 2011 91b; 123c. ST. PETER LINE: 220tr; ST. PETERSBURG METRO: 224br, 225cl; ST. PETERSBURG TIMES: 217tc.

Map Cover: SUPERSTOCK: Axiom Photographic Limited front.

Jacket: Front – SUPERSTOCK:: Axiom Photographic Limited; Back – DORLING KINDERSLEY: Rough Guides/ Jonathan Smith tl; Jon Spaull clb, bl; GETTY IMAGES:. Charles Bowman cla; Spine - SUPERSTOCK: Axiom Photographic Limited t.

All other images © Dorling Kindersley. For further information see:
www.dkimages.com

SPECIAL EDITIONS OF DK TRAVEL GUIDES

DK Travel Guides can be purchased in bulk quantities at discounted prices for use in promotions or as premiums. We are also able to offer special editions and personalized jackets, corporate imprints, and excerpts from all of our books, tailored specifically to meet your own needs.

To find out more, please contact:
(in the United States) **SpecialSales@dk.com**
(in the UK) **TravelSpecialSales@uk.dk.com**
(in Canada) DK Special Sales at **general@tourmaline.ca**
(in Australia) **business.development@pearson.com.au**

Phrase Book

In this guide the Russian language has been transliterated into Roman script following a consistent system used by the US Board on Geographic Names. All street and place names, and the names of most people, are transliterated according to this system. For some names, where a well-known English form exists, this has been used – hence, Leo (not Lev) Tolstoy.

In particular, the names of Russian rulers, such as Peter the Great, are given in their anglicized forms. Throughout the book, transliterated names can be taken as an accurate guide to pronunciation. The Phrase Book also gives a phonetic guide to the pronunciation of words and phrases used in everyday situations, such as when eating out or shopping.

GUIDELINES FOR PRONUNCIATION

The Cyrillic alphabet has 33 letters, of which only five (a, к, м, о, т) correspond exactly to their counterparts in English. Russian has two pronunciations (hard and soft) of each of its vowels, and several consonants without an equivalent.

The right-hand column of the alphabet, below, demonstrates how Cyrillic letters are pronounced by comparing them to sounds in English words. However, some letters vary in how they are pronounced according to their position in a word. Important exceptions are also noted below.

On the following pages, the English is given in the left-hand column, with the Russian and its transliteration in the middle column. The right-hand column provides a literal system of pronunciation and indicates the stressed syllable in bold. The exception is in the *Menu Decoder* section, where the Russian is given in the left-hand column and the English translation in the right-hand column, for ease of use. Because of the existence of genders in Russian, in a few cases both masculine and feminine forms of a phrase are given.

THE CYRILLIC ALPHABET

А а	a	alimony
Б б	b	bed
В в	v	vet
Г г	g	get (see note 1)
Д д	d	debt
Е е	e	yet (see note 2)
Ё ё	e	yonder
Ж ж	zh	leisure (but a little harder)
З з	z	zither
И и	i	see
Й й	y	boy (see note 3)
К к	k	king
Л л	l	loot
М м	m	match
Н н	n	never
О о	o	rob (see note 4)
П п	p	pea
Р р	r	rat (rolling, as in Italian)
С с	s	stop
Т т	t	toffee
У у	u	boot
Ф ф	f	fellow
Х х	kh	kh (like loch)
Ц ц	ts	lets
Ч ч	ch	chair
Ш ш	sh	shove
Щ щ	shch	fresh sheet (as above but with a slight roll)
ъ		hard sign (no sound, but see note 5)
Ы ы	y	lid
ь		soft sign (no sound, but see note 5)
Э э	e	egg
Ю ю	yu	youth
Я я	ya	yak

Notes

1) Г Pronounced as *v* in endings -oro and -ero.
2) E Always pronounced *ye* at the beginning of a word, but in the middle of a word sometimes less distinctly (more like *e*).
3) Й This letter has no distinct sound of its own. It usually lengthens the preceeding vowel.
4) O When not stressed it is pronounced like *a* in across.
5) ъ, ь The hard sign (ъ) is rare and indicates a very brief pause before the next letter. The soft sign (ь), marked in the pronunciation guide as ') softens the preceeding consonant and adds a slight *y* sound: for instance, *n'* would sound like *ny* in 'canyon'.

In Emergency

Help!	Помогите! *Pomogite!*	pamag**eet**-ye!
Stop!	Стоп! *Stop!*	stop!
Leave me alone!	Оставьте меня в покое! *Ostavte menya v pokoe!*	asta**vt'**-ye my**eny**a v pak**oy**e!
Call a doctor!	Позовите врача! *Pozovite vracha!*	pazav**eet**-ye vr**acha**!
Call an ambulance!	Вызовите скорую помощь! *Vyzovite skoruyu pomoshch!*	**vi**zaveet-ye skoru-yu p**omash**'!
Fire!	Пожар! *Pozhar!*	pazh**ar**!
Call the fire brigade!	Вызовите пожарных! *Vyzovite pozharnykh!*	**vi**zaveet-ye pazh**ar**nikh!
Police!	Милиция! *Militsiya!*	meel**eet**see-ya!
Where is the nearest...	Где ближайший... *Gde blizhayshiy...*	gdye bleezh**ay**sheey...
...telephone?	...телефон? *...telefon?*	...tyel**yef**on?
...hospital?	...больница? *...bolnitsa?*	...bal'n**eet**sa?
...police station?	...отделение милиции? *...otdelenie militsii?*	...atdyel**yen**ye meel**eet**see-ee?

Communication Essentials

Yes	Да *Da*	da
No	Нет *Net*	nyet
Please	Пожалуйста *Pozhaluysta*	paz**hal**sta
Thank you	Спасибо *Spasibo*	spas**eeb**a
You are welcome	Пожалуйста *Pozhaluysta*	paz**hal**sta
Excuse me	Извините *Izvinite*	eezveen**eet**-ye
Hello	Здравствуйте *Zdravstuyte*	zdra**st**vooyt-ye
Goodbye	До свидания *Do svidaniya*	da sveed**an**ya
Good morning	Доброе утро *Dobroe utro*	**dob**ra-ye **oot**ra
Good afternoon/day	Добрый день *Dobryy den'*	**dob**ree dyen'
Good evening	Добрый вечер *Dobryy vecher*	**dob**ree **vye**chyer
Good night	Спокойной ночи *Spokoynoy nochi*	spak**oy**noy **no**chee
Morning	утро *utro*	**oot**ra
Afternoon	день *den*	dyen'
Evening	вечер *vecher*	**vye**chyer
Yesterday	вчера *vchera*	fchy**era**
Today	сегодня *sevodnya*	syev**od**nya
Tomorrow	завтра *zavtra*	**zaf**tra
Here	здесь *zdes*	zdyes'

There	там	tam
	tam	
What?	Что?	shto?
	Chto?	
Where?	Где?	gdye?
	Gde?	
Why?	Почему?	pachyemoo?
	Pochemu?	
When?	Когда?	kagda?
	Kogda?	
Now	сейчас	seychas
	seychas	
Later	позже	pozhe
	pozzhe	
Can I...?	можно?	mozhna...?
	mozhno?	
It is possible/allowed	можно *mozhno*	mozhna
It is not possible/allowed	нельзя *nelzya*	nyelzya

Useful Phrases

How are you?	Как Вы Поживаете?	kak vee pozhivaete?
	Kak vee pozhivaete?	
Very well, thank you	Хорошо, спасибо	kharasho, spaseeba
	Khorosho, spasibo	
Pleased to meet you	Очень приятно	ochen' pree-yatna
	Ochen priyatno	
How do I get to...?	Как добраться до...?	kak dabrat'sya da...?
	Kak dobratsya do...?	
Would you tell me when we get	Скажите, пожалуйста, когда мы приедем в...?	skazheet-ye, pazhalsta, kagda mi pree-yedyem v...?
To...?	*Skazhite, pozhaluysta, kogda my priedem v...?*	
Is it very far?	Это далеко?	eta dalyeko?
	Eto daleko?	
Do you speak English?	Вы говорите по-английски?	vi gavareet-ye po-angleeskee?
	Vy govorite po-angliyski?	
I don't understand	Я не понимаю	ya nye paneema-yoo
	Ya ne ponimayu	
Could you speak more slowly?	Говорите медленнее	gavareet-ye myedlyenye-ye
	Govorite medlennee	
Could you say it again please?	Повторите, пожалуйста	paftareet-ye, pazhalsta
	Povtorite, pozhaluysta	
I am lost	я заблудился (заблудилась)	ya zabloodeelsya (zabloodeelas')
	Ya zabludilsya (zabludilas)	
How do you say... in Russian?	Как по-русски...?	kak pa-rooskee...?
	Kak po-russki...?	

Useful Words

big	большой	bal'shoy
	bolshoy	
small	маленький	malyen'kee
	malenkiy	
hot (water, food)	горячий	garyachee
	goryachiy	
hot (weather)	жарко	zharka
	zharko	
cold	холодный	khalodnee
	kholodnyy	
good	хорошо	kharasho
	khorosho	
bad	плохо	plokha
	plokho	
okay/fine	нормально	narmal'na
	normalno	
near	близко	bleezka
	blizko	
far	далеко	dalyeko
	daleko	
up	наверху	navyerkhoo
	naverkhu	

down	внизу	fneezoo
	vnizu	
early	рано	rana
	rano	
late	поздно	pozdna
	pozdno	
vacant (unoccupied)	свободно	svabodna
	svobodno	
free (no charge)	бесплатно	byesplatna
	besplatno	
cashier/ticket office	касса	kasa
	kassa	
avenue	проспект	praspyekt
	prospekt	
bridge	мост	most
	most	
embankment	набережная	nabyeryezhnaya
	naberezhnaya	
highway/motorway	шоссе	shasse
	shosse	
lane/passage	переулок	pyeryeoolak
	pereulok	
square	площадь	ploshat'
	ploshchad	
street	улица	ooleetsa
	ulitsa	
flat/apartment	квартира	kvarteera
	kvartira	
floor	этаж	etash
	etazh	
house/block	дом	dom
	dom	
entrance	вход	fkhot
	vkhod	
exit	выход	vikhot
	vykhod	
river	река	ryeka
	reka	
summer country house	дача	dacha
	dacha	
swimming pool	бассейн	basyeyn
	basseyn	
town	город	gorat
	gorod	
toilet	туалет	tooalyet
	tualet	

Making a Telephone Call

Can I call abroad from here?	Можно отсюда позвонить за границу?	mozhna atsyooda pazvaneet' za graneetsoo?
	Mozhno otsyuda pozvonit za granitsu?	
I would like to speak to...	Позвоните, пожалуйста...	pazaveet-ye, pazhalsta...
	Pozovite, pozhaluysta	
Could you leave him/her a message?	Вы можете передать ему/ей?	vi mozhet-ye pyeryedat' yemoo/yay?
	By mozhete peredat emy/yey?	
My number is...	Мой номер...	moy nomyer...
	Moy nomer...	
I'll ring back later	Я позвоню позже	ya pazvanyoo pozhe
	Ya pozvonyu pozzhe	

Sightseeing

castle	замок	zamak
	zamok	
cathedral	собор	sabor
	sobor	
church	церковь	tserkaf
	tserkov	
circus	цирк	tseerk
	tsirk	
closed for cleaning "cleaning day"	санитарный день *sanitarnyy den*	saneetarnee dyen'
undergoing restoration	ремонт *remont*	remont
exhibition	выставка	vistafka
	vystavka	
fortress	крепость	kryepost'
	krepost	
gallery	галерея	galeryeya
	galereya	

garden	сад _sad_	sad
island	остров _ostrov_	ostraf
kremlin/fortified stronghold	кремль _kreml_	kryeml'
library	библиотека _biblioteka_	beeblee-atyeka
monument	памятник _pamyatnik_	pamyatneek
mosque	мечеть _mechet_	myechyet'
museum	музей _muzey_	moozyey
palace	дворец _dvorets_	dvaryets
park	парк _park_	park
parliament	дума _duma_	dooma
synagogue	синагога _sinagoga_	seenagoga
zoo	зоопарк _zoopark_	zapark

Shopping

open	открыто _otkryto_	atkrita
closed	закрыто _zakryto_	zakrita
How much does this cost?	Сколько это стоит? _Skolko eto stoit?_	skol'ka eta stoeet?
I would like to buy......	Я хотел (хотела) бы купить... _Ya khotel (khotela) by kupit..._	ya khatyel (khatyela) bi koopeet'...
Do you have......?	У вас есть...? _U vas yest....?_	oo vas yest'...?
Do you take credit cards?	Кредитные карточки вы принимаете? _Kreditnye kartochki vy prinimaete?_	kryedeetnye kartachkee vy preeneemayetye?
What time do you open/close?	Во сколько вы открываетесь/ закрываетесь? _Vo skolko vy otkryvaetes/ zakryvaetes?_	Va skol'ka vy atkrivayetyes'/ zakrivayetyes?
This one	этот _etot_	etat
expensive	дорого _dorogo_	doraga
cheap	дёшево _deshevo_	dyoshyeva
size	размер _razmer_	razmyer
white	белый _belyy_	byelee
black	чёрный _chernyy_	chyornee
red	красный _krasnyy_	krasnee
yellow	жёлтый _zheltyy_	zholtee
green	зелёный _zelenyy_	zyelyonee
dark blue	синий _siniy_	seenee
light blue	голубой _goluboy_	galooboy
brown	коричневый _korichnevyy_	kareechnyevee

Types of Shop

bakery	булочная _bulochnaya_	boolachna-ya
bookshop	книжный магазин _knizhnyy magazin_	kneezhnee magazeen
butcher	мясной магазин _myasnoy magazin_	myasnoy magazeen

camera shop	фото-товары _foto-tovary_	foto-tavari
chemist	аптека _apteka_	aptyeka
delicatessen	гастроном _gastronom_	gastranom
department store	универмаг _univermag_	ooneevyermag
florist	цветы _tsvety_	tsvyeti
grocer	бакалея _bakaleya_	bakalye-ya
hairdresser	парикмахерская _parikmakherskaya_	pareekmakhyerskaya
market	рынок _rynok_	rinak
newspaper stand	газетный киоск _gazetniy kiosk_	gazyetnee kee-osk
post office	почта _pochta_	pochta
record shop	грампластинки _gramplastinki_	gramplasteenkee
shoe shop	обувь _obuv_	oboof'
travel agent	бюро путешествий _byuro puteshestviy_	byooro pootyeshestvee
bank	банк _bank_	bank

Staying in a Hotel

Do you have a vacant room?	У вас есть свободный номер? _U vas yest svobodnyy nomer?_	oo vas yest' svabodnee nomyer?
double room with double bed	номер с двуспальной кроватью _nomer s dvuspalnoy krovatyu_	nomyer s dvoospal'noy kravat'-yoo
twin room	двухместный номер _dvukhmestnyy nomer_	dvookhmyestnee nomyer
single room	одноместный номер _odnomestnyy nomer_	adnamyestnee nomyer
bath	ванная _vannaya_	vana-ya
shower	душ _dush_	doosh
porter	носильщик _nosilshchik_	naseel'sheek
key	ключ _klyuch_	klyooch

Eating Out

A table for two, please	Стол на двоих, пожалуйста	stol na dva-eekh, pazhalsta
I would like to book a table	Я хочу заказать стол _Ya khochu zakazat stol_	ya khachoo zakazat' stol
The bill, please	Счёт, пожалуйста _Schet, pozhaluysta_	shyot, pazhalsta
I am a vegetarian	Я вегетерианец (вегетерианка) _Ya vegeterianets (vegeterianka)_	ya vyegyetareeanyets (vyegyetareeanka)
breakfast	завтрак _zavtrak_	zaftrak
lunch	обед _obed_	abyet
dinner	ужин _uzhin_	oozheen
waiter!	официант! _ofitsiant!_	afeetsee-ant!
waitress!	официантка! _ofitsiantka!_	afeetsee-antka!
dish of the day	фирменное блюдо _firmennoe blyudo_	feermenoye blyooda
appetizers/starters	закуски _zakuski_	zakooskee

English	Russian	Pronunciation
main course	второе блюдо / *vtoroe blyudo*	ftaroye blyooda
meat and poultry dishes	мясные блюда / *myasnye blyuda*	myasniye blyooda
fish and seafood dishes	рыбные блюда / *rybnye blyuda*	ribniye blyooda
vegetable dishes	овощные блюда / *ovoshchnye blyuda*	avashshniye blyooda
dessert	десерт / *desert*	dyesyert
drinks	напитки / *napitki*	napeetkee
vegetables	овощи / *ovoshchi*	ovashshee
bread	хлеб / *khleb*	khlyeb
wine list	карта вин / *karta vin*	karta veen
rare (steak)	недожаренный / *nedozharennyy*	nyedazharenee
well done (steak)	прожаренный / *prozharennyy*	prozharenee
glass	стакан / *stakan*	stakan
bottle	бутылка / *butylka*	bootilka
knife	нож / *nozh*	nosh
fork	вилка / *vilka*	veelka
spoon	ложка / *lozhka*	loshka
plate	тарелка / *tarelka*	taryelka
napkin	салфетка / *salfetka*	salfyetka
salt	соль / *sol*	sol'
pepper	перец / *perets*	pyeryets
butter/oil	масло / *maslo*	masla
sugar	сахар / *sakhar*	sakhar

Menu Decoder

Russian	Pronunciation	English
абрикос / *abrikos*	abreekos	apricot
апельсин / *apelsin*	apyel'seen	orange
апельсиновый сок / *apelsinovyy sok*	apyel'seenavee sok	orange juice
арбуз / *arbuz*	arbooz	water melon
белое вино / *beloe vino*	byelaye veeno	white wine
бифштекс / *bifshteks*	beefshtyeks	steak
блины / *bliny*	bleeni	pancakes
борщ / *borshch*	borshsh	borsch (beetroot soup)
варенье / *varene*	varyen'ye	Russian syrup-jam
варёный / *varenyy*	varyonee	boiled
ветчина / *vetchina*	vyetcheena	ham
вода / *voda*	vada	water
говядина / *govyadina*	gavyadeena	beef
грибы / *griby*	greebi	mushrooms
груша / *grusha*	groosha	pear
гусь / *gus*	goos	goose
джем / *dzhem*	dzhem	jam
жареный / *zharenyy*	zharyenee	roasted/grilled/fried
икра / *ikra*	eekra	black caviar
икра красная/кета / *ikra krasnaya/keta*	eekra krasna-ya/kyeta	red caviar
капуста / *kapusta*	kapoosta	cabbage
картофель / *kartofel*	kartofyel'	potato
квас / *kvas*	kvas	kvas (sweet, mildly alcoholic drink)
клубника / *klubnika*	kloobneeka	strawberries
колбаса / *kolbasa*	kalbasa	salami sausage
кофе / *kofe*	kofye	coffee
красное вино / *krasnoe vino*	krasnoye veeno	red wine
креветки / *krevetki*	kryevyetkee	prawns
курица / *kuritsa*	kooreetsa	chicken
лук / *luk*	look	onion
малина / *malina*	maleena	raspberries
минеральная вода / *mineralnaya voda*	mineral'naya vada	mineral water
мороженое / *morozhenoe*	marozhena-ye	ice-cream
мясо / *myaso*	myasa	meat
огурец / *ogurets*	agooryets	cucumber
осетрина / *osetrina*	asyetreena	sturgeon
пельмени / *pelmeni*	pyel'myenee	meat or fish dumplings
персик / *persik*	pyerseek	peach
печенье / *pechene*	pyechyen'ye	biscuit
печёнка / *pechenka*	pyechyonka	liver
печёный / *pechenyy*	pyechyonee	baked
пиво / *pivo*	peeva	beer
пирог / *pirog*	peerok	pie
пирожки / *pirozhki*	peerashkee	small parcels with savoury fillings
помидор / *pomidor*	pameedor	tomato
морепродукты / *moryeproduktee*	moryeprodooktee	seafood
рыба / *ryba*	riba	fish
салат / *salat*	salat	salad
свинина / *svinina*	sveeneena	pork
сельдь / *seld*	sye'ld'	herring
сосиски / *sosiski*	saseeskee	sausages
сыр / *syr*	sir	cheese
сырой / *syroy*	siroy	raw
утка / *utka*	ootka	duck
фасоль / *fasol*	fasol'	beans
форель / *forel*	faryel'	trout
чай / *chay*	chai	tea
чеснок / *chesnok*	chyesnok	garlic
шашлык / *shashlyk*	shashlik	kebab
яйцо / *yaytso*	yaytso	egg
слива / *sliva*	sleeva	plum
фрукты / *frukty*	frookti	fruit
яблоко / *yabloko*	yablaka	apple

Transport

north	север *sever*	syever
south	юг *yug*	yook
east	восток *vostok*	vastok
west	запад *zapad*	zapat
airport	аэропорт *aeroport*	aeraport
aeroplane	самолёт *samolet*	samalyot
traffic police	ДПС *DPS*	day-pay-**ess**
bus	автобус *avtobus*	aftoboos
bus station	автобусная станция *avtobusnaya stantsiya*	aftoboosna-ya stantsee-ya
bus stop	остановка автобуса *ostanovka avtobusa*	astanofka aftoboosa
car	машина *mashina*	masheena
flight	рейс *reys*	ryeys
metro (station)	(станция) метро *(stantsiya) metro*	(stantsee-ya) myetro
no entry	нет входа *net vkhoda*	nyet fkhoda
no exit	нет выхода *net vykhoda*	nyet vikhada
parking	автостоянка *avtostoyanka*	aftostoyanka
petrol	бензин *benzin*	byenzeen
railway	железная дорога *zheleznaya doroga*	zhelyezna-ya daroga
railway station	вокзал *vokzal*	vagzal
return ticket	обратный билет *obratniy bilet*	obratnee beelyet
seat	место *mesto*	myesta
suburban train	пригородный поезд *prigorodniy poezd*	preegaradnee po-yezd
straight on	прямо *pryamo*	pryama
taxi	такси *taksi*	taksee
ticket	билет *bilet*	beelyet
token (for a single metro journey)	жетон *zheton*	zheton
to the left	налево *nalevo*	nalyeva
to the right	направо *napravo*	naprava
train	поезд *poezd*	po-yezd
tram	трамвай *tramvay*	tramvay
trolleybus	троллейбус *trolleybus*	tralyeyboos

Numbers

1	один/одна/одно *odin/odna/odno*	adeen/adna/adno
2	два/две *dva/dve*	dva/dvye
3	три *tri*	tree
4	четыре *chetyre*	chyetir-ye
5	пять *pyat*	pyat'
6	шесть *shest*	shest'
7	семь *sem*	syem'
8	восемь *vosem*	vosyem'
9	девять *devyat*	dyevyat'
10	десять *desyat*	dyesyat'

11	одиннадцать *odinnadtsat*	adeenatsat'
12	двенадцать *dvenadtsat*	dvyenatsat'
13	тринадцать *trinadtsat*	treenatsat'
14	четырнадцать *chetyrnadtsat*	chyetirnatsat'
15	пятнадцать *pyatnadtsat*	pyatnatsat'
16	шестнадцать *shestnadtsat*	shestnatsat'
17	семнадцать *semnadtsat*	syemnatsat'
18	восемнадцать *vosemnadtsat*	vasyemnatsat'
19	девятнадцать *devyatnadtsat*	dyevyatnatsat'
20	двадцать *dvadtsat*	dvatsat'
21	двадцать один *dvadtsat odin*	dvatsat' adeen
22	двадцать два *dvadtsat dva*	dvatsat' dva
23	двадцать три *dvadtsat tri*	dvatsat' tree
24	двадцать четыре *dvadtsat chetyre*	dvatsat' chyetir-ye
25	двадцать пять *dvadtsat pyat*	dvatsat' pyat'
30	тридцать *tridtsat*	treetsat'
40	сорок *sorok*	sorak
50	пятьдесят *pyatdesyat*	pyadyesyat'
60	шестьдесят *shestdesyat*	shes'dyesyat
70	семьдесят *semdesyat*	syem'dyesyat
80	восемьдесят *vosemdesyat*	vosyem'dyesyat
90	девяносто *devyanosto*	dyevyanosta
100	сто *sto*	sto
200	двести *dvesti*	dvyestee
300	триста *trista*	treesta
400	четыреста *chetyresta*	chyetiryesta
500	пятьсот *pyatsot*	pyat'sot
1,000	тысяча *tysyacha*	tisyacha
2,000	две тысячи *dve tysyachi*	dvye tisyachi
5,000	пять тысяч *pyat tysyach*	pyat' tisyach
1,000,000	миллион *million*	meelee-on

Time, Days and Dates

one minute	одна минута *odna minuta*	adna meenoota
one hour	час *chas*	chas
half an hour	полчаса *polchasa*	polchasa
day	день *den*	dyen'
week	неделя *nedelya*	nyedyel-ya
Monday	понедельник *ponedelnik*	panyedyel'neek
Tuesday	вторник *vtornik*	ftorneek
Wednesday	среда *sreda*	sryeda
Thursday	четверг *chetverg*	chyetvyerk
Friday	пятница *pyatnitsa*	pyatneetsa
Saturday	суббота *subbota*	soobota
Sunday	воскресенье *voskresene*	vaskryesyen'ye

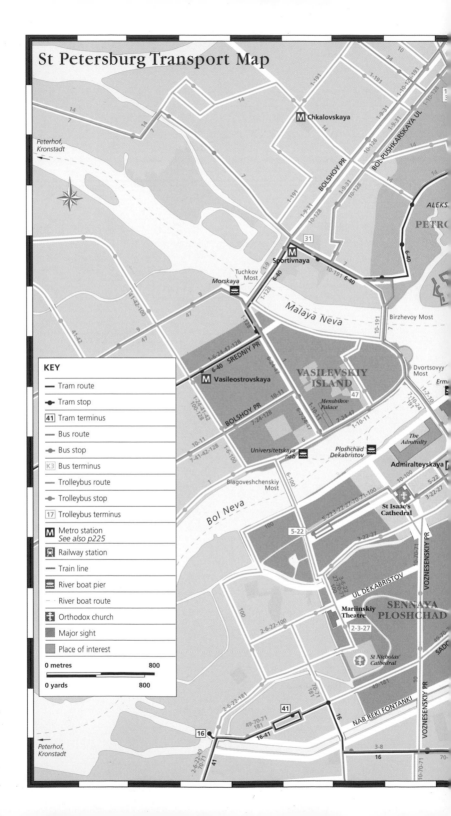
St Petersburg Transport Map

KEY

— Tram route

— Tram stop

[41] Tram terminus

— Bus route

— Bus stop

[K3] Bus terminus

— Trolleybus route

— Trolleybus stop

[17] Trolleybus terminus

[M] Metro station
See also p225

[R] Railway station

— Train line

— River boat pier

-- River boat route

[+] Orthodox church

Major sight

Place of interest

0 metres	800
0 yards	800

[M] Chkalovskaya

[M] Sportivnaya

Tuchkov
Most

Morskaya

Malaya Neva

Birzhevoy Most

[M] Vasileostrovskaya

VASILEVSKIY
ISLAND

*Menshikov
Palace*

SREDNIY PR

BOLSHOY PR

BOLSHOY PR

Dvortsovyy
Most

Erm

*The
Admiralty*

Admiralteyskaya

*Universitetskaya
nab*

*Ploshchad
Dekabristov*

Blagoveshchenskiy
Most

Bol Neva

St Isaac's
Cathedral

UL DEKABRISTOV

VOZNESENSKIY PR

Mariinskiy
Theatre

SENNAYA
PLOSHCHAD

St Nicholas'
Cathedral

NAB REKI FONTANKI

VOZNESENSKIY PR

BOL PUSHKARSKAYA UL

ALEKS.

PETRO

Peterhof,
Kronstadt

Peterhof,
Kronstadt